D1596149

Prosody in Interaction

Studies in Discourse and Grammar (SiDaG)

Studies in Discourse and Grammar is a monograph series providing a forum for research on grammar as it emerges from and is accounted for by discourse contexts. The assumption underlying the series is that corpora reflecting language as it is actually used are necessary, not only for the verification of grammatical analyses, but also for understanding how the regularities we think of as grammar emerge from communicative needs.

Research in discourse and grammar draws upon both spoken and written corpora, and it is typically, though not necessarily, quantitative. Monographs in the series propose explanations for grammatical regularities in terms of recurrent discourse patterns, which reflect communicative needs, both informational and socio-cultural.

Editor

Sandra A. Thompson
University of California at Santa Barbara
Department of Linguistics
Santa Barbara, CA 93106
USA

Volume 23

Prosody in Interaction
Edited by Dagmar Barth-Weingarten, Elisabeth Reber and Margret Selting

Prosody in Interaction

Edited by

Dagmar Barth-Weingarten
University of Freiburg

Elisabeth Reber
University of Erlangen-Nürnberg

Margret Selting
University of Potsdam

John Benjamins Publishing Company
Amsterdam / Philadelphia

™ The paper used in this publication meets the minimum requirements of American National Standard for Information Sciences – Permanence of Paper for Printed Library Materials, ANSI z39.48-1984.

Video clips (.mov) and audio files (.wav) of numerous examples in this volume can be found online, at http://dx.doi.org/10.1075/sidag.23.media

Library of Congress Cataloging-in-Publication Data

Prosody in interaction / edited by Dagmar Barth-Weingarten, Elisabeth Reber, Margret Selting.
      p. cm. (Studies in Discourse and Grammar, ISSN 0928-8929 ; v. 23)
Includes bibliographical references and index.
1. Prosodic analysis (Linguistics) 2. Grammar, Comparative and general--Phonology. I. Barth-Weingarten, Dagmar, 1971- II. Reber, Elisabeth. III. Selting, Margret.

P224.P758   2010
414'.6--dc22   2010039866
ISBN 978 90 272 2633 4   (Hb ; alk. paper)
ISBN 978 90 272 8846 2   (Eb)

John Benjamins Publishing Co. · P.O. Box 36224 · 1020 ME Amsterdam · The Netherlands
John Benjamins North America · P.O. Box 27519 · Philadelphia PA 19118-0519 · USA

Table of contents

Video clips (.mov) and audio files (.wav) of numerous examples in this
volume can be found online, at http://dx.doi.org/10.1075/sidag.23.media

This symbol marks the availability of a video clip of an example.

This symbol marks the availability of an audio file of an example.

Foreword

The appearance in 1996 of *Prosody in Conversation*, edited by Elizabeth Couper-Kuhlen and Margret Selting (Couper-Kuhlen and Selting 1996), was a landmark publication, drawing together, for the first time, a group of articles that explored the study of prosody in its 'home environment', everyday conversation.

The editors noted in their introduction to that volume the ways in which it represented a new development in the study of language and social organization, calling for new methodologies, new analytic approaches, and new interdisciplinary interactions. In retrospect, in fact, that volume can rightly be said to have heralded an entire new subfield, with practitioners from Conversation Analysis and Linguistics focusing their investigations on the role of prosody in social interaction.

Since that time a key figure has been providing consistently insightful leadership in developing these new methodologies, approaches, and interdisciplinary interactions, namely Elizabeth Couper-Kuhlen herself. The collection of papers in this volume, *Prosody in Interaction*, both celebrate her scholarship and provide eloquent testimony to the high standards which she has set for the entire field.

Inspired by Elizabeth Couper-Kuhlen's scholarship and example, the editors of this volume gathered the scholars represented here in Potsdam in September 2008 to present their research findings in her honor, and to express their admiration and esteem for her research and their appreciation for her as a teacher, mentor, and colleague. Those research findings, thoughtfully crafted into this volume, consider issues of prosody in interaction from a refreshing range of perspectives, including its phonetic properties and its role in sequence organization, radio commentary talk, child/caregiver talk, aphasia, and medical interviews.

These papers both show how far we've come and suggest countless fascinating research projects designed to further discover the way prosody works in human social encounters.

Sandra A. Thompson
Santa Barbara, California
spring 2010

References

Couper-Kuhlen, Elizabeth and Selting, Margret (eds.) 1996. *Prosody in conversation*. Cambridge: Cambridge University Press.

Preface

During the last quarter of a century, the empirical study of prosody in naturally occurring talk-in-interaction has evolved into a productive and internationally recognized field of study. To date, it has produced a large body of work in a wide range of subfields as well as a sound catalogue of research methods and principles adapted to its data and objectives. Research in this perspective has shown beyond doubt that prosody in interaction is systematically analyzable: It is deployed by participants in systematic ways in a context-sensitive fashion and functions as an essential resource in the management of social interaction. This means that, in addition to phonetic, morpho-syntactic, lexico-semantic, and visual-spatial signs and signals, prosody serves as the "prime contextualization cue" (Couper-Kuhlen 2001: 16) in the dynamic processes of communicative meaning-making. It is this perspective on 'prosody-as-contextualization cue' which distinguishes the study of prosody in interaction from "intonation-as-grammar" or "intonation-as-information-flow" approaches (cf. Couper-Kuhlen 2001: 15–16).

The present topical volume is the latest in a series of publications on the role of prosody in interaction (cf. Couper-Kuhlen and Selting 1996, Selting and Couper-Kuhlen 2001, Couper-Kuhlen and Ford 2004). In aiming to uncover the orderly use of linguistic resources by participants in achieving particular interactional goals, the papers in this volume are true contributions to the interactional-linguistic approach to the study of talk-in-interaction (cf., e.g., Couper-Kuhlen and Selting 1996, 2001, Selting and Couper-Kuhlen 2000, Couper-Kuhlen and Ford 2004, Hakulinen and Selting 2005). They, too, demonstrate the impressive progress research into prosody-in-interaction has made: on the one hand, the papers provide new insights into long-standing theoretical-methodological problems in the field, e.g. whether and/or how to employ mainstream-linguistic concepts, such as the intonation unit, in the description of interactional data, and how to deconstruct linguistic entities, which are produced and perceived as holistic entities by participants, into their constitutive parts. On the other hand, the perspective of prosody-in-interaction has widened: An increasing number of contributions looks at the *phonetics of interaction*, showing that "the potential interactional significance of … *all* audible aspects in and of speech that are produced by the human vocal apparatus" (Ford and Couper-Kuhlen 2004: 3, our emphasis) has been recognized. The study of prosody is now often being integrated into the study of more complex phenomena in interaction. One such phenomenon is represented as a major focus of contributions to the volume, namely the analysis of displays of affectivity in social interaction. Furthermore, with the rising interest in visual resources of face-to-face interaction, the volume offers several proposals on how prosodic-phonetic research can be linked to the study of visual-spatial conduct.

The contributions to this volume

The contributions to this volume range from the study of single prosodic-phonetic aspects to multimodal approaches to face-to-face interaction. Almost all the papers are complemented by a shorter commenting paper, putting the main contribution into perspective and raising further issues to be tackled.

Following a more general, introductory paper, the papers are divided into three main thematic sections:

1. Prosody and other levels of linguistic organization in interaction,
2. Prosodic units as a structuring device in interaction, and
3. Prosody and other semiotic resources in interaction.

In the introductory paper, *Margret Selting* defines the scope of the study of prosody in interaction and accounts for the relevance of the field by summarizing the functions of prosody in interaction. She outlines the main methodological approaches and principles, and sketches out major issues of current research. Listing challenges for future research, she names the varying views in the field as regards issues of categorization and the handling of categories from mainstream research. *Arnulf Deppermann,* in his commenting paper, postulates that in order to ensure the advancement of research on prosody in interaction, large corpora must be compiled and made accessible to the academic community. In addition, he lists criteria for such corpora, and discusses the viability of prosodic transcription.

  – *Prosody and other levels of linguistic organization in interaction*

Gareth Walker discusses a collection of rush-throughs from British and American video and audio data. He advocates an approach to the description of linguistic resources for the construction of turn-endings that encompasses more than just prosodic features. Observing the exploitation of phonatory and articulatory features at the juncture of the relevant TCUs, which collaborate with certain prosodic parameter changes (duration, but not pitch), he argues for a phonetic approach to the study of the vocal resources deployed in interaction. His discussant, *Susanne Günthner*, complements Walker's account by analyzing the syntactic and pragmatic levels of the rush-throughs discussed in order to gain a more holistic understanding of the notion of rush-through. She concludes that rush-throughs are not only used to link a syntactically complete unit to the next one but that they also connect one conversational activity to another.

    Richard Ogden also adopts a phonetic approach and explores the question whether there is a 'phonetics of complaining' by examining the turn design of complaints about third parties in English talk-in-interaction. He discerns two types of complaints, A-complaints and X-complaints, which clearly differ with regard to their prosodic-phonetic make-up, in particular in terms of pitch, loudness and articulatory configuration: A-complaints are used to seek an affiliative response, whereas X-complaints close down a sequence. He concludes that the phonetic designs identified for the two action formats are characteristic of 'seeking affiliation' and 'closing a sequence' rather than of 'complaining'. Further, he models the A- and X-complaints analysed as constructions. *Auli Hakulinen*, in her commenting paper, discusses the notion of (indirect) complaints as well as Ogden's conclusion that there is no phonetics of complaining.

Geoffrey Raymond shows that the production of type-conforming responses to yes/no-interrogatives in English (e.g., *yes* and *no* or equivalent tokens, such as e.g. *yeah*, or *nope*) generally orients to the syntactic format and the normative relevancies set up by the interrogative these tokens respond to. However, examining the prosody of type-conforming tokens, he finds that their prosodic formatting is used to project either more talk or turn completion. Similarly, actions beyond those originally accomplished can be added, or an aspect the original action would otherwise implement can be withheld.

In a joint paper on English and German talk-in-interaction, *John Local*, *Peter Auer* and *Paul Drew* describe their observations on the phonetic detail of speakers' 'trying again' when first attempts at launching an activity have failed. They distinguish three different types (retrieving, redoing, and resuscitating a previous first attempt) on the basis of sequential position, prosodic (pitch, loudness, duration) and lexico-syntactic features. In the case of retrievings and redoings, the different formats serve to downgrade or up-grade the repeated attempt respectively. The phonetic characteristics of resuscitating, in contrast, are related to the specific sequential and interactional position in which it occurs, presenting the unit as a second *first* attempt.

– *Prosodic units as a structuring device in interaction*

Beatrice Szczepek Reed's paper is concerned with the empirical grounding of intonation phrases in conversation. She claims that there are speech chunks smaller than turns, and potentially below the level of turn-constructional units, namely "turn-constructional phrases", which may, but need not, be co-extensive with intonation phrases. Based on English data, her contribution argues that turn-constructional phrases form a participant category, the extension of which can be deduced from prosodic, grammatical, semantic-pragmatic, turn-structural and sequence-organizational properties, although they may counter common syntactic phrasing. The latter issue is taken up by the paper's discussant, *Jan Anward*. He points out that chunks marked by incomplete syntax and continuing prosody are a frequent resource for turn-holding in spoken Swedish, for instance, which can be handled with more recent approaches to syntax. The real question, Anward claims, is rather the motivation for chunking.

Friederike Kern offers results from a study of German radio live commentaries of football matches. In particular, she examines the prosodic and syntactic resources radio reporters deploy in order to construct two types of what she calls "dramatic speech style", namely "building up suspense" and "presenting a climax". The activity of describing events on the football pitch, which is associated with dramatic speech style, differs from that of delivering background information in that both are contextualized by means of different bundles of prosodic resources. In his commenting paper, *Johannes Wagner* discusses whether Kern's findings can be generalized for other kinds of live sports commentaries. Distinguishing between "slow" and "fast" sports (horse racing vs. cricket, for instance), he suggests that while commentators may have the same set of prosodic resources available, they deploy them in specific ways.

In a study on the emergence of intonation systems in young children, *Bill Wells* examines English child-carer interactions. He compares instances of children's verbal repeats that imitate the tone, i.e. the pitch contour, of the carer's prior unit ("tonal repeat") with those that are done with a different prosodic design ("tonal contrast") and discusses the different contingencies that arise from these different formats: Whereas tonal repeat is treated as signaling alignment with the ongoing activity, tonal contrast serves to initiate something new. On the basis of these findings, implications for our understanding of the developing use of tone in 19–21 months-old children are proposed. The paper's discussant, *Traci Walker*, first raises the question whether the different formattings of repeat and contrast include variation in prosodic properties other than intonation. Secondly, she asks how much phonetic sameness is needed for a repeated unit to be analyzed as same or different. Finally, she corroborates Wells' point that tones only acquire meaning in specific sequential contexts.

– *Prosody and other semiotic resources in interaction*

In their paper based on material from German medical interaction, *Elisabeth Gülich* and *Katrin Lindemann* present a single-case study on the multimodal, and implicit, communication of fear of death in a patient's telling about her epileptic seizures in what they call "running-out-of-the-house episodes". The patient recounts the episode twice, displaying increasing emotional involvement through the increased expressiveness of multimodal resources such as, for example, direct eye-contact versus withdrawal of gaze. This kind of reframing in the second telling of the story episode and a final, actual labeling of the emotion are jointly achieved through the interactional work between therapist and patient. In her comment, *Elisabeth Reber* presents a closer analysis of the prosodic patterns deployed in the narrative reconstructions of the patient's seizures. She discusses whether and how prosody may contribute to the display of the patient's stance towards her tellings and the organization of local sequential moves.

Based on video-recorded Japanese talk-in-interaction, *Hiroko Tanaka*'s study on the response particle *huun* shows how the production of *huun* is accompanied by various vocal and visual displays. It makes visible the need for a unified account of response tokens, taking into consideration the co-occurring use of prosodic-phonetic and visual cues in particular sequential positions (cf. also Reber and Couper-Kuhlen 2010). The paper describes one of the core functions ascribed to the token, namely its use as a token that signals the *huun*-producer's involvement in, and appreciation of, the current talk, but at the same time it withholds active engagement in, or the expression of an explicit evaluative stance towards, other speaker's talk. Tanaka claims that in connection with certain multimodal resources it can even lead to topic attrition. It is the multimodal approach to the study of response tokens which the discussant, *Dagmar Barth-Weingarten*, considers the most important contribution of this paper to the present volume. She complements this by additional observations on visual cues which support the prosodic findings.

Cecilia Ford and *Barbara Fox* explore the phonetic-prosodic, visual and sequential construction of "laughables", that is, conversational objects inviting recipient laughter or other kinds of humorous actions. On the basis of material from American English video-recorded face-to-face conversations, they find that it is the interplay of particular phonetic, lexico-semantic and bodily practices, together with the sequential positioning of these practices, that are treated as contextualizations of laughables. In conclusion, they call for a more refined transcription system, which is needed to account for the fine details of phonetic practices involved in the construction of laughables. In her comment, *Karin Birkner* points out that Ford and Fox's paper implements a range of desiderata for future research: for instance, examining laughables in a cross-cultural perspective, exploring contexts where laughter serves other functions than indicating amusement, and uncovering possible gender differences in the multimodal design of laughables.

The constitutive role of prosody and gesture in interactional meaning-making is also emphasized in *Charles Goodwin*'s paper. With a detailed single-case analysis, Goodwin illustrates how a participant suffering from severe aphasia compensates for his very restricted vocabulary by deploying additional semiotic resources, namely prosody and gesture. Through the mutual interactional work of all participants building on, and making sense of, all of his communicative signals ("cooperative semiosis"), the patient is able to accomplish meaningful actions. While this may be particularly striking in the case of aphasia, Goodwin claims that in essence similar phenomena can be observed in the interaction of language-unimpaired participants. *Helga Kotthoff*'s comment addresses the prospects of Goodwin's work for two other types of interaction in which a fully competent speaker compensates for the linguistic and conversational deficits of a not fully competent speaker: with children and with second language learners. These interactive processes, too, she argues, can be captured with Goodwin's concept of cooperative semiosis.

The event inspiring this volume

The great majority of the contributions to this volume are based on papers presented by their authors on the occasion of the international conference "Prosody and Interaction", held at the University of Potsdam, Germany, in September 2008.[1] Besides taking stock of roughly 25 years of research in the field of prosody in interaction, the conference was organized in order to celebrate Elizabeth Couper-Kuhlen's 65th birthday and her outstanding academic achievements.

The conference participants, including the contributors to this volume, gathered in the true spirit of the person to be honored: The work of Elizabeth Couper-Kuhlen has had a major impact on the emergence and evolution of *Interactional Linguistics* and on the development of research on prosody in interaction in particular. It is to her this volume is dedicated. We gratefully acknowledge that it has been, and still is, an honor and a pleasure to work with her as an advisor, colleague and friend. She influenced our approach to linguistics and still inspires our way of thinking about language. She points out directions for future research to her colleagues, and she sets standards in scholarly inquisitiveness, meticulousness and sharpness in thought and presentation for everyone.

May many more adherents of your field of expertise be able to enjoy your guidance and friendship and share your thoughts.

Acknowledgements

We would like to extend our sincere thanks to the participants of the conference and to the contributors to this volume, who not only authored their own papers but also acted as reviewers of other contributions. Thanks is also due to a number of external reviewers, who were willing to share their expertise with us, sometimes even more than once: Pia Bergmann, Peter Gilles, Andrea Golato, John Heritage, Wolfgang Imo, Elise Kärkkäinen, K.K. Luke, Yael Maschler, Jörg Peters, Reinhold Schmitt, Helmut Spiekermann, Anja Stuckenbrock, Traci Walker, Anne Wichmann and, of course, Sandy Thompson, who also supported the publication of this volume in the series "Studies in Discourse and Grammar". Last but not least, thanks is due to Isja Conen and Martine van Marsbergen from Benjamins, who went with us through the potential cliffs of publishing. All of you made this "present" possible.

Dagmar Barth-Weingarten
Elisabeth Reber
Margret Selting

Braunschweig, Erlangen, Potsdam in spring 2010

---

1.   The conference was generously funded by, among others, the German Research Foundation (DFG). For a more detailed conference report see Barth-Weingarten and Reber (2009).

References

Barth-Weingarten, Dagmar and Reber, Elisabeth 2009. "International conference 'Prosody and Interaction': 15–17 September 2008, Potsdam University, Germany – Conference report". *Gesprächsforschung. Online-Zeitschrift zur verbalen Interaktion* 10: 118–130 [http://www.gespraechsforschung-ozs.de/heft2009/tb-barth.pdf].

Couper-Kuhlen, Elizabeth 2001. "Intonation and discourse: Current views from within". In: *The handbook of discourse analysis*, Deborah Schiffrin, Deborah Tannen and Heidi E. Hamilton (eds.), 13–34. Oxford: Blackwell Publishing.

Couper-Kuhlen, Elizabeth and Ford, Cecilia E. (eds.) 2004. *Sound patterns in interaction. Cross-linguistic studies from conversation*. Amsterdam: Benjamins.

Couper-Kuhlen, Elizabeth and Selting, Margret (eds.) 1996. *Prosody in conversation: Interactional studies*. Cambridge: Cambridge University Press.

Ford, Cecilia E. and Couper-Kuhlen, Elizabeth 2004. "Conversation and phonetics: Essential connections." In: Sound patterns in interaction. Cross-linguistic studies from conversation, Elizabeth Couper-Kuhlen and Cecilia E. Ford (eds.), 3–25. Amsterdam: Benjamins.

Hakulinen, Auli and Selting, Margret 2005. *Syntax and lexis in conversation*. Amsterdam: Benjamins.

Reber, Elisabeth and Couper-Kuhlen, Elizabeth 2010. "Interjektionen zwischen Lexikon und Vokalität: Lexem oder Lautobjekt?" In: *Sprache intermedial: Stimme und Schrift, Bild und Ton* (Jahrbuch des Instituts für Deutsche Sprache 2009), Arnulf Deppermann and Angelika Linke (eds.), 69–96. Berlin: de Gruyter.

Selting, Margret and Couper-Kuhlen, Elizabeth 2000. "Argumente für die Entwicklung einer interaktionalen Linguistik". *Gesprächsforschung – Online-Zeitschrift zur verbalen Interaktion* 1: 76–95 [http://www.gespraechsforschung-ozs.de/heft2000/ga-selting.pdf].

Selting, Margret and Couper-Kuhlen, Elizabeth (eds.) 2001. *Studies in interactional linguistics*. Amsterdam: Benjamins.

List of contributors

Jan Anward
Department of Culture and Communication
Linköping University
581 83 Linköping
Sweden
email: jan.anward@liu.se

Peter Auer
Freiburg Institute for Advanced Studies
(FRIAS)
School of Language & Literature
University of Freiburg
Albertstr. 19
79104 Freiburg
Germany
email: peter.auer@germanistik.uni-freiburg.de

Dagmar Barth-Weingarten
Hermann Paul School of Language
Sciences
University of Freiburg
Starkenstr. 44
79104 Freiburg
Germany
email: dagmar.barth-weingarten@hpsl.uni-freiburg.de

Karin Birkner
Sprach- und Literaturwissenschaftliche
Fakultät
University of Bayreuth
Universitätsstraße 30
95440 Bayreuth
Germany
email: karin.birkner@uni-bayreuth.de

Arnulf Deppermann
Institute for the German Language (IDS)
Postfach 10 16 21
68016 Mannheim
Germany
email: deppermann@ids-mannheim.de

Paul Drew
Department of Sociology
University of York
York YO10 5DD
United Kingdom
email: wpd1@york.ac.uk

Cecilia Ford
Department of English
University of Wisconsin-Madison
600 N. Park Street
Madison WI 5370
United States
email: ceford@wisc.edu

Barbara Fox
Department of Linguistics
University of Boulder at Colorado
Campus Box 295
Boulder, CO 80309
United States
email: barbara.fox@colorado.edu

Charles Goodwin
Applied Linguistics
University of California, Los Angeles
3300 Rolfe Hall
Los Angeles, CA 90095-1531
United States
email: cgoodwin@humnet.ucla.edu

Elisabeth Gülich
Fakultät für Linguistik und Literaturwis-
senschaft
University of Bielefeld
Postfach 10 01 31
33501 Bielefeld
Germany
email: elisabeth.guelich@uni-bielefeld.de

Susanne Günthner
Germanistisches Institut
University of Muenster
Hindenburgplatz 34
48143 Münster
Germany
email: susanne.guenthner@uni-muen-
ster.de

Auli Hakulinen
Department of Finnish, Finno-Ugric
and Nordic Languages and Literatures
University of Helsinki
P.O. Box 3
Fabianinkatu 33
FIN00014 Helsinki
Finland
email: auli.hakulinen@helsinki.fi

Friederike Kern
Institut für Germanistik
Universität Potsdam
Am Neuen Palais 10
14469 Potsdam
Germany
email: fkern@uni-potsdam.de

Helga Kotthoff
Deutsches Seminar I
University of Freiburg
Postfach
79085 Freiburg
Germany
email: helga.kotthoff@germanistik.
uni-freiburg.de

Katrin Lindemann
Deutsches Seminar
Universität Zürich
Schönberggasse 9
8001 Zürich
Switzerland
email: katrin.lindemann@ds.uzh.ch

John Local
Department of Language and Linguistic
Science
University of York
Heslington
York YO10 5DD
United Kingdom
email: lang4@york.ac.uk

Harrie Mazeland
Department of Language
and Communication/Center for Lan-
guage and Cognition Groningen (CLCG)
Faculty of Arts
University of Groningen
Oude Kijk in 't Jatstr. 26
PO 716
9700 AS Groningen
The Netherlands
email: h.j.mazeland@rug.nl

Richard Ogden
Department of Language & Linguistic
Science
University of York
YORK YO10 5DD
United Kingdom
email: rao1@york.ac.uk

Leendert Plug
Department of Linguistics
and Phonetics
University of Leeds
Woodhouse Lane
Leeds LS2 9JT
United Kingdom
email: L.Plug@leeds.ac.uk

Geoffrey Raymond
Department of Sociology
2834 Ellison Hall
University of California, Santa Barbara
Santa Barbara
CA 93106-9430
United States
email: graymond@soc.ucsb.edu

Elisabeth Reber
Institut für Anglistik und Amerikanistik
University of Erlangen-Nürnberg
Bismarckstraße 1
91054 Erlangen
Germany
email: Elisabeth.Reber@angl.phil.
uni-erlangen.de

Margret Selting
Institut für Germanistik
Universität Potsdam
Am Neuen Palais 10
14469 Potsdam
Germany
email: selting@rz.uni-potsdam.de

Beatrice Szczepek Reed
Department of Educational Studies
University of York
York
YO10 5DD
United Kingdom
email: bsr504@york.ac.uk

Hiroko Tanaka
Department of Sociology
University of Essex
Wivenhoe Park
Colchester
Essex CO4 3SQ
United Kingdom
email: htanaka@essex.ac.uk

Sandra A. Thompson
Department of Linguistics
South Hall 3607
University of California, Santa Barbara
Santa Barbara
CA 93106-3100
United States
email: sathomps@linguistics.ucsb.edu

Johannes Wagner
IFKI
University of Southern Denmark
Engstien 1
6000 Kolding
Denmark
email: jwa@sitkom.sdu.dk

Gareth Walker
School of English Literature, Language
and Linguistics
University of Sheffield
Jessop West
1 Upper Hanover Street
Sheffield S3 7RA
United Kingdom
email: g.walker@sheffield.ac.uk

Traci Walker
Department of Language and Linguistic
Science
University of York
Heslington
York YO10 5DD.
United Kingdom
email: tsc3@york.ac.uk

Bill Wells
Department of Human Communication
Sciences
University of Sheffield
31 Claremont Crescent
Sheffield S10 2TA
United Kingdom
email: bill.wells@sheffield.ac.uk

Introduction

Prosody in interaction

State of the art*

Margret Selting
University of Potsdam, Germany

This paper gives an overview of the field of prosody in interaction, classifying research areas and questions as they have developed since the start of the field in the mid 1980s. The overview is organized by the following questions:

1. What is prosody?
2. Why should scholars and students concerned with the analysis of conversation or interaction study prosody?
3. Why should phoneticians and phonologists study the forms and uses and/or functions of prosody in interaction?
4. Who studies prosody in interaction currently in what way?
5. What are our current research questions and our future tasks in research in prosody?
6. What are the challenges of research in prosody and interaction that we still need to come to terms with?

Introduction and overview

Since the 1980s, prosody has become both a nationally and internationally noticed and productive field of enquiry. Prosody is being studied within nearly every linguistic school and tradition, such that there is now a rich multiplicity of approaches and methodologies of research on prosody. This paper will focus on only one particular

* I am grateful to Arnulf Deppermann and the organizers of the March 2007 Annual Conference on 'Gesprächsforschung' for getting me started into the topic of this paper. I profited from comments on the talk I gave at the conference that this paper is based on. Furthermore, I am grateful to the participants of the 'Kolloquium zur linguistischen Kommunikationsforschung' at the University of Potsdam for helpful comments on an earlier version of this paper, and in particular to Elizabeth Couper-Kuhlen and Dagmar Barth-Weingarten who contributed important ideas and suggestions. Last, but not least, I am very grateful to Dagmar Barth-Weingarten and Elisabeth Reber as well as to Sandy Thompson and an anonymous reviewer for their innumerable comments and suggestions that helped the paper to arrive at its present form.

family of approaches to the study of prosody, namely on the research that emerged from or is incorporated into the analysis of natural conversation or interaction. In this research tradition, prosodic descriptions of single phenomena are now part of many studies; and to consider all of them is beyond this paper. Instead, I will focus on the approaches and studies that deal with prosody as their main subject.[1]

This paper will give an overview of the field of prosody in interaction, trying to identify and classify research areas and research questions as they have developed since the start of the blossoming of the field in, say, the mid 1980s. My aim is to show the broadness and richness that characterizes our field of research. The person to be honored with and in the papers of this volume, Elizabeth Couper-Kuhlen, has played a very important role in initiating and developing the course of this field.

My overview will be organized by the following questions:

1. What is prosody? How do we define and conceive of it?
2. Why should scholars and students concerned with the analysis of conversation or interaction study prosody? Or in other words: what relevance does the study of prosody have for the grammar of spoken language and for the analysis of conversation and/or interaction?
3. Why should phoneticians and phonologists study the forms and uses and/or functions of prosody in interaction?
4. Who studies prosody in interaction currently in what way? What are the approaches and methodological principles that we follow?
5. What are our current research questions and our future tasks in research in prosody?
6. What are the challenges of research in prosody and interaction that we still need to come to terms with?

1.   What is prosody?

Currently, two definitions are most relevant for research on prosody in interaction: Crystal's and Firth's.

In the West European research tradition following Crystal (1969), 'prosody' is understood to encompass all (suprasegmental) phenomena that are produced by the interplay of pitch, loudness and duration in syllable-sized or larger segments and that are realized in an "essentially variable relationship to the words selected" (ibid.: 5). While this definition implies that lexically determined word stress does not fall into the domain of prosody, it comprises the following phenomena and parameters:

---

1.   It is unavoidable even for overview papers to reflect the author's position in the limited amount of space available. My apologies go out to all who feel themselves misrepresented or unduly disregarded.

- primary (linguistic) prosodic systems: pitch direction, pitch range, pause, loudness, tempo, rhythmicality,
- secondary (paralinguistic) phenomena:
  - 'voice qualifiers' (for example whisper, breathiness, huskiness, creak, etc.) and
  - voice qualifications (such as laughter, giggle, tremolo, sobbing or crying),

with tension (for instance lax, tense, slurred or precise voice) belonging to both prosodic as well as paralinguistic systems (Crystal 1969: 131, cf. also Auer and Selting
2001: 1122).

As the differentiation between Crystal's 'linguistic' und 'paralinguistic' phenomena, and especially the classification of pause, seem to be problematic, some researchers
(such as Kelly and Local 1989, Couper-Kuhlen 2000: 2) go back to Firth (1957) for a
more extensive definition of the subject area of 'prosody'. Firth conceived of *'prosodies'*
as all types of syntagmatic relationships between syllables that are not determined by
the structure of words and utterances. These encompass syllable structures, stress/ac-
centuation, tone, quality and quantity, and, if applicable, also phenomena like glottal-
ization, aspiration, nasalization, whisper etc.

Following Firth, all suprasegmental phenomena that are constituted by the interplay of pitch, loudness, duration and voice quality can be understood as prosodic, as
long as they are used – independently of the language's segmental structure – *as communicative signals*. This broader definition of prosody is most useful for the study of
prosody in interaction.

2.   Why should scholars and students concerned with the analysis of conversation or interaction study prosody?

Most students of prosody in interaction work within conversation analysis (CA) and/
or interactional linguistics (IL). This kind of research is important for several reasons.

Firstly, research in prosody in interaction has filled a research gap since about the
mid-1980s: data from natural social interaction had rarely been the basis for systematic studies of prosody before that time. While older approaches to the investigation of
prosody had mostly been based on introspective or experimental data, researchers in
the field of prosody in interaction have decided to ground their work on data from
natural conversational or other interactional contexts and follow the rigorous methodological principles of CA, as they were first set out in the work of Sacks, Schegloff and
Jefferson (esp. 1974, cf. Section 4). With this decision, researchers in prosody in interaction started their own new field of enquiry, which has by now developed into a rich
field with its own family of approaches (cf. Section 4).

Secondly, prosody has been shown to be relevant and indispensable for the description of the organization and function of social interaction. While in principle
every researcher should be free to include or exclude prosody in their own research,

the inclusion of prosody is nevertheless crucial for some specific research questions. If we are concerned with *basic research questions* (*Grundlagenforschung*) and want to describe the basic, constitutive parameters and principles involved in the production and interpretation of verbal actions in conversation, we simply cannot neglect prosody. Otherwise, the analysis would be at best incomplete – and, in many cases, even incorrect, because prosody accomplishes two basic functions:

a. In spoken language, prosody is *always (co)constitutive*:
    Because prosody is always co-occurring with grammar (morpho-syntax) and lexis in utterances in their sequential contexts, it is always co-constitutive in the expression and achievement of interactional meaning. There is no spoken language without prosody, and disregarding prosody in the study of spoken language means disregarding an integral part of spoken language itself.
b. Furthermore, *in some cases*, prosody even fulfills a *distinctive* function in the production of interactional meanings: It has been shown for some activity/action types and practices that prosody is used to accomplish some actions in a *specific* or even *distinctive* way. This is demonstrated in Example (1).

Example (1)
In German, the item *was* (English 'what') as an open-class repair initiator can be formatted in at least the three following ways: [2]

	was,	vs.	was.	vs.	<<h>!WAS!?>

a. was,   with rising pitch and normal loudness and length signals a problem in acoustic decoding,
b. was.   with falling pitch and normal loudness and length signals a problem of referential understanding,
c. <<h>!WAS!?> on a higher tone register and with greater loudness, sometimes also greater length, signals a problem of expectations, i.e. surprise or astonishment.

With differing prosody, the same lexical item can thus initiate different types of other-initiated self repair which are also handled in different ways in the sequences to follow (cf. Selting 1996b).

This shows that, at least for basic research questions, prosody cannot be disregarded. To what extent prosody has to be considered for other research questions and in particular for applications in fields of practice – this of course depends on the specific research questions.

If we want to say something more specific about the role that prosody plays in the organization of interaction, we can look at the *general tasks and practices that have to be accomplished by participants for the organization of interaction* and focus on the role

---

2. Transcription here is adapted to the GAT transcription system, cf. Selting et al. (1998, 2009).

of prosody therein. This leads to the following conclusions: Prosody is relevant for the following recurrent tasks and practices in interaction:

2.1   The construction of units

In their description of a "simplest systematics for the organization of turn-taking for conversation", Sacks et al. (1974) distinguish between turns and turn-constructional units (TCUs). Turns-at-talk can be composed of a single unit (single-unit turns) or of several units (multi-unit turns).

Let us first consider the construction of single units, TCUs, and single-unit turns and their possible expansions.

Example (2) (Selting 1995a: 94–95):

```
a.  geNAU;
    precisely;
    precisely

    da      musst   ich  ARbeiten;
    then    must    I    work
    I had to work then
```

vs.

```
b.  genau da         musst ich ARbeiten  un   dann war ich noch  auf
    precisely then   must  I   work       and  then was I   PART  to
    precisely then I had to work and then I was PART

    ner Andern fete eingeladen.
    another party invited
    invited to another party
```

In the two utterances in Example (2), produced by the same speaker, the same sequence of words *genau da musst ich arbeiten* ('precisely then I had to work') is packaged into two separate units in the first case and into one single unit in the second case. The two versions perform quite different actions: In (a), *geNAU* ('precisely') is deployed as a response token to agree with the prior speaker's locating the time of a particular event, namely a concert he gave, before the current speaker goes on to give more information on her own whereabouts at that particular time. In (b), *genau* is deployed as a modifier to specify the indexical time adverbial *da* at the beginning of the speaker's account why she was not present at that particular concert.

In connection with the construction of single units, here are some of the more detailed practices that have to be accomplished by prosody:

–   Signaling the internal cohesion and delimitation of single TCUs (cf. Local 1992, Selting 1995a, 1996a, 2000a, 2001a, 2005, Auer 1996, Fox 2001, Couper-Kuhlen 2004).

- Signaling a unit's semantic focus through the interplay of syntax, lexis and accentuation (cf. Selting 1995a).
- In cases of internal trouble, distinguishing between the continuation of the TCU-in-production and the beginning of a new unit (cf. Local 1992, Selting 1995a, 1996a).
- In cases of possible pivot-constructions (apokoinu), distinguishing between genuine pivot-constructions and the abandoning of a fragment and the beginning of a new unit (cf. Selting 1995c).
- In cases of syntactic expansion, differentiating constructions on the continuum between prosodically integrated extensions of the "old" unit and prosodically exposed additions as new units (cf. Auer 1996, Couper-Kuhlen and Ono 2007a).
- Contributing to distinguishing grammatical constructions and their variants (along the lines of an empirical, interactionally oriented construction grammar; cf. Günthner and Imo 2006), used as unit-constructing practices or devices.

2.2   The construction of multi-unit turns

In the construction of multi-unit turns, prosody can be deployed to signal the type of combination of units in the turn. See Example (3).

Example (3) (Selting et al. 1998: 116, lines 16–18):

```
das letzte  kind   (.) endlich  aus m         HAUS,
the last    child      finally  out of the    house

zum stuDIERN, (-)
for studying

WEGgegangen,
left
```

Example (3) shows a few units from a longer story. Here, the only way the speaker signals that she intends her phrasing of this part of the story to be understood not as one or two, but as three separate units, is through prosody. Each of these units ends with pitch rising-to-mid, and for the beginning of the next unit the speaker creates a prosodic break by dropping in pitch and thus starting a new prosodic unit. A pause between units reinforces the separation of the stretch of speech into different units. At the same time, by repeatedly using rising pitch, she signals cohesion between the units. With an altogether different prosody, the same wording could very well be used to phrase one single unit: *das letzte kind endlich aus m haus zum studiern weggegangen* (i.e. 'the last child finally (had) left the house for studying'). In comparison to a possible phrasing in one single unit, the phrasing in three units achieves the following: instead of one single unit with one single accented syllable to suggest the semantic focus of that unit, a phrasing in three separate units results in the constitution of three accented syllables with each accented syllable signaling a separate focus of its own. This phrasing can be used, for instance, to signal emphasis, to create suspense, etc.

This brief analysis suggests the following:

- Whether grammatical elements belong to the prior unit or to a new unit may be signaled only through prosodic packaging (see above).
- The kind of combination between units in turns may be conveyed only through prosody. Examples of this are:
  - the signaling of causal clauses with *weil* ('because') or of concessive clauses with *obwohl* ('although') as either prosodically integrated or not integrated with their "main" clauses, which each signal different interactional meanings (Günthner 1993, 1996a, Couper-Kuhlen 1996b), or
  - the signaling of the following TCU's topical relation to the prior TCU or turn as a continuation of the prior topic or as a new topic (Couper-Kuhlen 2001a, 2004).

2.3   The organization of turn-taking

On approaching the end of a turn-final TCU (more precisely: after the turn-final TCU's transition relevance place (TRP)), the allocation of the next TCU has to be negotiated (for the rules of turn-allocation see Sacks et al. 1974). Apart from these rules, at the end of turns, current speaker can deploy syntax and prosody in order to project either turn-holding or turn-yielding. Next speakers can go along with this or they can come in with contributions not projected by current speaker: non-competitive and competitive incomings. In all these practices, speakers realize specific bundles of phonetic and prosodic cues in order to distinguish between the particular practice at hand and other possible practices at this location in the interactional sequence.

Prosody differentiates – inter alia – between:

- Turn holding and turn yielding at turn endings (Local et al. 1986, Selting 1995a, 1996a, 2000a),
- non-competitive and competitive incomings (French and Local 1983, Selting 1995a).

Related to this, prosody also signals opportunities for minimal responses, such as continuers and collaborative completions (cf. Selting 2000a, Lerner 1996, Local 2005).

In most varieties of German, in the appropriate sequential and action context, level or slightly rising final pitch at the end of turn constructional units may be used to signal turn holding, i.e. project a continuation by the same speaker. Consider the following examples:

Example (4) (cf. Couper-Kuhlen and Selting 1996a: 34; adapted to GAT):

```
a.  ich  mach  das   jetz  hier  zu  ↑¯ENde¯
    I    make  this  now   here  an  end
    I'm going to finish this here now

b.  ich  mach  das   jetz  hier  zu  `EN´de,
    I    make  this  now   here  an  end
    I'm going to finish this here now
```

In order to yield the turn, however, the speaker must choose a pitch other than level or slightly rising in German (Selting 1995a, 2000a).

The beginning of the transition relevance place or space (TRP) is signaled by the unit's *final* accent. While the accentuation itself, i.e. the choice of the syllable that carries the pitch accent, is closely linked to grammatical principles, the final accent can often be deduced from syntactic and pragmatic projection. It is here where the contextualization of the designed turn holding or yielding starts, involving pitch movement, loudness, duration, speech rate and perhaps other prosodic parameters. Example (5) is an illustration.

Example (5) (Selting 1995a: 202, adapted at GAT):

```
1  Nat:   Ich  würd   AU     nich fahrn  wenn  ich  so:
          I    would  also   not  drive  if    I    so

2         LEUte     hier  hätte
          people    here  had

3         <<all> mit  deman    was      am       wochenende
                 with whomone things    at the weekend

4         mAchen    k[önnte   oder  so,>
          do        could     or    so
          I also wouldn't drive home if I knew people here with whom one could do some-
          thing on the weekends

5  Ida:              [nee DANN:  wär   ja    alles:  (.) in ORDnung;
                      no  then   were  PART  everything in order
                      no then everything would be okay
```

In the context which this turn is taken from, neither the first possible syntactic clause alone, *Ich würd AU nich fahrn* ('I also wouldn't drive home', line 1), nor this syntactic clause plus its continuation *wenn ich so: LEUte hier hätte* ('if I knew people here', lines 1–2) are possibly complete TCUs, since in the given context the final relative clause of the TCU, *mit deman was am wochendende mAchen könnte* ('with whom one could do something on the weekends', lines 3–4), is crucial to make this turn a coherent response to the prior one (not shown here). Under these conditions, the accent in the word *mAchen* in line 4 of Nat's turn, which can be anticipated as the final accent because of the unit's syntactic structure, opens up the transition relevance place. The second speaker Ida makes use of this with an early start of her response.

Finally, prosody can also organize potentially problematic turn-taking. French and Local (1983) showed that a recipient's incomings produced in overlap with a current speaker's turn are treated differently according to their prosodic make-up: Somewhat simplified, the principle is the following: overlapping talk formatted with high and forte prosody is heard and treated as competitive, i.e. an (attempted) interruption designed to usurp the floor, whereas overlapping talk formatted with low and quiet prosody is heard and treated as non-competitive, i.e. something like a mere background remark, designed to not take the floor (cf. Selting 1995a for a similar analysis on the basis of German data).

2.4   The construction of actions

While linguistics often tends to focus on the units of language, it needs to be kept in mind that the purpose of interaction is the accomplishment of actions and activities. In this way, the specific syntax and prosody of units seems to play a crucial role for the signaling and interpretation of action types such as, for instance, questions and initiations of repair.

Consider again the single-word unit and turn *was* ('what') in Example (1):

Example (1)':

```
was,          vs.    was.             vs.     <<h>!WAS!?>
```

Each of these variants opens up a particular type of repair sequence in which a particular response is thus made relevant (cf. Selting 1996b):

a. `was,`   makes relevant something like a repetition of the prior turn;
b. `was.`   makes relevant the explication of the referential term that the item locates;
c. `<<h>!WAS!?`   makes relevant the explication of background information in order to clarify a clash of expectations.

As various studies have shown, prosody is realized to differentiate between at least the following practices and actions:

– the initiation of different types of repair, which are also treated differently in the next turn, as seen above (Kelly and Local 1989, Selting 1995a, 1996b),
– different types of questions and enquiries, i.e. second questions (Selting 1992, 1995a),
– repetition vs. mimicry of an interlocutor's prior contribution (Couper-Kuhlen 1996a),
– repetition for understanding checks, displays of recognition or mulling over (Kelly and Local 1989),
– continuation of a prior vs. initiation of a new topic or a new sequence (Couper-Kuhlen 2001a, 2004),
– signaling and/or negotiation of agreement and disagreement in, e.g., assessment sequences (Ogden 2006),
– signaling affiliation or non-affiliation with prior talk (Szczepek Reed 2006).

2.5   The contextualization of genres (*kommunikative Gattungen*),
modalities, styles, emotive involvement etc.

Prosody is used to suggest the interpretation of different genres and styles, but also modalities, attitudes and emotive involvement (Couper-Kuhlen 1992, 2006, Selting 1994, 1995a, b, 1996b, Freese and Maynard 1998). See, for instance, <<h>!WAS!?> in Example (1), which contextualizes surprise.

In general, the function of prosody in conversation can be described as follows: Prosody is relevant for the *projection* (predominantly in a prospective orientation) and *contextualization* (in a retrospective <u>and</u> a prospective orientation) of units and their relations and interactive meanings within the interaction (Selting 1995a, Couper-Kuhlen 2007b).

In addition, prosody shows, at least partially, *regionalized forms and functions* (Local, Kelly and Wells 1986, Local, Wells and Sebba 1985, Wells and Peppé 1996, Gilles 2005, Peters 2006) and *characteristics and usages specific to and constitutive of interactional styles* (Selting 1995b, 1997, Kern and Selting 2006a, b, Kern and Simsek 2006).

3   Why should phoneticians and phonologists study the forms
and uses and/or functions of prosody in interaction?

In general, approaches to prosody and phonetics differ fundamentally in their research strategies: While many researchers start with more idealized data and assume that the results can ultimately be transferred to natural data, others do not believe in this and insist on starting from natural data from "real" social interactions, which means: interactions which were consequential for the participants at the time.

3.1   New technological possibilities allow new
methodologies in research on prosody

Traditionally, when it was still impossible to record and analyze data acoustically, phoneticians used to rely on their own intuitions or their auditive perceptions and transcriptions of data obtained from selected informants. Later, when technological inventions made recording possible, but the machinery was so large that it could not be taken out into the field, phoneticians either recorded their own pronunciation of words and sentences with, e.g., an oszillograph, or they invited selected speakers into the phonetic laboratory to produce data for them to register and analyze. Sometimes, these selected speakers were performers such as speakers of radio news or actors, who were trained in speaking in public. Data samples obtained from these speakers were thought of as reasonably reliable realizations of the standard language (cf. also Gessinger 1994).

With the advent of modern sociolinguistics, however, during the 1960s, it became generally recognized that language variation is subject to – inter alia – class and situational constraints (cf. Labov 1972). At about the same time, recording technology had developed so far that it became much easier to record the speech of speakers in their actual natural environments. While at first, machinery was still quite big and thus noticeable and intrusive for the situation to be recorded, recording devices became smaller almost by the year. The smaller the equipment was, the easier it became for the researcher to move away from settings such as reading aloud (word lists, sentences, or even texts) or formal interviews as their settings for data collection (cf. also Auer 1993).

Today, recordings can be made virtually everywhere, and recording has become more a problem of ethics than of possibility. At the same time, acoustic analysis is no longer performed by hardware but by software, and the new programs (for instance PRAAT, developed by Paul Boersma and David Weenink at the Institute of Phonetic Sciences at the University of Amsterdam, see www.praat.org) are so powerful that they usually allow the analysis of natural speech from natural interactional settings. Thus, if the aim of linguistic and phonetic analysis is to describe natural speech, there are no obstacles any more to record this kind of speech within its natural "home", natural situations of interaction.

In conclusion: The advent of modern audio and video recording technology as well as modern speech and acoustic analysis software has made the restriction of data to a laboratory environment unnecessary.

3.2   Limitations of some other approaches' preference of more idealized data

Some researchers still work on the basis of their own intuitions. Other researchers continue to record and analyze speech produced in the laboratory, in order to control variables and samples of speech. It is argued that the analysis of speech from such controlled situations allows the researcher to isolate the most basic descriptive facts about language which can then later be transferred to and checked with data from natural situations (cf. Mayer 1999).

However, such a transfer is hardly possible (cf. Labov 1972 on situationally specific styles of speaking), since if we were to follow this research strategy, we would tackle speech from natural interaction with a severe laboratory speech bias (see 3.3. below and also Section 6.).

Work with controlled, semi-natural data like those from, for instance, map-task dialogues (cf. Anderson et al. 1991) has bridged the gap between the approaches to a certain extent, but not really closed it. Here experimental subjects engage in semi-natural tasks with set-up problems in which they respond rather spontaneously to each other. Nevertheless, the situations are too restricted to be comparable to natural talk-in-interaction.

If we look at the categories and results from such studies of prosody in non-natural settings, we simply do not know whether they are relevant for the analysis of speech in natural interaction. The tasks to be fulfilled by participants in natural interaction through speech are very different from those to be fulfilled in laboratory settings. Thus, it comes as no surprise that traditional intonation theory is mostly concerned with sentences – often without making explicit that the underlying data came from sentences read aloud in the laboratory. Conversational issues such as turn taking or sequence organization simply do not come up in such a setting. For natural data, the results of laboratory studies might turn out as at best irrelevant or incomplete, but they might also be wrong. In any case they give us an inappropriate starting point and perspective for the analysis of data from natural interaction.

To understand and describe the prosody of speech from natural interaction, then, it behooves us to base our analyses on data from these very settings as well as to orient to the interactional tasks which speakers attend to in these settings and the role of prosody in accomplishing these tasks.

3.3   Some advantages of starting from natural data in the first place

The approaches concerned with prosody in interaction represented in this paper, and in this volume, insist on starting from data from natural social interactions. They require both analyzing natural data as well as validating analyses with reference to these data, applying rigorous conversation analytic and phonetic methodology. (The methodological principles involved in this will be outlined in Section 4 below.)

Students of prosody in interaction argue that starting from natural data allows the researcher to isolate the basic categories and parameters that are relevant for the participants in their organization of social interaction. Adopting Harvey Sacks' (1984; cf. also 1992) maxim of 'order at all points', they have been able to show that the use and treatment of phonetic and prosodic detail in interactional data is highly systematic and relevant for the participants.

4.   Who studies prosody in interaction currently in what way?

4.1   Approaches

Current research to prosody in interaction can be grouped according to four approaches, which originate from different traditions.

4.1.1   *Phonetics and phonology for conversation*

The first researchers to deal with prosody systematically on the basis of conversation-analytic theory and methodology were phoneticians at the University of York (UK), in particular Local and Wells (for early work see French and Local 1983, Local et al. 1985, Local et al. 1986 etc.). They created the research program of a 'phonology-for-conversation', in which phonetic features of spoken language are described in terms of their relevance for the organization of conversation. This implies a combination of Firthian-inspired detailed phonetic analysis (Firth 1957, "detailed qualitative and quantitative parametric phonetic techniques", Local and Walker 2005: 120) with a conversation-analytic sequential analysis of the social actions in which the participants are engaged; by which "it seeks to identify the interactional tasks managed by clusters of phonetic events" (ibid.: 120f.). At present, it is in particular the names of Local, Wells, Ogden, Curl and Walker which are most associated with this research school.

4.1.2 *Prosody as a contextualization device*
Approximately at the same time as the York phoneticians, Gumperz (cf. Gumperz 1982, 1990) developed his contextualization theory. This assumes that the content of a contribution, the *what*, is being made interpretable through the design of the contribu-tion, the *how*. The *how*, i.e. the particular presentation of the *what*, is deployed to sug-gest and make available interpretive frames. Conversation analysts used this approach in addition to CA, in order to integrate the analysis of prosody, but also language vari-ation (in terms of code- and style shifting and switching), syntax and lexis, gestures, facial expressions etc., into the sequential analysis of verbal interaction (cf. Auer 1992, Auer and di Luzio 1992). The work by Couper-Kuhlen (1993) and Auer, Couper-Kuhlen and Müller (1999) on rhythm and tempo in conversation, and that by Selting (1995a) primarily on intonation in conversation, are based on this approach. (See this volume as well as, for instance, Couper-Kuhlen and Selting 1996.)

4.1.3 *Interactional Linguistics*
Since the mid 1990s, both Ford et al. (especially ibid. 1996, 2002, 2003) as well as Couper-Kuhlen and Selting (especially Selting and Couper-Kuhlen 2001, Couper-Kuhlen and Selting 2001) have been developing an approach which they call *Interac-tional Linguistics*. This approach aims at an analysis of the structures of spoken lan-guage in interaction, in particular structures of syntax, prosody/intonation and pragmatics with respect to their functions for the sequential organization of natural talk-in-interaction. In their sequential analysis, they are oriented towards CA. In this approach, too, some work is specifically aimed at the analysis of prosody in conversa-tion (Fox 2001, Rabanus 2001, Jasperson 2002, Ford et al. 2004, Couper-Kuhlen and Ford 2004, Gilles 2005, cf. also, Wichmann 2000, Wennerstrom 2001, Hakulinen and Selting 2005, and papers in this volume).

4.1.4 *CA work on prosody in conversation*
Work on prosody in conversation usually builds on "foundations" of CA descriptions of the sequential organization of conversation, but also takes up work by practitioners of CA which is devoted to prosodic phenomena in particular. To name but a few, Sacks, Schegloff and Jefferson pointed to the relevance of intonation for turn-taking as early as 1974; Jefferson (1988) dealt with prosodic phenomena such as, for example, pauses; Schegloff (1982) described prosodic details of hesitation phenomena and (1987) pitch peaks in their function as signals for the opening up of transition relevance places at turn endings. Freese and Maynard (1998) published work on 'Prosodic features of bad

news and good news in conversation". In his 1998 article entitled 'Reflections on study-ing prosody in talk-in-interaction', Schegloff conceives of prosody as "one set of re-sources and practices among many by which participants interactively produce con-versation and other talk-in-interaction" (1998: 235). On the basis of three examples, he shows how prosody can contribute to the organization of conversation: (1) pitch peaks can project a forthcoming designed turn completion, (2) pitch levels in the opening turns of telephone conversations are used for the negotiation of tenor, "for subtly shad-ed displays of state and stance, of mood and relationship, of topic priorities and topical allusion, of sequence organization and interactional exigency" (ibid.: 244), and (3) prosody contributes to the constitution of actions, as

> "we must suppose that there is some 'methodic way' – some mechanism – by which some prosodic practice (not some particular prosodic realization) enters into the constitution and recognition of an utterance as an instance of some type of action, and that 'way' – that mechanism – calls for analysis and explication" (ibid: 247).

4.2   Methodological principles

The methodological principles for the analysis of prosody in conversation have been explicitly formulated primarily by Couper-Kuhlen and Selting (1996a) and Local and Walker (2005). They will be summarized here in a list-like form:

Couper-Kuhlen and Selting (1996a: 25–39) propose the following catalogue:

1. Give priority to the analysis of naturally occurring talk.
2. Treat the data as an integral part of the context in which it occurs.
3. Treat the data as emergent in the real time of ongoing interaction.
4. Ground analytic categories in the data itself.
    Use, following Wootton (1989), types of evidence such as the following:
    a. The relationship of the device to just prior turns.
    b. Co-occurring evidence within the turn.
    c. Subsequent treatment of the interactional device in question.
    d. Discriminability of the interactional device.
    e. Deviant cases in the use of the device.
5. Validate analytical categories by demonstrating participants' orientation to them.

Local and Walker (2005: 121–123) put forward the following "(m)ethodological im-peratives (...) for the investigation of the phonetic organization and phonological structures of spontaneous speech:

1. Only use data drawn from talk-in-interaction. [...]
2. Conduct phonetic and interactional analysis in parallel and not serially. [...]

3. Demonstrate the orientation of participants to any categories posited or analytic claims made. [...]
4. Ensure that any analytic account handles single cases as cogently as it does the aggregate. [...]
5. Subject each fragment to close inspection during repeated listenings. [...]
6. Treat all details at all levels as of potential relevance to the participants. [...]
7. Be attentive to place in sequence and to place in structure. [...]."

Furthermore, Local and Walker (2005: 128) draw the following general conclusions:

> "if we wish to advance understanding of speech communication and account for the organization and functioning of phonetic detail in everyday talk-in-interaction, we need to
> (1) treat all phonetic resources equally and not give analytic privilege to one kind of phonetic parameter over another;
> (2) provide rigorous analytic evidence for the observable orientations of interlocutors to the phonetic characteristics described, and
> (3) develop a theory of phonetic exponency which relates to a sequential action-based analysis of talk-in-interaction."

The approaches detailed above in Section 4 have a number of *indisputable principles of prosodic analysis* in common:

1. The analysis should be based on data from naturally occurring talk.
2. The development of categories should be data-based.
3. The analysis combines sequential analysis and phonetic-prosodic analysis.
4. Analyses must be 'warranted', i.e., they have to be based on evidence that participants orient to the categories at hand, that the analyses are relevant for them rather than only for the analyst.

5. What are our current research questions and our future tasks in research on prosody?

'Prosody in conversation' has developed into a fine-grained field of research today. Within interactional linguistics and research in prosody and interaction, there is – in my view – a need for further detailed and precise phonetic-prosodic analysis, for different sequential contexts. Such analyses always imply at least the following two goals:

a. the *de*construction of holistically interpreted units in their sequences into their constitutive prosodic cues and parameters,
b. the *re*construction of the functioning of phonetic-prosodic cues and parameters in co-occurrence with all other relevant verbal and non-verbal structures in their sequential context.

*De*constructing holistically interpreted units, in turns or actions in their sequential environments, means isolating the fundamental formal resources, i.e. formal features, parameters or structures which a speaker deploys in co-occurrence with other formal features in making her utterances interpretable in their sequential environment. The deconstruction of the formal resources allows us to then investigate and reconstruct the ways in which these formal resources are deployed to fulfill their functions in the organization of interaction. *Re*construction thus aims at describing the mechanisms and principles according to which participants are able to deploy the formal resources in order to make their units, in turns or actions, interpretable in their sequential context. And again, in this reconstruction of the mechanisms and principles of meaning-making in interaction, prosody is but one of the resources. It has to be considered as deployed with other resources in their sequential context, to contribute to, and in some cases distinguish between, the construction of (particular) units, practices, actions, in order to fulfill recurrent tasks in the organization of interaction.

The major research areas outlined in the following overview illustrate interactionally relevant tasks that recurrently need to be organized in interaction. I will list the major research areas and their central research questions, and I will put forward the research questions that in my opinion require further systematic research, presenting them under the sub-heading 'desiderata'.[3]

5.1   Prosody in the organization of natural interaction

Present major research areas and desiderata are as follows.

5.1.1   *The construction of units*
Analysis of the role that phonetic-prosodic phenomena play in the projection and organization of single unit- and multi-unit-turns, in their interplay with – primarily – grammar (morpho-syntax), including a comparative perspective comparing different languages and language types (cf. Selting 2001a).

Desiderata:
This work should be combined and integrated with work on the visual and non-verbal resources being deployed in organizing interaction into recipient-designed chunks and units in time.

---

3.   In order not to overload this paper, I refrain from referring to the relevant literature for all the areas mentioned here. The list of references contains many sources relevant here, not all of which are actually referred to in the text. For directions for future research cf. also Couper-Kuhlen (2000: 15, 2001b: 29–30).

5.1.2   *The construction of turns and the organization of turn-taking*

- Analysis of the role phonetic-prosodic phenomena play in the projection and organization of designed turn endings (cf. Selting 2000a);
- Analysis of 'increments', i.e. expansions at possible turn completions, including a language (type) comparative perspective (cf. Walker 2004a, b, Couper-Kuhlen and Ono 2007);
- Analysis of different types of turn-taking: smooth turn transition, the use and signaling of "hesitation", the structure and use of overlap, break-off/abandonment of units and turns, the signaling of non-competitive versus competitive incomings (i.e., interruptions of current by next speaker) (Walker 2004a, b, Wells and Corrin 2004, Szczepek Reed 2004, Tanaka 2004, Ogden and Routarinne 2005, etc.);
- Description of the accomplishment of collaborative completion (Local 2005).

Desiderata:
- Further research on the role and relevance of phonetic and prosodic parameters in their co-occurrence with syntax and lexico-semantics for the projection of turn continuation and turn ending.
- What cross-linguistic differences manifest themselves?

5.1.3   *The contextualization of practices and actions*

Comparative analyses of the syntax and prosody of practices and actions in conversation, for example conversational questions, repairs, assessments, informings, announcements, repetitions, quoting, reported speech (*Redewiedergabe*), reproaches, devices and practices of topic organization, recipient behavior, etc. (cf., inter alia, M. H. Goodwin 1996, Couper-Kuhlen 1999, Günthner 2005a, Ogden 2006, Mori 2006, Selting 2007)

Desiderata:
What role do phonetic variation and prosody play in the signaling and production, in the making interpretable of actions in conversation: apart from the practices and actions mentioned above, also e.g. in requests, invitations, news receipts, recipient tokens, confirmation tokes, rejection tokens, response cries?

5.1.4   *The organization and internal structuring of sequences*

Analysis of prosody in question-answer-sequences, assessment sequences, request sequences, informing sequences, teasing sequences, lists, topic organization sequences, resumption of sequences after inserted activities, etc. (cf. Couper-Kuhlen 2004, Ford et al. 2004, Hellermann 2005, Mazeland 2007)

Desiderata:
- How are first pair parts and second pair parts of adjacency pairs prosodically related?

– Are expansions before, in, and after sequences prosodically related to the host sequence – and how? Here, all of the sequence structures described by Schegloff
(2007) can profit from an underpinning with phonetic and prosodic analysis to
discover the role of (different kinds of) phonetic-prosodic relations in accomplishing interactional meaning.

5.1.5   *The handling of 'trouble'*

Analysis of prosody in repair sequences, in the handling of "trouble" in interaction,
etc. (cf. Curl 2003, 2004, 2005, Curl et al. 2006).

Desiderata:
Further research on the role of prosody in the organization of repair sequences and the
handling of trouble. How does the differential prosodic formatting of the initiation of
repair condition the repair itself? How does the prosodically differential organization
of repair and trouble sequences matter to the sequence's contribution to the ongoing
interaction – as well as to the repair's functioning in the interaction?

5.1.6   *Interaction transcending single turns and sequences*

It has been shown that interlocutors very closely orient to each other in their usage of
phonetic and prosodic cues in interaction. Wennerstrom (2001) writes about *tone con-
cord*, and Szczepek Reed (2006) describes *pitch matching* between speakers. Prosody is
one of the most subtle devices for suggesting and negotiating interactional meaning as
well as the relationship between the speakers.

Desiderata:
Further research on the role of prosody in *cross-speaker interaction*, e.g. in the signaling of *alignment* and *affiliation*.

5.1.7   *The construction and contextualization of genres, modalities*
and/or styles in interaction

Analysis of prosody in *big packages* such as story telling, arguing, disputing, lecturing,
etc. (cf. Kern 2007, Selting 2008a, b).

Desiderata:
– Further research on the role of prosody in constituting such big packages, also in
teasing, joking, gossiping and in institutional talk such as classroom-talk, and so on.
– Is it possible to find more general patterns, i.e. prosodically indexed modalities
and styles, transcending single actions and/or genres?

5.2   Prosody and grammar/syntax in conversation

Analysis of the co-occurrence and interplay of syntactic, lexico-semantic and prosodic
features of units of spoken language in general and in specific constructions and their

variants in particular; always studied in their sequential contexts; early examples have been syntactic sentences and clauses, so-called "elliptical" phrases, causal clauses, concessive clauses, and so on (for a description and references to older work see Selting and Couper-Kuhlen 2001, for recent work, see, e.g., Birkner 2007, 2008). Currently, work is being done that integrates prosodic analysis into empirical approaches to the grammar of constructions (cf. Couper-Kuhlen and Thompson 2005, the contributions in Günthner and Imo 2006, Günthner 2005b).

Desiderata:
- If there are conventionalized patterns between syntax and lexico-semantics that exhibit both fixed and open slots, do these constructions co-occur with specific phonetic-prosodic structures? Are there fixed prosodic "patterns"?
- What role do stylized intonation contours play in interaction? Can they be looked upon as "prosodic constructions"?
- Is prosody relevant for the description of single grammatical constructions or does it take on construction-transcending interactional functions?

5.3   Prosody and semantics: Signaling of information structure

Study of accent placement and its relevance for the meaning and interpretation of TCUs, turns and sequences. Local and Walker (2005: 129) point out that "Wells and MacFarlane (1998) provide a radical deconstruction of prosodic accentuation and its phonological status as projecting turn-transition relevance or not".

Desiderata:
Although accentuation has been an important area of research in phonology, very little work has been done on its relevance and function in natural interaction. What is the relevance of accentuation, i.e. accent placement, in relation to grammatical structures? What is its relevance for signaling the semantic structure of units in terms of information structure? How does this relate to the relevance of accentuation for the organization of turn taking? What is the relevance of accentuation in the design of turns and sequences? What role do multiple accents play in TCUs, turns and sequences?

5.4   Prosody and language variation/language comparison/typology

a. *Constitution and contextualization of speech styles and conversational styles,*
    e.g. styles in cooperative story telling and controversial argumentation, dramatization of story climaxes (cf. Selting 2008a, b)
b. *Regionalized structures and functions of prosody in conversation*
    (cf. Auer 2001, Gilles 2005, Peters 2006, Selting 2000b, 2001c, 2004a, b etc.)
c. *The role of prosody for the construction of ethnic styles*
    (cf. Kern and Selting 2006a, b, Kern 2008, Kern and Simsek 2006, Simsek 2008)

d. *Comparative studies of the prosody of different languages in conversation,*
    e.g. German-English-Chinese (cf. Li forthc.)
e. *Comparative studies of 'increments' in different language-types/families*
    (cf. Couper-Kuhlen and Ono 2007, Tanaka 1999)

Desiderata:
There is a need for further comparative studies of prosody in talk in different varieties/
(ethnic) styles, and languages and language types/families, with reference to its use in
practices and activities, such as the organization of turn-taking and the management
of comparable activities and sequences:
–   Can we find similarities and differences in the use of phonetic-prosodic resources
    across languages or language types?
–   Do certain practices and actions require a certain verbal and also prosodic
    organization?
–   What kind of relation do interactional requirements bear to language structure
    and language type and their prosodic organization?
–   To what extent does language structure demand or facilitate certain interactive
    practices, for instance certain types of projecting turn-completion, repair, and re-
    cipient behavior?

5.5   Prosody in conversation with specific kinds of participants

a. Prosody in conversations between adults and children and among children
    (Tarplee 1996, Wells and Corrin 2004)
b. Prosody in conversations with and among people with language impairments
    (Wells and Peppé 2003, Catterall et al. 2006, Goodwin 2003, 2006, this volume)

Desiderata:
We need further studies of language acquisition and language impairment from an in-
teractional point of view and with an interactional prosodic/linguistic methodology:
–   In what way is prosody acquired in the processes of first and second language
    acquisition?
–   In what way is prosody deployed in difficult communicative situations, say with
    participants with restricted linguistic competence (e.g., L1 or L2 language learn-
    ers) or with language impairment? How can prosody be deployed to compensate
    for the loss or non-availability of other linguistic resources?

5.6   Prosody and the contextualization of affect

Prosodic contextualization of emotive involvement, affect and stance in conversation:
Signaling of, e.g., anger, joy, grief, disappointment, indignation, emphasis, astonishment, agreement vs. disagreement/dissonance, and the prosodic structure and use of

emotive *sound objects* (Reber 2007, 2008) such as *erkh.* to express disgust and recipient responses such as *ah:::;* or *wow:::;* to express delight or enthusiasm (cf. Selting 1994, 1996b, Deppermann and Lucius-Hoene 2005, Couper-Kuhlen 2009, Selting 2010).

Desiderata:
- What role do phonetic-prosodic parameters and bundles of features play in the signaling of emotive involvement, affect and stance in interaction?
- Which phonetic-prosodic parameters are used to signal which affects?
- What is the relation between phonetics-prosody and other verbal and non-verbal signaling devices in the display and management of affectivity in interaction?

5.7   Prosody and the multimodality of interaction

Analysis of the relation between vocal, i.e. verbal and prosodic, and non-verbal/vocal signaling cues in interaction, especially the relation between prosodic resources on the one hand and non-verbal/vocal gesture such as gaze, facial expression, posture, on the other hand, for the projection and contextualization of units, turns, actions, and sequences (cf. Schönherr 1997, Selting in prep).

On the relation between prosodic and non-verbal signaling cues, in a study of the deployment of gesture and gaze in the construction of complex sentences, parenthetical clauses, and repair in Austrian-German talk-in-interaction, Schönherr (1997) came to the following conclusions:

"Prosodie und Gestik sind eng miteinander verbunden" (ibid.: 207 [*Prosody and gesture are closely tied to each other;* translation MS.]).

"Das Verhältnis zwischen prosodischen und nonverbalen Signalen kann als Implikationshierarchie beschrieben werden: Wenn Diskontinuitätssignale auftreten, ist die Prosodie üblicherweise daran beteiligt" (ebd.: 212 [*The relation between prosodic and nonverbal signals can be described as an implicational hierarchy: If signals of discontinuity are used, prosody usually is part of them;* translation MS.]).

Another issue is this: Is there an additive or an implicational relation between verbal-vocal and non-verbal-visual cues, such that in face-to-face interaction, as compared to telephone interaction, the visual channel is added to the auditory one, or is there an entirely different *semiotic field* or *semiotic ecology* in telephone and in face-to-face interaction, as Goodwin (2000: 1494, 2007, this volume) suggests.

Desiderata:
It has become clear by now that for the study of face-to-face interaction research has to be based on video recordings. Recently, the study of multimodality in interaction has become an important field of research (cf., e.g., Goodwin 2000, Sidnell and Stivers 2005, Mondada 2007, Schmitt 2007). This research implies analyzing the relation between the verbal, vocal and non-verbal/vocal modes of interaction, i.e. the study of the co-occurrence and interplay between the segmental, prosodic and paralinguistic, and visual resources of interactions in the process of managing

interaction. Which gestures are related to which prosodic categories, e.g. accented syllables, unit boundaries, and how are they connected to each other? Are there systematic and/or conventional co-occurrences between prosody and non-vocal/verbal signaling cues?[4]

In order to be able to accurately describe the practices participants employ and the functions for which they employ these resources, prosody should be integrated in the sequential and multimodal analysis of interaction. Almost all the research fields listed above offer themselves as starting points for such an integration.

Moreover, apart from the desiderata with respect to the open questions in the fields of research mentioned above, structured around the tasks to be fulfilled in interaction, there are some more basic desiderata which relate to our ways of transcribing and analyzing the data in the first place. In order to provide for the tackling of the above mentioned future research questions, we should also (further) develop the following more basic tools and categories for data representation and analysis:

- the transcription of prosody
- the transcription and categorization of voice qualities
- the transcription of non-verbal/vocal aspects of talk: gaze, facial expression, gesture, posture, etc.

Some of these issues will be taken up again in the next section.

6.   What are the challenges of research in prosody and interaction that we still need to come to terms with?

6.1   General problems

6.1.1   *Differences in the aims of the relevant approaches*[5]
In some of the relevant CA literature, the focused and systematic analysis of prosody (as well as that of e.g. grammar or gesture) is rejected (cf. Schegloff 2005).[6] From an interactional linguistics perspective, however, the systematic analysis of single signaling systems of interaction, such as syntax or prosody or gesture, does not necessarily conflict with the analysis of the interaction as a whole. It rather serves to enlarge and deepen our knowledge about the systematic basis of interaction and about the practices and resources that participants deploy in interaction. Therefore, the systematic

---

4.   I am grateful to Peter Gilles for some of these ideas.

5.   Spelling out some of the differences between the approaches to prosody in interaction here is not meant to separate or criticize them. Rather, positions and differences need to be made transparent.

6.   Cf. also Levinson (2005), who criticizes Schegloff's approach as *interactional reductionism* and advocates his own perspective of an *interactional constructivism*, which he takes to be more realistic.

analysis of vocal and visual signaling systems is absolutely necessary to the study of talk-in-interaction, and integrated into the analysis of interaction as a whole (cf. also Section 6.2.5.).

6.1.2 *Practical problems*

The complexity of research on prosody is both overestimated and underestimated: It is underestimated when young researchers believe prosodic analysis and description to be possible without a background in articulatory and acoustic phonetics and without the help and critical guidance by experts in the field. It is overestimated when young researchers do not even dare to approach the research field: Prosodic analysis and description are demanding, but learnable. Even students who think of themselves as not musical or not musically gifted can use acoustic-phonetic software such as PRAAT (www.praat.org) to both train their own perception as well as to back up and refine their auditory analysis of prosody. In this way, as for most of us, steady practice may lead to expertise in the field.[7]

With the easy availability of programs such as PRAAT, authors of prosodic analyses are increasingly expected to present acoustic evidence of their findings. For most analyses this is indeed a way to visualize auditory phonetic-prosodic analyses and to increase the trustworthiness of the results. For the systematic analysis of phonetic and prosodic details, though, an instrumental analysis is absolutely necessary (cf. principle (3) in Section 4.2).

6.2   Specific open questions

6.2.1 *Differences in terms of categorization*

Approaches to the study of prosody in interaction differ with respect to their aims in notating and describing data. One of the issues can be phrased in the following question:

What actually do we want to transcribe and describe: Do we want to transcribe and analyze *everything observable* – or rather only those phenomena that (intuitively) seem *relevant* to the participants and therefore to us?

The York phoneticians, in their *Phonetics and Phonology for Conversation* (see Section 4.1.1) practice impressionistic observation and description of all perceivable phonetic parameters, i.e. prosodic and segmental parameters. They argue that we need to do this, because we cannot know in advance what will turn out to be relevant at the

---

7.   Having made this point, a note is in order: The relation between auditory perception and acoustic-phonetic measurements is not always straightforward. For example, auditory perception of pitch is relational and interpretative, but acoustic measurement is not, even in a logarithmic presentation. And acoustic measurements can be faulty. In general, we can make use of acoustic measurements to back up and refine our auditory analysis, but in cases of discrepancy between auditory and acoustic analysis, we should perhaps better trust our (trained) perception and search for explanations of apparently anomalous measurements. For introductions to acoustic phonetics see, e.g., Ladefoged (1992), Clark and Yallop (1990).

end of the analysis. Others argue that in principle there is no limit to the perceivable and observable, and maximally detailed notation of everything observable will obscure our recognition of the relevant parameters. Therefore, they argue, we should concentrate on the parameters relevant for the research question and description at hand.

6.2.2 *Differences in how to deal with traditional or established categories*
One of the methodological principles in Section 4.2 suggests grounding analytic categories in the data themselves. Yet, in particular in prosodic and phonetic research there are many categories and concepts already available. Can traditional and more holistic categories such as *intonation unit/prosodic unit/intonation phrase* or *accent* be used and adapted for the analysis of natural interaction – or do we need to start with a new analysis and create new categories appropriate for the description of spoken language in interaction?

After all, the traditional categories have originated from a linguistic tradition that was based and designed to study written language, read language or – as Abercrombie (1965: 4) once put it – "spoken prose" (cf. also Linell 2005). In particular, the traditional categories of the "nucleus" of the "intonation/tone unit" and of "tones" or "final intonation contours" have been designed to capture the distinctive prosodic choices associated with different functional interpretations of decontextualized sentences such as "statement", "question" and the like, and they try to attribute meanings or functions to tones and other intonational choices (cf. Selting 1995a: 22–23). Yet, the categories advocated by these approaches are not necessarily the kinds of categories that we need for the analysis of the participants' use of prosody for the management of interaction.

Scholars in *Phonology for Conversation*, for instance, object to the use of traditional and holistic categories like, e.g., accent. As the following examples with two differing accent placements intuitively show, each accentuation suggests a different semantic meaning of the unit in its sequential context. The second example occurred briefly after the first one:

(6)   Examples of two differing accent placements
      (cf. Selting 1995a: 121, transcription adapted to GAT)

   a.   (Context: After Nat has just told her interlocutors that she works in a restaurant in the evenings, Ida asks her:)

```
Ida:   wIe   lange   GEHT   das   da?
       how   long    GOES   that  there
```
       how long is that OPEN

   b.   (Context: After Nat has told her interlocutors that she has to work in the restaurant till very late, Ida has mentioned that she works in a bistro, too. Now, Nat addresses Ida and asks her:)

```
Nat:   und   wIe   lange   geht   das   DA:?
       and   how   long    goes   that  THERE
```
       and how long is THAT one open

The accentuation in (a) suggests this question as the first one of its kind and Ida wants to know how long the restaurant that Nat works in is open. The accentuation in (b), however, takes question (a) for granted and Nat now focuses on the contrast between her own restaurant and the one where Ida works.

The position of the phoneticians in the *Phonology for Conversation* approach regarding accent would be: Accent is already an interpretation, not a purely observational parameter. The approach of a *Phonology for Conversation* should not base its descriptions on such (already holistic) interpretations. On the descriptive level, only those phonetic parameters should be taken into account that can be registered objectively: Pitch (movement), (shifts in) loudness, (shifts in) duration, (shifts in) speech rate, vowel qualities, voice qualities, etc.

In contrast to this, many (interactional) linguists and prosodists who would not identify themselves as phoneticians look at the use of holistically interpreted concepts like accent as mid-level abstractions that are unproblematic for many research questions.

In my own opinion, the level of abstraction of categories that are being used should be adjusted to the research question pursued: If the analysis is aimed at describing such functions of prosody as, for instance, the signaling of the semantic meaning of units via accent placement, i.e. questions of accentuation and information structure, or at the description of dense accentuation as one feature among others constitutive of a communicative style (cf. Selting 1994), it is sufficient to differentiate between accentuation and non-accentuation of syllables. However, if the aim is to analyze in detail in which way holistic interpretations like *stressed, accented, foregrounded, focused-on* or the like are achieved at all, we need a more precise description of the constitutive prosodic and phonetic parameters involved.

Hence, the question is rather: which old and which new categories are *necessary*? What categories can we adapt to our purposes – and what categories do we have to reject and find new ways of thinking about? For an answer to this question, the specific research question dealt with may provide us with some guidance.

6.2.3 *Improved transcription as a task and challenge*

Following from the prior issues, the next one is: How can we *represent* what is relevant for the participants?

On the relevance of transcriptions, Walker (2004b: 38) reminds us of the following:

> "(...) any transcription should be considered an *aide memoir* i.e. as a readable reference point and as a tool to facilitate discussion of phonic material both orally and in print. Most importantly, the transcription should not be considered to be 'the data' (...)."

The Jeffersonian style of transcription is the one predominantly used and oriented to by researchers in CA and IL, including researchers in the field of prosody and interaction. Jefferson indeed was an expert at perceiving and notating details of talk in interaction. Her transcription system set a well-recognized standard for the field of

CA. (For recent representations see Jefferson 2002: 1377–1383 and Schegloff 2007: 265–269.)[8]

Yet, from a linguistic point of view, Jefferson's transcription system is not ideal. Especially the notation of phonetic and prosodic details is not compatible with linguistic ways of analyzing and representing these structures (cf. Couper-Kuhlen and Selting 1996a: 40–45, Walker 2004b: 39–44). Therefore, in 1998, a group of German interactional linguists published a new transcription system, GAT, which is as compatible as possible with the CA-Jeffersonian transcription system, but suggests additional conventions for the notation of prosody (GAT is an acronym for *Gesprächsanalytisches Transkriptionssystem*; devised and published by Selting, Auer, Couper-Kuhlen and many others, see Selting et al. 1998).

This transcription system has been revised and adapted to the needs of today's and future research in IL, on the basis of large corpora, in areas such as prosody in interaction, the study of affectivity in talk-in-interaction as well as the study of the multimodality of interaction (see GAT 2, published as Selting et al. 2009). The transcription system differentiates between three different levels of delicacy which are relevant for different research purposes: the *minimal transcript*, appropriate as a working transcript or for non-linguistic research questions; the *basic transcript*, a presentation appropriate for sequential analyses; and the *fine transcript*, appropriate for the analysis of phonetic-prosodic and/or non-verbal details. Just like the first version of GAT, GAT 2 is intended to offer suggestions for the transcription of data from social interaction, the conventions are of course open to be adapted to the research questions at hand.

There will also be an English version of GAT 2, translated by Elizabeth Couper-Kuhlen and Dagmar Barth-Weingarten (see Selting et al. in press). GAT 2 is accompanied by a tutorial tool and a transcription editing program. For both see the websites given in Selting et al. (2009, in press). The tutorial is intended to – among others – provide tools and exercises for the transcription of prosody.

Nevertheless, the revised transcription system GAT 2 is still lacking in some respects. Especially in the domain of voice qualities, many cues relevant for our interpretation of actions and their style or affective quality can so far only be captured intuitively and with the help of interpretive commentaries such as <sounding disappointed>, <sounding happy> or <sounding sad>.

With somewhat similar intentions to those that led to the development of GAT, Walker (2004b) develops a mode of transcription that consists of two parts: an *unadorned orthographic transcription*, "used in discussing aspects other than fine phonetic details, e.g. the sequential organisation of talk", and an *enhanced orthographic transcription*, "used principally where fine phonetic details are being discussed" (ibid.: 45).

---

8.   For some more information about transcription systems currently used in IL, cf. also http://www.linguistics.ucsb.edu/faculty/sathomps/bibliographies/bibliog-interactional-linguistics.htm.

6.2.4 *The description of voice qualities as a challenge for future research[9]*
Many of the parameters of research in prosody are fairly clear and their physical properties can be measured – we can use, e.g., PRAAT, to measure the fundamental frequencies (F0) underlying the perception of pitch, the wave amplitudes underlying the
perception of loudness, and the duration underlying the perception of length, etc.
These parameters might not be deployed in a categorical way and they may only in
some cases be used for distinctive functions (see above) – categorization has to reflect
their gradient and fuzzy nature. But nevertheless, research so far has shown that these
prosodic parameters are analyzable and describable.

However, there is a neighboring field which is much less developed still: For the
description of voice qualities (Stimmqualitäten) such as *creaky, breathy, tense, lax,* or
hyperarticulated, hypoarticulated (for the latter cf. Ogden 2006), we cannot even revert
to descriptive terms that researchers have agreed upon. There might be acoustic correlates of such voice qualities as *creaky* and *breathy* voice, but for most voice qualities there
are no certain results regarding their acoustic-phonetic analysis, let alone in spoken
language in natural interaction. Yet, as research in prosody and interaction moves on,
the inclusion of voice qualities into the analysis is expected to become more tractable.

The same is true for the notation of non-verbal practices and actions in the domains
of gaze, facial expression, gesture, posture, etc. As this, however, opens up an area well
beyond the scope of prosody and interaction, I will not go into details on this here.

6.2.5 *Different paths of analysis and their findings*
In conversation analysis, the analysis usually starts from interaction sequences, (verbal
or non-verbal) actions, or functions. In research on prosody, interactional linguistics
and constructions, however, the analysis often starts from particular forms or structures of utterances, for example particular intonation contours or grammatical constructions. What are the implications of an analysis that takes forms or prosodic structures as its starting point? How can a particularistic analysis of forms or structures be
reconciled with the analysis of interaction sequences?

The problem we encounter when we start from forms or constructions is this:

By starting our analysis from particular forms such as particular intonation contours, we arrive at a number of different actions that may be constructed with this intonation contour. If we then try to look for a common meaning and function of the intonation contour, the functional and interactional analysis often remains unsatisfactory.

A way out might be to restrict the kinds of actions and sequences that, e.g., the
intonation contour in question is studied in, e.g. well-defined practices and sequences
such as, for instance, turn-taking, adjacency pairs, repair sequences, lists, assessment
sequences, news reports, storytelling, etc. By starting our analysis from forms in well-
defined sequences, we can analyze the relevance and interplay of cues from prosody,

---

9.   I am grateful to Elizabeth Couper-Kuhlen for pointing out this problem to me.

lexis, syntax, etc., i.e. we can study the co-occurrence of cues for the construction of actions such as assessments and responses to them in assessment sequences.

But, as Ogden (2006) has shown, the prosody of assessments and their responses does not depend on their lexis or syntax, or even on the action itself, but on the preference structure that has been suggested with the first assessment as well as on the other speaker's talk. While an analysis starting from actions and sequences can capture this, an analysis starting from the prosodic or other linguistic form might well miss this generalization.

The conclusion from this is: While we can always look at the details of prosody and other forms of utterances as an intermediate step, we always in the end need to come back to the systematic analysis of actions and sequences in interaction and integrate our more form-related analyses into this. Otherwise, the functional analysis of interactional meaning will remain unsystematic.

7.   Conclusions

As I have tried to show, research in prosody and interaction has developed into a broad and rich research field. It is being recognized for its value all over the world. I want to thank Elizabeth Couper-Kuhlen very much for her work and cooperation in founding and developing the field and also for contributing to many special areas within this field.

References[10]

Abercrombie, David 1965. *Studies in phonetics and linguistics.* Third impression, 1971. London: Oxford University Press.

Anderson, Anne H.; Bader, Miles; Gurman Bard, Ellen; Boyle, Elizabeth; Doherty, Gwyneth M.; Garrod, Simon; Isard, Stephen; Kowtko, Jacqueline; McAllister, Jan; Miller, Jim; Sotillo, Catherine; Thompson Henry S. and Weinert, Regina 1991. "The HCRC map task corpus". *Language and Speech* 34: 351–366.

Anward, Jan 2002. "Other voices, other sources." In: *Jagen och rösterna: Goffman, Viveka och samtalet/ Selves and Voices: Goffman, Viveka, and Dialogue,* Per Linell and Karin Aronsson (eds.), 128–147. Linköping.

Auer, Peter 1990. "Rhythm in telephone closings." *Human Studies* 13: 361–392.

Auer, Peter 1991. "Vom Ende deutscher Sätze." *Zeitschrift für Germanistische Linguistik* 19 (2): 139–157.

Auer, Peter 1992. "Introduction: John Gumperz' Approach to contextualization." In: *The contextualization of language,* Peter Auer and Aldo di Luzio (eds.), 1–38. Amsterdam: Benjamins.

---

10.   The following list gives all the references referred to in the text, but also many others relevant to the field. Nevertheless, it is not intended as a comprehensive bibliography.

Auer, Peter 1993. "Über ↄ". *Zeitschrift für Literaturwissenschaft und Linguistik 23* (90–91) (Special Issue on "Materiale Bedingungen der Linguistik", ed. by Brigitte Schlieben-Lange): 104–138.

Auer, Peter 1996. "On the prosody and syntax of turn-continuations." In: *Prosody in conversation. Interactional studies,* Elizabeth Couper-Kuhlen and Margret Selting (eds.), 57–100. Cambridge: Cambridge University Press.

Auer, Peter 2001. "'Hoch ansetzende' Intonationskonturen in der Hamburger Regionalvarietät." *Zeitschrift für Germanistische Linguistik* (157–158): 125–165.

Auer, Peter and Couper-Kuhlen, Elizabeth 1994. "Rhythmus und Tempo konversationeller Alltagssprache." *Zeitschrift für Literaturwissenschaft und Linguistik* 24 (96): 78–106.

Auer, Peter; Couper-Kuhlen Elizabeth and Müller, Frank E. 1999. *Language in time. The rhythm and tempo of spoken interaction.* Oxford: Oxford University Press.

Auer, Peter and di Luzio, Aldo (eds.) 1992. *The contextualization of language.* Amsterdam: Benjamins.

Auer, Peter and Rönfeldt, Barbara 2004. "Prolixity as adaptation: Prosody and turn-taking in German conversation with a fluent aphasic." In: *Sound patterns in interaction,* Elizabeth Couper-Kuhlen and Cecilia Ford (eds.), 171–200. Amsterdam: Benjamins.

Auer, Peter and Selting, Margret 2001. "Der Beitrag der Prosodie zur Gesprächsorganisation." In: *Text- und Gesprächslinguistik. Ein internationales Handbuch zeitgenössischer Forschung, Volume 2: Gesprächslinguistik*, Klaus Brinker, Gerd Antos, Wolfgang Heinemann and Sven F. Sager (eds.), 1122–1131. Berlin: de Gruyter.

Barth-Weingarten, Dagmar 2009. "When to say something – some observations on prosodic-phonetic cues to the placement and types of responses in multi-unit turns." In: *Where prosody meets pragmatics,* Dagmar Barth-Weingarten, Nicole Dehé and Anne Wichmann (eds.), 143–181. Bingley: Emerald.

Birkner, Karin 2007. "Semantik und Prosodie von Relativsätzen im gesprochenen Deutsch." *Deutsche Sprache* 35: 271–285.

Birkner, Karin 2008. *Relativ(satz)konstruktionen im gesprochenen Deutsch: Syntaktische, prosodische, semantische und pragmatische Aspekte.* Habilitationschrift (Post-doctoral thesis), Universität Freiburg.

Catterall, Catherine; Howard, Sara; Stojanovik, Vesna; Szczerbinski, Marcin and Wells, Bill 2006. "Investigating prosodic ability in Williams syndrome." *Clinical Linguistics and Phonetics* 20 (7–8): 531–538.

Clark, John and Yallop, Colin 1990. *An introduction to phonetics and phonology.* Oxford: Blackwell.

Couper-Kuhlen, Elizabeth 1986. *An introduction to English prosody.* Tübingen: Niemeyer.

Couper-Kuhlen, Elizabeth 1992. "Contextualizing discourse: The prosody of interactive repair." In: *The contextualization of language,* Peter Auer and Aldo di Luzio (eds.), 337–364. Amsterdam: Benjamins.

Couper-Kuhlen, Elizabeth 1993. *English speech rhythm. Form and function in everyday verbal interaction.* Amsterdam: Benjamins.

Couper-Kuhlen, Elizabeth 1996a. "The prosody of repetition: On quoting and mimicry." In: *Prosody in conversation. Interactional studies*, Elizabeth Couper-Kuhlen and Margret Selting (eds.), 366–405. Cambridge: Cambridge University Press.

Couper-Kuhlen, Elizabeth 1996b. "Intonation and clause-combining in discourse. The case of *because.*" *Pragmatics* 6 (3): 389–426.

Couper-Kuhlen, Elizabeth 1999. "Coherent voicing: On prosody in conversational reported speech." In: *Coherence in spoken and written discourse: How to create it and how to describe it,* Wolfgang Bublitz and Ulla Lenk (eds.), 11–32. Amsterdam: Benjamins.

Couper-Kuhlen, Elizabeth 2000. "Prosody." In: *Handbook of pragmatics 2000,* Jef Verschueren, Jan-Ola Östman, Jan Blommert and Chris Bulcaen (eds.), 1–19. Amsterdam: Benjamins.

Couper-Kuhlen, Elizabeth 2001a. "Interactional prosody: High onsets in reason-for-the-call turns." In: *Language in Society* 30: 29–53.

Couper-Kuhlen, Elizabeth 2001b. "Intonation and discourse: Current views from within." In: *The Handbook of discourse analysis,* Deborah Schiffrin, Deborah Tannen and Heidi E. Hamilton (eds.), 13–34. Malden: Blackwell.

Couper-Kuhlen, Elizabeth 2004. "Prosody and sequence organization in English conversation." In: *Sound patterns in interaction,* Elizabeth Couper-Kuhlen and Cecilia E. Ford (eds.), 335–376. Amsterdam: Benjamins.

Couper-Kuhlen, Elizabeth 2005. "Prosodische Stilisierungen im Gespräch." In: *Zwischen Literatur und Anthropologie: Diskurse, Medien, Performanzen,* Aleida Assmann, Ulrich Gauer and Gisela Trommsdorff (eds.), 315–337. Tübingen: Narr.

Couper-Kuhlen, Elizabeth 2006. *A sequential approach to affect: The case of 'disappointment'.* Paper read at the ICCA 06 (International Conference on Conversation Analysis), Helsinki, May 10–14, 2006.

Couper-Kuhlen, Elizabeth 2007a. "Situated phonologies: patterns of phonology in discourse contexts." In: *Phonology in context,* Marina C. Pennington (ed.), 186–218. Palgrave: Macmillan.

Couper-Kuhlen, Elizabeth 2007b. "Prosodische Prospektion und Retrospektion im Gespräch." In: *Gespräch als Prozess. Linguistische Aspekte der Zeitlichkeit verbaler Interaktion,* Heiko Hausendorf (ed.), 69–94. Tübingen: Narr.

Couper-Kuhlen, Elizabeth 2009. "A sequential approach to affect: The case of 'disappointment'". In: *Talk in interaction – comparative dimensions,* Markku Haakana, Minna Laakso and Jan Lindström (eds.), 94–123. Helsinki: Finnish Literature Society (SKS).

Couper-Kuhlen, Elizabeth and Auer, Peter 1991. "On the contextualizing function of speech rhythm in conversation: question-answer sequences." In: *Levels of linguistic adaptation. Selected Papers of the 1987 International Pragmatics Conference. Vol. II,* Jeff Verschueren (ed.), 1–18. Amsterdam: Benjamins.

Couper-Kuhlen, Elizabeth and Ford, Cecilia E. (eds.) 2004. *Sound patterns in interaction.* Amsterdam: Benjamins.

Couper-Kuhlen, Elizabeth and Ono, Tsuyoshi (eds.) 2007. "Turn continuation in cross-linguistic perspective." *Pragmatics* 17 (4).

Couper-Kuhlen, Elizabeth and Ono, Tsuyoshi 2007a. "'Incrementing' in conversation. A comparison of practices in English, German and Japanese." In: Turn continuation in cross-linguistic perspective, edited by Elizabeth Couper-Kuhlen and Tsuyoshi Ono. *Pragmatics* 17 (4): 513–552.

Couper-Kuhlen, Elizabeth and Selting, Margret (eds.) 1996. *Prosody in conversation. Interactional studies.* Cambridge: Cambridge University Press.

Couper-Kuhlen, Elizabeth and Selting, Margret 1996a. "Towards an interactional perspective on prosody and a prosodic perspective on interaction." *Prosody in conversation. Interactional studies,* Elizabeth Couper-Kuhlen and Margret Selting (eds.), 11–56. Cambridge: Cambridge University Press.

Couper-Kuhlen, Elizabeth and Selting, Margret 2001. "Introducing interactional linguistics." In: *Studies in interactional linguistics.* Margret Selting and Elizabeth Couper-Kuhlen (eds.), 1–22. Amsterdam: Benjamins.

Couper-Kuhlen, Elizabeth and Thompson, Sandra A. 2005. "A linguistic practice for retracting overstatements: concessive repair." In: *Syntax and lexis in conversation,* Auli Hakulinen and Margret Selting (eds.), 257–288. Amsterdam: Benjamins.

Crystal, David 1969. *Prosodic systems and intonation in English.* Cambridge: Cambridge University Press.

Curl, Traci S. 2003. "The phonetics of repetition in other-initiated repair sequences." In: *Proceedings of the 15th International Congress of Phonetic Sciences,* Maria-Josep Solé, Daniel Recasens and Joaquin Romero (eds.), 1843–1846. Barcelona: Universidad Autonoma de Barcelona.

Curl, Traci S. 2004. "'Repetition' repairs: The relationship of phonetic structure and sequence organization." In: *Sound patterns in interaction.* Elizabeth Couper-Kuhlen and Cecilia E. Ford (eds.), 273–298. Amsterdam: Benjamins.

Curl, Traci S. 2005. "Practices in other-initiated repair resolution: The phonetic differentiation of 'repetitions'". *Discourse Processes* 39 (1): 1–43.

Curl, Traci S.; Local, John and Walker, Gareth 2006. "Repetition and the prosody-pragmatics interface." *Journal of Pragmatics* 38 (10): 1721–1751.

Deppermann, Arnulf and Lucius-Hoene, Gabriele 2005. "Trauma erzählen – kommunikative, sprachliche und stimmliche Verfahren." *Psychotherapie & Sozialwissenschaft* 1: 35–73.

Firth, J.R. 1957. *Papers in linguistics, 1934–1951.* Oxford: Oxford University Press.

Ford, Cecilia E. 2004. "Contingency and units in interaction." *Discourse Studies* 6 (1): 27–52.

Ford, Cecilia E. and Couper-Kuhlen, Elizabeth 2004. "Conversation and phonetics. Essential connections." In: *Sound patterns in interaction,* Elizabeth Couper-Kuhlen and Cecilia E. Ford (eds.), 3–25. Amsterdam: Benjamins.

Ford, Cecilia E.; Fox, Barbara A. and Hellermann, John 2004. "Getting past *no*: Sequence, action and sound production in the projection of *no*-initiated turns." In: *Sound patterns in interaction,* Elizabeth Couper-Kuhlen and Cecilia E. Ford (eds.), 233–269. Amsterdam: Benjamins.

Ford, Cecilia E.; Fox, Barbara A. and Thompson, Sandra A.1996. "Practices in the construction of turns: The "TCU" revisited." *Pragmatics* 6 (3): 427–454.

Ford, Cecilia E.; Fox, Barbara A. and Thompson, Sandra A. (eds.) 2002. *The language of turn and sequence.* Oxford: Oxford University Press.

Ford, Cecilia E.; Fox, Barbara A. and Thompson Sandra A. 2002a. "Introduction." In: *The language of turn and sequence,* Cecilia E. Ford, Barbara A. Fox and Sandra A. Thompson (eds.), 3–13. Oxford: Oxford University Press.

Ford, Cecilia E.; Fox, Barbara A. and Thompson, Sandra A. 2002b. "Constituency and the grammar of turn increments." In: *The language of turn and sequence,* Cecilia E. Ford, Barbara A. Fox and Sandra A. Thompson (eds.), 14–38. New York: Oxford University Press.

Ford, Cecilia E.; Fox, Barbara A. and Thompson, Sandra A. 2003. "Social interaction and grammar." In: *The new psychology of language, Vol. 2,* Michael Tomasello (ed.), 119–143. Mahwah, N.J.: Lawrence Erlbaum.

Ford, Cecilia E. and Thompson, Sandra A. 1996. "Interactional units in conversation: syntactic, intonational, and pragmatic resources for the management of turns." In: *Interaction and grammar,* Elinor Ochs, Emanuel A. Schegloff and Sandra A. Thompson (eds.), 134–184. Cambridge: Cambridge University Press.

Fox, Barbara A. 2001. "An exploration of prosody and turn projection in English conversation." In: *Studies in interactional linguistics.* Margret Selting and Elizabeth Couper-Kuhlen (eds.), 287–315. Amsterdam: Benjamins.

Freese, Jeremy and Maynard, Douglas W. 1998. "Prosodic features of bad news and good news in conversation." *Language in Society* 27: 195–219.

French, Peter and Local, John 1983. "Turn-competitive incomings." *Journal of Pragmatics* 7: 701–715.

Gessinger, Joachim 1994. *Auge and Ohr. Studien zur Erforschung der Sprache am Menschen 1700–1850.* Berlin: de Gruyter.

Gilles, Peter 2005. *Regionale Prosodie im Deutschen. Variabilität in der Intonation von Abschluss und Weiterweisung.* Berlin: de Gruyter.

Goffman, Erving 1981. *Forms of talk.* Oxford: Basil Blackwell.

Goodwin, Charles 2000. "Action and embodiment within situated human interaction." *Journal of Pragmatics* 36: 1489–1522.

Goodwin, Charles 2003. "Conversational frameworks for the accomplishment of meaning in Aphasia." In: *Conversation and brain damage,* Charles Goodwin (ed.), 90–116. Oxford: Oxford University Press.

Goodwin, Charles 2006. "Human sociality as mutual orientation in a rich interactive environment: Multimodal utterances and pointing in aphasia." In: *Roots of human sociality,* Nick Enfield and Stephen C. Levinson (eds.), 96–125. London: Berg Press.

Goodwin, Charles 2007. "Environmentally coupled gestures." In: *Gesture and the dynamic dimensions of language.* Susan Duncan, Justine Cassel and Elena Levy (eds.), 195–212. Amsterdam: Benjamins.

Goodwin, Marjorie Harness 1996. "Informings and announcements in their environment: Prosody within a multi-activity work setting." In: *Prosody in conversation. Interactional studies,* Elizabeth Couper-Kuhlen and Margret Selting (eds.), 436–461. Cambridge: Cambridge University Press.

Gumperz, John J. 1982. *Discourse strategies.* Cambridge: Cambridge University Press.

Gumperz, John J. 1990. "Contextualization and understanding." In: *Rethinking context. Language as an interactive phenomenon,* Alessandro Duranti and Charles Goodwin (eds.), 229–252. Cambridge: Cambridge University Press.

Gülich, Elisabeth and Couper-Kuhlen, Elizabeth 2007. "Zur Entwicklung einer Differenzierung von Angstformen im Interaktionsverlauf: Verfahren der szenischen Darstellung." In: *Koordination. Analysen zur multimodalen Kommunikation,* Reinhold Schmitt (ed.), 293–338. Tübingen: Narr Francke Attempto.

Günthner, Susanne 1993. "'...weil – man kann es ja wissenschaftlich untersuchen' – Diskurspragmatische Aspekte der Wortstellung in WEIL-Sätzen." *Linguistische Berichte* 143: 37–59.

Günthner, Susanne 1996a. "From subordination to coordination? Verb-second position in German causal and concessive constructions." *Pragmatics* 6 (3): 323–356.

Günthner, Susanne 1996b. "The prosodic contextualization of moral work: an analysis of reproaches in 'why'-formats." In: *Prosody in conversation. Interactional studies,* Elizabeth Couper-Kuhlen and Margret Selting (eds.), 271–302. Cambridge: Cambridge University Press.

Günthner, Susanne 1999. "Polyphony and the 'layering of voices' in reported dialogues: An analysis of the use of prosodic devices in everyday reported speech." *Journal of Pragmatics* 31: 685–708.

Günthner, Susanne 2005a. "Fremde Rede im Diskurs: Formen und Funktionen der Polyphonie in alltäglichen Redewiedergaben." In: *Zwischen Literatur und Anthropologie: Diskurse,*

Medien, Performanzen, Aleida Assmann, Ulrich Gaier and Gisela Trommsdorff (eds.), 339–359. Tübingen: Gunter Narr.

Günthner, Susanne 2005b. "Dichte Konstruktionen". *InLiSt (Interaction and Linguistic Structures)* 43 (<http://www.uni-potsdam.de/u/inlist/issues/43/index.htm>).

Günthner, Susanne and Imo, Wolfgang (eds.) 2006. *Konstruktionen in der Interaktion*. Berlin: de Gruyter.

Hakulinen, Auli and Selting, Margret (eds.) 2005. *Syntax and lexis in conversation*. Amsterdam: Benjamins.

Hellermann, John 2005. "Syntactic and prosodic practices for cohesion in series of three-part sequences in classroom talk." *Research on Language and Social Interaction* 38 (1): 105–130.

Jasperson, Robert 2002. "Some linguistic aspects of closure cut-offs." In: *The language of turn and sequence*, Cecilia E. Ford, Barbara A. Fox and Sandra A. Thompson (eds.), 257–286. Oxford: Oxford University Press.

Jefferson, Gail 1983. "Another failed hypothesis: Pitch/loudness as relevant to overlap resolution." *Tilburg Papers in Language and Literature* 38: 1–24. Tilburg: Tilburg University.

Jefferson, Gail 1986. "Notes on 'latency' in overlap onset." *Human Studies* 9: 153–183.

Jefferson, Gail 1988. "Preliminary notes on a possible metric which provides for a 'standard maximum' silence of approximately one second in conversation." In: *Conversation: An interdisciplinary perspective*, Derek Roger and Peter Bull (eds.), 166–196. Clevedon: Multilingual Matters.

Jefferson, Gail 2002. "Is 'No' an acknowledgement token? Comparing American and British uses of (+)/(–) tokens." *Journal of Pragmatics* 34: 1345–1383.

Kelly, John and Local, John 1989. *Doing phonology. Observing, recording, interpreting*. Manchester: Manchester University Press.

Kern, Friederike 2007. "Prosody as a resource in children's game explanations: Some aspects of turn construction and recipiency." *Journal of Pragmatics* 39 (1): 111–133.

Kern, Friederike 2008. *Das Zusammenspiel von Prosodie und Syntax am Beispiel von Türkendeutsch*. Habilitationsschrift (Post-doctoral thesis), Universität Potsdam.

Kern, Friederike and Selting, Margret 2006a. "Einheitenkonstruktion im Türkendeutschen: Grammatische und prosodische Aspekte." *Zeitschrift für Sprachwissenschaft* 25 (2): 239–272.

Kern, Friederike and Selting, Margret 2006b. "Konstruktionen mit Nachstellungen im Türkendeutschen." In: *Grammatik und Interaktion*, Arnulf Deppermann, Reinhard Fiehler and Thomas Spranz-Fogasy (eds.), 319–347. Radolfzell: Verlag für Gesprächsforschung.

Kern, Friederike and Simsek, Yazgül 2006. "Türkendeutsch: Aspekte von Einheitenbildung und Rezeptionsverhalten." In: *Mehrsprachige Individuen – vielsprachige Gesellschaften*, Dieter Wolff (ed.), 101–119. Frankfurt/Main: Lang.

Klewitz, Gabriele and Couper-Kuhlen, Elizabeth 1999. "Quote-unquote. The role of prosody in the contextualization of reported speech sequences." *Pragmatics* 9 (4): 459–485.

Labov, William 1972. *Sociolinguistic patterns*. Philadelphia: University of Pennsylvania Press.

Ladd, D. Robert 1996. *Intonational phonology*. Cambridge: Cambridge University Press.

Ladefoged, Peter 1992. *A course in phonetics*. Second Edition. New York: Harcourt Brace Jovanovich.

Lerner, Gene H. 1996. "On the "semi-permeable" character of grammatical units in conversation: conditional entry into the turn space of another speaker." In: *Interaction and grammar*, Elinor Ochs, Emanuel A. Schegloff and Sandra A. Thompson (eds.), 238–276. Cambridge: Cambridge University Press.

Levinson, Stephen C. 2005. "Living with Manny's dangerous idea." *Discourse Studies 7* (4–5): 431–453.

Li, Xiaoting (forthcoming). *Prosody, syntax, and body movements in turn management in Mandarin Chinese conversation.* PhD Dissertation, Peking University.

Lindström, Anna Karin 1997. *Designing social actions: Grammar, prosody, and interaction in Swedish conversation.* PhD dissertation, UCLA.

Linell, Per 2005. *The written language bias in linguistics. Its nature, origins, and transformations.* London: Routledge.

Local, John 1992. "Continuing and restarting." In: *The contextualization of language,* Peter Auer and Aldo di Luzio (eds.), 273–296. Amsterdam: Benjamins.

Local, John 1996. "Conversational phonetics: Some aspects of news receipts in everyday talk." In: *Prosody in conversation. Interactional studies,* Elizabeth Couper-Kuhlen and Margret Selting (eds.), 177–230. Cambridge: Cambridge University Press.

Local, John 2003. "Phonetics and talk-in-interaction." In: *Proceedings of the 15th International Congress of Phonetic Sciences,* Maria-Josep Solé, Daniel Recasens and Joaquin Romero (eds.), 115–118. Barcelona: Universidad Autonoma de Barcelona.

Local, John 2004. "Getting back to prior talk: *and-uh(m)* as a back-connecting device in British and American English." In: *Sound patterns in interaction,* Elizabeth Couper-Kuhlen and Cecilia E. Ford (eds.), 377–400. Amsterdam: Benjamins.

Local, John 2005. "On the interactional and phonetic design of collaborative completions." In: *A figure of speech: A Festschrift for John Laver,* William J. Hardcastle and Janet Mackenzie Beck (eds.), 263–282. New Jersey: Lawrence Erbaum.

Local, John and Kelly, John 1986. "Projection and 'silences': Notes on phonetic and conversational structure." *Human Studies* 9: 185–204.

Local, John; Kelly John and Wells, William H.G. 1986. "Towards a phonology of conversation: turn-taking in Tyneside English." *Journal of Linguistics* 22: 411–437.

Local, John and Walker, Gareth 2004. "Abrupt-joins as a resource for the production of multi-unit, multi-action turns." *Journal of Pragmatics* 36: 1375–1402.

Local, John and Walker, Gareth 2005. "Methodological imperatives for investigating the phonetic organization and phonological structures of spontaneous speech." *Phonetica* 62: 120–130.

Local, John; Wells, William H.G. and Sebba, Mark 1985. "Phonology for conversation. Phonetic aspects of turn delimitation in London Jamaican." *Journal of Pragmatics* 9: 309–330.

Martínez-Castilla, Pastora and Peppé, Sue 2008. "Intonation features of the expression of emotions in Spanish: Preliminary study for a prosody assessment procedure." *Clinical linguistics phonetics* 22 (4): 363–370.

Mayer, Jörg 1999. "Prosodische Merkmale von Diskursrelationen." *Linguistische Berichte* 177: 65–86.

Mazeland, Harrie 2007. "Parenthetical sequences." *Journal of Pragmatics* 39: 1816–1869.

Mondada, Lorenza 2007. "Multimodal resources for turn-taking. Pointing and the emergence of possible next speakers." In: *Discourse Studies* 9 (2): 195–226.

Mori, Junko 2006. "The workings of the Japanese token hee in informing sequences. An analysis of sequential context, turn shape, and prosody." *Journal of Pragmatics* 38 (8): 1175–1205.

Müller, Frank E. 1994. "Rhythmus in formulaischen Paradigmen der Alltagssprache." *Zeitschrift für Literaturwissenschaft und Linguistik* 24 (96): 53–77.

Müller, Frank E. 1996. "Affiliating and disaffiliating with continuers: prosodic aspects of recipiency." In: *Prosody in conversation. Interactional studies,* Elizabeth Couper-Kuhlen and Margret Selting (eds.), 131–176. Cambridge: Cambridge University Press.

Ogden, Richard 2004. "Non-modal voice quality and turn-taking in Finnish." In: *Sound patterns in interaction*, Elizabeth Couper-Kuhlen and Cecilia E. Ford (eds.), 29–62. Amsterdam: Benjamins.

Ogden, Richard 2006. "Phonetics and social action in agreements and disagreements." *Journal of Pragmatics* 38: 1752–1775.

Ogden, Richard; Hakulinen, Auli and Tainio; Liisa 2004. "Indexing 'no news' with stylization in Finnish." In: *Sound patterns in interaction*, Elizabeth Couper-Kuhlen and Cecilia E. Ford (eds.), 299–234. Amsterdam: Benjamins.

Ogden, Richard and Routarinne, Sara 2005. "The communicative function of final rises in Finnish intonation." *Phonetica* 62: 160–175.

Peters, Jörg 2006. *Intonation deutscher Regionalsprachen*. Berlin: de Gruyter.

Rabanus, Stefan 2001. *Intonatorische Verfahren im Deutschen und Italienischen. Gesprächsanalyse und autosegmentale Phonologie*. Tübingen: Niemeyer.

Reber, Elisabeth 2007. *Managing affectivity in talk-in-interaction: The case of sound objects in informings*. Paper presented at the 40th Annual Meeting of the Societas Linguistica Europaea.

Reber, Elisabeth 2008. *Affectivity in talk-in-interaction: Sound objects in English*. PhD Dissertation, University of Potsdam.

Sacks, Harvey 1984. "Notes on methodology." In: *Structures of social action. Studies in conversation analysis*, J. Maxwell Atkinson and John Heritage (eds.), 21–27. Cambridge: Cambridge University Press.

Sacks, Harvey 1992. *Lectures on conversation*. Vol. 1. (Ed. by Gail Jefferson). Oxford: Blackwell.

Sacks, Harvey; Schegloff, Emanuel A. and Jefferson, Gail 1974. "A simplest systematics for the organization of turn-taking in conversation." *Language* 50: 696–735.

Schegloff, Emanuel A. 1982. "Discourse as an interactional achievement: some uses of 'uh huh' and other things that come between sentences." In: *Analyzing discourse: Text and talk, Georgetown University Round Table on Languages and Linguistics 1981*, Deborah Tannen (ed.), 71–91. Washington, D.C.

Schegloff, Emanuel A. 1987. "Analyzing single episodes of interaction. An exercise in conversation analysis." *Social Psychological Quarterly* 50 (2): 101–114.

Schegloff, Emanuel A. 1996. "Turn organisation: one intersection of grammar and interaction." In: *Interaction and grammar*, Elinor Ochs, Emanuel A. Schegloff and Sandra A. Thompson (eds.), 52–133. Cambridge: Cambridge University Press.

Schegloff, Emanuel A. 1998. "Reflections on studying prosody in talk-in-interaction." *Language and Speech* 41 (3–4): 235–263.

Schegloff, Emanuel A. 2005. "On integrity in inquiry ... of the investigated, not the investigator." *Discourse Studies* 7 (4–5): 455–480.

Schegloff, Emanuel A. 2007. *Sequence organization in interaction. A primer in conversation analysis*. Cambridge: Cambridge University Press.

Schmitt, Reinhold (ed.) 2007. *Koordination. Analysen zur multimodalen Interaktion*. Tübingen: Narr.

Schönherr, Beatrix 1993. "Prosodische und nonverbale Signale für Parenthesen. 'Parasyntax' in Fernsehdiskussionen." *Deutsche Sprache* 21: 223–243.

Schönherr, Beatrix 1997. *Syntax – Prosodie – nonverbale Kommunikation*. Tübingen: Niemeyer.

Selting, Margret 1987. "Reparaturen und lokale Verstehensprobleme. Oder: Zur Binnenstruktur von Reparatursequenzen." *Linguistische Berichte* 108: 128–149.

Selting, Margret 1991. "w-Fragen in konversationellen Frage-Antwort-Sequenzen." In: *Fragesätze und Fragen*, Marga Reis und Inger Rosengren (eds.), 263–288. Tübingen: Niemeyer.

Selting, Margret 1992. "Prosody in conversational questions." *Journal of Pragmatics* 17: 315–345.

Selting, Margret 1993. "Voranstellungen vor den Satz. Zur grammatischen Form und interaktiven Funktion von Linksversetzung und Freiem Thema im Deutschen." *Zeitschrift für Germanistische Linguistik* 21: 291–319.

Selting, Margret 1994. "Emphatic speech style – with special focus on the prosodic signalling of heightened emotive involvement in conversation." *Journal of Pragmatics* 22: 375–408.

Selting, Margret 1995a. *Prosodie im Gespräch. Aspekte einer interaktionalen Phonologie der Konversation.* Tübingen: Niemeyer.

Selting, Margret 1995b. "Sprechstile als Kontextualisierungshinweise. Die sprechstilistische Kontextualisierung konversationeller Aktivitäten, am Beispiel mündlicher Erzählungen in Gesprächen." In: *Stilfragen. Jahrbuch 1994 des Instituts für deutsche Sprache.* Gerhard Stickel (ed.), 225–256. Berlin: de Gruyter.

Selting, Margret 1995c. "Der 'mögliche Satz' als interaktiv relevante syntaktische Kategorie." *Linguistische Berichte* 158: 298–325.

Selting, Margret 1996a. "On the interplay of syntax and prosody in the constitution of turn-constructional units and turns in conversation." *Pragmatics* 6 (3): 357–388.

Selting, Margret 1996b. "Prosody as an activity-type distinctive cue in conversation: The case of so-called 'astonished' questions in repair." In: *Prosody in conversation. Interactional studies,* Elizabeth Couper-Kuhlen and Margret Selting (eds.), 231–270. Cambridge: Cambridge University Press.

Selting, Margret 1997. "Interaktionale Stilistik: Methodologische Aspekte der Analyse von Sprechstilen." In: *Sprech- und Gesprächsstile,* Margret Selting and Barbara Sandig (eds.), 9–43. Berlin: de Gruyter.

Selting, Margret 1999. "Communicative style." In: *Handbook of pragmatics 1999,* Jef Verschueren, Jan-Ola Östman, Jan Blommaert and Chris Bulcaen (eds.), 1–24. Amsterdam: Benjamins.

Selting, Margret 2000a. "The construction of units in conversational talk." *Language in Society* 29: 477–517.

Selting, Margret 2000b. "Berlinische Intonationskonturen: Der 'Springton'." *Deutsche Sprache* 28 (3): 193–231.

Selting, Margret 2001a. "Fragments of units as deviant cases of unit-production in conversational talk." In: *Studies in interactional linguistics,* Margret Selting and Elizabeth Couper-Kuhlen (eds.), 229–258. Amsterdam: Benjamins.

Selting, Margret 2001b. "Probleme der Transkription verbalen und paraverbalen/prosodischen Verhaltens." In: *Text- und Gesprächslinguistik. Ein internationales Handbuch zeitgenössischer Forschung, Vol. 2: Gesprächslinguistik,* Klaus Brinker, Gerd Antos, Wolfgang Heinemann and Sven F. Sager (eds.), 1059–1068. Berlin: de Gruyter.

Selting, Margret 2001c. "Berlinische Intonationskonturen: Die 'Treppe aufwärts'." *Zeitschrift für Sprachwissenschaft* 20 (1): 66–116.

Selting, Margret 2004a. "Regionalized intonation in its conversational context." In: *Regional variation in intonation,* Peter Gilles and Jörg Peters (eds.), 49–73. Tübingen: Niemeyer.

Selting, Margret 2004b. "The 'upward staircase' intonation contour in the Berlin vernacular: An example in the analysis of regionalized intonation as an interactional resource." In: *Sound patterns in interaction,* Elizabeth Couper-Kuhlen and Cecilia E. Ford (eds.), 201–231. Amsterdam: Benjamins.

Selting, Margret 2005. "Syntax and prosody as methods for the construction and identification of turn-constructional units in conversation." In: *Syntax and lexis in conversation,* Auli Hakulinen and Margret Selting (eds.), 17–44. Amsterdam: Benjamins.

Selting, Margret 2007. "Lists as embedded structures and the prosody of list construction as an interactional resource." *Journal of Pragmatics* 39: 483–526 (<http://dx.doi.org/10.1016/j.pragma.2006.07.008>).

Selting, Margret 2008a. "Interactional stylistics and style as a contextualization cue." In: *Rhetorik und Stilistik. Rhetoric and Stylistics. An international handbook of historical and systematic research*, Ulla Fix and Andreas Gardt (eds.), 1038–1053. Berlin: de Gruyter.

Selting, Margret 2008b. "Linguistic resources for the management of interaction." In: *Handbook of applied linguistics. Vol. 2: Handbook of interpersonal communication*, Gerd Antos, Eija Ventola and Tilo Weber (eds.), 217–253. Berlin: de Gruyter.

Selting, Margret 2010. "Affectivity in conversational storytelling. An analysis of displays of anger or indignation in complaint stories." *Pragmatics* 20 (2): 229–277.

Selting, Margret; Auer, Peter; Barden, Birgit; Bergmann, Jörg; Couper-Kuhlen, Elizabeth; Günthner, Susanne; Quasthoff, Uta; Meier, Christoph; Schlobinski, Peter and Uhmann, Susanne 1998. "Gesprächsanalytisches Transkriptionssystem (GAT)." *Linguistische Berichte* 173: 91–122.

Selting Margret; Auer, Peter; Barth-Weingarten, Dagmar; Bergmann, Jörg; Bergmann, Pia; Birkner, Karin; Couper-Kuhlen, Elizabeth; Deppermann, Arnulf; Gilles, Peter; Günthner, Susanne; Hartung, Martin; Kern, Friederike; Mertzlufft, Christine; Meyer, Christian; Morek, Miriam; Oberzaucher, Frank; Peters, Jörg; Quasthoff, Uta; Schütte, Wilfried; Stukenbrock, Anja and Uhmann, Susanne 2009. "Gesprächsanalytisches Transkriptionssystem 2 (GAT 2)." *Gesprächsforschung – Online-Zeitschrift zur verbalen Interaktion* 10: 353–402 (www.gespraechsforschung-ozs.de).

Selting Margret; Auer, Peter; Barth-Weingarten, Dagmar; Bergmann, Jörg; Bergmann, Pia; Birkner, Karin; Couper-Kuhlen, Elizabeth; Deppermann, Arnulf; Gilles, Peter; Günthner, Susanne; Hartung, Martin; Kern, Friederike; Mertzlufft, Christine; Meyer, Christian; Morek, Miriam; Oberzaucher, Frank; Peters, Jörg; Quasthoff, Uta; Schütte, Wilfried; Stukenbrock, Anja and Uhmann, Susanne (in press). "A system for transcribing talk-in-interaction: GAT 2 (translated and adapted for English by Elizabeth Couper-Kuhlen and Dagmar Barth-Weingarten)." To appear in *Gesprächsforschung - Online-Zeitschrift zur verbalen Interaktion* (www.gespraechsforschung-ozs.de).

Selting, Margret and Couper-Kuhlen, Elizabeth (eds.) 2001. *Studies in interactional linguistics.* Amsterdam: Benjamins.

Selting, Margret and Couper-Kuhlen, Elizabeth 2001a. "Forschungsprogramm 'Interaktionale Linguistik." *Linguistische Berichte* 187: 257–287.

Selting, Margret 2010. "Emotive involvement in conversational storytelling." *Pragmatics* 20 (2): 229–277.

Sidnell, Jack and Stivers, Tanya 2005. "Multi-modal interaction." *Semiotica* 156 (1): 1–20.

Simsek, Yazgül 2008. *Sequenzielle und prosodische Aspekte der Organisation der Sprecher-Hörer-Interaktion im Türkendeutschen.* Doctoral dissertation, University of Potsdam.

Szczepek Reed, Beatrice 2004. "Turn-final intonation in English." In: *Sound patterns in interaction,* Elizabeth Couper-Kuhlen and Cecilia E. Ford (eds.), 97–117. Amsterdam: Benjamins.

Szczepek Reed, Beatrice 2006. *Prosodic orientation in English conversation.* London: Palgrave Macmillan.

Tanaka, Hiroko 1999. *Turn-taking in Japanese conversation: A study in grammar and interaction.* Amsterdam: Benjamins.

Tanaka, Hiroko 2000. "Turn-projection in Japanese talk-in-interaction." *Research on Language and Social Interaction* 33 (1): 1–38.

Tanaka, Hiroko 2004. "Prosody for marking transition-relevance places in Japanese conversation: The case of turns unmarked by utterance-final objects." In: *Sound patterns in interaction,* Elizabeth Couper-Kuhlen and Cecilia E. Ford (eds.), 63–96. Amsterdam: Benjamins.

Tarplee, Clare 1996. "Working on young children's utterances: prosodic aspects of repetition during picture labelling." In: *Prosody in conversation,* Elisabeth Couper-Kuhlen and Margret Selting (eds.), 406–435. Cambridge: Cambridge University Press.

Uhmann, Susanne 1991. *Fokusphonologie.* Tübingen: Niemeyer.

Uhmann, Susanne 1992. "Contextualizing relevance: On some forms and functions of speech rate changes in everyday conversation." In: *The contextualization of language,* Peter Auer and Aldo di Luzio (eds.), 297–336. Amsterdam: Benjamins.

Uhmann, Susanne 1993. "Das Mittelfeld im Gespräch." In: *Wortstellung und Informationsstruktur,* Marga Reis (ed.), 313–354. Tübingen: Niemeyer.

Uhmann, Susanne 1996. "On rhythm in everyday German conversation: beat clashes in assessment utterances." In: *Prosody in conversation. Interactional studies,* Elizabeth Couper-Kuhlen and Margret Selting (eds.), 303–365. Cambridge: Cambridge University Press.

Uhmann, Susanne 1997. *Grammatische Regeln und konversationelle Strategien.* Tübingen: Niemeyer.

Walker, Gareth 2004a. "On some interactional and phonetic properties of increments to turns in talk-in-interaction." In: *Sound patterns in interaction,* Elizabeth Couper-Kuhlen and Cecilia E. Ford (eds.), 147–170. Amsterdam: Benjamins.

Walker, Gareth 2004b. *The phonetic design of turn endings, beginnings, and continuations in conversation.* PhD thesis, University of York.

Wells, Bill and Corrin, Juliette 2004. "Prosodic resources, turn-taking and overlap in children's talk-in-interaction." In: *Sound patterns in interaction,* Elizabeth Couper-Kuhlen and Cecilia E. Ford (eds.), 119–144. Amsterdam: Benjamins.

Wells, Bill and Macfarlane, Sarah 1998. "Prosody as an interactional resource: Turn-projection and overlap." *Language and Speech* 41 (3–4): 265–294.

Wells, Bill and Peppé, Sue 1996. "Ending up in Ulster: Prosody and turn-taking in English dialects." In: *Prosody in conversation. Interactional studies,* Elizabeth Couper-Kuhlen and Margret Selting (eds.), 101–130. Cambridge: Cambridge University Press.

Wells, Bill and Peppé, Sue 2003. "Intonation abilities of children with speech and language impairments." *Journal of Speech Language and Hearing Research* 46: 5–20.

Wennerstrom, Ann 2001. *The music of everyday speech.* Oxford: Oxford University Press.

Wichmann, Anne 2000. *Intonation in text and discourse.* London: Longman.

Wichmann, Anne 2001. "Spoken parentheticals." In: *A wealth of English.* Karin Aijmer (ed.), 177–193. Gothenburg: University Press.

Wootton, Anthony J. 1989. "Remarks on the methodology of conversation analysis." In: *Conversation: An interdisciplinary perspective,* Derek Roger and Peter Bull (eds.), 238–258. Clevedon: Multilingual Matters.

Wright, Melissa 2007. "Clicks as markers of new sequences in English conversation." In: *Proceedings of the 16th International Congress of Phonetic Sciences. Vol. 2,* Jürgen Trouvain and William John Barry (eds.), 1069–1072. Saarbrücken: Universität des Saarlandes.

Future prospects of research on prosody: The need for publicly available corpora

Comments on Margret Selting
"Prosody in interaction: State of the art"*

Arnulf Deppermann
Institute for the German Language (IDS), Mannheim, Germany

In her overview, Margret Selting makes the case for the claim that dealing with authentic conversation necessarily lies at the heart of an interactional-linguistic approach to prosody (see Selting this volume, Section 3.3). However, collecting and transcribing corpora of authentic interaction is a time-consuming enterprise. This fact often severely restricts what the individual researcher is able to do in terms of analysis within the scope of his or her resources. Still, for dealing with many of the desiderata Margret Selting points out in Section 5 of her extensive overview, the use of larger corpora seems to be required. In this commenting paper, I want to argue that future progress in research on prosody in interaction will essentially rest on the availability and use of large public corpora. After reviewing arguments for and against the use of public corpora, I will discuss some upshots regarding corpus design and issues of transcription of public corpora.

1. Publicly available corpora: Pros and cons

Although in a rudimentary fashion, the need for a larger corpus already becomes visible in the first steps of a close sequential analysis of single cases. In research on prosody, we find it especially hard to follow the basic conversation-analytic maxim that it is our duty as an analyst to show that conversationalists orient to some putative device (cf. Selting this volume, Section 4.2). This is because in analyzing single cases, it often is not plainly evident that interactants orient to prosodic features as such – in contrast to, e.g. sequential actions or lexical categorizations. It is a major challenge to find out

---

* I thank Dagmar-Barth-Weingarten and Elisabeth Reber for helpful comments on an earlier version of this paper.

and to show that they react specifically to some prosodic feature – and not to some other contingently co-occurring feature in the turn, patterns of multimodal participation and/or the sequential environment. We often need larger collections of cases in order to see and to show that they exhibit systematic practices of using and responding to prosodic features which cannot be accounted for on the grounds of, e.g., lexical items or action type properties. Equally, the single case often does not show clearly if and how some prosodic feature might resonate with other co-occurring features which can be said to necessarily accompany the prosodic device in question in order to achieve some interactional effect or which can be seen to determine systematically the interactional import of the prosodic device.

In other words, the size and the composition of the researcher's own corpus often severely limits what can be achieved. Larger corpora are needed in order to discover the range of variants of some device in question, their factual import (or, just to the contrary, the fact that some variation does not matter) and the generic, context-free properties of prosodic practices in contrast to their context-sensitive adaptations. While single-case analysis may not even allow for noticing a possibly distinct phenomenon and for developing testable hypotheses, corpora often exhibit patterns which inspire the inductive discovery of some phenomenon (which then in turn needs close single-case analysis).

As Margret Selting makes clear, co-occurring grammatical constructions, sequential environments, (e.g., institutional) genres, communities of practice, kinds of speakers and languages/language types will be the major candidates for comparative and contrastive studies (cf. Selting this volume: Sections 5.1.7, 5.2, 5.4, 5.5), which look for context-sensitive contrasts and specializations as well as for commonalities and generalizations which transcend the individual context. Turning to larger corpora thus will not only lead to a differentiation of findings, but may as well open our eyes to even more general structures than can become obvious in a small corpus. Larger corpora are thus indispensable for refining analyses, testing the robustness of findings in different contextual environments and checking how general some phenomenon or mechanism actually is. Finally, only large corpora allow for providing statistical evidence. According to conversation-analytic standards, however, codings necessary for such quantification should only be assigned after having carefully worked through a large collection of cases by hand. This is needed as the basis for discovering the relevant emic categories which can serve as codes (cf. Schegloff 1993).

Yet, many researchers with a conversation-analytic background refuse to work with public corpora. I will deal with two major objections and possible counter-arguments against them:

1. The researcher does neither have comprehensive knowledge of the interactional context nor of its ethnographic background. This may lead to an inadequate analysis. If we do not know exactly conversational histories and ethnographic

prerequisites for action and interpretation, we may not be able to arrive at a comprehensive analysis of the single instance, i.e., we may miss some delicate details of what exactly is indexed by the single token in its context (e.g., disappointment because of the deception of hopes that had priorly been inspired by the interlocutor; prosodic escalation in overlap because of claims to superior expertise because of professional history...). However, the availability of the recording of the whole encounter and ethnographic background knowledge seem to be relevant only if culture-specific contextualization conventions (Gumperz 1982), which do not exhibit direct sequential repercussions, matter or if phenomena relating to larger sequences, like contrastive prosodic packaging of different larger activities, are at issue.

In most cases we will still be able to identify generic, "context-free" functional uses and potentials which matter for the prosodic practice as such and which account for the possibility to use it in an infinite range of individual contexts. An example is glottal closure at the end of candidate turn constructional units. While motivations for the use of glottal closure in this position of the construction of a turn are multifaceted and highly context-dependent, glottal closure is invariably used to contextualize the unit as an unfinished fragment (see Selting 2001). Admittedly, if the corpus does not allow for more than a KWIC-concordance with severely limited access to the sound surrounding the focal phenomenon, it will be impossible to carry out a serious sequential analysis. Therefore, a public corpus must provide access to the whole communicative event or at least "big packages" within complex speech events. This is a requirement which is, e.g., in contrast to corpora suited for applications in speech technology (cf. Wichmann 2008).

2.   Another objection against public corpora is the indexicality of transcription practices (Mondada 2007). Transcripts inevitably vary with respect to the research question at hand and also with regard to theoretical commitments about impressionistic vs. selective transcription, the nature of units and boundaries, the adequacy of categories like '(focal/nucleus) accent', the relevance of formal vs. functional features in transcripts, etc (cf. Selting this volume: Section 6.2). The objection against a public corpus thus is that researchers are faced with transcripts, which may be too coarse, too selective, too fine-grained or laden with theoretical commitments and therefore distort possibly relevant features of the original sound or make them inaccessible. Still, I will argue below that it is possible to define a base standard for searchable public data bases which are useful for all different concerns of prosodic research in Interactional Linguistics.

In what follows, I will sketch some considerations for the design of public corpora which comply with the needs of Interactional Linguists.

2.   Criteria for the design of publicly available corpora

There are some basic corpus-linguistic criteria which apply to spoken corpora in general (see Merkel and Schmidt 2009, Bird and Simons 2002, Baude et al. 2006). They are also relevant for corpora suited for research on prosody. Among the most important criteria are:

–   The corpus needs to be publicly available via internet or on CD/DVD as a machine-readable and searchable data-base,
–   it should use interoperable data-formats (preferably XML for text and WAV for sound),
–   it needs to include audio- and possibly video-files,
–   they should be aligned with the transcript so that the sound can be played immediately from the transcript,
–   the corpus should include meta-data concerning speakers and speech events,
–   the corpus should be managed by a data base which allows for browsing the corpus and for searches using (combinations of) meta-data and features of the transcripts.

For interactional research on prosody, the development of corpora which are equipped with search tools which address aspects of sequential structure of interactions, such as turn-beginnings and -endings, turn-transition or overlap, is a major task.[1] Data-bases for research on prosody in interaction should allow for reading transcripts and listening to recordings of whole interactions. The download of segments of sound and transcript needs to be possible in order to submit them to subsequent analysis in other programs such as PRAAT. In this way, the corpus should allow for a systematic overview of the corpus, multi-criteria searches, the exhaustive retrieval of candidate tokens for building a collection, the possibility of refining transcripts according to the researchers' needs and for analyzing the original sound data.

3.   The adequate level of detail of transcription in publicly available corpora

I will now return to the issue of transcription. Wichmann (2008: 205) makes a plea for richly annotated corpora: "One hopes that future spoken corpora will provide linguistically sophisticated syntactic, pragmatic and discourse annotation together with an equally sophisticated prosodic annotation that can then be complemented by automatic analysis of global trends, such as pitch, pause, loudness and voice quality." Prosodic annotation allows for the possibility to search prosodic features directly in the

---

1.   A model in this respect is the French data-base "Corpus de langues parlées en interaction" (CLAPI): http://clapi.univ-lyon2.fr/.

transcripts.[2] This seems to be a major requirement for a systematic prosodic analysis of large data-bases. However, a closer look at the problems associated with the search for a "generic level" of prosodic transcription in a public corpus suggests that prosodic transcription causes too many problems to be advisable:

–   There is no common agreement on the degree of granularity of prosodic transcription: Which phenomena are to be included? In how much detail?
–   There are competing standards, conventions, and philosophies of transcription (see Selting this volume). IPA, GAT, TOBI, and CA (just to name the most commonly used systems) focus on different phenomena, presuppose different categories for coding and "lumping together" what are considered to be the "same phenomena", make different theoretical assumptions regarding relevant distinctions and prosodic systems in speech and interaction. In sum, not one of these systems can be taken as an undisputed base representation complying with all needs of Interactional Linguistics, being compatible with all possible theoretical commitments. Each transcript inevitably implies some kind of categorization and thus interpretation of observable phenomena, which may be disputed or refused on theoretical grounds.
–   The reliability and validity of prosodic transcripts is quite poor in practice (see, e.g., the London-Lund corpus; cf. also O'Connell and Kowal 1999). In part, deficits arise from problems inherent in the transcription systems, such as lacking, imprecise or polysemous definitions of transcription conventions, multiplication of signs for the same phenomena, etc. Still more important are problems associated with the transcribers, i.e., differences in individual styles of transcription, lack of training, lack of knowledge in phonetics and prosody, and lack of time and of runs of correction and validation. These problems are aggravated if large corpora have to be transcribed by students in a relatively short time, with little training and with no specific research goal in mind.

In sum, problems of searchability (most importantly, resulting in false negatives) and dependency on non-shared theoretical decisions taken by the corpus-designers and transcribers are inevitable when relying on prosodic transcriptions. Most serious researchers on prosody probably would not rely on pre-transcribed prosodic transcripts, but they would adapt the transcription according to their own research interests and theoretical convictions.

Because of the various problems of prosodic transcripts, orthographic transcripts offer the best basis for searches. At first sight, this may seem paradoxical because orthographic transcripts do not contain any prosodic annotation at all. But it is precisely this lack which makes them suitable for many kinds of comprehensive searches which

---

2.   I will not discuss Wichmann's suggestion that corpora should contain pragmatic and discourse annotation, which seems to me at least as problematic as prosodic annotation from a conversation-analytic point of view.

do not discard relevant phenomena because of transcription decisions. Automatic searches in orthographic transcripts inevitably result in false positives, which have to be discarded by the researcher by hand, but they run the risk of false negatives (exclusion of relevant phenomena) to a much lesser extent than all other kinds of transcripts (prosodic, eye dialect, etc.). Still, many interesting phenomena cannot be searched using orthographic transcripts. If we are, e.g., interested in identifying interactional, prosodic and phonetic properties of different kinds of intonation phrases, we cannot resort to orthographic transcripts for creating collections via automatic searches. Using prosodically annotated transcripts, however, would presuppose that we already know most of the details relevant to the boundaries of intonation phrases, whose detection is precisely the goal of the study. So, while the possibility to dispose of large publicly available corpora will serve many research interests, the benefit of automatic procedures of retrieval and analysis will depend crucially on research goals.

Today, public corpora suited for Interactional Linguistics are still rare (for overviews see Merkel and Schmidt 2009, Wichmann 2008, McCarthy and O'Keefe 2008).[3] Moreover, not one of the few corpora that are available does conform to all of the criteria outlined in this paper. Thus, the construction of public corpora of interactional data and the advancement of their standards is a major task. If it is accomplished, it can also foster future research in Interactional Linguistics.

References

Baude, Olivier et al. 2006. *Corpus oraux.* Paris: CNRS.

Bird, Steven and Simons, Gary 2002. "Seven dimensions of portability for language documentation and description." *Language* 79: 557–582.

Gumperz, John J. 1982. *Discourse strategies.* London: Cambridge University Press.

McCarthy, Michael and O'Keefe, Anne 2008. "Corpora and spoken language." In: *Corpus Linguistics. Vol.2,* Anke Lüdeling and Merja Kytö (eds.), 1008–1024. Berlin: de Gruyter.

Merkel, Silke and Schmidt, Thomas 2009. "Korpora gesprochener Sprache im Netz – eine Umschau." *Gesprächsforschung* 10: 70–93 (http://www.gespraechsforschung-ozs.de/heft2009/px-merkel.pdf).

Mondada, Lorenza 2007. "Commentary: transcript variations and the indexicality of transcribing practices." *Discourse Studies* 9 (6): 809–821.

O'Connel, Daniel C. and Kowal, Susanne 1999. "Transcription and the issue of standardization." *Journal of Psycholinguistic Research* 28: 103–120.

---

3.   From 2011 onwards, a large public corpus (Forschungs- und Lehrkorpus Gesprochenes Deutsch: FOLK) of conversations in German with audio files and transcripts aligned will be available via internet: http://agd.ids-mannheim.de/html/folk.shtml.

Schegloff, Emanuel A. 1993. Reflections on quantification in the study of conversation. In: Research on Language & Social Interaction 26 (1): 99–128.

Selting, Margret 2001. "Fragments of units as deviant cases of unit-production in conversational talk." In: *Studies in Interactional Linguistics*, Margret Selting and Elizabeth Couper-Kuhlen (eds.), 229–258. Amsterdam: Benjamins.

Wichmann, Anne (2008) "Speech corpora and spoken corpora." *In: Corpus Linguistics. Vol. 1, Anke Lüdeling and Merja Kytö (eds.), 187–207. Berlin: de Gruyter.*

PART I

Prosody and other levels of linguistic organization in interaction

The phonetic constitution
of a turn-holding practice
Rush-throughs in English talk-in-interaction*

Gareth Walker
University of Sheffield, UK

There is a need to get to grips with the phonetic design of talk in its totality and without a separation of prosodic and non-prosodic aspects. Features of duration, phonation and articulation are all shown to be systematic features of rush-throughs, and bound up with the turn-holding function of the practice. Data are drawn from audio and video recordings made in a range of interactional settings, all involving speakers of English from the UK or the US. The paper concludes by reviewing some of the reasons why this holistic approach is desirable, namely: empirical findings, the parametric nature of speech, and a commitment to a mode of enquiry which takes seriously observable details of all kinds.

1. Introduction

There are at least three reasons to look at the phonetic design of talk in its totality and without a separation between prosodic and non-prosodic aspects.[1] First, a range of details is involved in the production and interpretation of talk. Any part of an utterance can be described in terms of articulatory and phonatory quality, frequency (pitch), loudness and duration (Laver 1994). Because all of these features are always

---

* I am grateful to John Local for the generous sharing of data and ideas during the formation of this paper; I take full responsibility for how I may have incorporated or overlooked those data and ideas. Dagmar Barth-Weingarten, Susanne Günthner, Elisabeth Reber, Hiroko Tanaka, Traci Walker, Bill Wells and an anonymous reviewer gave useful comments on earlier drafts and revisions.

1. Definitions of 'prosody' in the literature are surprisingly hard to come by, and when they are given they may refer to different parts of the speech signal. A survey of the literature on 'prosody and interaction' (e.g. papers in Couper-Kuhlen and Selting 1996, Couper-Kuhlen and Ford 2004) suggests that for all practical purposes within that field prosody refers to variations in loudness, duration and (especially) pitch. Those are the features which 'prosody' is taken to refer to here. This is not meant to suggest that this is the only use of the term: this is clearly not the case.

'there' in the speech signal, they could conceivably have interactional relevance at any given point. Second, numerous studies describe practices in which clusters of phonetic features are implicated, and these feature-clusters can incorporate both prosodic and non-prosodic features (see e.g. Curl 2005, Curl et al. 2006, Kelly and Local 1989a, Local 1996, 2004, Walker 2004, 2007). The empirical nature of these analyses mean that their findings pose an important challenge for segmental analytic frameworks which focus on lexical contrast at the expense of other sorts of meaning (Ogden 2001). Indeed, these findings have arisen from studies which approach talk-in-interaction from a well-established non-segmental perspective (for overviews and analyses in this Firthian phonological tradition, see e.g. Kelly and Local 1989b, Kelly and Plug 2005, Ogden and Local 1994). Third, one principle of interactional phonetics (incorporated from conversation analysis; CA) is that "no order of detail in conversational interaction can be dismissed a priori as disorderly, accidental, or interactionally irrelevant" (Heritage 1989: 22). There is no reason that this principle should not be followed in the study of the phonetic design of talk, just as it is followed in the study of other aspects of interaction (sequential organisation, lexical choice, grammatical structure, body position, gaze, gesture and so on). This principle provides a warrant for inspecting all aspects of the speech signal for their possible interactional relevance.

In what follows part of an account is presented of a practice – the rush-through – which is regularly referred to in the literature but which is yet to receive sustained analytic attention. In the course of the phonetic analysis a range of phonetic details is described without affording primacy to either prosodic or non-prosodic aspects (Local and Walker 2005). It will be argued that both prosodic (durational) and non-prosodic (articulatory and phonatory) features are systematic in the practice, and relate to its function in interaction.

The production of more talk by a current speaker following a point of possible completion may require some kind of interactional 'work' (Schegloff 1987a). One practice designed to handle this work has been dubbed the rush-through. Both the label given to this practice and existing descriptions of individual cases suggest that the practice is describable in phonetic terms. However there is as yet no technical phonetic examination of the practice. Furthermore, descriptions given to date have been provided as part of other analytic enterprises (e.g. Ford and Thompson 1996: 165–166, Kitzinger 2000: 185–186, Roberts 2002, Schegloff 1982: 76, 1987b: 78, 1996: 93, 1998: 241). This means that both the (phonetic) form of the rush-through and its function in interaction has remained under-explored. This paper attempts to fill these gaps somewhat by providing a technical phonetic account of some instances of rush-throughs (Section 2) and by offering some remarks on interactional aspects of a small set of cases (Section 3). Some concluding comments are given in Section 4.

The sample of data presented here is taken from a range of types of interaction (an everyday conversation over the telephone, a recording of face-to-face interaction, off-air recordings of television and radio interviews). All interactants are native speakers of British or American English with no known relevant pathologies. As has become standard in conversation analysis and interactional phonetics, detailed analysis of a small number of fragments is presented; aggregate measures are given at appropriate points. The fragments discussed in detail have been selected as exemplars of more general patterns: the data presented here are a representative sample of a larger collection of 20 instances of rush-throughs.

2.   Phonetic analysis

The following sections provide observations concerning the phonetic design of rush-throughs in terms of the following characteristics: duration (Section 2.1), juncture (Section 2.2) and pitch (Section 2.3). It is important to note that these were not the only features considered in the course of the phonetic analysis: rather, they are those features which are either systematic, or of interest for other reasons. The phonetic analysis involves careful and repeated parametric listening, and inspection of acousti-co-graphic records using the Praat computer analysis package (http://www.fon.hum. uva.nl/praat).

2.1   Duration

Fragment 1 is taken from a broadcast television interview between Michael Parkinson and actress Joanna Lumley. The rush-through occurs in line 13; the join between the turn-constructional unit (TCU; see Schegloff 1996, 2007) ending with the rush-through – henceforth the *first TCU*, even where this is not the first TCU in the turn – and the TCU which follows (the *second TCU*) is marked with the ⌢ symbol; the main conventions are listed in the appendix to this chapter. With the exception of the transcription of Fragment 3 (which is taken directly from an existing transcription in circulation in the academic community) the transcriptions are prepared in such a way as to reflect aspects of the sequential organization of the talk, and to balance readability and detail. They are relatively systematized presentation transcriptions derived from more detailed working transcriptions (Ball and Local 1996, Kelly and Local 1989a, 1989b): readers are therefore encouraged to consult the audio recordings which accompany this volume for independent listening and analysis.

(1) **Parkinson**, 27/10/2007, Part 2, 0:03 (cf. sound file [WAL-1-Parkinson.wav])
     (UK TV interview; Michael Parkinson [MP] interviewing actress Joanna Lumley [JL])

```
1   MP:  you were this child of the Raj weren't you
2            (0.4)
3   JL:  I was I wa[s born
4   MP:            [yeah (.) and it's interesting we've
5        had quite a few people who (0.2) had that
```

```
 6             similar backgrou[nd in:-:-
 7   JL:                      [mm
 8   MP:   coming up in:-:- growing up in India .hhhh and
 9          it seems to me that it produces a remarkable
10          (0.6) child a remarkable person much more .hhhhh
11          self sufficient (.) resilient (.) and with a
12          different kind of approach to life than .hhhh
13          other people⌒↘it is discernible
14                   (.)
15   JL:   is it=
16   MP:   =mm:[:
17   JL:       [.hhh=
18   MP:   =very much so
19   JL:   I wonder how much of that is to do with the
20          travelling which was immense cos you never flew
21          in those days you always went .hh long boat
22          journeys
```

MP's talk approaches a point of possible syntactic and pragmatic (action) completion with his "…different kind of approach to life than .hhhh other people" (lines 12–13).[2] MP's talk up to this point makes a response from JL relevant (a response concerning the matter of why growing up abroad may produce a "remarkable person": see JL's eventual response along these lines beginning at line 19). However, rather than yield his turn at this point of possible completion, MP speeds up his talk on "other people" and goes on to produce a further TCU ("it is discernible", line 13) without delay.

MP's "other" in line 13 is faster than his preceding talk, and his following "people" is faster still. This rushed production of "people" is even significantly faster than his earlier turn-medial token of "people" at line 5: that earlier version has a duration of 393 milliseconds (ms), while the rushed version has a duration of 146 ms. This rushed version is therefore roughly twice as fast as the earlier version. That a TCU-final token should be so much faster than a TCU-medial token is especially remarkable as the ends of units of talk typically exhibit a slowing down (see e.g. Local et al. 1986, Turk and Shattuck-Hufnagel 2007, see also Barth-Weingarten 2009 where it is argued that a lack of final lengthening may provide for the production of the second element in a bi-clausal 'parallel-opposition' construction).

A second instance of a rush-through is shown in Fragment 2. The rush-through occurs at the end of CF's "…healthy environment" (line 9).

---

2.   There may be other points of possible syntactic and pragmatic completion preceding the rush-through in the same turn, as in Fragment 1. However, it is the point of possible completion at which the rush-through occurs which is the focus of discussion.

(2) **Today environment**, 28/02/2006, 5:10 (cf. sound file [WAL-2-Today-environ-ment.wav])

(UK radio interview; Edward Stourton [ES] interviewing Caroline Flint MP [CF], then Minister for Public Health, on the day a report into childhood obesity was published; ES and CF are in different studios)

```
 1   CF:   and that carries on through school but it's also
 2         what happens I think .hhhh in terms of
 3         addressing these issues .hhh when a family turns
 4         up in the doctor's surgery .hhh and (.) all
 5         different (.) other areas of our lives .hh where
 6         it can make an impact .hh y'know access to our
 7         parks .hh access to sport .hh but ge[nerally
 8   ES:                                       [.hhhh
 9   CF:   creating that he[althy environment⌒now n[o one
10   ES:                   [uhn-                    [ah-
11   CF:   person .hh can take responsibility for all
12   CF:   [of that  [.hh [but what w]e do need (.) if
13   ES:   [but it's [prec[isely     ]
14   CF:   I could just make this point
```

CF brings her talk to possible syntactic and pragmatic completion with her "generally creating that healthy environment" (lines 7–9). At the end of her first TCU there is a significant and audible speeding-up on "environment" of about the same magnitude as the speeding-up in Fragment 1.

Fragment 3 is taken from a telephone call. The rush-through occurs in line 26.

(3) **MDE-MTRAC.60.1.3**, 0:07 (cf. sound file [WAL-3-MTRAC.wav])

(US telephone; Joey has recent arrived at his father's – Tony's – home following a stay with his mother, Marsha)

```
 4   Tony:     Joe got here I just wan'duh letchu kno:w
 5             'ee uh [(        )
 6   Marsha:          [Oh thank you fer callin,h
 7   Tony:     He stepped outta the house longih- I
 8             thought'e wz g'nna be back i:n en I would
 9             remind him tuh ca:ll b't uh apparently he
10             wz going with Ilene tih the movies 'r
11             something (like that I didn't check=).
12   Marsha:   ehh hha hha hhuh .hhhh She call(s)/(ed)
13             him evry ni:ght.
14                 (0.3)
15   Tony:     Ha:h?
16   Marsha:   She call(s)/(ed) him evry ni[:ght.
17   Tony:                                  [Oh really?
18   Marsha:   An' he wz out evry n(h)i(h)gh(h)t hnh
19                 (0.4)
```

```
20  Tony:    Tha:t's uh,hh (0.4) They're rilly quite
21           a nice couple.
22  Marsha:  At's w't evrybuddy says I haven't met her
23           but I- .hhh I guess I- I ↑wi:ll, hh
24  Tony:    Yeh probly you will,
25  Marsha:  .hhh Ah that's so nice'v you tih call
26           Tony I appreciate it⌢what time did'e get
27           on the pla:ne.
28  Tony:    Uh::: (0.2) I: do:n't know exactly I
29           think ih wz arou:nd three uh'clo:ck or
30           something a' that sort.
```

Marsha approaches a point of possible syntactic and pragmatic completion with her "appreciate it" (line 26), making a response from Tony relevant as she does so. While the tempo characteristics of her talk up to the fricative of "appreciate" are not especially remarkable, Marsha speeds up her talk significantly from this point. The talk which follows in that TCU is much faster than might have been anticipated on the basis of the tempo characteristics of the talk up to that point.

What can be heard in each of Fragments 1–3 is the current speaker approaching a point of possible syntactic and pragmatic completion, but rather than yielding their turn at that point, speeding up the talk and continuing into further talk without delay. Indeed, this speeding-up localised to the end of a TCU and continuation without delay are hallmarks of the rush-through. While this speeding-up can be clearly heard, inspection of acoustico-graphic records makes it possible to provide independently verifiable measures of this speeding-up and quantified measures of its magnitude.

Figure 1 shows articulation rate plots for the talk leading up to the end of the first TCU in each of Fragments 1–3. The figure gives a visual representation of how quickly the sounds in each metrical foot are being produced. (A foot consists of a stressed syllable and all unstressed syllables following it up to, but not including, the next stressed syllable; Abercrombie 1964.) It is appropriate to take the foot as a domain of measurement for articulation rate as each foot contains exactly one stressed syllable: in English, stressed syllables are typically longer (produced more slowly) than unstressed syllables (Crystal and House 1990). The articulation rate for each foot is calculated in phonological segments per second, or sps; $sps = n(1/time)$, where n = number of segments, and $time$ = duration of foot in seconds. Articulation rate is expressed in sps because units containing more segments tend to have a longer duration than those with fewer segments (Crystal and House 1990). The results of these calculations can then be plotted on a chart. Each foot is represented by a dot centred over an orthographic label; the higher the dot, the faster the articulation rate.

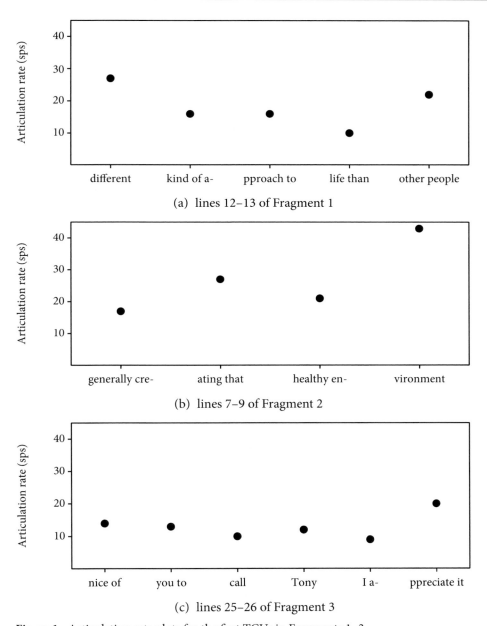

(a) lines 12–13 of Fragment 1

(b) lines 7–9 of Fragment 2

(c) lines 25–26 of Fragment 3

Figure 1. Articulation rate plots for the first TCUs in Fragments 1–3

It can be seen from Figures 1a-c that the final foot of the first TCU has a considerably faster articulation rate than the foot which preceded it. For each of the cases shown, the articulation rate of the final foot is roughly twice that of the penultimate foot. Neither the occurrence of this speeding-up, nor its magnitude, is particular to these three cases:

the mean change in articulation rate from the penultimate foot to the final foot across a set of instances is +81% (min = 25%, max = 133%, standard deviation = 37, n = 14). This speeding-up is all the more remarkable given that we would expect a turn-final foot to be *slower* than a penultimate foot. Rush-throughs involve not just an absence of slowing down, but rather a marked speeding up. Of course, one thing which this localised speeding-up around the possible end of a TCU provides for is starting up the post rush-through talk sooner than might have been anticipated by a co-participant. Evidence that these second TCUs begin earlier than co-participants anticipate will be presented in Section 3. Before that, some further consideration of phonetic aspects of the practice willfollow; namely juncture (Section 2.2) and pitch (Section 2.3).

2.2   Juncture

The join between the first and second TCUs (i.e. those joined by the rush-through) routinely exhibits features of close juncture. Specifically, the two TCUs can be bound together by features of phonation (actions of the vocal folds) and articulation (movements of other vocal organs). Note that features of phonation and articulation would not typically be considered 'prosodic'. This binding together of the two TCUs works against a co-participant coming in 'in the clear' (i.e. without incoming talk occurring in overlap) after the first TCU.

In each of Fragments 1–3, and as part of the rush-through, there is continued vocal fold vibration (voiced phonation) across the join between the two units. This continued vocal fold vibration can be heard in each case and identified visually in acoustico-graphic displays. Figure 2 provides visual representations of part of Fragment 3. In the figure, time runs along the x-axis. At the top of the figure are orthographic labels and a phonetic (IPA) transcription of Marsha's talk. The IPA symbols are centred over the relevant portion of the figure. Beneath the transcriptions is a spectrogram, which shows changes in frequency and intensity over time. (In a spectrogram, frequency is shown on the y-axis; intensity shows up as relative darkness.) Beneath the spectrogram is a fundamental frequency (F_0), or 'pitch' trace. Pitch is the perceptual correlate of fundamental frequency. The fundamental frequency of a sound corresponds to the rate at which the vocal folds vibrate: the higher the rate of vocal fold vibration, the higher the F_0; the higher the F_0, the higher the perceived pitch. The F_0 trace is presented on a logarithmic scale to take into account the non-linear perception of pitch whereby listeners perceive greater changes in pitch at lower frequencies. To give an indication of placement in the speaker's pitch range the F_0 trace is plotted on a y-axis which represents Marsha's baseline and topline pitches, established on the basis of one minute of representative speech. Beneath the F_0 trace is a (sound pressure) waveform. All portions of the figure are time-aligned with one another.

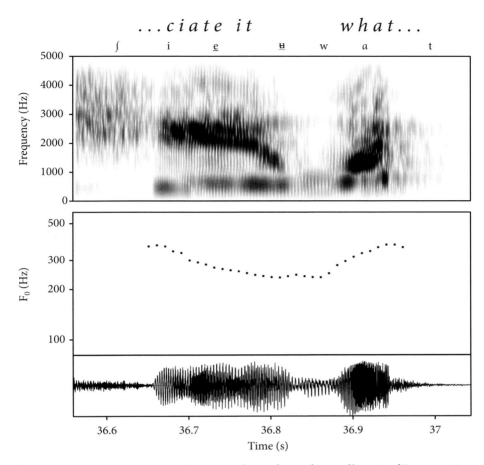

Figure 2. Labelled spectrogram, F_0 trace and waveform of part of line 26 of Fragment 3

In addition to the continuation of voiced phonation being audible, there is evidence in each part of the figure that vocal fold vibration continues between the first and second TCUs in Fragment 3. This is especially remarkable given that, in citation form, "appreciate it" would be expected to end with a voiceless [t]. First, the waveform remains periodic across the join around 36.85 s. (Periodicity in a waveform is indicative of vocal fold vibration.) Second, Praat's pitch tracking algorithm can reliably locate voiced frames (and hence F_0 values) across the join. Third, in the spectrogram there are vertical striations throughout this portion, which correspond to vibrations of the vocal folds.

Fragment 4 contains a further case of a rush-through, at the point of possible syntactic and pragmatic completion on "doing things" (line 6).[3]

---

3.   The speeding-up on the final foot of CB's first TCU is in line with the speed-up observed in Fragments 1–3. The penultimate foot ("better ways of") has an articulation rate of 18.4sps and the final foot ("doing things") has an articulation rate of 27sps: an increase of 47.2%.

(4) **Today things,** 11/08/2003, 8:42 (cf. sound file [WAL-4-Today-things.wav])
(UK radio interview; Sarah Montague [SM] interviewing Chris Bryant MP [CB]
shortly after the death of Dr David Kelly, a British UN weapons inspector: the BBC and
the government were investigated as part of the inquiry into the circumstances surrounding his death)

```
1   CB:  I- I don't think it's a g:reat gladiatorial
2        battle between the BBC .hhh and government I-
3        (0.2) I think there are specific issues that
4        need to be answered and need to be looked at and
5        .hh and we need to ascertain whether there are
6        better ways of doing things⌢so
7        there'[s   ac]tually I th]in-]
8   SM:       [but is] Ming      ] Ca]mpbell right the
9        luhh Liberal Democrat foreign affairs spokesman
10       when he says .hh that uh- the result of this
11       could have a direct effect on the next election
```

In Fragment 4, the vocal folds can be heard to vibrate throughout the final sound of
"things" at the end of the first TCU (line 6): the final /z/ is fully voiced. A time-aligned
spectrogram and sound-pressure waveform of a relevant portion of the recording is
shown in Figure 3. That there is simultaneous friction and voicing for [z] is evident
from both the spectrogram and the waveform. The spectrogram shows high frequency
noise (above c. 3.5 kHz) indicative of turbulent airflow, and regularly occurring vertical striations which correspond to vocal fold vibrations; likewise, the waveform is periodic with a frequency of c. 80 Hz, corresponding to low frequency vibrations of the
vocal folds, and also shows random (aperiodic) higher frequency noise, indicative of
turbulence. In utterance-final ('pre-pausal') position /z/ would usually be either partially or fully voiceless ('devoiced'). Smith (1997) reports that in an experimental study
of devoicing of /z/ in American English, all tokens of sentence final /z/ by all speakers
were fully devoiced; fully voiced tokens were only found when /z/ was followed by a
sonorant consonant or vowel. (Smith 1997 deals with American English data, though
the findings are consistent with descriptions of fricative voicing in British English, too:
see e.g. Abercrombie 1967: 138, Docherty 1992, Gimson 2001: 282, Jones 1962: 203,
Laver 1994: 340–342, Ward 1945: 129.) Furthermore, in other pre-pausal productions
of /z/ by the same speaker in the same interview, /z/ is not fully voiced. Figure 4 shows
a time-aligned spectrogram and waveform of the word "intentions", where /z/ exhibits
final devoicing i.e. it is voiceless at its end. Figure 4 shows that only the first 20 ms or
so of friction associated with /z/ is accompanied by vocal fold vibration. After that
there is turbulent airflow without vocal fold vibration (note the high frequency noise
above c. 3.5 kHz in the spectrogram and aperiodicity in the waveform, but no vertical
striations in the spectrogram or periodicity in the waveform). The key point concerning the fully voiced /z/ in Fragment 4 is this: fully voiced tokens of /z/ only occur where
a current speaker speaks next; in pre-pausal position /z/ is fully, or partially, devoiced.

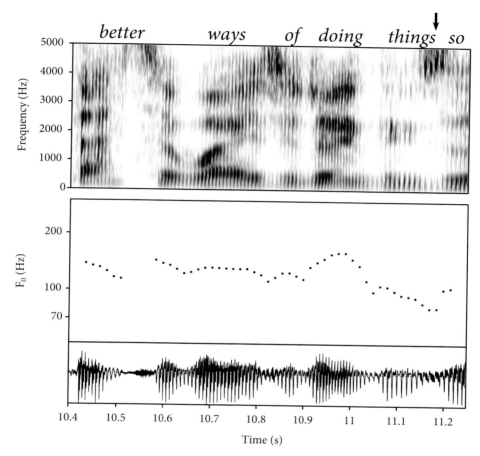

Figure 3. Labelled spectrogram, F_0 trace and waveform of line 6 of Fragment 4. The arrow indicates the midpoint of the final voiced /z/

Therefore, the fully voiced [z] at the end of "things" in Fragment 4 projects more talk from the current speaker.

This maintaining of vocal fold vibration – which is a regular property of rush-throughs, including those in Fragments 1 and 2 as well as in Fragments 3 and 4 – makes it impossible for a co-participant to find any kind of gap (period of no vocal activity) in which they might begin their talk. If they do begin their talk, they will find that their co-participant is already 'making noise', i.e. their vocal folds are continuing to vibrate.

In addition to showing how phonation can be bound up with the practice, Fragment 3 also shows how articulatory details may be bound up in doing a rush-through. At the end of *appreciate it* there is considerable reduction of the articulatory gestures when compared with those which might occur in citation forms of the same words. For instance, there are no closure portions associated with either /t/. Furthermore,

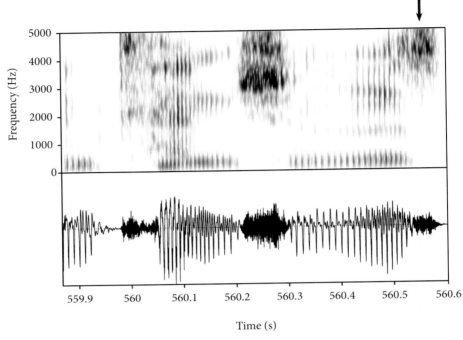

Figure 4. Spectrogram and waveform of "intentions" produced by CB (Fragment 4). The arrow indicates the midpoint of the final voiceless /z/ (cf. sound file [WAL-5-bryant-intentions.wav])

towards the end of *appreciate it* Marsha's lips become rounded and the tongue is re-tracted. (Evidence for this is shown in the spectrogram, where there is a fall in F2 from about 2000 Hz to about 1200 Hz beginning at about 36.77 s and lasting until about 36.82 s.) This retraction of the tongue body and rounding of the lips cannot be ac-counted for by the segmental make-up of *appreciate it*, since all of the vowel sounds in these words are front and unrounded. Rather, the tongue retraction and lip rounding is being done in anticipation of what is to come: the [w] of *what*.

These anticipatory gestures allow the current speaker to project more talk will fol-low. Furthermore, it means that while one TCU is being brought to an end, another has already begun. This point is returned to in Section 3.

2.3   Pitch

Up to this point it has been argued that localised manipulation of articulation rate, phonation and articulatory details are among those features which figure in the execu-tion of a rush-through. It is plausible that all of these features provide for the produc-tion of talk beyond a point of possible syntactic and pragmatic completion by (a) al-lowing talk to begin sooner than would have been anticipated (duration), (b) removing

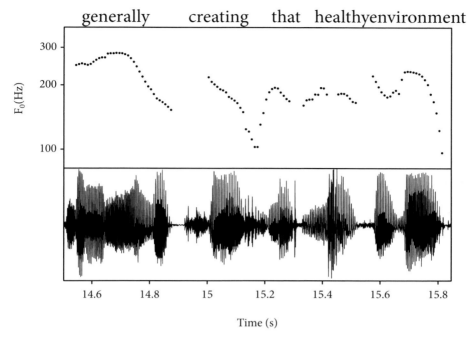

Figure 5. Labelled F_0 trace and waveform of part of lines 7–9 of Fragment 2

any gap between the first TCU and the following talk (phonation), and (c) the projection of more talk (phonation and articulation).

Pitch, however, seems to play no such role in the projection of more talk to come from that speaker beyond the end of the first TCU. First TCUs have the pitch characteristics of complete intonation phrases. Figure 5 shows a labelled F_0 trace and waveform of the end of the first TCU in Fragment 2.

Figure 5 shows that there is a large fall in pitch on the final foot of the first TCU in Fragment 2 (...*vironment*). Note also the fall in pitch over ...*ciate it* in Fragment 3 (Figure 2); in Fragment 4 (Figure 3) there is a fall in pitch over the final foot of CB's first TCU (*doing things*).

In addition to their production as complete intonation phrases, first TCUs may exhibit pitch characteristics (including contour, excursion and terminal pitch) of other complete turns. For instance, Fragment 2 (Figure 5) and Fragment 4 (Figure 3) both exhibit final falling pitch (with falls of 15 ST and 12.1 ST respectively), in each case terminating in the lower quartile of the speaker's range. Such large and clearly audible falls-to-low in pitch makes these TCUs comparable with other designed-to-be and treated-as complete units described in the literature (Ford and Thompson 1996, Local et al. 1986, Szczepek Reed 2004). To illustrate the point that first TCUs may be comparable with other complete turns in terms of their final pitch characteristics, Figure 6 shows a F_0 trace and waveform of the end of the first TCU in Fragment 4 (Figure 6a)

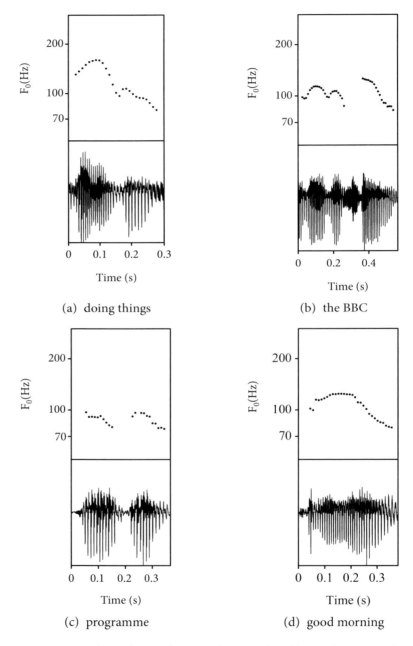

Figure 6. F_0 traces and waveforms of TCU endings produced by CB (Fragment 4) (cf. sound file [WAL-6-bryant-pitch-comparisons.wav])

alongside F_0 traces and waveforms of TCU endings from the same interview as Fragment 4 (Figure 6b–d).

It can be seen that in each case, including the rush-through, the TCU ends with a falling pitch: the final falls in Figure 6a-d measure 12.1 ST, 7.9 ST, 7.4 ST and 4.0 ST respectively. They also all end in the lower quartile of the speaker's pitch range, and all four end within 1 ST of each other. It is important to note that Figures 6b-d show TCU ends which were followed just after by speaker transition which occurred 'in the clear', i.e. without overlap. In other words, the final pitch characteristics of the first TCU may be directly comparable with those of other treated-as-complete TCUs.

In summary, whatever work (if any) is being done by pitch in the rush-throughs, pitch does not seem to play a systematic role in the projection of more talk (cf. duration, articulation and phonation). This finding that pitch doesn't project more talk is especially interesting given that pitch seems to be taken as a turn holding device *par excellence*: witness the use of stock phrases such as "continuing intonation" in the literature.

2.4   Summary

It has been argued that rush-throughs involve an approximate doubling of articulation rate in the final foot of the first TCU. There is also close juncture between the first and second TCUs. This may involve the continuation of voiced phonation across this join and articulatory anticipation of the second TCU. (It is, of course, quite possible for close juncture to occur between TCUs where there is no rush-through: it is the co-occurrence of close juncture with localised speeding-up around the possible end of a TCU which are the hallmarks of a rush-through.) It has been argued that pitch features do not play a systematic role in the projection of more talk beyond the first TCU. Rather, the pitch features of the first TCUs seem designed to mark them out as complete, coherent units. While some of these phonetic features (localised speeding-up, continued phonation) are either stated or hinted at in existing descriptions of rush-throughs, other features (assimilation, the possibility of the first TCU exhibiting those pitch features found in other designed-to-be and treated-as complete utterances) are not. In any case, one aim of the preceding sections has been to offer a more rigorous phonetic account of rush-throughs, the descriptions of which have previously had an "informal, quasi-phonetic tenor" (Schegloff 2005: 470).

The next section presents an examination of some sequential aspects of the practice, and particularly those which relate to rush-throughs as a resource for continuing a turn past a point of upcoming possible completion.

3.   Sequential organisation

The features of duration, phonation and articulation described in the preceding sections each militate against a co-participant starting up with reference to the end of the first TCU. The temporal compression at the end of the TCU provides for the starting of the second TCU sooner than the co-participant might have anticipated. Starting sooner than a co-participant anticipates puts the current speaker at an advantage in terms of talking past a point of upcoming possible completion at which a co-participant would otherwise be able to start their talk. As part of their basic set of rules of turn construction, Sacks et al. (1974) make the following observation:

> "If the turn-so-far is so constructed as not to involve the use of a 'current speaker selects next' technique, then self selection for next speakership may, but need not, be instituted; *first starter acquires rights to a turn*" (Sacks et al. 1974: 704, emphasis added)

The speeding-up which forms part of the rush-through provides for current speaker to be first starter following the first TCU. The phonatory and articulatory aspects of rush-throughs also seem designed to ensure that the current speaker is first starter. The continuation of voiced phonation means that at whatever point a co-participant begins their talk they will find that the current speaker is already speaking and may have already projected more talk to come via particular anticipatory articulatory gestures.

Given its design features it seems entirely plausible that rush-throughs represent a resource for talking past a point of upcoming possible completion. Indeed, it has been argued that 'rush-throughs' provide for the current speaker "to interdict another speaker's starting up" (Schegloff 2000: 51). However, published evidence in support of this claim is relatively sparse, presumably because where rush-throughs have been discussed this has been as part of other analytic endeavours. Within the current collection of instances, there are three principle forms of evidence that the rush-through represents a resource for turn-holding along the lines assumed up to this point.

One piece of evidence in support of rush-throughs as a turn-holding device is relatively straightforward: co-participants do not usually come in with reference to the end of the first TCU. This is the state of affairs in Fragments 1 and 3: in neither case do the co-participants begin their talk with reference to the end of the first TCU. Of course, this absence of start-ups with reference to the end of the first TCU does not necessarily mean that the co-participants were in any sense *prohibited* from coming in at that point: it could be that they chose not to speak at that point. While this might account for some cases, it certainly does not offer a plausible account for all of the cases in the collection. Fragment 1 provides some evidence that the absence of an incoming from JL at the end of the TCU ending with the rush (line 13) is not because she chose not to come in at that point, or was otherwise unable to e.g. through a problem of comprehension. First, JL's eventual response to this TCU (beginning at line 19) doesn't suggest any difficulty in understanding MP's talk leading up to the rush-through, and neither participant's intervening conduct (lines 15–18) suggests any problem of understanding. Second, given the nature of the interview (a TV interview) JL is obliged to respond to MP's talk leading up to the rush-through, or at least not responding to it would be an accountable course of action (Clayman and Heritage 2002). A more plausible account for why JL doesn't come in at the end of MP's *...other people* (line 13) is that the design of MP's talk, i.e. the deployment of the rush-through towards its end, militates against the start-up from JL which MP's talk made relevant: there would seem to be no other sequential or pragmatic factors for JL not coming in around the end of MP's *...other people* (line 13).[4]

The kinds of environments in which rush-throughs are deployed also provide a second form of evidence in support of the rush-through as a turn-holding device. In this regard, consider again Fragment 2. In Fragment 2 CF deploys a rush-through at the end of *generally creating that healthy environment* (lines 7–9). Just prior to the deployment of the rush-through there have been two audible indications from ES that he will start up talk at the next transition relevance place (TRP): his sharp inbreath during CF's *generally* (line 8) and his *uhn-* (line 10) which ends with glottal closure which is held until his start-up just after CF's rush-through (Local and Kelly 1986). CF's deployment of a rush-through can therefore be understood as responsive to ES's displayed intention to start up his own talk at the next TRP.

A third kind of evidence for rush-throughs as a turn-holding device comes from those occasions where co-participants do come in with reference to the end of the first TCU. When co-participants do come in with reference to the end of the first TCU, they begin their talk some way into the second TCU. In Fragment 2 ES makes a start on his own responsive talk (*ah-*, line 10) with reference to the end of CF's first TCU. By the time that ES begins his talk, CF is already a little way into her second TCU and clearly projecting more talk with her adverb *now*. By deploying the rush-through at the end of the first TCU, CF has been able to reach a point of "maximum grammatical control" (Schegloff 1996: 92) before ES has been able to produce a response. Note, too, that ES's start-up occurs at just that point where CF's *healthy environment* might have ended had it not been for the speeding up on the last word. Examples like Fragment 2 provide evidence to support the claim that rush-throughs allow the current speaker to start up their post-rush-through talk sooner than the co-participants themselves anticipate. A final point to note concerning Fragment 2 is that on finding himself talking in overlap with CF he drops out suggesting an orientation to CF being the "first starter" and therefore as having acquired rights to the turn by the time he begins.

The only case in the collection where incoming speaker holds on to bring talk to completion is Fragment 4. Following CB's rush-through at the end of *doing things*, and a short way into his next TCU, SM starts up talk (line 8). This however does not contradict

---

4.   A reviewer raised the intriguing possibility that MP's inbreath at the end of line 12 "might be heard as projecting a rather longer stretch of talk than an imminent TRP." This may be the case: however, given that MP still deploys a rush-through at the next point of possible completion, he doesn't seem to have deemed the inbreath alone to have secured the space to produce more talk beyond that point of possible completion. The deployment of the rush-through shows an orientation to that point as one of transition relevance, irrespective of the presence of an inbreath relatively late in the ongoing TCU.

the notion that rush-throughs secure for the current speaker rights to produce more talk past a point of upcoming possible completion. Unlike ES's incoming in Fragment 2, SM's talk in Fragment 4 is hearable as turn competitive (French and Local 1983). It is hearable as competitive principally due to the production of talk in overlap with high pitch. The first two syllables (*but is*, line 8) are not especially high for the beginning of a turn. However, the next (*Ming*) and the start of the syllable after that (*Camp*) do exhibit high pitch. This high pitch begins at roughly the point where SM would be able to recognise that CB has elected to continue rather than yielding his turn after *things*. So, rather than drop out at this point (as ES did in Fragment 2), SM produces talk designed as competitive. CB drops out midway through the production of the first vowel in *Campbell*, and SM's talk returns to something more like her expected norms for talk produced in the clear.

It is possible, therefore, to locate cases where a co-participant starts up talk in response to the first TCU, but on doing so they find themselves talking in overlap with the current speaker who, by that point, is some way into their second, post-rush-through, TCU. This lends support to the notions that as a result of their phonetic design these second TCUs really are begun sooner than might have been anticipated, and that the temporal compression evident in rush-throughs has interactional relevance. Also, in order to overcome the primary rights to speakership which the rush-through is designed to secure by virtue of the early start it provides for, an incoming speaker's talk must be designedly competitive.

While rush-throughs, it is argued, represent a turn-holding device, it is not always the case that they are deployed where there is vigorous competition for the floor. Consider again Fragment 3. Marsha deploys a rush-through in line 26, at the end of the TCU in which she offers an appreciation of Tony having called her. Note though that this is not the first time that Marsha has thanked Tony for calling her: her talk in lines 25–26 is a redoing of her earlier appreciation at line 6 (*Oh thank you fer callin,h*). Rather than receiving the kind of acceptance from Tony that Marsha's turn at line 6 made relevant (e.g. "no problem" or "you're welcome"), Tony began to produce an account for why he, rather than their son Joey, has called Marsha (line 7 on). That this appreciation was not overtly receipted by Tony adumbrates the possibility that the reissued appreciation, i.e. the appreciation ending with the rush-through at line 26, will also fail to secure overt receipt. By moving without delay into further talk following the appreciation, Marsha avoids the occurrence of any kind of gap in which a response from Tony might be noticeably absent (cf. Schegloff 1995).

In summary, there are at least three kinds of evidence that rush-throughs represent a resource for the production of more talk past an upcoming point of possible completion: (1) co-participants do not generally come in with reference to the end of the first TCU; (2) rush-throughs may be deployed in response to bids to take the floor at the next TRP; and (3) where co-participants do come in, they come in some way into the second TCU.

4.   Summary and implications

One aim of this paper has been to provide a more technical and rigorous phonetic account of rush-throughs: a practice which has been mentioned from time to time in the literature but which has not got beyond loose and inconsistent phonetic descriptions. On the basis of auditory and acoustic parametric phonetic analysis it has been shown that rush-throughs involve (1) an approximate doubling of articulation rate in the final foot of a TCU, relative to the preceding foot; (2) close juncture of the first and second TCUs, which incorporates features of phonation and articulation. Consideration has also been given to sequential aspects of rush-throughs in terms of their deployment and their treatment as a turn-holding device. The analysis presented here has shown that while certain prosodic features (duration) are systematic in the practice, others (pitch) are not. Furthermore, certain non-prosodic features (phonation, articulation) are systematic.

The paper began by setting out some of the reasons why analysts should consider the phonetic design of talk in its entirety, and without *a priori* decisions to focus on some particular phonetic parameter(s). These reasons were: the nature of the speech signal, previous (and present) empirical findings, and a commitment to an analytic framework which, being grounded in the principles of CA, should be conscientiously inclusive in terms of the details it deals with. In their introduction to *Sound patterns in interaction* (Couper-Kuhlen and Ford 2004), also Ford and Couper-Kuhlen (2004) outline the generally skeptical approach that CA takes towards categories of both social and linguistic orders. On the basis of the findings of this study, and previous studies which reach much the same conclusion, it is suggested that the same skepticism should be applied to the category 'prosody'. If we keep our minds – and our ears – open to the possibility that any aspect could in principle have interactional relevance at any given moment, we will be able to build a more complete understanding of how talk-in-interaction is organised. I take it that this is the goal of interactional phonetics.

References

Abercrombie, David 1964. "A phonetician's view of verse structure." *Linguistics* 6: 5–13. Reprinted in Abercrombie (1965), 16–25.
Abercrombie, David 1965. *Studies in phonetics and linguistics.* Oxford: Oxford University Press.
Abercrombie, David 1967. *Elements of general phonetics.* Edinburgh: Edinburgh University Press.
Ball, Martin J. and Local, John 1996. "Current developments in transcription." In: *Advances in clinical phonetics,* Martin J. Ball and Martin Duckworth (eds.), 51–89. Amsterdam: Benjamins.
Barth-Weingarten, Dagmar 2009. "Contrasting and turn transition: Prosodic projection with parallel-opposition constructions." *Journal of Pragmatics* 41: 2271–2294.
Clayman, Steven E. and Heritage, John 2002. *The news interview: Journalists and public figures on the air.* Cambridge: Cambridge University Press.

Couper-Kuhlen, Elizabeth and Ford, Cecilia E. (eds.) 2004. *Sound patterns in interaction.* Amsterdam: Benjamins.

Couper-Kuhlen, Elizabeth and Selting, Margret (eds.) 1996. *Prosody in conversation.* Cambridge: Cambridge University Press.

Crystal, Thomas H. and House, Arthur S. 1990. "Articulation rate and the duration of syllables and stress groups in connected speech." *Journal of the Acoustical Society of America* 88: 101–112.

Curl, Traci S. 2005. "Practices in other-initiated repair resolution: The phonetic differentiation of 'repetitions.'" *Discourse Processes* 35: 1–43.

Curl, Traci S.; Local, John and Walker, Gareth 2006. "Repetition and the prosody-pragmatics interface." *Journal of Pragmatics* 38: 1721–1751.

Docherty, Gerard J. 1992. *The timing of voicing in British English obstruents.* Berlin: Foris.

Ford, Cecilia E. and Couper-Kuhlen, Elizabeth 2004. "Conversation and phonetics: Essential connections." In: *Sound patterns in interaction,* Elizabeth Couper-Kuhlen and Cecilia E. Ford (eds.), 3–25. Amsterdam: Benjamins.

Ford, Cecilia E. and Thompson, Sandra A. 1996. "Interactional units in conversation: Syntactic, intonational, and pragmatic resources for the management of turns." In: *Interaction and grammar,* Elinor Ochs, Emanuel A. Schegloff and Sandra A. Thompson (eds.), 134–184. Cambridge: Cambridge University Press.

French, Peter and Local, John 1983. "Turn competitive incomings." *Journal of Pragmatics* 7: 701–715.

Gimson, A.C. 2001. *Gimson's pronunciation of English.* London: Arnold, 6th edn. Revised by Alan Cruttenden.

Heritage, John 1989. "Current developments in conversation analysis." In: *Conversation: An interdisciplinary perspective,* Derek Roger and Peter Bull (eds.), 21–47. Clevedon: Multilingual Matters.

Jones, Daniel 1962. *An outline of English phonetics.* Cambridge: Heffer, 9th edn. First published 1918.

Kelly, John and Local, John 1989a. "On the use of general phonetic techniques in handling conversational material." In: *Conversation: An interdisciplinary perspective,* Derek Roger and Peter Bull (eds.), 197–212. Clevedon: Multilingual Matters.

Kelly, John and Local, John 1989b. *Doing phonology.* Manchester: Manchester University Press.

Kelly, John and Plug, Leendert 2005. *Seventy years of Firthian phonology: prospect and retrospect.* Special issue of *York Papers in Linguistics* 2 (4). York: University of York.

Kitzinger, Celia 2000. "Doing feminist conversation analysis." *Feminism & Psychology* 10: 163–193.

Laver, John 1994. *Principles of phonetics.* Cambridge: Cambridge University Press.

Local, John 1996. "Some aspects of news receipts in everyday conversation." In: *Prosody in conversation: Interactional studies,* Elizabeth Couper-Kuhlen and Margret Selting (eds.), 177–230. Cambridge: Cambridge University Press.

Local, John 2004. "Getting back to prior talk: and-uh(m) as a back-connecting device." In: *Sound patterns in interaction,* Elizabeth Couper-Kuhlen and Cecilia E. Ford (eds.), 377–400. Amsterdam: Benjamins.

Local, John and Kelly, John 1986. "Projection and 'silences': Notes on phonetic and conversational structure." *Human Studies* 9: 185–204.

Local, John; Kelly, John and Wells, Bill 1986. "Towards a phonology of conversation: turn-taking in Tyneside English." *Journal of Linguistics* 22: 411–437.

Local, John and Walker, Gareth 2005. "Methodological imperatives for investigating the phonetic organisation and phonological structures of spontaneous speech." *Phonetica* 62: 120–130.

Ogden, Richard 2001. "Turn transition, creak and glottal stop in Finnish talk-in-interaction." *Journal of the International Phonetic Association* 31: 139–152.

Ogden, Richard and Local, John 1994. "Disentangling autosegments from prosodies: a note on the misrepresentation of a research tradition in phonology." *Journal of Linguistics* 30: 477–498.

Roberts, Felicia 2002. "Qualitative differences among cancer clinical trial explanations." *Social Science & Medicine* 55: 1947–1945.

Sacks, Harvey; Schegloff, Emanuel A. and Jefferson, Gail 1974. "A simplest systematics for the organization of turn-taking for conversation." *Language* 50: 696–735.

Schegloff, Emanuel A. 1982. "Discourse as an interactional achievement: Some uses of 'uh huh' and other things that come between sentences." In: *Georgetown University Round Table on Linguistics 1981. Analysing Discourse: Text and Talk*, Deborah Tannen, (ed.), 71–93. Washington: Georgetown University Press.

Schegloff, Emanuel A. 1987a. "Analyzing single episodes of interaction: An exercise in conversation analysis." *Social Psychology Quarterly* 50: 101–114.

Schegloff, Emanuel A. 1987b. "Recycled turn beginnings: A precise repair mechanism in conversation's turn-taking organisation." In: *Talk and social organisation*, Graham Button and John R.E. Lee (eds.), 70–85. Clevedon: Multilingual Matters.

Schegloff, Emanuel A. 1995. "Discourse as an interactional achievement III: The omnirelevance of action." *Research on Language and Social Interaction* 28 (3): 185–211.

Schegloff, Emanuel A. 1996. "Turn organization: One intersection of grammar and interaction." In: *Interaction and grammar*, Elinor Ochs, Emanuel A. Schegloff and Sandra A. Thompson (eds.), 52–133. Cambridge: Cambridge University Press.

Schegloff, Emanuel A. 1998. "Reflections on studying prosody in talk-in-interaction." *Language and Speech* 41: 235–263.

Schegloff, Emanuel A. 2000. "Overlapping talk and the organization of turn-taking for conversation." *Language in Society* 29: 1–63.

Schegloff, Emanuel A. 2005. "On integrity in inquiry...of the investigated, not the investigator." *Discourse Studies* 7: 455–480.

Schegloff, Emanuel A. 2007. *Sequence organization in interaction: A primer in conversation analysis 1*. Cambridge: Cambridge University Press.

Smith, Caroline L. 1997. "The devoicing of /z/ in American English: effect of local and prosodic context." *Journal of Phonetics* 25: 471–500.

Szczepek-Reed, Beatrice 2004. "Turn-final intonation in English." In: *Sound patterns in Interaction*, Elizabeth Couper-Kuhlen and Cecilia E. Ford (eds.), 97–117. Amsterdam: Benjamins.

Turk, Alice E. and Shattuck-Hufnagel, Stefanie 2007. "Multiple targets of phrase-final lengthening in American English words." *Journal of Phonetics* 35: 445–472.

Walker, Gareth 2004. "On some interactional and phonetic properties of increments to turns in talk-in-interaction." In: *Sound patterns in interaction*, Elizabeth Couper-Kuhlen and Cecilia E. Ford (eds.), 147–169. Amsterdam: Benjamins.

Walker, Gareth 2007. "On the design and use of pivots in everyday English conversation." *Journal of Pragmatics* 39: 2217–2243.

Ward, Ida C. 1945. *The phonetics of English*. Cambridge: Heffer and Sons, 4th edn.

Appendix: Transcription conventions

Turns at talk run down the page with the speaker identified at the left hand edge. The onset of overlapping talk is indicated by left-hand square brackets, "["; the end of overlap may be indicated by right-hand square brackets, "]". Silences are measured in seconds and enclosed in parentheses, e.g. (0.2); a period in parentheses indicates a silence of less than one tenth of a second (100 ms). Audible breathing is indicated by "h", with each "h" indicating one tenth of a second (100 ms); audible inbreathing is indicated by "h", or sequences of "h", preceded by ".": .hhh. A hyphen, "-", indicates oral or glottal 'cut-off'. A colon, ":", indicates the sustention of sound: the more colons, the longer the sound. Where descriptions are provided, these are placed in double parentheses and italicized, *((like this))*.

Rush-throughs as social action

Comments on Gareth Walker "The phonetic constitution of a turn-holding practice: Rush-throughs in English talk-in-interaction"*

Susanne Günthner
University of Muenster, Germany

1. Rush-throughs as a "kind of bridging between TCUs"

Even though "rush-throughs" have been mentioned sporadically in research on turn-taking, their description has remained rather impressionistic.

In their classical paper on turn-taking, Sacks at al. (1978: 13) describe "rules governing turn construction". Concerning *transition-relevance places*, they make the following observation:

> "If the turn-so-far is so constructed as not to involve the use of a 'current speaker selects next' technique, self selection for next speakership may, but need not, be instituted; with first starter acquiring rights to a turn, transfer occurring at that place." (Sacks et al. 1978: 13)

In cases in which current speaker plans to build a multi-unit turn (and to prevent next speaker from taking over), s/he can speed up just before the possible transition-relevance-place and, thus, indicate that s/he is not willing to give up the turn. For this, Schegloff (1982) introduced the term *rush-through*:

> "Speakers may also employ methodical devices for achieving a multi-unit turn at positions other than the beginning of the turn in question. There is, for example, what can be called a 'rush through' – a practice in which a speaker, approaching a possible completion of a turn-constructional unit, speeds up the pace of the talk, withholds a dropping pitch or the intake of breath, and phrases the talk to bridge what would otherwise be the juncture at the end of a unit." (Schegloff 1982: 76).

---

*   Thanks to Dagmar Barth-Weingarten and Elisabeth Reber for useful comments, and thanks to Lisa Roebuck for checking the English.

In his description of this kind of bridging between TCUs, Schegloff (2005: 470) refers to the "informal, quasi-phonetic tenor" of *rush-throughs*. Furthermore, he considers the study of *rush-throughs* a promising "place to explore the possible convergence of phonetic and conversation-analytic work".

2.   Convergences of phonetic and conversation-analytic work: Gareth Walker's promising analysis

Gareth Walker's paper presents a rigorous phonetic account of *rush-throughs*,[1] revealing various convergences between phonetics and CA. His analysis, thus, fills an important gap concerning the organization of turn-taking and the production of multi-unit turns.

Based on data from audio and video recordings in various contexts (broadcast television interviews, radio interviews and telephone calls, etc.), involving speakers of British and American English, Walker explores the phonetic, prosodic and sequential characteristics of *rush-throughs*. His close-up phonetic account shows that specific phonological and prosodic features are systematically used in a combined way to prevent co-participants from coming in at a point of syntactic and pragmatic completion (Walker this volume):

i.   a nearly doubling of articulation rate in the final foot of the TCU,
ii.   close juncture of the first and second TCUs.

What is striking about Walker's in depth-analysis is the fact that pitch plays no significant role in this practice. This result contradicts Schegloff's (1982: 76) assumption that speakers withhold "a dropping pitch" when approaching a possible completion of a turn-constructional unit in order to bridge a juncture at the end of a unit. Walker's prosodic account reveals that speakers do not withhold a dropping pitch, but instead use final pitch movements to mark the first TCU as a complete intonation unit. This finding is a strong argument in favour of his plea to study a/the "phonetic design of talk in its totality" (Walker this volume: 51) and not to separate prosodic from phonological features.

Drawing upon Harvey Sacks (1964/92) and John Heritage (1989: 22) that "no order of detail in conversational interaction can be dismissed a priori as disorderly, accidental, or interactionally irrelevant", Walker claims that this principle also holds for phonetic features and provides a warrant for including "all aspects of the speech signal for their possible interactional relevance" (this volume: 52).

However, one is inclined to ask: What is meant by "all"? Why stop at phonetic and prosodic means and exclude syntactic or lexical "signals", features of the ongoing conversational action, mimics, gestures, etc.? Participants' inferences of interactional

---

1.   This paper uses Walker's understanding of phonetics as comprising prosodic, articulatory and phonatory features.

meaning surely do not stop at phonetics and prosody. Thus, the question arises: how do phonological and prosodic features interact with other verbal features (or "speech signals", as Walker would put it)? And how do they interact with gestural or mimic "signals"?

3. Phonetics and beyond: *Rush-throughs* as social actions

In a somewhat impressionistic way, Walker points out that *rush-throughs* appear at points of possible syntactic and pragmatic completion. However, we get no hint as to what is meant by syntactic and pragmatic completions.

According to Ford and Thompson (1996: 143–144) a turn completion includes the following features:

i.   syntactic completion
ii. intonational completion
iii. completion of the ongoing action (i.e. an utterance is being interpretable "as a complete conversational action within its specific sequential context").

Does Walker's vague reference to "pragmatic completions" hint at completions of on-going actions?

In the following, we shall have a closer look at Walker's data and explore the so-called *pragmatic completions* involved in rushing through, in order to obtain a more holistic picture of *rush-throughs* as social actions. Consider the following examples:

(1) **Parkinson**, 27/10/2007, Part 2, 0:03 (cf. sound file [WAL-1-Parkinson.wav])

```
 9  MP: it produces a remarkable
10      (0.6) child a remarkable person much more .hhhhh
11      self sufficient (.) resilient (.) and with a
12      different kind of approach to life than .hhhh
13      other people⌒˅it is discernible
14          (.)
```

(2) **Today environment**, 28/02/2006, 5:10 (cf. sound file [WAL-2-Today-environ-ment.wav])

```
 6  CF: .hh y'know access to our
 7      parks .hh access to sport .hh but ge[nerally
 8  ES:                                     [.hhhh
 9  CF: creating that he[althy environment⌒˅now n[o one
10  ES:                 [uhn-                     [ah-
11  CF: person .hh can take responsibility for all
12  CF: [of that
```

(3)   **MDE-MTRAC.60.1.3**, 0:07 (cf. sound file [WAL-3-MTRAC.wav])

```
22  Marsha:   At's w't evrybuddy says I haven't met her
23            but I- .hhh I guess I- I ↑wi:ll, hh
24  Tony:     Yeh probly you will,
25  Marsha:   .hhh Ah that's so nice'v you tih call
26            Tony I appreciate it⌢what time did'e get
27            on the pla:ne.
28  Tony:     Uh::: (0.2) I: do:n't know exactly I
29            think ih wz arou:nd three uh'clo:ck or
30            something a' that sort.
```

(4)   **Today things**, 11/08/2003, 08m42s (cf. sound file [WAL-4-Today-things.wav])

```
1  CB:   I- I don't think it's a g:reat gladiatorial
2        battle between the BBC .hhh and government I-
3        (0.2) I think there are specific issues that
4        need to be answered and need to be looked at and
5        .hh and we need to ascertain whether there are
6        better ways of doing things⌢so
7        there'[s    ac]tually I th]in-]
8  SM:         [but is] Ming      ] Ca]mpbell right the
```

In all four fragments, when speakers reach points of possible completion (line 13 in (1); line 9 in (2), lines 26–27 in (3) and line 6 in (4)), they put in some extra effort – starting from a little before possible completion with speeding up in combination with close juncture – indicating that they intend to keep the floor and build a multi-unit turn. Furthermore, as the data reveal, *rush-throughs*, which are used as practices for transcending boundaries, show projective as well as retractive features: In all four cases, speakers use them to tie a new TCU back to the preceding one; at the same time, contextualizing more to come. And in all four fragments, already initiated syntactic *gestalts* (clauses or phrases) are being closed with the beginning of the *rush-through*. With the new TCU, speakers also start new syntactic units. Thus, in rushing through, speakers – by means of phonological and prosodic features – link syntactically quasi independent segments.

However, speakers not only rush into next syntactic units, but – as the data show – they also rush into new conversational activities.

Ad Example 1: MP first provides an argument concerning people growing up in India, and lists these people's characteristics in comparison with *other people* (lines 11–12). He speeds up his talk on *other people*, and without delay rushes through from a listing activity to an assessment.

Ad Example 2: CF is also involved in producing a list, which she concludes with a general statement (lines 5–9). However, at the end of her general statement, she produces a significant and audible speeding-up (on *environment*), connecting the listing activity with a new activity; a moral statement (lines 9 and 11). The use of the discourse marker *now* indexes the break of these activities.

Ad Example 3: Even though the speaker (Marsha) uses regressive assimilation and an increase in tempo to indicate that the two parts (lines 25–27) belong together, the two TCUs form different communicative activities. In the first TCU, Marsha thanks Tony for calling and utters her appreciation (lines 25–26). Then, she not only rushes into another sentences type (from a statement to a wh-question) but also from an appreciation to a question for information (and thus to a first pair part of an adjacency pair).

Ad Example 4: CB lists up arguments, before he rushes into a concluding statement. Again, by means of duration and juncture, present speaker indicates that while his present TCU is being brought to an end, the next one has already begun. However, in contrast to the other three fragments, this is the only example in Walker's collection where – despite of the *rush-through* – the co-participant comes in and starts a turn competitive activity. (The fact that incoming speaker's talk is designed competitively, is treated as an indication of the interactional relevance of *rush-throughs*.)

In all four cases, the present TCU is interpretable as "a complete conversational action within its specific sequential context" (Ford and Thompson 1996: 150). In contrast to increments which – according to Couper-Kuhlen and Ono (2007: 513) – are grammatical extensions of the prior unit, *rush-throughs* form practices speakers use to introduce a new conversational activity in a multi-unit turn.

Returning to Ford and Thompson's (1996: 143–144) criteria for turn completion, we can conclude that in the data presented, the first TCUs show (i) syntactic completion (in the sense of syntactic *gestalts* being closed); (ii) intonational completion (in all four cases, speakers use final pitch movements to mark the first TCU as a complete intonation unit) and (iii) completions of ongoing social actions. Even though these criteria are fulfilled in the fragments presented, speakers still manage to cancel the upcoming transition relevance place, and thus, prevent their co-participants from taking over. Accordingly, in fragment 4, where next speaker tries to overcome "the primary rights to speakership which the rush-through is designed to secure by virtue of the early start it provides for" (Walker this volume: 68), the incoming speaker's turn is designedly competitive. They achieve this by employing some extra work: i.e. by speeding up their talk (despite of various indications of possible completion) and rushing into the next turn unit, "interdicting (so to speak) the otherwise possibly relevant starting up of talk by another at that point." (Schegloff 1987: 104). In other words: these multi-unit turns form methodologically achieved outcomes (Schegloff 1987: 104), which interactants use to construct themselves as legitimate speakers of the next TCU. As the reactions of co-participants show, they tend to orient to these phonological and prosodic cues by accepting speakers' rights to continue (or by competitively fighting for next turn).

This indicates that certain phonological and prosodic cues – such as increase of articulation rate – in combination with close juncture of the first and second TCUs – may override other cues (such as dropping pitch and syntactic completions), thereby indicating that sequences of talk belong together, despite intonational and syntactic boundaries. Moreover, *rush-throughs* not only form ways of building multi-unit turns, but also multi-unit activity turns.

Walker's study achieves a stimulating and insightful presentation of phonetic features involved in moments in which current speakers try to prevent their co-participants from taking over the turn at a next possible completion. In highlighting the relevance of phonetic features in the construction of turn-endings, Walker succeeds in demonstrating how prosodic and non-prosodic features are part of social action in everyday talk.

I shall conclude my comments with some questions:

–   As talk-in-interaction is a multi-level activity, one wonders about gestural/mimical indications speakers provide in preventing their co-participants from taking over.
–   Are *rush-throughs* systematically connected to the introduction of new communicative activities? I.e. are they mainly used in cases in which participants introduce changes in social actions?
–   Since the data provided are rather heterogeneous – ranging from informal everyday interactions (telephone talk) to multi-media data (TV- and radio interviews) and thus, including different genres (interview, gossip etc.) – one wonders whether the different settings with their differing ways of organizing talk and their particular participation frameworks have an influence on formal and functional features of *rush-throughs*? E.g. do phonetic cues play more major roles in interactions such as telephone or radio interviews, where participants have no gestural and mimical cues available?

References

Couper-Kuhlen, Elizabeth and Ono, Tsuyoshi 2007. "'Incrementing' in conversation. A comparison of practices in English, German and Japanese." *Pragmatics* 17 (4): 513–552.
Ford, Cecilia E. and Thompson, Sandra A. 1996. "Interactional units in conversation: syntactic, intonational, and pragmatic resources for the management of turns." In: *Interaction and grammar*, Elinor Ochs, Emanuel A. Schegloff and Sandra A. Thompson (eds.), 134–184. Cambridge: Cambridge University Press.
Heritage, John 1989. "Current developments in conversation analysis." In: *Conversation: An interdisciplinary perspective*, Derek Roger and Peter Bull (eds.), 21–47. Clevedon: Multilingual Matters.
Sacks, Harvey 1964–68/1992. *Lectures on conversation. Vol I.* Cambridge, Mass.: Blackwell.
Sacks, Harvey; Schegloff, Emanuel A., and Jefferson, Gail 1978. "A simplest systematics for the organization of turn-taking for conversation." In: *Studies in the organization of conversational interaction,* Jim Schenkein (ed.), 7–55. New York: Academic Press.

Schegloff, Emanuel A. 1982. "Discourse as an interactional achievement: Some uses of 'uh huh' and other things that come between sentences." In: *Georgetown University Roundtable on Languages and Linguistics 1981: Analyzing discourse: Text and talk,* Deborah Tannen (ed.), 71–93. Washington D.C.: Georgetown University Press.
Schegloff, Emanuel A. 1987. "Analyzing single episodes of interaction: An exercise in Conversation Analysis." *Social Psychology Quarterly* 50: 101–114.
Schegloff, Emanuel A. 2005. "On integrity in inquiry...of the investigated, not the investigator." *Discourse Studies* 7: 455–480.

Prosodic constructions in making complaints

Richard Ogden
University of York, UK and University of Helsinki, Finland

What sorts of actions have phonetic exponents? Turn-taking and stance-marking can be handled phonetically: discontinuity (e.g. Couper-Kuhlen 2004a); prosodic stylisation (e.g. Ogden et al. 2004); *and-uhm* constructions (Local 2003); the use of 'upgrading' and 'downgrading' to mark types of agreement (Ogden 2006). Here I consider the linguistic construction of complaints based on a collection of complaints about third parties (Drew and Walker 2008). Two turn formats convey complaints. One format is designed to receive an affiliative response; the other is designed to close down a sequence. These turn types are phonetically distinct. Complaints are analysed as constructions: units of linguistic organisation that unite elements of linguistic form (including phonetics) with elements of meaning, including seeking affiliation and sequence management.

1. Constructing turns at talk

It is a truism that when speakers speak, they are conveying many messages at once. A speaker's gender, age, and physical state (such as breathlessness or tension) may all be hearable, even if their words are unintelligible. Firth (1957: 226) said, "it is part of a Frenchman's meaning to sound like one": there are many linguistic resources speakers can use to mark their belonging to a particular part of society, such as through their choice of words or their pronunciation (see Foulkes and Docherty 2006 for a socio-phonetic overview). Interactants in conversation are also managing their interaction on many levels: the moment-by-moment contingencies of turn-taking, or marking the relation of one turn at talk to another, are quite different sorts of activity from e.g. the social norms of giving and receiving compliments or displaying alignment (or not) with another person's position.

Phonetic material is usually conceived of as the audible manifestation of (or in Firthian terms the *exponents* of; Ogden and Local 1994, Ogden 1999, Local 2003) meaningful but abstract elements. Traditional phonetics and phonology place particularly great emphasis on words and utterances (the audible forms of sentences), relegating much of the object of inquiry of this and other volumes (e.g. Couper-Kuhlen and Ford 2004, Couper-Kuhlen and Selting 1996) to the status of paralinguistic features.

One of the crucial aspects of work on interactional linguistics has been to demonstrate how meaningful actions, as oriented to by conversationalists, work in tandem with phonetic resources to reveal recurrent, normative methods by which interactants can solve a range of problems particular to talking in the here and now.

It has been shown that aspects of sequence organisation have phonetic exponents. For example, Couper-Kuhlen (2004a) shows how one kind of sequential discontinuity is phonetically marked; Walker (2007) discusses the form and function of 'pivots', places in talk which serve as both beginnings and endings; Local (2004) demonstrates that *and-uhm*, when used to skip over immediately prior talk to refer to some earlier talk has particular segmental, rhythmical and intonational properties; Ogden (2001, 2004) shows how voice quality in Finnish is an exponent of transition relevance.

Other work on the phonetics of conversation shows how things like 'affect' can be given a more concrete explanation in terms of interactional and sequential organisation. For example, Ogden (2006) shows that various strengths of agreement and disagreement involve fine-tuning the phonetic details of talk in a second pair part relative to a first pair part (cf. Levinson 1983, Pomerantz 1984); and Ogden et al. (2004) argue that one form of prosodic stylisation in Finnish, alongside lexical and grammatical features marks that the current turn expresses something already known, familiar or obvious.

Organising sequences of talk, managing aspects of turn-taking and or marking a stance are actions with a generic function. Complaints are a more specific action type. This paper explores two common turn designs in complaint sequences. These designs relate to the whole turn constructional unit (TCU) (Sacks et al. 1974). The two constructions raise some interesting questions about what kinds of meaning – or here more specifically what kinds of *action* – have phonetic exponents, perhaps opening up the way for more theoretically inclined linguists to have an understanding of conversation which obviates the need for paralinguistic features, while giving a fuller interactionally grounded specification to them, and for more CA-oriented linguists to think more formally about matters of meaning and representation.

We start with a brief overview of complaint sequences; describe the commonest type of complaint construction and show how it appears in sequences of talk, and what its interactional implications are; we then look at a different type of complaint, which proposes sequence closure, and then move on to discuss possible cases of self-initiated, self-repair within a complaint; and finally, we consider some of the implications of the findings, notably that the construction of complaints may be a composite of other types of construction. In common with much other work on complaints, the term is used here as a vernacular category, rather than a technical one (cf. Edwards 2005: 7).

2.   Complaining and complaints

One of the major findings of Drew and Walker (2008) is that complaints, rather than having an adjacency pair structure, are often extended sequences of talk. They are often carefully constructed so as to increase the likelihood of securing an affiliative response from the complaint recipient. Once affiliation from the recipient is achieved, the door to further complaining may be opened (cf. Traverso 2008), leading to an extended sequence in which complainant/recipient roles can be shifted or the boundaries between them blurred. Complaints can also be disattended, and so not affiliated with, even in the face of several attempts by the complainant to secure an affiliative response. In these cases, affiliation is 'on the table' to the extent that it is proposed as a relevant action, but not taken up by the recipient.

As Schegloff points out (2005: 464), "[v]irtually any situation, any current state or history of a relationship – indeed, virtually anything – can be treated as a complainable." This begs the question of how a complaint is recognised as a complaint; and in turn one possibility is that complaints 'sound like' complaints, by virtue of e.g. the use of paralinguistic features, or some kind of prosodic marking. For instance, Kohler and Niebuhr (2007) claim that in German intensifying emphasis has both a 'positive' and a 'negative' form, where the 'negative' form marks the speaker's negative affective stance towards the thing they are talking about. An understanding of how complaints are constructed may help us to understand better how 'paralinguistic' features work in talk; and how activities such as complaining are constructed in conversation.

In this paper, we consider a collection of TCUs which deliver complaints. Two sequentially, interactionally and phonetically distinct types of complaint are considered, and we conclude with a discussion of how to account for the phonetics of each type.

2.1   Data

The data in this paper are taken from a collection of approximately 80 complaint sequences taken from roughly 20hr of phone calls (the same material as in Drew and Walker 2008). The speakers are from Britain and the USA. The complaints in this collection are all complaints about third parties or external events (like the weather); complaints about the co-participant, which hold them morally answerable for their transgressions – often called 'reproaches' (Günthner 2000), or 'direct complaints' (Edwards 2005) – are excluded.

The phonetic analysis combines auditory and acoustic techniques. Where f0 data is presented, a speaker's average f0 is calculated on the basis of a representative sample of approximately two minutes of their talk, with the estimated pitch hand-corrected; the average is the median, to overcome any distortions caused by exceptionally high or low samples.

3.   Overview of A-complaints

On a first pass, many turns which deliver complaints are produced loud with pitch high in the speaker's range. A lay hearing of this might treat such turns as expressions of an affective stance such as 'outrage'. In this section, we consider a more subtle explanation of such complaints.

In making a complaint about a third party, a complainant offers the recipient an opportunity to display affiliation with the complainant against a third party (Drew 1998: 302–303). These kinds of TCUs will be called *A-complaints*, where A is mnemonic for 'affiliation'. An A-complaint is a TCU where a complainable is topicalised and an affiliative response by the recipient is made relevant as a next action. Affiliative responses include matching assessments; second stories about similar events; or displays of sympathy with the complaint. Affiliative responses tend to extend the complaint sequence, and may lead to a blurring of the complainant/recipient roles (Drew and Walker 2008).

Fragment 1 – discussed by Drew and Walker (2008) – provides a simple example: Lesley complains at A→ about the number of people the telephone company has cut off, to which Mum replies with an affiliative expression of sympathy (lines 30, 32), and an assessment of the phone company (line 34) followed by an escalation of the complaint (not shown).

(1)   #12 Holt X (Christmas) 1: 1: 6[1]

```
27 Les A→  but ap\/parently | they cut /fi:ve↑ ↑\people off in
28     A→  Gal/hampto[n (.) on[: /Thursday-
29 Mum             [( ) !   [          )
30 Mum       ↑oh lo:ve
31           (0.4)
32 Mum       that's a nuisance isn't it
33 Les       ye[s
34 Mum         [they're getting terrible
```

In a complaint sequence, there may be individual TCUs where the complaint is only incipient and is not oriented to as a complaint by either participant; nonetheless, the turn is part of a complaint sequence. (2) is one such example. Here, Lesley's complaint is delivered through a story which is launched in line 1, and whose punch-line is at lines 8–9.

(2)   #5 Holt 1:8 shopping

```
1   Les     and-uhm I did Granny Field's shopping for her at
2           the beginning of the /week
3   Mum     oh yeh
4           (.)
```

---

1.   Transcription conventions can be found at the end of the paper.

```
 5   Les              ↑but (.) I'm \not going to do it \/now
 6                    she was up and about and out in the garden
 7                    and there's ↑nothing the ↑\matter with her
 8          A→        and ↑there was ↑me going and doing all her
 9          A→        flipping \shoppin[g
10   Mum                             [ah ha!
```

Lines 1–2, *I did Granny Field's shopping for her at the beginning of the week*, propose to launch a story-telling, an action which Mum aligns with in line 3. As it turns out, lines 1–2 also contain an incipient version of Lesley's complaint, which is brought to the fore and is the point of the story in lines 8–9. Line 1, then, does identify a complainable, from Lesley's point of view, but is not yet overtly oriented to as such.

The TCU at lines 8–9 is constructed to secure an affiliative response from Mum. Note how it mirrors the story launch in lines 1–2, with the addition of a few features: (1) Lesley presents herself as a victim (*there was me going and doing...*) rather than an agent (*I did...*); (2) it contains a mild expletive, *flipping*; (3) it is an extreme formulation (see Pomerantz 1986 on the relevance of these to complaints), *all her flipping shopping*, vs. *[Granny Field's] shopping*; (4) it is a recognisable possible ending of the story, where the recipient can be expected to display an understanding of the story-so-far. It is produced with sustained high pitch with a fall with a wide pitch span at the end (Figure 1). In this case, the story ending reflects its beginning, but with the addition of features (and context) which highlight Granny Field's complainable behaviour (cf. Sacks 1992: 228). As we shall see, many of these features turn out to be recurrent in A-complaints.

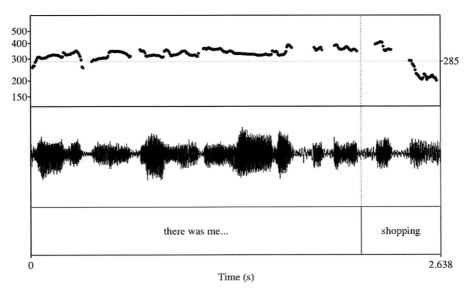

Figure 1. Lines 8–9 of Fragment 2, scaled to the speaker's maximum and minimum F0. Right axis: speaker's average F0

The TCUs in lines 1 and 7–8, then, provide an interesting contrast. They contain much the same propositional content, but project and make relevant quite different next actions. The TCU in lines 7–8 exemplifies the particular interest of this paper, because it is an instance where a complaint is made explicit. It is an A-complaint because it makes affiliation from the recipient a relevant next action.

4.   Analysis of data fragments

4.1   A-Complaints which get affiliative responses

We begin our consideration of the phonetics of complaint sequences with (3), starting with a sequence where an A-complaint is receipted with affiliation immediately on its completion, opening the way for further complaining.

```
(3)   #56 NB:II:5:R eight hundred dollars
      1   L        what's new with you
      2   E        .hhhh oh:: I went to the dentist and [uh:: G]od
      3   L                                              [yeah  ]
      4   E        he wanted to pull a tooth and [make me a] new
      5   L                                       [((t'hhhh))]
      6   E        gold uh: .hhhh (.) ↑bridge for
      7            (.)
      8   E   A→   ↑ei:ght hundred \dollars
      9   L        oh:: sh::i[:t ]
      10  E                  [shi]:t
      11           (0.2)
      12  E        is right
      13  L        that's a big (.) that's a big uh:::=
      14  E        =.p.hhh=
      15  L        =[gimmick]
      16  E        [((continued complaining by E))
```

In lines 2–8, Emma starts a complaint in response to Lottie's inquiry *what's new*. This begins with a factual description (*oh I went to the dentist*), but immediately after this, Emma uses a mild expletive, *God*, before launching into the substance of her complaint. Firstly, she complains that *he wanted to pull a tooth* (of which Emma later says *he ought to try to save it, it's not bothering me, I said God no I'm not ready to have my tooth pulled today*); secondly, that he wanted to make a new gold bridge (she later says *who in the hell wants a gold bridge*). But the main focus of the complaint at this point in the telling is the cost of the proposed work, *eight hundred dollars*.

The cost of the dental work is the third – therefore projectably the last (Jefferson 1990) – of a list of three complainables about Emma's visit to the dentist. *Eight hundred dollars* is prosodically, pragmatically, and syntactically complete, and once completed, Emma stops talking. This turn is designed as the 'punch-line' of Emma's story, and a relevant next action for Lottie is to demonstrate her understanding of the story, and, through that, her affiliation with Emma's complaint.

In line 9, Lottie does just this, with an expletive: *oh shit*. This aligns with the activity of complaining and explicitly affiliates with the complaint, by offering a strong assessment which is commensurate with the strength of the complaint. Emma accepts this alignment by building the same expletive into her next turn and affirming it: *shit (0.2) is right*. Having secured Lottie's affiliation with her complaint, Emma expands on the complaint. Here we see both participants treat an expression of a complaint as an opportunity to display affiliation; and once this is secured, the complaint is expanded upon.

Table 1 shows some of the key intonational features of Emma's TCUs. Note that the A-complaint *eight hundred dollars* has an average and peak f0 markedly higher than prior turns, as well as a much wider pitch span. It is also otherwise offset from surrounding talk: the word 'for' ends with glottal closure, followed by a silence of approximately 125ms. The glottal closure is released into a period of creaky voice: [fə? (0.125) ?eɪt-]. Figure 2 shows a pitch trace for the last two TCUs in Table 1. This A-complaint, like others we will consider, is delivered higher in the speaker's register than her prior turns (as well as relatively high in her overall register), and is phonetically off-set from prior talk. It is prosodically constructed as a different kind of object than prior turns. Figure 2 shows a pitch trace of lines 6–8.

This example is a canonical case of an A-complaint. Its sequential location (last item in a list, an obvious story end), lexical design (an expletive, mention of an inappropriate quantity of money), and aspects of its phonetic design (loud; off-set from the immediately prior talk; high f0 peaks) – all these work to produce a turn that seeks an affiliative response from the recipient.

We will now look at other cases, where an affiliative response is not forthcoming, and show that the properties we have identified for A-complaints are normal in the construction of many complaints.

Table 1. Median f0, peak f0 and pitch span in Fragment 3

speaker's overall median = 219 Hz	median f0 (Hz)	peak f0 (Hz)	span (st)
oh I went to the dentist	254	283	14
and-uh god he wanted to pull a tooth	213	274	7
and make me a new gold bridge for	229	315	7.7
eight hundred dollars	297	388	19.1

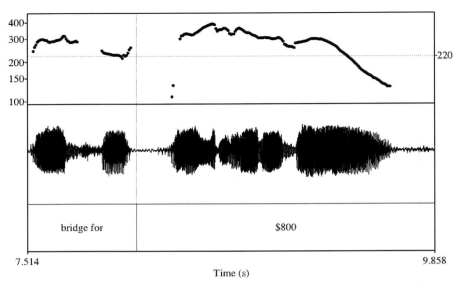

Figure 2. F0 trace of lines 6–8 of Fragment 3, scaled to the speaker's maximum and minimum. Right axis: speaker's average F0

4.2   Reformulation of the complaint after a non-affiliative response

Commonly, A-complaints are receipted with non-affiliative responses. Non-affiliative responses include silence; minimal responses such as *uh-huh*, *mmm*, which acknowledge the turn without taking an affiliative stance to the complaint embedded within; treating the complaint as something else, such as news; and challenges. One way for a complainant to handle a non-affiliative response is to offer the recipient another opportunity to provide such an affiliative response. In doing this, the complainant often reformulates some aspect of the complaint, or repeats the essence of the complaint. Thus we find sequences with the following organisation, which is recursive:

A: [A-complaint]
B: [no affiliation]
A: [A-complaint]

These sequences of repeated A-complaints are evidence that the prior A-complaint(s) did indeed make relevant an affiliative response from the recipient, and by offering another opportunity to the recipient to affiliate, the complainant foregrounds the activity of affiliation as a relevant next action. This is somewhat parallel with the reformulation of invitations (Davidson 1984).

(4)   #28 Heritage I Call 3 six o'clock

(Ilene has called Lisa to discuss when she should pick up her dog from Lisa.)

```
 1   Lis A→  she gets me up at six every ↑morning
 2             she- p- (.) ↑welcome to /go
 3   Ile       ehh hheh heh h[eh
 4   Lis                      [he-he-[he
 5   Ile                             [.hh why does she get you
 6             up a[t six
 7   Lis           [I d'↑\know
 8       A→  but it /seems her time for getting ↑\up is
 9             six o'↑\clock
10   Ile       u-well does she /bark
11   Lis A→  ↑\yeh she ↑\yips
12   Ile       oh well she doesn't do that here
12   Lis       ↑(well) well she wants to get down to the \boys
13       A→  think about -six o'clock -she has th-
14       A→  .hh ↑she has the \urge
15   Ile       {oh I \see | yes yeah}p
16             yeah no she doesn't [do] that here
17   Lis                          [uh]
18   Lis       oh well [just as] well for ↑\you
19   Ile               [yeah   ]
20   Lis       [you wouldn't ↑\like her very much
21   Ile       [eh
22   Lis       if she did it every mor[ning
23   Ile                              [ehh heh heh heh e- [heh
24   Lis                                                  [(*)
25   Ile       .hh .pt well look uhm (0.8) .ptk Kah-
26   Ile       tomorrow's Friday isn't it
```

Fragment 4 contains a series of complaints from Lisa about Ilene's dog, which are met with Ilene by laughter (line 3), requests for an explanation (lines 5–6, 9), and a denial (lines 11, 16). Lisa formulates her complaint first in line 1. *Every morning* is an extreme formulation (cf. Fragment (2) *all her flipping shopping*). A common feature of A-complaints is that they highlight a quantity or time as inappropriate. The specific formulation of the time as *six o'clock* here and in several other turns can be understood as 'too early', and as an inappropriate time to be woken: note the similarity to (3), *eight hundred dollars*, where an inappropriate expense was raised as part of the complaint or (1) *five people*. The precision given by numbers, rather than terms such as 'very early', or 'several people', contributes to the complainer's construction of offence.

Ilene laughs off the first formulation of the complaint, and then challenges it by asking *why* (lines 5–6). Lisa responds with a claim not to know, and repeats her complaint about the time she is woken in line 8. Ilene treats this turn as an inadequate response to her question *why* and challenges – i.e. does not affiliate with – the complaint

Table 2. Median f0, peak f0 and pitch span in Fragment 4

	median f0 (Hz)	peak f0 (Hz)	span (st)
she gets me up a six every morning she's welcome to go	(poor quality)	470	(poor quality)
I don't know	462	663	23.6
it seems her time for getting up is six o'clock	400 (lowest f0 not reliable)	630	18.0 (lowest f0 not reliable)
yeh she yips	502	629	17.3
think about six o'clock she has the- she has the urge	284	543	21.5
it's just as well for you	442	590	14.6
you wouldn't like her very much if she did it every morning	193	571	27.4

in lines 5–6: *does she bark*. Lisa responds to this by modifying the generic *bark* to *yip*, a louder, more piercing noise than *bark*. In this response and by reformulating the terms of the question in this way, Lisa continues and extends her complaint by highlighting a new element of it. Ilene rebuts this complaint by claiming that her dog's behaviour as described by Lisa is not one she has witnessed at home. In lines 12–14, Lisa provides another possible answer to Ilene's 'why' question, an answer which Ilene also dismisses as behaviour she has not witnessed at home.

Here, then, we have a series of turns where a speaker pursues a complaint despite a series of non-affiliative responses. The substance of the complaint – the time at which the dog wakes Lisa up by barking – is repeated at several places, despite the lack of any affiliation with this part of the complaint by Ilene.

Phonetically, Lisa's A-complaints in this sequence are characterised by wide pitch spans – all over one octave – with very high f0 peaks. Some figures in Table 2 are only estimates because the quality of the recordings is not good enough to allow for precise measures. Nonetheless, the f0 peak values are reasonably accurate, and the pitch spans are cautious estimates, because some low f0 values are not measurable.

Thus, again, we see that A-complaints are TCUs with high f0 and wide pitch span. The A-complaints in this fragment contain specific and repeated references to a time which is 'too early'. In the face of non-affiliation, the complainer reformulates and repeats her complaint, while retaining many aspects of its linguistic (including prosodic) design.

4.3   The recipient exits the sequence in place of affiliating

When a series of A-complaints fails to elicit any affiliative response from the recipient, the exit from the complaining sequence is sometimes initiated by the recipient with an explicit change of topic. This is the case in Ilene's turn at lines 25–26 in Fragment 4, *hh*

.pt well look uhm (0.8) .ptk Kah- tomorrow's Friday isn't it. Thus, one possible sequence for exiting a complaint sequence is like this:

A: [A-complaint]
B: [no affiliation]
A: [A-complaint]
B: [initiate exit from the sequence]

Such exits can be seen as a strategy for disengaging from an activity in which the co-participants are unlikely to reach agreement (cf. Couper-Kuhlen 2004b): by withdrawing from the activity of complaining, the recipient places herself in a position where she will no longer withhold affiliation.

Fragments 4 and 5 illustrate this sequence. We will consider Fragment 5 in more detail. Lesley has been complaining to Mum about how some relatives do not reciprocate Lesley's generosity in exchanging Christmas presents. For extensive discussion, see Couper-Kuhlen (2004b: 209–214).

(5)   #9 Holt:X (Christmas) 1: Side 1: Call 1

```
 9   Mum       well you know the: thih- these days things're ↑so
10             ex↑\pensive aren't they
11   Les A→    ↑oh ↑yes but she ex↑pects it the other ↑\way
12   Mum       Mm hm
13   Les       or you wouldn't mind
14   Mum       hm
15             (0.2)
16   Mum       mm
17   Les       and she /gets ↑it the other way
18             but she['s ne- ij
19       A→    but we get nasty remarks about not being able to
20       A→    afford uh \Christmas presents
21             (.)
22   Mum       ah hah dear dear dear hn
23             (0.6)
24             hm (.) never mind
25   Les       .hhhhhh
26   Mum       oh now what was I going to say eh
```

The sequence shown comes after a series of complaints (not shown here) that the relative *only sends a very little* (money), *all that talk about generosity, ... she hasn't been at all generous to them* (Lesley's children) *in that way.* Lesley then apparently closes the sequence down herself; next, Mum (lines 9–10) offers an account of why the relatives might send presents that seem ungenerous. This is countered by another series of turns highlighting the non-reciprocity (thus not denying the truth of Mum's counter, but highlighting the lack of reciprocity as the complainable), culminating in a complaint about the remarks made by the relatives (lines 19–20). These turns are met with

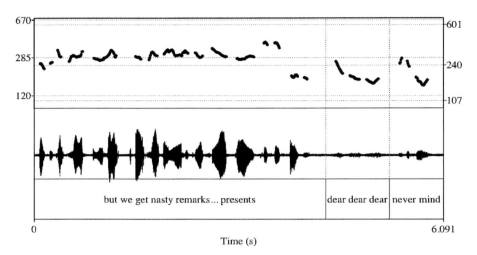

Figure 3. F0 trace of lines 19–24 of Fragment 5. Left axis: Lesley's minimum, average and maximum F0. Right axis: Mum's minimum, average and maximum F0

responses that are not congruent with the strength of the presented complaint (Couper-Kuhlen 2004b: 211). Mum's response here is only mildly affiliative: she does not join in with Lesley's expressions of outrage, but expresses mild sympathy (*dear dear dear*) before proposing a closure (*never mind*, Couper-Kuhlen 2004b), and then moving on to a new sequence at line 26. The design and timing of Mum's turns, and the way she navigates her way out of the sequence, are indicative of the dispreferred status of non-affiliation as a response to a complaint.

Phonetically, there is a mismatch between Lesley's turns and Mum's, both in use of their pitch range and loudness. Lesley's turn at lines 19–20 is at a sustained high level, and is relatively high in volume. Mum's response is low in volume, and low in her pitch range (Figure 3).

This fragment shows how a complainant can orient to lack of affiliation by repeating the complaint, while one way for the recipient to handle what might be a difficult situation is to negotiate their way out of it, in this case by easing her way into a new sequence of talk.

5.   A second complaint construction: Overview of X-complaints

A-complaints are so frequent that they may create the impression that complaints are *normatively* associated with sustained high f0, and falling intonation contours with wide pitch span. However, a small number of turns which apparently deliver complaints are *not* delivered with such phonetic characteristics, and these turns also need an explanation.

Some TCUs which deliver complaints propose sequence closure, and so make relevant as a next action not affiliation with the complaint, but an acceptance to close the complaint sequence down. Such complaints are followed by a change of topic (rather than, e.g. continued pursuit of the complaint); they have the quality of summarising prior talk, e.g. by recycling prior turns; they are often a summary of the complaint. These turns also have very different phonetic properties from A-complaints, which prevents them from being heard as proposing a continuation of the complaint sequence. They are designed to exit a sequence and will be referred to as X-complaints, mnemonic for 'exit'. Note that the exit in these cases is initiated by the complainant, and not by the recipient.

Fragments 6 and 7 contain examples of X-complaints, marked X→ .

(6)   CH en_4310.743–760

(A is complaining to B, as part of a longer sequence about a baby's birth, that the adoptive parents' lawyer did not show up as arranged. 'She' in line 12 is the birth mother.)

```
 1   A        we had uh- we ↑had some difficult times with the
 2            lawyer down there
 3      A→ he [was supposed to show up
 4   B          [mhm
 5            (0.3)
 6   B        mhm=
 7   A  A→ =and we waited all \/day and he never: (.) bloody
 8      A→ showed ↑\up
 9            (0.2)
10   B        °oh no°
11   A        and-uhm ((swallow)) he-
12      A→ and also ↑\she was expecting him \too
13            (0.2)
14   B        mhm
15   A  X→ you know and so \that was fru[\strating
16   B                                  [yeah
17   A        but anyway we waited all day and uhm
18            but then five twenty-five Niamh was born
```

This sequence, part of a much longer story, focuses on A's complaint about the lawyer who was supposed to meet her and her partner, along with the birth mother of a baby that A and her partner are adopting at the hospital. Line 7 is an A-complaint, constructed with extreme formulations, *all day*, *never*, and an expletive, *bloody*. Line 12 extends the complaint by suggesting that the lawyer let the birth mother down as well, i.e. the complaint is not just on her behalf. B's responses to A's turns in lines 6, 10 and 14 have a dispreferred format: they are delayed and minimal, and display no affiliation. In line 15, A summarises by spelling out her own assessment of the situation as *frustrating*, and then changing the trajectory of her telling in lines 17–18 to the main thrust of her longer story, which is about the baby's birth. The turn at line 15 therefore closes down one trajectory of the sequence while presenting to the recipient the complainant's own understanding of this aspect of the story before moving on to another.

Table 3. Key features of f0 in Fragment 6. (Values in parentheses indicate values when creaky voice, with a very low f0, is left out of the calculation.)

speaker's overall median = 198 Hz	median f0 (Hz)	peak f0 (Hz)	span (st)
we had some difficult times with the lawyer down there	195 (195)	374	17.3 (17.3)
and we waited all day	187 (189)	341	23.7 (14.95)
and he never bloody showed up	204 (204)	400	24.3 (14.03)
and also she was expecting him too	203 (203)	483	21.1 (21.1)
you know and so that was frustrating	169 (175)	276	21.1 (11.6)

B responds to this summary of the story in overlap with the minimal response *yeah*: note that she does not produce a second assessment, but merely accepts A's assessment. In offering a minimal response and not e.g. an assessment of her own, or overt affiliation with the negative assessment, B also positions herself as a recipient of a further telling; and A treats this as an adequate response by continuing with the next part of the story.

How is it that line 15 is not treated by either participant as providing an opportunity for an extension of the complaining sequence about the lawyer? Firstly, it presents a summary assessment (*so...*), rather than a new complaint. Secondly, it does not contain an extreme formulation, and no expletive (both common features of A-complaints). Thirdly, prosodically, this turn is unlike an A-complaint: it is relatively quiet, it is fast, and the speaker's pitch is not at the upper end of her range. The f0 of the highest peak is lower than the peaks of preceding turns, and (discounting creak), the turn has a narrower pitch span than the A-complaint turns. It therefore contrasts phonetically with her prior turns.

Fragment (7) is discussed in more detail in Ogden (2007). As with the prior fragment, (7) is a series of complaints which the recipient, Lottie, refrains from aligning with.

(7)   #68 NB:IV:10:R gone to pot
       (Emma is complaining about a hotel where Emma and her husband have stayed.)

```
 5   E        ((complaints about lack of air conditioning, and
 6            only two staff to serve breakfast))
 7   L        yeah?
 8   E        because (.) uy Bud couldn't even eat his breakfast
 9      A→    he ↑ordered he waited ↑forty-five minutes and he had
10            to be out there to tee \off so I gave it to-uh (.)
11            Karen's little boy
12            (0.7)
13 E A→       ((swallow)) I mean that's how bad the service was.h
14            .hh
```

```
15   X→  .hh it's gone to pot
16 L     ?oh y[eah
17 E          [but it's a beautiful golf course
```

Emma's full complaint has been abbreviated here, in order to focus on the X-complaint in line 15. In data omitted here, Emma details a number of deficiencies with the hotel. Lottie does not display any affiliation with any of these complaints, although at line 7, her *yeah* aligns with the complaining activity. In her next turn, Emma expands the complaint, mentioning the amount of time they were kept waiting. At line 12 is a 0.7sec gap where Lottie withholds any kind of affiliation. Emma's turn in line 13 orients to Lottie's lack of talk at line 12 and starts with *I mean*, making it explicit what the complaint was about. This provides Lottie with another opportunity to display her affiliation, but again (line 14) she withholds any.

In line 15, Emma produces a summary assessment showing the egregious nature of the service she has received using an idiomatic expression, *it's gone to pot* (Drew and Holt 1988). This idiomatic expression is another summary of what the thrust of the complaint was. Lottie's response, whether affiliative or not, is followed by a shift away from complaining initiated by the complainant (Drew and Holt 1998). Thus the complaint in line 15 initiates a move out of the complaint sequence by the complainant.

Figure 4 shows an f0 trace of *it's gone to pot*. Note that the f0 is below the speaker's average, and it falls into creak. Compared to the turns marked A→, this turn is quiet and slow, and in a markedly different register from the prior turns. Table 4 shows overall values for the TCUs in this complaint sequence. What is noteworthy here (as in the

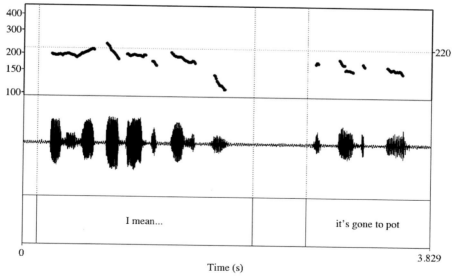

Figure 4. F0 trace of the X-complaint in Fragment 7, lines 13–15, scaled to the speaker's maximum and minimum. Right axis: speaker's average F0

Table 4. Key features of f0 in Fragment (7). (Values in parentheses indicate values when creaky voice, with a very low f0, is left out of the calculation. This is a more accurate reflection of the perceived pitch span.)

speaker's overall median = 219 Hz	median f0 (Hz)	peak f0 (Hz)	span (st)
previous turns, not shown	221	348	18.6
lines 5–6	229	330	15.3
I mean that's how bad the service was	194	234	13.28
it's gone to pot	154 (155)	184	15.49 (5.5)

previous example) is the lower peak in the X-complaint and the lower average f0 through the TCU as compared to the prior turns. As in Fragment 6, disengagement from the complaint is marked prosodically as well.

There are very few X-complaints in the collection. Mostly, the exit from the complaint sequence is initiated by the recipient, rather than the complainant. Why this should be is a matter for another study.

6.   Repair in A-complaints

One piece of evidence for the phonetic format of A-complaints as being high in the speaker's pitch register is instances of self-repair. The analysis of these repairs is not always straightforward, since often not only the prosodic shape of the turn, but also other aspects of the turn design, are repaired. Here we consider two cases of repair, where the only linguistic difference between the trouble source and the repair is in the prosodic shape of the two. In this data, the speaker repairs not just e.g. word fragments, but whole phrases. Thus we see that the production of the TCU is repaired as a whole; this is important, since the domain of the prosodic format of A-complaints is a whole prosodic phrase, and not just e.g. the height of an f0 peak on one accented item.

(8)   #28 Heritage I call 3 six o'clock
       (Ilene has called Lisa to discuss when she should pick up her dog from Lisa.)

```
12  Lis        well wel she wants to get down to the boys
13       TS→   think about six o'clock she has th-
14       R→    .hh she has the urge
```

Fragment 8 contains a trouble source at line 13 and a repair at line 14. The repair uses exactly the same lexical items as the trouble source, but there are significant intonational differences in the production of the two. The in-breath between the trouble source and the repair may be one way for Lisa to ensure she has enough air to produce the repair at volume and with high pitch. The repair has a noticeable upward shift in pitch register, as shown in Figure 5. In the trouble source *she has th-*, the average f0 is

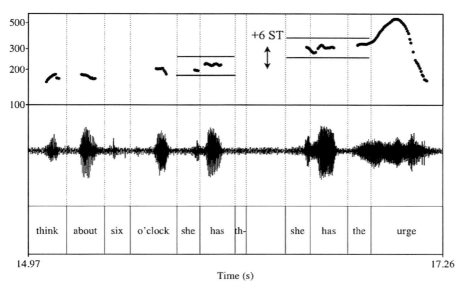

Figure 5. FO plot of the repair in lines 13–14 of Fragment 8

around 210 Hz, in the repair, *she has the*, the average f0 is around 300 Hz, an upstep of approximately 6 semitones. The pitch span of *she has the urge* is approximately 21.5 semitones, consistent with the wide pitch spans seen in many other A-complaints. The upwardly reset pitch on *she has the* is consistent with the high sustained pitches seen in other A-complaints.

The domain of the repair here is a whole intonation phrase, and not just one of the accented items within a phrase: this accounts for the in-breath and the up-step in pitch: | she `has th- | .hh ↑she `has the \urge |

Here, then, is a case where a speaker repairs her own talk in the same turn, and does not repair the syntax or lexis of the turn, but rather its prosodic shape. By upgrading the pitch register, the complainant perhaps upgrades the appeal for an affiliative response to the complaint presented in the turn.

The next fragment is slightly more complex, because the repair is carried out on talk in overlap. Therefore, it may be possible to analyse this data as a more audible redoing of the same turn (cf. Schegloff 2000), or a shift from one kind of complaint turn to another. Some of the prosodic differences between the trouble source and the repair are very dramatic, and the outcome of the repair is a piece of talk at a pitch level and with other intonational features consistent with an A-complaint.

(9)   #58 NB:II:5:R smog

```
40  E      so I had to come home wash my hair and go with Bud
41         to something and I said oh my God I got home my face
42         was so red I thought I was gonna die
```

```
43              (0.3)
44  E  TS→    So[u it's  terr]ible up
45  L           [° oh : : : °]
46  E  R→     t's terrible up .hhh we lie:- (0.4)
              we absolutely lie stark naked on the bed
```

The trouble source at line 44 is part of an on-going complaint about the hot weather. It has several features of an X-complaint. Firstly, it starts with *so*, which presents the assessment as a summary of previous talk. Secondly, the turn is produced around Emma's average f0, which is around 218 Hz. Thirdly, the turn comes after a sequential location where Lottie, the recipient, could have shown (but did not, in line 43) affiliation with Emma's description of how the heat made her feel.

Lottie comes in at line 45 with *oh*, which is produced quietly, and in overlap with Emma's talk. The 'oh' is only weakly affiliative, thanks to its delayed production, its quietness, and the fact that it treats Emma's story as news, rather than as a complaint with which to affiliate (e.g. by displaying sympathy or by joining in with the complaint).

In re-doing her turn, at line 46, Emma is able to recast her overlapped turn not as closing-implicative, but rather as a possible continuation of the complaint. She steps up both the pitch and volume levels, and although the turn is not syntactically complete when it finishes, Emma goes on to provide evidence, in strong terms (*lie*, repaired to *absolutely lie, stark naked*), of how unbearable she finds the heat. Emma places complaining back on the agenda, having possibly projected an end to the complaining sequence in what retrospectively turns out to be a trouble source. In other words, this

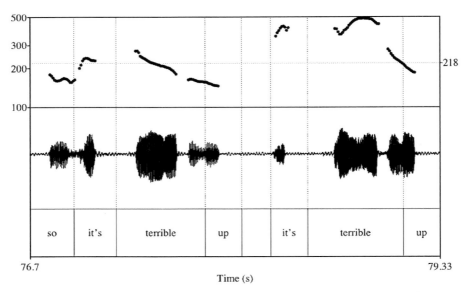

Figure 6. F0 trace of lines 44 and 46 of Fragment 9. Note the upward resetting of F0 in the repair

repair shifts the turn away from being one kind of complaint to another, and in part it does so through the repair on the prosodic features of the turn.

These two cases of repair, then, highlight the reality of the prosodic design of A-complaints for complainants themselves. In the cases we have considered here, only the prosodic features are repaired, and the repair foregrounds complaining for an affiliative response.

7. Discussion

I have argued that there are at least two distinct turn designs which deliver complaints. A-complaints make affiliation a relevant next action, thus proposing a continuation of the complaint sequence; while with an X-complaint, a complainant can propose closure of their own complaint sequence. The sequential, lexical and phonetic properties of these turn designs are summarised in Table 5.

How can we account for these findings? I will offer a construction-based account, based on Croft and Cruse (2004: 258). Constructions relate form and meanings, and are therefore similar to signs in Head-Driven Phrase Structure Grammar (see Ogden 1999 for an application of this to phonology). The 'Form' part of constructions consists of linguistic elements such as syntax, phonology, lexis and (I would argue) sequential location. The 'Meaning' part of the construction is expressed in semantic and pragmatic

Table 5. Summary of features of A-complaints and X-complaints

	A-complaint	X-complaint
Lexis	– extreme formulations	– summary
	– expletives	– idiomatic expression
	– negative assessment	– lexical recycling
	– reference to inappropriate quantity (e.g. too much, too little, too long time...)	
Sequence	– at a place where affiliation is a relevant next action, e.g. first assessment, story completion	– at a possible sequence ending; proposes termination of complaint sequence
	– proposes continuation of the complaint	– followed by change of topic
Phonetics	– f0 sustained above speaker's average	– f0 low in speaker's range; lower than in preceding turns
	– loud	– relatively quiet
	– f0 peaks high in speaker's range	– overall 'lax' setting (e.g. creaky voice quality)
	– wide pitch span, usually because of a final fall to low from high	– no wide pitch span

terms; and for the purposes of a CA-oriented approach, actions such as 'complaining' also belong here. This means that, for example, 'complaining' (on the 'meaning' side) can have formal exponents, such as lexis, on the 'form' side.

The turns identified so far as A- and X-complaints result from the unification (∪) of several constructions, including three we could initially describe as [CLOSE DOWN SEQUENCE], [SEEK AFFILIATION] and [COMPLAIN ABOUT THIRD PARTY]:

A-Complaint: [COMPLAIN ABOUT THIRD PARTY] ∪ [SEEK AFFILIATION]
X-Complaint: [COMPLAIN ABOUT THIRD PARTY] ∪ [CLOSE SEQUENCE]

Since A-complaints and X-complaints have mutually exclusive phonetic properties, at least some of these properties are ascribable to the actions [SEEK AFFILIATION] and [COMPLAIN...]. Thus we can sketch partial constructions for these two actions, based on the material in Table 5. These are shown in tables 6–8, which are partial descriptions.

A-complaints are the unification of two components: the component of making a complaint; and the component of making affiliation a relevant response. 'Complaining about a third party' has as its exponents the particular formulation of something as a complainable; the action of 'seeking an affiliative response' has as its exponents the sequential features identified, and (let us hypothesise) phonological exponents such as 'f0 sustained above the speaker's average', 'loud', 'wide pitch span', and so forth. Further evidence for this interpretation is that A-complaints have some features in common

Table 6. Sketches of partial constructions to account for A- and X-complaints

CLOSE SEQUENCE	
PHON	f0: low in speaker's range; lower than preceding turns; no wide span
	setting: relatively quiet; lax
LEX	{idiomatic expression, lexical recycling...}
ACTION	*close sequence*

SEEK AFFILIATION	
PHON	f0: sustained above speaker's average; lower than preceding turns; wide span
	setting: relatively loud; lax
SEQ	place where affiliation is relevant: {first assessment; story completion}
ACTION	*make affiliative response relevant*

COMPLAIN ABOUT THIRD PARTY	
PHON	
LEX	{negative assessment...}
ACTION	*complain about (non-present) third party*

with e.g. strong agreements or disagreements (Ogden 2006): this means that the action of [SEEKING AFFILIATION] is a more general one which combines with other actions; and [COMPLAIN ABOUT THIRD PARTY] has formal exponents such as lexis, but no phonological ones.

X-complaints also have the component of making a complaint; but more specifically, they summarise a complaint and have the component of proposing to close a sequence down. The action of 'complaining' is achieved through the sequential and lexical formulation of the TCU; the action of 'proposing to close down the sequence' is also achieved through the lexical and sequential formulation of the turn, but also through its phonological formulation. The reason this is likely is that the phonetics of 'X-complaints' is identifiable with other kinds of sequence-closing turns, such as have been described by Couper-Kuhlen (2004a). Thus, the phonetics of X-complaints is a property of the 'X' part of their name (exiting the sequence) rather than a property of complaining. Further evidence for this is that X-complaints are phonetically similar to the sequence-closing turns described in Couper-Kuhlen (2004a) and elsewhere.

Thus, one conclusion from this paper is that the phonetic properties initially associated with 'complaining' are most likely the exponents of at least two other actions. In the case of A-complaints, it is the action of seeking an affiliative response; in the case of X-complaints, it is the action of exiting a sequence. What makes turns 'hearable' as complaints is not just their phonetic properties, but their lexical construction, shared knowledge or assumptions between conversationalists about what constitutes a complainable, and the sequential organisation of the complaint.

In producing a complaint, interactants do more than just 'complain' (cf. Drew 1998, Drew and Walker 2008, Edwards 2005). They also project (and monitor for) possible turn-completion; places where talk of a particular kind is relevant; and their complaint may be nuanced in particular ways, in response to the development of the sequence. An account which disaggregates the many levels of linguistic construction in such complex activities increases the explanatory power of the device, and allows us to understand the composition of the aggregate. For this reason, it is a positive result to be able to say that 'complaints have no special phonetics'.

Acknowledgements

Thanks to Paul Drew, Auli Hakulinen, John Local, Leendert Plug, Geoff Raymond, Marja-Leena Sorjonen, Gareth Walker, Traci Walker, the editors and two reviewers for their comments on earlier versions of this paper. This work was supported by ESRC grant RES-000-23-0035 and the Marie Curie Research Training Network Sound to Sense.

Appendix: Transcription conventions

Transcriptions are left relatively unadorned; more precise information about the data is presented in tables and figures. Some symbols are used to convey a sense of the intonation contours in targeted turns:

↑	unexpectedly high f0
\	falling contour
/	rising contour
\/	fall-rise contour
underlining	accentually prominent syllable

References

Couper-Kuhlen, Elizabeth 2004a. "Prosody and sequence organization: The case of new beginnings." In: *Sound patterns in interaction*, Elizabeth Couper-Kuhlen and Cecilia E. Ford (eds.), 335–376. Benjamins: Amsterdam.

Couper-Kuhlen, Elizabeth 2004b. "Analyzing language in interaction: the practice of *never mind.*" *English Language & Linguistics* 8: 207–237.

Couper-Kuhlen, Elizabeth and Ford, Cecilia. E. 2004. *Sound patterns in interaction.* Amsterdam: Benjamins.

Couper-Kuhlen, Elizabeth and Selting, Margret 1996. *Prosody in conversation.* Cambridge: Cambridge University Press.

Croft, William and Cruse, D. Alan 2004. *Cognitive linguistics.* Cambridge: Cambridge University Press.

Davidson, Judy 1984. "Subsequent versions of invitations, offers, requests and proposals dealing with potential or actual rejection." In: *Structures of social action. Studies in conversation analysis,* J. Maxwell Atkinson and John Heritage (eds.), 102–128. Cambridge: Cambridge University Press.

Drew, Paul 1998. "Complaints about transgressions and misconduct." *Research on Language and Social Interaction* 31: 295–325.

Drew, Paul and Holt, Elizabeth 1988. "Complainable matters: the use of idiomatic expressions in making complaints." *Social Problems* 35: 398–417.

Drew, Paul and Holt, Elizabeth 1998. "Figures of speech: figurative expressions and the management of topic transition in conversation." *Language in Society* 27: 495–522.

Drew, Paul and Walker, Traci 2008. "Going too far: complaining, escalating and disaffiliation." *Journal of Pragmatics* 41: 2400–2414.

Edwards, Derek 2005. "Moaning, whinging and laughing: the subjective side of complaints." *Discourse Studies* 7: 5–29.

Firth, J. R. 1957. *Papers in linguistics 1934–1951.* Oxford: Oxford University Press.

Foulkes, Paul and Docherty, Gerard 2006. "The social life of phonetics and phonology." *Journal of Phonetics* 34: 409–438.

Günthner, Susanne 2000. *Vorwurfsaktivitäten in der Alltagsinteraktion. Grammatische, prosodische, rhetorisch-stilistische und interaktive Verfahren bei der Konstitution kommunikativer Muster und Gattungen.* Tübingen: Niemeyer.

Jefferson, Gail 1990. "List construction as a task and interactional resource." In: *Interactional competence*, George Psathas (ed.), 63–92. New York: Erlbaum.

Kohler, Klaus J. and Niebuhr, Oliver 2007. "The phonetics of emphasis." In: *Proceedings of 16th ICPhS*, Saarbrücken, 2145–2148.

Levinson, Stephen R. 1983. *Pragmatics.* Cambridge: Cambridge University Press.

Local, John 2003. "Variable domains and variable relevance: interpreting phonetic exponents." *Journal of Phonetics* 31: 321–339.

Local, John 2004. "Getting back to prior talk: and-uh(m) as a back-connecting device." In: *Sound patterns in interaction*, Elizabeth Couper-Kuhlen and Cecilia E. Ford (eds.), 377–400. Amsterdam: Benjamins.

Ogden, Richard 1999. "A declarative account of strong and weak auxiliaries in English." *Phonology* 16: 55–92.

Ogden, Richard 2001. "Turn-transition, creak and glottal stop in Finish talk-in-interaction." *Journal of the International Phonetic Association* 31: 139–152.

Ogden, Richard 2004. Non-modal voice quality and turn-taking in Finnish. In: *Sound patterns in interaction*, Elizabeth Couper-Kuhlen and Cecilia E. Ford (eds.), 29–62. Amsterdam: Benjamins.

Ogden, Richard 2006. "Phonetics and social action in agreements and disagreements." *Journal of Pragmatics* 38: 1752–1775.

Ogden, Richard 2007. "Linguistic resources for complaints in conversation." *Proceedings of 16th ICPhS*, Saarbrücken, 1321–1324.

Ogden, Richard and Local, John 1994. "Disentangling autosegments from prosodies: A note on the misrepresentation of a research tradition in phonology." *Journal of Linguistics* 30: 477–498.

Ogden, Richard; Hakulinen, Auli and Tainio, Liisa 2004. "Indexing 'nothing much' with stylisation in Finnish." In: *Sound patterns in interaction*, Elizabeth Couper-Kuhlen and Cecilia E. Ford (eds.), 299–334. Benjamins: Amsterdam.

Pomerantz, Anita 1984. "Agreeing and disagreeing with assessments: Some features of preferred/dispreferred turn shapes." In: *Structures of social action. Studies in conversation analysis*, J. Maxwell Atkinson and John Heritage (eds.), 57–101. Cambridge: Cambridge University Press.

Pomerantz, Anita 1986. "Extreme case formulations: A way of legitimizing claims." *Human Studies* 9: 219–229.

Sacks, Harvey 1992. Lectures on conversation. Vol. 2. Edited by Gail Jefferson. Oxford: Blackwell.

Sacks, Harvey; Schegloff, Emanuel A. and Jefferson, Gail 1974. "A simplest systematics for the organization of turn-taking for conversation." *Language* 50: 696–735.

Schegloff, Emanuel A. 2000. "Overlapping talk and the organisation of turn-taking for conversation." *Language in Society* 29: 1–63.

Schegloff, Emanuel A 2005. "On complainability." *Social Problems* 52: 449–476.

Traverso, Véronique 2008. "The dilemmas of third-party complaints in conversation between friends." *Journal of Pragmatics* 41: 2385–2399.

Walker, Gareth, 2007. "On the design and use of pivots in everyday conversation." *Journal of Pragmatics* 39: 2217–2243.

The relevance of context
to the performing of a complaint
Comments on Richard Ogden "Prosodic constructions in making complaints"

Auli Hakulinen
University of Helsinki, Finland

Introduction

The paper by Richard Ogden opens a new and little investigated aspect of the study of complaints in trying to find out whether there is a phonetics of complaining. Another thing it opens up is a possible link between empirically oriented interactional studies and the more theoretical approach of construction grammar. As a whole, the paper nicely illustrates what a long distance and winding path there is from the vernacular notion of 'complaint' to suggesting a formalisation of a 'construction' of complaint.

My comments will begin with a discussion of what a complaint is. I will then say a few words about the difficulty of distinguishing between 'direct' and 'indirect' complaints. Third, I am going to take up Ogden's claim that there is no (specific) phonetics of complaining. In conclusion, I move to a territory which I am not too familiar with, the question of how to decide on and describe the constitutive elements in a construction.

1. Complaints and their receipt

Ogden starts with the complaint as a vernacular category, which means that he does not offer a definition of the phenomenon he is focusing on. However if a complaint is recognised as one by the recipients, there must be some recurrent features that help in the recognition. We can take it as one of his hypotheses that a complaint is one if it sounds like one. Another one would be that a complaint is what is treated as a complaint. The data that form his collection consist of some 80 *complaint sequences* that share the feature of being complaints about third parties or external events. Thus, in Edwards' (2005) terms, he focuses on 'indirect' complaints. However, Ogden's criterion of a complaint has most likely been lexical rather than prosodic or sequential. Lexical, because the very difference between what he calls *A-complaints* and *X-complaints* lies in their prosody (cf. his Examples 3 and 6). Although he does consider the receipt of the respective complaints, the conclusion of the sequential analysis could be a different one from the one he in fact has drawn. In my view, his X-complaints, at the end of a story, may be hearable as representing something else and not 'complaints'.

On the basis of the different kinds of receipt, Ogden has divided the complaints into two groups: A-complaints, which make an affiliative response relevant, and X-complaints, which make exit relevant, i.e. behave as closing-implicative turns. Canonical instances of A-complaints are offered e.g. by his Examples 2 and 3. They are presented as story punch lines, they are syntactically bounded TCUs and they have specific prosodic characteristics – wide pitch span and very high f0 peaks – which presumably carry the burden of being identified as complaints (cf. Couper-Kuhlen 2004: 360). All in all, they could be viewed as instances of complaint constructions. As predicted, they are typically – but not necessarily – received with an affiliative response.

2.   Reformulating and repairing a complaint

A more intricate case is provided by Ogden's Example 4, where the complaint that shares the phonetics previously characterised does not receive an affiliative response. Rather, it is challenged or rebutted by the recipient and leads to subsequent reformulations and efforts at pursuing the expected response. One explanation for this may be that – as I see it – we are dealing here with an instance of a complaint that should rather be viewed as a 'direct' one; a complaint about the co-participant, as it is about the behaviour of a dog that the recipient possesses. A dog is not a 'third party' but an intimate part and parcel of its owner's life. Interestingly here, then, even though the phonetics indexes that an affiliation-seeking complaint has been delivered, the recipient refuses to affiliate as she has a different perspective on the behaviour of her own dog[1]. Presumably, the line of division between complaints directed to the co-participant and those about third parties is an empirical and a local issue. It is the recipient who in the end will judge whether s/he experiences the complaint as being about her/himself or not.

In the section titled "Repair in A-complaints", Ogden discusses the example I just mentioned. He makes the important observation that while the complaint speaker repairs the pitch span, she in fact repairs the whole intonation phrase which forms the complaint and thereby upgrades it into an appeal for an affiliative response. More interestingly, in Ogden's Example 9, the speaker repairs a turn which began as a summary

---

1.   The term affiliation here means that the recipient displays that s/he literally shares the perspective of the co-participant. For a discussion of the difference between affiliation and alignment see Stivers (2008).

into a prosodically canonical, affiliation-seeking complaint, thereby re-opening the topic for elaboration. If we go along with what speakers do, I think these two instances of repair convincingly show that prosody is indeed a constitutive part of complaints, or at least what I take to be the canonical ones, the A-complaints.

3.   Performing complaints

We are back at the issue of what a complaint *is*. I find it difficult to agree with Ogden's view that the so called X-complaints are to be understood as complaints as well. If prosody is relevant, these kinds of turns are not performing, or acting out, a complaint. In bringing complaint sequences or narratives to an end, they are hearable as summaries and just that. I assume that they share the phonetics and possibly also some lexical characteristics of other idiomatically composed closing-implicative summaries (cf. Drew and Holt 1998). On the other hand, even if A-complaints according to Ogden share *some* prosodic features (N.B. not all!) with strong agreements and disagreements, this, in my mind, does not warrant his conclusion that "complaints have no special phonetics". Well, perhaps not special in the sense of unique but at least recognisable as a constitutive component of a construction. This, I think, he has in fact elegantly shown.

A next task could be to compare the prosody of affectively produced *first* assessments with that of the A-complaints. If they are found to share components such as loudness, high pitch peak relative to the speaker's range and wide pitch span within a TCU, one could suggest that 'affiliation seeking' is a more general feature of a turn than complaining. Also, it would be interesting to see if direct complaints that are presented as reproaches of the co-participant, typically encompass the same kind of affiliation-seeking prosody as was found in the indirect ones.

Irrespective of whether any reader agrees with me in the issue of X-complaints not being *real* complaints, one of the outcomes of Ogden's work serves to further deconstruct the mundane category of complaints. Edwards (2005) shows that there are many different ways of presenting a complaint: objectification; displacement, laughter and irony. Ogden's paper raises the question of what to call 'complaints' in different sequential positions *within a sequence of complaining*: when used as announcements in story prefaces, as punch lines or as summaries.

4.   Complaint and construction grammar

A more serious problem at least for the description of construction grammar is probably raised by the fact that a turn is often used to perform more than one task (Ogden this volume: 101).

If construction grammar cannot at the moment take sequential context into account in any systematic way, it will have to delimit the construction to encompass a turn or a TCU. Sacks (1992: 359) remarked that a turn separated from its context is sometimes no longer "recognisable as a complaint". This seems to hold for Ogden's X-complaints. For example, the turn *so that was frustrating* (in Example 6) could equally well be produced by a story recipient. The utterance *it's gone to pot* (Example 7) could be a remark by someone standing in the street and looking at a dilapidated warehouse.

A first attempt at taking context into account is offered by Ogden on p. 100, where features like "close sequence" resp. "seek affiliation" are suggested to form part of a complaint construction. Even if one did not agree with this suggestion, it is a thought provoking one and, hopefully, leads to subsequent efforts to include sequential features/components in the descriptions of constructions.

Unlike creak or other attributes of voice quality, where it is not always easy to tell exactly where they begin or end, the prosodic features that Odgen has described in this paper seem to fall on bounded segments. For this reason, I would happily go along with the suggestion that prosody is part of a complaint Gestalt or construction, where the other formal components are lexical. Both the prosody and the lexical choices could be taken as manifestations of an affective component that is included in the 'partial description' of a complaint. The meaning part of a construction could thus be broadened to include an interactional component like 'seeking affiliation' and an expressive/affect component that would have action exponents like 'performing a complaint'.

As Richard Ogden has argued elsewhere (2006), phonetics does not go hand in hand with a propositional content of an utterance. In this paper he has shown where to look instead: in my opinion he has shown the relevance of phonetics for a certain kind of *action*. Because of this, I found the last sentence of his paper somewhat surprising.

References

Couper-Kuhlen, Elizabeth 2004. "Prosody and sequence organization in English conversation: The case of new beginnings." In: *Sound patterns in interaction. Cross-linguistic studies from conversation*, Elizabeth Couper-Kuhlen and Cecilia E. Ford (eds.), 335–376. Amsterdam: Benjamins.

Drew, Paul and Elizabeth Holt 1998. "Figures of speech: figurative expressions and the management of topic transition". *Language in Society* 27: 495–522.

Edwards, Derek 2005: "Moaning, whining and laughing: the subjective side of complaints." *Discourse Studies* 7 (1): 5–29.

Ogden, Richard 2006: "Phonetics and social action in agreements and disagreements." *Journal of Pragmatics* 38: 1752–1775.

Sacks, Harvey 1992: *Lectures on conversation. Vol. I.* Edited by Gail Jefferson. Oxford: Blackwell.

Stivers, Tanya 2008. "Stance, alignment, and affiliation during storytelling: when nodding is a token of affiliation". In: *Research on Language and Social Interaction* 41: 31–57.

Prosodic variation in responses

The case of type-conforming responses to yes/no interrogatives

Geoffrey Raymond
University of California, Santa Barbara, United States

Highly structured sequential environments in which speakers manage complex (or divergent) relevancies constitute a perspicuous site for explicating the role of prosody in action-formation because a range of turn constructional resources are regularly pressed into service to manage distinct aspects of them. To illustrate this, I focus on three prosodic practices used to form type-conforming tokens (e.g., *yes* and *no*) deployed in responses to yes/no-type interrogatives (Raymond 2000, 2003). The environment for such responses are highly structured: the choice between alternative tokens establishes the basic valence of the responding action. Nevertheless, the relevancies they must manage can be complex – as in the case of 'double-barreled' actions. In conclusion I compare two of these practices with others that exploit different elements of turn construction to highlight the specificity of prosodic resources, per se and note other similarly structured environments that might permit similar analyses.

1. Prosody as a sequentially sensitive resource for action formation: The case of *yes* and *no* as responses

As many students of talk-in-interaction have noted, the very sound patterns out of which utterances are built pose serious analytic challenges for anyone who would move past the most formal, physiological approach to them. They are notoriously slippery, and virtually demanding an impressionistic approach to both description *and* analysis. Therefore, for too long analysts struggled without making much headway in tackling their systematic organization. Spurred by Local and Kelly's (1986) early efforts, however, Elizabeth Couper-Kuhlen, and her colleagues (Selting, Ford, and Thompson, among others) and students, have done much to open up this most impenetrable, and yet fundamental and important, domain of inquiry.

The broad conceptual approach to prosody Couper-Kuhlen articulated in her books (with Margret Selting 1996 and Cecilia Ford 2004) simultaneously circumscribes the relevant domain of inquiry and identifies an analytic approach to it, that is then expertly exemplified in subsequent chapters and publications. In the first of these, Couper-Kuhlen and Selting compare their approach to prosody to Schegloff's analysis of a syntax-for-conversation. They note that:

> "Viewing prosody context-sensitively ... means paying attention to the fact that its carrier is a turn at talk ... which itself has a sequential location. Just as Schegloff states that a syntax-for-conversation must 'recognize that its sentences will be in turns and will be subject to the organization of turns and their exigencies' (1979: 281), so a prosody-for-conversation must recognize that its basic unit – whether expounded by intonational, rhythmic, pausal or dynamic means – co-occurs with, and will be interpreted in relation to, a turn-constructional unit. Similar to turn-constructional units, which may be situated parts of larger 'projects', prosodic units will be sensitive to their location in a series. And similar to turns, which occur in sequence, prosodic units can be expected to demonstrate sensitivity to their sequential location... All the types and orders of organization that operate in and on turns in conversation can operate on the basic prosodic unit." (Couper-Kuhlen and Selting 1996: 26)

The import of these observations warrant some elaboration: Rather than simply attempting to isolate specific sound patterns, and describing them by reference to their production in isolated mouths or speakers, *interaction* is recognized as the natural home of sound patterns that are social in origin and orientation. It is this fundamentally important insight that establishes a structural, analytic basis for explicating of how basic sound patterns, which are partly constitutive of talk itself, figure in interaction. As with any other basic resource in interaction, progress in understanding sound patterns depends on attending to how speakers deploy (1) a specific resource in (2) a specific sequential context.

In this chapter, I advance our understanding of prosody as a context-sensitive resource by describing one sequential environment in which a cluster of prosodic practices have emerged: "type-conforming" (i.e., "yes" and "no") responses to yes/no interrogatives (hereafter, YNI; Raymond 2003). After recounting the broader framework within which these responses are produced, I show that this sequential environment is a highly propitious one for deploying – and thus understanding – prosodic practices since it is both highly structured *and* complex: on the one hand, the basic or default resources for responding are fairly *simple* since the choice between alternative tokens (e.g., *yes* and *no*) establishes the basic valence of the responding turn; on the other, the range of relevancies those tokens must manage are frequently *complex* since they derive from (at least) three, distinct sources: the relevancies set in motion by the grammatical form of the YNI, the normative constraints embodied in the type of action it initiates (or the course of action in which it participates), and the turn-taking implications these, together, have for the structure of response. Speakers can manage these complexities by exploiting a 'division of labor' enabled by the multiple constituents of turn design: sequential positioning, word selection, grammar and prosody/intonation. In this chapter, I specifically focus on practices that exploit prosody, describing three separate practices as a basis for illustrating the broad range of matters that prosody can be used to manage in this sequential context. In conclusion, I note a range of other highly structured environments within which a similar proliferation of prosodic practices has emerged, suggesting that responses to YNIs are but one of many environments that might be investigated in this way.

2.   YNIs, type-conforming responses and the "structure of responding"

This chapter focuses on "yes" and "no" as responses to YNIs, produced as part of what I call type-conforming responses (Raymond 2003). As I have noted in other work (Raymond 2000), each element of such responses can be varied to shape the action they deliver; in this chapter I focus specifically on variations in the sound patterns used to produce "yes" and "no". For example, consider (and better, listen to) the following: *yeh, ye↑AH, ↑YE↓ah, yep, yea:::h, nah, no, nope, ↑NO!, ↑No↓, no:::,* etc. (arrows indicate marked shifts in pitch). Each of these variations is orderly: each one systematically alters a different aspect of the response underway, and thereby intervenes consequentially in the course of action to which it contributes. So what do these versions of "yes" and "no" do?

To address this question we will need some basic analytic resources. First, we will briefly need to understand basic features of YNIs and responses to them, and especially the difference between nonconforming and type-conforming responses. Second, we will develop a more fine-grained analysis of the latter, for such responses constitute one location in which prosodic variations come to have a special, and very pronounced, import.

2.1   Type-conforming vs. nonconforming responses

Recipients of grammatically formed YNIs face an immediate choice in formulating their responses: will they conform to the constraints embodied in its grammatical form, or not? Previous research (Raymond 2000, 2003) has focused on the basic alternative response types speakers can produce in this sequential location – type-conforming and nonconforming responses – by describing the alternative actions they implement and the relationship between these actions in the most general terms possible: (unmarked) type-conforming responses (e.g., "yes" or "no" or equivalent tokens) accept the course of action initiated by a YNI, including its terms and presuppositions as adequate while nonconforming responses indicate some trouble with it. As a consequence, even disconfirming type-conforming responses may nevertheless ratify some elements proposed by it. For example, if one friend asks another (apropos a long phone conversation he had with a young woman), "did you talk about your future?" even a "no" response will tacitly confirm that the two, in fact, do have a future to have talk about. This basic difference in response types is further reflected in a basic asymmetry between them: Insofar as type-conforming responses accept the design of an interrogative as unproblematic, no special warrant is required to produce them. Conversely, if a speaker wishes to challenge a presuppositions entailed by an interrogative, treat some element of its design as problematic, or otherwise produce an action not contemplated by it, they can depart from the terms established by its grammatical form to produce a nonconforming response. Insofar as speakers only produce such nonconforming responses "for cause" (cf. Raymond 2003), participants may inspect the design of a nonconforming response for the trouble or resistance indicated by it – the "cause" that prompted the departure it implements.

In light of these differences, it may appear that type-conforming responses are rather monolithic and uninteresting when compared to the variety of outcomes speakers can accomplish by responding to YNI with something other than "yes" or "no". Indeed the very term 'conforming' suggests it. However, as Schegloff (1986) has noted in another connection the routine and its achievement is often the site of the most intricate, interactively organized work. And so too in these sequences.

A dense array of activities can be accomplished by type-conforming responses through speakers' variations: of the (i) design of the turns they are embedded in; (ii) the tokens used to implement them; and (iii) the prosodic contours through which those tokens are realized. In what follows I describe a basic or default response form, and then consider systematic departures from it, focusing on both the technical composition of such responses and the underlying ground in practice for the accomplishment of the actions that compose the upshot, the tenor, and the texture of interaction.

2.2   Unmarked type-conforming responses

The grammatical form of a yes/no type interrogative sets a range of parameters for responding turns beyond simply making a "yes" or "no" relevant next; specifically, to satisfy the normative relevancies mobilized by a YNI without challenge or change to the course of action it implements, YNIs make relevant the position in which such type-conforming tokens should be delivered, and the prosodic contour through which they should be delivered. In fact, such responses are coordinated by reference to two concurrently relevant structures.

First, YNIs establish a highly structured sequential environment, setting in motion a fine-grained interpretive framework within which variations in the progressive realization of a type-conforming token are meaningful and consequential. Specifically, by projecting a determinate structure for the production of a responsive token, participants can monitor a responding speaker's progressive realization of her turn, tracking whether she produces a (i) fully articulated type-conforming token (e.g., *yes* or *yeah* articulated to completion) (ii) placed in turn initial position (iii) by itself in that slot (iv) delivered with either flat or terminal intonation.

As a consequence, the continuing moment-by-moment unfolding of the material elements out of which a type-conforming response is formed (such as its pace, volume, pitch, and the prosodic contour that carries it) can be inspected for the progressive realization (suspension, deflection, or abandonment) of what has been projected so far. In this respect, the highly projectable character of such responses constitutes a proximate normative structure within which a range of other organizational contingencies can be coordinated and managed (including the timing and design of action by others, cf. Lerner 1996). It is precisely this progressively realized structure that makes any deflections in a response's locally projected course a site of action, a recognizable form of action, and a site of action and interpretation by others. Thus, in sequences initiated by YNIs, the projectability of conduct (across turns and within them), and the moment-by-moment progressive realization of what has been projected so far (cf. Raymond and Lerner 2007), constitute key interpretive structures within which prosody, and prosodic variation, are organized.

Second, in producing such responses, speakers must also contend with two, alternative sequential contexts. In some cases, YNIs make relevant responses that can be completed with a simple "yes" or "no"; more often however, YNIs serve as a vehicle for another action, such as a request, an invitation, and the like, thereby initiating what Schegloff (2007) calls "double-barreled" actions. Such double-barreled actions make relevant a response to both the YNI and the action it delivers. Excerpts (1–2) contain examples of 'unmarked' type-conforming responses in these two sequential contexts. In excerpt (1), Alan initiates a sequence with the FPP (lines 1–2), *did Bruce Leave you a note?* In response, Karen produces a simple *no* delivered with terminal (or falling) intonation (indicated by the period).

(1) **Kamunsky 1** (cf. sound file [RAY-1-Kamunsky1-did bruce.mov])

```
1 I->  ALA:  Okay uhm (B- dih jid )/(did-B-didya) Bruce leave
2            you a no:te¿
3 R->  KAR:  nNo.
4  ->  ALA:  Oka:y. The party is on fer Saturda:y,
```

By launching his turn accepting Karen's response immediately on its completion, Mark's *okay* (line 4) treats that response as having satisfied the relevancies set in motion by his query.

Alternatively, sequences where the action initiated by a YNI makes talk relevant beyond a "yes" or "no" regularly attract type-conforming tokens with "flat" intonation, as in excerpt (2). In this case, Alan's query constitutes a virtual request; as a "double barreled" action, Alan's query makes relevant a response to both the question and the request for which it is a vehicle.

(2) **Kamunsky 1** (cf. sound file [RAY-2-Kamunsky1-is karen.mov])

```
1  I->  ALA:  Hi.=Is Karen there?
2  R->  MB:   Yea Just a minute please=
3   ->  ALA:  =Mhm
```

We can note that MB responds to both aspects of the sequence in response: *yea* confirms Karen's presence, and *just a minute* projects his immanent retrieval of her. We
can further note that MB exploits prosody to manage the distinct components of his
response. Although MB's *Yea* does not come to a full completion, the stress on the
early part of it (the underlining of the *ye*) and the stress on the start of the next word
(the underlining of the *j*) reflect the speakers parsing of her turn into distinct intonational contours associated with the two parts of the response: {response to interroga-
tive} + {response to action}. Alan accepts MB's response with *mmhm*, treating it as
possibly complete at *please*, an early, if not first, transition relevance place.

In sum: across excerpts (1–2) speakers design their responsive turns to implement
unmarked responses to yes/no type interrogatives insofar as they provide what that
grammatical form has provided a place for: a fully formed type-conforming token
placed in turn initial position and delivered with either flat or falling intonation. In
excerpt (2), where the YNI delivered an action that made talk relevant beyond the
type-conforming token, speakers *first* satisfied the constraints embodied in the grammatical form of the FPP before responding to the action delivered by it (Raymond
2000, 2003). In this way, responding speakers produce simple responses that satisfy the
relevancies mobilized by the initiating action without challenge or change to the course
of action initiated by it.

In these examples, speakers use YNIs to initiate adjacency pair sequences that
pose systematic interpretive constraints on the talk they make relevant: the grammatical form of such YNIs – and the actions they deliver – set interpretive constraints on
each of the basic constituents of turn organization responding speakers can use in
designing their utterances: the timing and placement of it's initiation, the words selected to compose it, the syntax or grammar used to organize it, and – especially important for the purposes of this chapter – the basic prosodic contours of the type-
conforming tokens they make relevant. In cases involving what I will call "unmarked"
type-conforming responses, responding speakers treat the various relevancies set in
motion by the YNI as aligned such that they permit a response – or at least its initiation – in a simple type-conforming token.

The complex relevancies set in motion by YNIs, the actions they implement, and
the relations they pose for speaker and recipient do not always align so neatly, however. In type-conforming responses, the first opportunity to manage such complexity
is the production of the type-conforming token itself. By posing a choice between alternative tokens – prototypically "yes" and "no" – the grammatical form of yes/no type
interrogatives makes the production of such tokens literally pivotal in the sequence
because such tokens supply the terms around which the remainder of the responsive

turn will be organized. As a consequence, speakers can strategically manipulate the realization of such tokens to manage a range of contingencies: in the first place they can be used to manage basic exigencies of turn-construction, being deployed to project more talk, or turn completion; but they can also be manipulated to transform the action a "yes" or "no" delivers in the sequence, and thereby intervene (more directly) in the business of the sequence itself. In what follows we will consider practices relevant to each of these organizational domains, tracking how speakers' manipulate the shape and pitch of the sound pattern used to deliver a type-conforming token, thereby shaping the action it delivers in response, and thus the relevancies it sets in motion.

3. Prosodic variations in the delivery of type-conforming tokens

3.1 Prosody and turn taking: Variations in prosody can project more talk

Insofar as type-conforming tokens themselves manage central relevancies mobilized by YNIs, they can be manipulated to manage the most basic exigencies confronted by speakers. For example, by giving a determinate form to the conditional relevance of a second pair part (a response or SPP cf. Schegloff 1968, 2007) on a first pair part (or FPP), the relevancies established by the grammatical form of a yes/no type interrogative can enable a type-conforming token, by itself, to deliver a possibly complete response. Moreover, insofar as the completion of that response token satisfies the relevancies mobilized by the YNI (as FPP), its completion can have implications for the larger sequence, or even occasion, in which it participates. To forestall these possibilities, speakers can modulate the production of such type-conforming tokens to avoid their being heard as possibly complete. That is, speakers can manipulate the transition relevance a type-conforming token's completion may otherwise indicate, and the attendant relevancies the completion of that token would otherwise set in motion.

Excerpt (3) involves just such a case. This excerpt comes from a call between a sister and brother, Joyce and Stan, which has been primarily devoted to satisfying his requests for help in shopping. That project completed, Stan initiates a pre-closing sequence (line 1), *well okay, that's all I wanted to bug you with today*, a move ratified by Joyce in the following turn (line 3), *okay Stan*. Before moving to actually close the call, however, but still in the shadow of this pre-closing sequence (on closings, see Schegloff and Sacks 1973, Button 1987, 1990), Stan asks Joyce (line 4), *so are you okay?*

(3) **Joyce and Stan (modified)** (cf. sound file [RAY-3-Joyce-Stan.mov])

```
      1        S:    ·hhhh We:ll okay: at's about all I wannid tuh (0.7)
      2              bug you with. (tod[ay).
      3        J:                      [uhhahhahh hh Okay Stan:,
      4  I->  S:    So are ^you okay?
      5  R->  J:    Yeah,
      6              (0.4)
```

```
7                 um: (0.2) whatta ya doing like: s: late Saturday
8                 afternoo:n.=
9        S:       =·hhhhh Well late Sa- I pra- a friend a'mine just
```

By asking Joyce to confirm that she is *okay*, the design of Stan's FPP projects a 'no news' response. In the sequential context initiated by his use of a YNI, such a response could be delivered by a "yes", upon which closing the call could be resumed. Indeed Joyce is fine, and so delivers a type-conforming 'no news' response (line 5), *yeah* (cf. sound file [RAY-3.1-Joyce-Stan-yeah.wav]). Despite this, Joyce manages to stall the resumption of closing that her response would otherwise make relevant by manipulating its pro-sodic delivery; she produces her *yeah* with a slightly rising intonation contour, using a prosodic contour (English) speakers regularly use to project more talk (cf. Ford and Thompson 1996, Schegloff 1996). In contrast to the FPP speaker's conduct in excerpt (1), Stan does not treat Joyce's type-conforming response as possibly complete. Having succeeded in her bid to stall Stan's resumption of the call's closing, Joyce then launches what turns out to be a pre-request sequence (line 7). Thus, in a call mostly devoted to satisfying Stan's interests, Joyce exploits Stan's (minimal) display of interest in her cir-cumstances to launch what turns out to be a request of her own. The initial seeds of that course of action are realized in the manipulated contour of her type-conforming response, a move that forestalls both the imminent close of the sequence, and (potentially) the call itself, providing Joyce with an opportunity to assess Stan's willing-ness to cooperate with her request.

In this case Joyce's manipulation of the delivery of her type-conforming response withholds one aspect of what an unmarked response would have delivered: she at-tempts to thwart its treatment as a possibly complete answer and the attendant rele-vancies such a response would have invoked in this sequential context (e.g. resuming the close of the call). She does this by realizing the type-conforming token, *yeah*, with slightly rising, or continuing, intonation.[1]

In a second case of this practice below, the responding speaker uses several re-sources to mitigate the full compliance otherwise indicated by a preferred type-con-forming response. In this sequence, Mum initiates a possible pre-sequence (either a pre-invitation or pre-request/offer) by asking whether Leslie's family have left her. The unmarked polarity of Mum's YNI establishes "yes" as the preferred response in this sequence. After a brief delay (that may adumbrate the problems Leslie notes in line 5), Leslie delivers such a response, see *yes* in line 3.

---

1.   The brief pause following Joyce's *yeh*, likely reflects a range of contingencies, at least one is worth mentioning explicitly: the talk projected by the prosody of her *yeh* is not part of the same sequence (i.e., that Stan initiated), and thus must be distinguished from it (*uhm* may have simi-lar consequences). More generally, the use of prosody to project additional talk should not be taken to mean that a speaker will proceed without delay; rather such practices project that con-tinuation is immanent or forthcoming (even if it is delayed).

(4)   **Holt 1.1** (cf. sound file [RAY-4-Holt1.1.mov])

```
1  I->  Mum:  'Av your family gone o:ff?
2             (.)
3  R->  Les:  Ye:s,
4        Mum:  Oh ^goo:d,
5        Les:  <A:t um: half past three: this morning.
6             (0.3)
7        Mum:  ˘Oh my wo:rd.
```

As in excerpt (3), Leslie delivers her type-conforming token with slightly ising intonation(as indicated by the comma). In contrast to (3), however, Mum immediately registers Leslie's response (with an assessment). Rather than undermining the claim that such prosodically manipulated SPPs project more talk however, what Leslie does next underscores this relationship. Immediately following Mum's uptake of her SPP, Leslie produces an addition to the response delivered by the type-conforming token: *At uhm half past three in the morning.* Two features of it are remarkable. First, its beginning is 'rushed,' as indicated by the left-pointing caret. Second, she packages the addition as an increment to Mum's FPP (Schegloff 1996), thereby producing it 'as if' it directly followed her type-conforming token. The design of this addition appears aimed at connecting it to the type-conforming token that Leslie produced to project more talk in the first place, thus sequentially deleting Mum's appreciation of their departure. We can note then, that Mum revises her up-take, now registering Leslie's response as having delivered bad news (*oh my word*, in line 7). Although Mum treated Leslie's marked type-conforming token as possibly complete, Leslie's subsequent conduct suggests that she had used its prosodic contour to project the relevance of more talk in the first place.

The manipulation of type-conforming tokens in excerpts 3 and 4 involve one instantiation of a more general practice: as both Ford and Thompson (1996) and Schegloff (1998) have noted, (English) speakers in other environments can use slightly rising prosody to project more talk and thereby forestall a recipient's treatment of a *possibly* complete utterance as *actually* complete. And it is not only "yes" that can constitute a complete response; in many cases "no" can do so as well. As Ford et al. (2004) note, speakers have a range of practices to "get past *no*".

Before moving to other matters, I should add that speakers can manipulate type-conforming responses to manage the opposite contingency as well. That is, instead of projecting additional talk at a point of possible completion, speakers can indicate that a possible completion is an actual one. In responses to YNIs, speakers can rely on a combination of prosody and word selection to show that their type-conforming tokens constitute complete responses. For example, as Heritage and Sorjonen (1994) have noted, speakers can use *yep*, *nope* and *mm*, produced with falling intonation to indicate that their responses will take no elaboration (see also, Heritage and Greatbatch 1991). The exploitation of this resource is most explicit when *yep* or *nope* are used to deliver

unelaborated dispreferred responses since they project that talk which might otherwise have been anticipated (or relevant) will *not* be produced (see Raymond 2000).

Together, these alternative methods for producing type-conforming tokens provide for the two basic stances that a turn-so-far can project regarding its course and
duration: does the turn-so-far project more talk, or turn completion? In addition,
these observations specify one part of a claim made earlier: by making "yes" and
"no" the vehicle for delivering the action made relevant by a FPP, the grammatical
form of a YNI makes those tokens pivotal for how the remainder of the sequence
will be organized. As Couper-Kuhlen anticipated, then, at least some sound patterns
– and perhaps a great many – will find their home in managing the exigencies of
turn taking.

But prosodic variations in type-conforming tokens are not limited to this domain;
prosodic manipulations of type-conforming tokens can directly participate in the
business of the sequence as well. In these cases, while the prosody of the type-conforming token is produced within a turn, its locus of organization – its source and
import – can be found in the larger course of action in which it participates.

3.2   Prosody in Action: Using prosody to shape sequential trajectories

The sound patterns used to deliver type-conforming tokens can be manipulated as a
method for shaping the *actions* such tokens deliver, thereby enabling speakers to manage a range of other contingencies posed by YNI initiating actions. Such prosodic manipulations are primarily deployed in circumstances where a YNI FPP is the vehicle
for another action, and thus where responding speakers must use type-conforming
tokens to manage more than one set of contingencies.

3.2.1   *More than "yes" or "no": Anticipating and/or projecting good news/bad news*
with type-conforming tokens
Perhaps the most straightforward (and common) cases can be found in responses to
YNIs that either *project* (good or bad) news *for* recipients – as in the case of pre-an-
nouncements – or that *anticipate* news *from* those recipients (on the organization of
good and bad news, see Maynard, 1997, 1998, 2003). Such YNIs not only make relevant
a response to the query itself, but they regularly occasion the responding speaker's appreciation of the news that has been projected, or her foreshadowing of the news that
has been anticipated. To the extent that both of these jobs are managed (at least initially) in a single lexical item, speakers can exploit a division of labor, using the selection
of a token to manage the response to the sequence initiated by the YNI, while using the
prosodic contour and pitch of that token to appreciate or foreshadow the news.

The practices for manipulating type-conforming tokens examined in this section
vary on at least two dimensions: First, the shape and duration of the sound patterns
through which the type-conforming token is realized can provide a method for speakers to register or project news; and second, in a subset of such cases speakers use

markedly high pitch as a method for occasioning a departure from the sequential trajectory that the token might have otherwise made relevant. Due to space limitations
we will consider only the first set here.

    In excerpt (5) a speaker uses a marked type-conforming token to register a bit
of good news, reflecting the simplest version of this practice. In this stretch of talk,
two friends (Dorothy and Terri) turn to catching up after discussing some recent
news reported by Dorothy. After Terri declines (over several opportunities) to report anything about herself, she begins a sequence in which she ultimately solicits
Dorothy's advice regarding her clothing for an awards banquet. Just after she launches it (in line 10, *I am-*), however, she stops its production, and produces a possible
pre-announcement YNI designed to establish whether she has already told Dorothy
about the award she has won (line 10), (which is relevant for understanding the request for advice).

(5)   **May 1.2** (cf. sound file [RAY-5-May1.2.mov])

```
 1        Dorothy:   ˙hhhh (1.9) ˙h so- en- hows yer
 2                   personal life going?
 3                   (0.5)
 4        Terri:     ˙hhh (0.3) ˙h fine i guess.
 5        Dorothy:   uh huh.=
 6        Terri:     u::m. °yeah. fine.°
 7        Dorothy:   yeah.=
 8        Terri:     =nothing new. (0.3)
 9        Dorothy:   no, (0.4)
10 I->    Terri:     no. (0.5) i am- (0.2) did i tell
11                   you (0.3) i got this award at werk?
12 R->    Dorothy:   #ye:::ah.#
13        Terri:     yeah so the banquets u:::::m- (0.4)
14                   not next week its january seventh
15                   so i got a dress en im tryin
16                   tuh dec(hhh)ide if i can
17                   w(h)ear it er n(h)ot.=
```

Evidently, *did I tell you I got this award at work* (a canonical pre-announcement sequence, cf. Schegloff 2007) projects news, and specifically good news. Dorothy can
invite Terri to tell her about it with "no", and thereby provide an occasion to celebrate
Terri's achievement. As it happens, however, Terri has *already* told Dorothy. In conveying this with a "yes" (cf. sound file [RAY-5.1-May1.2-yeah.wav]), however, Dorothy
blocks the projected announcement, virtually ensuring that a prepared sequential location for appreciating Terri's good news will never arrive. Dorothy manages these
countervailing concerns by producing her type-conforming token in a distinctive
fashion. She stretches her *yeah* considerably, very gradually lowering its pitch over the
course of its production; at the same time she forms her mouth into a smile, producing

so-called 'smile voice'. Through these features, Dorothy conveys her appreciation for Terri's accomplishment even as she blocks further elaboration of it.[2]

As noted above, this practice for prosodically marking type-conforming tokens can also be used to foreshadow the valence of news solicited from a recipient. For example, consider (6), taken from a call between a young woman (Cindy) and her partner's mother (Pam) that largely concerns Pam's son, Mark. In a previous conversation, Pam has enlisted Cindy (the "daughter-in-practice", if not in-law) in an effort to facilitate a family vacation; apparently she requested that Cindy asks Mark whether he would go on a family cruise. After discussing a range of other matters, Pam (in line 1) unilaterally introduces a new topic, asking whether Cindy has broached the subject. Pam's conspiratorially formed query in line 1 (*Hey, did you ask him about going on a cruise*) sets in motion a complex course of action by making relevant a response to the proximate question while also anticipating Mark's response to the question about the cruise. In designing her YNI to prefer a "yes", Pam anticipates that Cindy has talked with Mark, while her hopeful expression of it anticipates that he has responded positively. In these respects, Mom's FPP conveys her anticipation of a positive response: not just that Cindy talked to Mark, but that he will want to join the family on a cruise. In contrast to the last case, then, Pam's query *anticipates* news *from* Cindy (instead of *projecting* news *for* her).

(6)   **Munoz 1.2** (cf. sound file [RAY-6-Munoz1.2.mov])

```
1  I->  Pam:    .hhh Hey did you ask him about going on a
2              cruise,
3  R->  Cindy:  [.hhhh YEa::h]=
4       Pam:    [(or d-)]
5       Cindy:   = I dont think hes gonna go for
6              *tha:t*.
5       Pam:    oh that booger head. hh=
```

In this sequential context, a preferred response by Cindy may have to manage both of these contingencies: conveying whether she has talked to Mark, and if she has, whether he wants to go. The preferred, type-conforming response Cindy composes uses a form that mirrors the last case: she produces a stretched, low pitch *yea::h* that slowly decays over its course (cf. sound file [RAY-6.1-Munoz1.2-yea.wav]). Unlike the last case, however, Cindy produces this pattern without smile voice, and thus the relatively low pitch of the turn produces a deflated effect. In this way Cindy conveys that she talked to Mark while simultaneously projecting the bad news that follows directly: he doesn't want to go (see Freese and Maynard (1998) for an analysis of prosody and emotions in good news/bad news sequences).

---

2.   It is worthy noting as well that the features of this "appreciation" are very different from those found in Freese and Maynard (1998) and the "prosodic correlates of emotions" described in Couper-Kuhlen (1986: 181) perhaps owing to the fact that the token in this excerpt is doing "double duty", and thus does not convey an unalloyed emotion.

We can note, then, that Cindy exploits these features of her response to manage its complex relationship to the preference structure established by Pam's query: on the one hand, Cindy delivers her *yeah* as a preferred response, producing it early (with a minimal delay comprised of the in-breath that precedes it) in (partial) overlap with Pam's completion of her query; she did, after all, ask Mark about the cruise as Pam had requested. On the other hand, there is no question that the response from Mark that she will convey disappoints the larger project of which it is a part, a fact which she projects by delivering her token with a long, drawn-out, falling contour. In this respect, Cindy manages to transform the action her type-conforming response might have otherwise delivered so that it anticipates the bad news she goes on to produce. By successfully projecting trouble in this case, Cindy manages to avoid the sort of premature uptake of a preferred response, and consequent misalignment, that we discussed in our analysis of excerpt (4).

Across these cases we can appreciate the complex interplay between the multiple relevancies set by speakers uses of YNI FPPs to initiate sequences, and the division of labor enabled by the possibility of using word selection and variations in prosody to manage different aspects of those sequences in response. In each case, speakers initiated sequences that posed alternative, cross-cutting relevancies for responding speakers to manage with a simple type-conforming token. Responding speakers managed these relevancies via a kind of division of labor, using the type-conforming token itself to respond to one set and the manipulation of its prosodic packaging to manage another. But of course neither is entirely separate from the other: in each case, the issues managed by the prosodic contour was made specially relevant by the action the type conforming token delivered; for example in excerpt 5 the registering of good news in a turn-initial type-conforming token was specifically relevant because that token blocked its further telling, and thus its production might provide the only chance to appreciate it; and in excerpt 6 the preferred response delivered by a type-conforming token may have inadvertently foreshadowed good news (as in excerpt 4), making the projection of bad news before its completion specially relevant. Thus, the consequences of these distinct elements of turn construction are intertwined insofar as they reshape the sequential trajectory that an unmarked type-conforming token would have otherwise encouraged.

3.2.2   *Less than "yes" or "no": Type-conforming Responses that challenge elements of a FPP*
Once we have noticed that speakers can exploit their type-conforming tokens to do "double duty" by varying their prosodic realization, we can begin to search for other possible practices. As it happens, there are many. In an effort to keep this account brief, I will focus on one of the more interesting ones I have come across. Speakers can shape their type-conforming tokens to adumbrate a challenge to the relevance or appropriateness of a FPP, or the trajectory it projects, even as they conform to the constraints set by it. See for example, excerpt (7). This stretch of talk comes from one call in a series of calls during which Alan phones friends to invite them to a party he will host,

and, if they accept, request that they bring either food or drink. Karen's question at line 1 comes after Alan's request that she bring chips and dip and his description of what he has asked others to bring. By asking whether Alan has the party *really planned out*, Karen may simply be asking about what he has organized for the occasion. Her use of *really* as an intensifier of *planned*, however suggests that, more likely, the question effectively chides him for either 'over-planning' or 'under-planning' his party. In either of these latter possibilities, the query constitutes a challenge to, or critique of, Alan's efforts. This is how Alan hears it, in any case.

(7) **Kamunsky 1** (cf. sound file [RAY-7-Kamunsky1-planned-out.mov])

```
1  I->  KAR:  D'you have this really planned out?
2            (0.2)
3  R->  ALA:  Yea:h, why:,
4        KAR:  Oh I w'js wunnering,
```

In response (after some delay, which may be an early harbinger of trouble), Alan produces a *yeah* with a very marked stress pattern (cf. sound file [RAY-7.1-Kamunsky1-planned-out-yeah.wav]). In contrast to the stretched type-conforming tokens in excerpts (5–6), Alan's token is more abrupt; also unlike the long, smooth decay that characterized those earlier cases, Alan's *yeah* includes a perturbation in its progressive realization: the early portion of it is stressed, *Yea:h*, and then it shifts or curves lower. In effect, although Alan's response delivers a preferred action, his production of the type-conforming token *yeah* rises to meet the challenge he hears in Karen's question. This stance is further revealed in the TCU he follows up his type-conforming response with – *why*? *Why* commonly serves as a 'post-pre,' (Schegloff 2007: 31, note 3). In this sequential context it makes explicit that Alan understood Karen's FPP was 'leading up to something.' By using it after a preferred type-conforming response (which, in most circumstances would promote a next action on its own), Alan displays his understanding that the way he delivered his response potentially thwarted such an outcome. By first thwarting the trajectory projected by Karen's FPP, and then inviting it on his terms, Alan effectively turns the tables; his SPP challenges Karen to make her complaint explicit. It is noticeable that Karen's utterance suggests that she understands this sequence much as I have described it: on hearing Alan's response, she backs down by claiming an innocent motivation for her query (*wondering*). The *just* in particular suggests she hears a challenge in Alan's turn insofar as it appears designed to rebut Alan's claim that something other than 'mere' curiosity prompted her query. Thus, Alan's delivery of a type-conforming token in this sequence shapes yet another aspect of what it would otherwise deliver: he undercuts the alignment that a preferred type-conforming response would have delivered (a move first indicated by his brief delay in responding). As in the cases of news-appreciating type-conforming tokens discussed in the prior section, the import of this practice is to (a) manage the complex relevancies set by a YNI FPP, and (b) thereby re-shape the sequential trajectory that an unmarked type-conforming token would have otherwise encouraged.

A second instance of this practice can be found in excerpt (8)[3], taken from an extended family discussion regarding whether Virginia, the youngest daughter, should be allowed to get a new summer dress. In this argument, Virginia argues quite strongly that she should be allowed to get the dress; her mother steadfastly maintains that she should not. The excerpt begins with the intrusion of a third party, Virginia's brother Wesley who notes *well you buy her clothes anyway*. The tag question he tacks on to the end of this statement, *don't you?*, makes Mom's acceptance of his formulation relevant next. The resulting form of this query is potentially equivocal. While the content of the statement appears to provide materials for a challenge to Virginia's claims (insofar is it positions Mom as the one who decides "anyway"), his use of a negatively formed tag question designed to hearably challenge its recipient, *don't you?* (Heritage 2002),[4] complicates matters because it is directed to Mom. Thus, although Wesley may have designed his query to challenge *Virginia's* presumption that Mum should buy her a dress, because he selects *Mom* as a recipient (and directs the tag question to her), just whom he is challenging may not be clear.

(8) **Virginia 4:23–27** (cf. video file [RAY-8-Virginia.mov]))

```
1  I->   WES:   Wu'you-y[ou buy 'er clothes anyway, dontchyuh?
2        PRU:           [eh heh huh °uh uh
3               (0.3)
4        PRU:   ·hhhk!=
5  R->   MOM:   =^Yea:h. But I've bought 'er all the
6               clothes that she ne:e:ds.
```

As the selected speaker, Mom begins a type-conforming response. Notably, however, the sound pattern and pitch with which she packages it suggests a different stance than would otherwise be indicated by a simple "yeah" (cf. sound file [RAY-8.1-Virginia-yeah.wav]). Mom uses very high pitch, delivering her token with a marked perturbation in its progressive realization. Although this results in a sounds pattern that sounds like the previous case, Mom actually uses stress (or intensity) to break the smooth production of her "yeah" so that the first part of it is stressed by comparison to its completion, which abruptly curves lower at its end (rather than simply fading or decaying to completion). By delivering her type-conforming token with this prosodic pattern, Mom "returns the challenge" embodied in her son's utterance. In effect, Mom

---

3. The FPP in excerpt (8) involves a different interrogative form. In this case Wesley uses a FPP consisting of a declarative + tag question to make "yes" or "no" relevant on its completion. See Raymond 2009 for a discussion of this and related forms.

4. Stan's use of the tag question *don't you?* can be heard as challenging in this context for two reasons: (i) the use of an interrogative form asks Mom to confirm what he has proposed while (ii) the negative form of the query with high rising intonation embodies an implicit claim that she has already (or would likely) deny/ied such a claim. Thus *don't you?* solicits an admission, and as such, can be heard as challenging the current position of the person targeted by it.

confirms that she buys Virginia's clothes, but constrains whatever inferences Wesley – or Virginia – might make from that confirmation.

Although speakers use slightly different aspects of speech production used to produce the prosodically marked type-conforming tokens in excerpts 7 and 8, the resulting effect (or sound pattern) is the same: the progressive realization of the token (produced with high pitch relative to the surrounding talk) is modified mid-course so that the single syllable of the token is produced with a distinctive rise-fall pattern. And just as important, the outcomes they achieve are also comparable. In both cases, speakers use these distinctively formed type-conforming tokens to respond to challenges tacitly embodied in the YNIs to which they are responding using a type-conforming token in turn-initial position to deliver the action its form made relevant (thereby accepting the query/action as adequate), while using the prosodic contour of that token to modify (or withhold) the alignment, or agreement, its unmarked production would otherwise implement. In effect, these stressed type-conforming tokens confirm the facts questioned in their FPP, while resisting the implication given them by the FPP speaker. In this way, the inflected, or prosodically curved, realization of *yeah* constrains the inferences that a preferred type-conforming response would have otherwise encouraged, thereby treating the trajectory projected by the FPP as problematic and establishing an alternative one in its place. Thus, if the marked type-conforming tokens in excerpts (3) and (4) withheld one basic aspect of what the type conforming token would otherwise deliver in the sequence – its status as a possibly complete response – these withhold another: the alignment that "yes" as a preferred, type-conforming response would otherwise implement.[5]

In excerpts (7–8), speakers relied on type-conforming tokens produced with a curved (up/down) intonation contour to resist a potential inference that the responsive action delivered by it – even when it confirmed the facts queried – might have otherwise permitted. Specifically, in excerpts (7) and (8) the inflected, or curved, realization of *yeah* was used to resist the trajectory that a preferred type-conforming response would otherwise have made relevant. In each of these cases, the immediate consequence of the prosodically manipulated type-conforming token was to project more talk, while the action delivered by their response as a whole resisted the trajectory projected by the FPP.[6]

4.   Discussion

The observations and claims in this paper have been premised on a comparison of alternative prosodic practices for realizing type-conforming tokens. Though analytically

---

5.   The same prosodic pattern can also be used to deliver dispreferred actions. See Raymond (2000) for a more substantial discussion of these and other cases.

6.   Lindström (1997) and Hakulinen (2001) have described similar intonation contours that achieve the same outcome in both Swedish and Finish.

sound, such a comparison can only be part of the picture – a "first order" contrast, as it were. Such marked prosodic practices might also be usefully contrasted with practices of responding that involve a *different set of resources* being used to manage a *similar set of contingencies*. That is, instead of focusing on resources for action formation, and asking how variations in its realization can be consequential for the action(s) an utterance delivers – as we have so far – a different perspective is offered by focusing on *alternative resources for action formation*, and asking how their deployment might reflect a speaker's effort to *manage related contingencies* in a different way. For surely this too is a way in which prosody is "context sensitive". One practice for prosodically manipulating a turn or token is not merely an alternative to other ways of doing so; it is also an alternative to practices of word selection (as noted above), the use of prefaces, and actions built using wholly different grammatical forms. If we consider the alternative actions enabled by nonconforming responses, for example, we may gain some insight into the specificity of prosody as a resource for action formation in type-conforming responses.

For example, we might note that the action accomplished by the speakers type-conforming tokens in (7) and (8) can be usefully compared with alternatives practices for registering trouble with the terms of a FPP. As we noted above in describing the organization of type-conformity, speakers can challenge the presupposition of a FPP, or otherwise register troubles with it, using nonconforming responses. Thus, in excerpts (7–8), the fact that speakers registered trouble with a FPP by manipulating the prosodic contour of their type-conforming token reflects a choice regarding how to register such trouble in a response form that otherwise conforms with the relevancies set by the YNI FPP to which they respond. Given these alternatives, we might ask: how are we to understand a speakers' selection of one practice over another? One possibility is that the tacit registering of trouble enabled by the use of prosody in excerpts 7 and 8, and the "double duty" responses such manipulation enables, is directly fitted to the circumstances targeted by these turns. In each case, the challenges posed by the FPP were either merely potential in excerpts 7, or (possibly) inadvertent (8). Thus, to register a challenge explicitly in the surface design of the turn – as a nonconforming response would do – would be to expose a potentially "partial" or disputable hearing of the prior utterance, thereby setting the participants on a quite different sequential trajectory. By registering these troubles tacitly, speakers can avoid letting them pass altogether without committing themselves, their recipients, and the sequence itself, to explicitly realized conflict.

5.   Concluding remarks

The prosodic practices we have examined in this paper demonstrate a deep link between the relevancies mobilized by the grammatical form of yes/no type interrogatives, the prosodic contours of the tokens speakers offer in response, and the actions they implemented. By posing a choice between alternative tokens the grammatical form of yes/no type interrogative FPPs makes the production of such tokens central to the organization of the sequence and the course of action organized through it. As a consequence of this centrality – and the highly structured sequential environment set by YNIs – responding speakers can manipulate their type-conforming tokens to shape the actions they deliver. Beyond unmarked type-conforming responses (i.e., responses that accomplish responding alone), we noted that speakers can vary the realization of such type-conforming tokens using slightly rising intonation to project more talk or use closed forms (*yep*, *nope*, and *yeah* with glottal stop) to project turn completion. In addition, we examined two other practices that speakers use to intervene directly in the business of the sequence itself, either to convey an action over and above what a type-conforming token would deliver on its own (as in cases 5–6), or to withhold an aspect of the action such a token would otherwise deliver (as in excerpts 7–8). Collectively, these practices suggest that virtually any movement away from the form of response made relevant by the grammatical form of a YNI will entail some modification of the action the type-conforming response would deliver, or the stance it would take up toward the course of action in which it participates.

This latter point bears some elaboration: We can ask, what about these sequential locations established by YNIs make responses to them such a rich ecological niche for the proliferation of prosodic practices? The sequential environment set in motion by the YNIs we have examined are remarkable for the ways in which participants must manage multiple, simultaneously relevant contingencies (some of which may be "cross-cutting") while using a highly restricted (or simplified) set of alternatives: the relatively basic actions made possible by a choice between alternative tokens ("yes" and "no"). If it is this feature of these sequences – that the resources available to speakers are highly structured while the contingencies they must manage are complex – makes them ideal for the proliferation of prosody-based practices, then we should expect a similar proliferation of prosodic practices in other environments with the same features. There are at least a few: For example, as Schegloff notes (1998) the exchange of greetings in the opening of conversations is both highly structured and very complex; perhaps it is not surprising then that practices of prosodic manipulation are also prominent in the delivery of greetings that do more than simple greeting. Similarly, the use of names in summons sequences, in identification and recognition sequences, and to a lesser extent in addressing and person reference, is also highly structured and potentially complex (see Schegloff 1986). These too, are regularly shaped to do more than summoning, recognizing, or referring by virtue of their prosodic realization. Finally, the initiation of repair in next turn (i.e., NTRIs, see Schegloff et. al. 1977) is also both highly structured, and regularly exploited to do more than manage problems in hearing and understanding (Schegloff 2000). In each of these environments, participants rely on a fairly circumscribed range of tokens – ones that are virtually dedicated, as in the case of "yes" and "no", greetings, and NTRIs, or, in the case of names, ones that are special to the participants in many different ways. The combination of a highly

structured sequential environment and a limited range of specialized tokens or devoted terms may encourage the proliferation of action-specific sound patterns as one
of a range of methods for projecting, reflecting, or otherwise managing and manipulating the sort of action, sequence, or interaction underway since many of the resources typically available to speakers (word selection, grammar, sequential positioning,
and so on) are either constrained, or already pressed into service in managing some
other aspect of them.

These observations, in turn, suggest that the omni-relevant forms of organization
that structure the real-time production of action in interaction, namely projectability
–, the capacity to project the course and duration of an in-progress action from its in-
ception – and progressivity – the moment-by-moment material realization of, or departure from, what has been projected – provide interpretive keys that are central to
understanding prosody as a resource for action formation in talk (cf. Raymond and
Lerner 2007). Indeed, if we revisit a key passage from the Couper-Kuhlen and Selting
(1996: 26) quote that I began with, we can note that they anticipated as much in their
observation that "basic units of sounding patterning can be expounded by intonational, rhythmic, pausal or dynamic means" in a turn at talk. In this chapter, I hope to have
made some sources of this fundamental linkage more explicit, and thereby invite others to unpack how sound is formed up and patterned in interaction more generally.

References

Button, Graham 1987. "Moving out of closings." In: *Talk and social organization*, Graham Button
    and J.R.E. Lee (eds.), 101–151. Clevedon: Multilingual Matters.
Button, Graham 1990. "On varieties of closings." In: *Interaction competence,* George Psathas
    (ed.), 93–148. Lanham, MD: University Press of America.
Couper-Kuhlen, Elizabeth 1986. *An introduction to English prosody.* London: Edward Arnold.
Couper-Kuhlen, Elizabeth and Selting, Margaret 1996. "Towards and interactional perspective on
    prosody and a prosodic perspective on interaction." In: *Prosody in conversation,* Elizabeth
    Couper-Kuhlen and Margaret Selting (eds.), 11–56. Cambridge: Cambridge University Press.
Couper-Kuhlen, Elizabeth and Ford, Cecilia E. 2004. *Sound patterns in interaction.* Amsterdam:
    Benjamins.
Ford, Cecilia E. and Thompson, Sandra A. 1996. "Interactional units in conversation: Syntactic,
    intonational and pragmatic resources for the management of turns." In: *Interaction and
    grammar*, Elinor Ochs, Emmanuel A. Schegloff and Sandra A. Thompson (eds.), 134–184.
    Cambridge: Cambridge University Press.
Ford, Cecilia E.; Fox, Barbara and Hellerman, John 2004. "'Getting past *no*': Sequence, action
    and sound projection of *no*-initiated turns." In: *Sound patterns in interaction,* Elizabeth
    Couper-Kuhlen and Cecilia E. Ford (eds.), 233–269. Amsterdam: Benjamins.
Freese, Jeremy and Maynard, Douglas W. 1998. "Prosodic features of good and bad news in
    conversation." *Language in Society* 27 (2), 195–219.
Gardner, Rod 1997. "The conversation object mm: A weak and variable acknowledging token."
    Research on Language and Social Interaction 30: 131–156.

Hakulinen, Auli 2001. "On some uses of the particle 'kyl(la)' in Finnish conversation." In: *Studies in interactional linguistics*, Margaret Selting and Elizabeth Couper-Kuhlen (eds.), 171–198. Amsterdam: Benjamins.

Heritage, John 2002. "The limits of questioning: Negative interrogatives and hostile question content." *Journal of Pragmatics* 34: 1427–1446.

Heritage, John and Greatbatch, David 1991. "On the institutional character of institutional talk: The case of news interviews." In: *Talk and social structure*, Deidre Boden and Don H. Zimmerman (eds.), 93–137. Berkeley: University of California Press.

Heritage, John and Sorjonen, Marja-Leena 1994. "Constituting and maintaining activities across sequences: And-prefacing as a feature of question design." *Language in Society* 23: 1–29.

Lerner, Gene H. 1996. "On the place of linguistic resources in the organization of talk-in-interaction: "Second person" reference in multi-party conversation." *Pragmatics* 6 (3): 281–294.

Lindström, Anna 1997. *Designing social actions: Grammar, prosody and interaction in Swedish conversation.* Unpublished Ph.D. dissertation. Department of Sociology, University of California Los Angeles.

Local, John K. and Kelly, John 1986. "Projection and silences: notes on phonetic and conversational structure." *Human Studies* 9: 185–204.

Maynard, Douglas 1997. "The news delivery sequence: Bad news and good news in conversational interaction." *Research on Language and Social Interaction* 30: 93–130.

Maynard, Douglas 1998. "Praising versus blaming the messenger: Moral issues in deliveries of good and bad news." *Research on Language and Social Interaction* 31: 359–395.

Maynard, Douglas 2003. *Bad news, good news: Conversational order in everyday talk and clinical settings.* Chicago: University of Chicago Press.

Raymond, Geoffrey 2000. *The structure of responding: Type-conforming and nonconforming responses to YNIs.* Unpublished PhD dissertation. Department of Sociology, UCLA.

Raymond, Geoffrey 2003. "Grammar and social organization: Yes/No interrogatives and the structure of responding." *American Sociological Review* 68: 939–967.

Raymond, Geoffrey 2009. "Grammar and social relations: Alternative forms of Yes/No-type initiating actions in health visitor interactions" In: *"Why do you ask?": The function of questions in institutional discourse,* Alice F. Freed and Susan Ehrlich (eds.), 87–107. Oxford: Oxford University Press.

Raymond, Geoffrey and Lerner, Gene 2007. "Managing multiple involvements in a material world of practical, situated action." Paper presented at the center for Language, Interaction, Mind and Body (LIMB), UCSD.

Schegloff, Emanuel A. 1968. "Sequencing in conversational openings." *American Anthropologist* 70: 1075–1095. [Reprinted 1972. In: *Directions in sociolinguistics: The ethnography of communciation*, John J Gumperz and Dell Hymes (eds.), 346–380. New York: Holt, Rinehart and Winston.]

Schegloff, Emmanuel A. 1979. "The relevance of repair to syntax-for-conversation." In: *Syntax and semantics, Volume 12: Discourse and syntax*, Talmy Givon (ed.), 261–286. New York: Academic Press.

Schegloff, Emanuel A. 1986. "The routine as achievement." *Human Studies* 9: 111–151.

Schegloff, Emanuel A. 1996. "Turn organization: One intersection of grammar and interaction." In: *Interaction and grammar*, Elinor Ochs, Sandra A. Thompson and Emmanuel A. Schegloff (eds.), 52–133. Cambridge: Cambridge University Press.

Schegloff, Emanuel A. 1998. "Reflections on studying prosody in talk-in-interaction." *Language and Speech* 41: 235–263.

Schegloff, Emanuel A. 2000. "When 'others' initiate repair," *Applied Linguistics* 21 (2): 205–243.

Schegloff, E. A. 2005. "On integrity in inquiry...of the investigated, not the investigator." *Discourse Studies* 7 (4–5): 455–480.

Schegloff, Emanuel A. 2007. *Sequence organization: A primer in conversation analysis.* Cambridge: Cambridge University Press.

Schegloff, Emanuel A. and Sacks, Harvey 1973. "Opening up closings." *Semiotica* 8: 289–327.

Schegloff, Emanuel A.; Jefferson, Gail and Sacks; Harvey 1977. "The preference for self-correction in the organization of repair in conversation," *Language* 53 (2): 361–382.

Retrieving, redoing and resuscitating turns in conversation[*]

John Local, Peter Auer and Paul Drew
Department of Language & Linguistics, University of York, United Kingdom,
Freiburg Institute for Advanced Studies, University of Freiburg, Germany
and Department of Sociology, University of York, United Kingdom

Not infrequently in conversation, a speaker launches an activity which in some way or other is intercepted by another co-participant, or is otherwise unsuccessful, such that it receives no proper uptake. Activities of this kind may simply be lost. However, speakers who did not succeed may also 'try again'. In this paper, we describe three ways of 'trying again'. We will show that apart from occurring in different sequential positions, they also display different constellations of prosodic and other formal features. While two of the relaunchings are related to the preceding first attempt by a systematic form shift, either upgrading or downgrading them, the third type appears in a variety of forms and will be shown to be formally unrelated to the resuscitated first activity.

1. Introduction

One kind of 'disturbance' to the orderliness of sequences of turns in conversation occurs when a speaker says something that is 'lost' in the subsequent interaction. The following is a particularly clear example; a bunch of (student) friends are sitting informally around a table eating dinner, and at this point the talk has turned to a friend of some of them (Rob) who is presently absent, but who may show up later. Shane has just said that Rob – the 'he' in line 1 – has problems; and Nancy has asked whether he uses "his bathroom as a darkroom". So two things about this person – his personality, and that he is a photographer – have been mentioned immediately before Michael refers again to Rob being a photographer (lines 1–2), which Shane subsequently

---

[*] We gratefully acknowledge the support of FRIAS in working at this paper.

merges back into Rob's problematic personality (*still won't keep him from being an asshole*, line 11).[1]

(1)   [Chicken Dinner:8:423–465]

```
         1    Mic:   He might be: ˙hhhh (0.6) well known photographer some
         2           day
         3           (0.2)
         4    Sha:   that's true=
         5    Mic:   =you know
         6           (1.7)
         7    Sha:   it's tru[e
         8    Viv:           [you could s-]
         9    Mic:           [s: t r a_:]nger things have happ[ened
        10    Sha:                                          [that's ri:ght
        11           and it still won't keep him from being an asshole
        12    Viv:   hnh
        13    (1.2)
        14    Sha:   ˚hn˚
        15    Mic:   hnuh=
        16    Sha:   =uh y(h)uh
        17           (2.7)
  ->    18    Nan:   what kind of c[amera does he have]
        19    Viv:                 [that's not even fair ] though they
        20           didn't [even meet him yet
        21    Sha:          [n no
        22           (0.7)
        23    Mic:   who Rob
        24           (0.3)
        25    Viv:   ye:ah.
        26    Mic:   w[ell    I    met Rob ]
        27    Viv:    [have you met him]
        28    Mic:   I met him
        29    Sha:   nuh he's a nice guy he's [j's s[orta dumb. ]
        30    Mic:                            [( [  )         ]
        31    Nan:                               [I've talked to him on the phone
```

In her highlighted turn, in line 18, Nancy asks what kind of camera Rob has. However, her enquiry is intersected by Vivian's comment (lines 19–20) concerning the unfairness

---

1.   In this paper we will be using English and German extracts. The different transcription conventions have not been homogenised. The English transcripts are orthographically simplified versions of Jefferson's system, while the German ones follow GAT (see *www.gespraechsforschung-ozs.de/heft2009/px-gat2.pdf*).

of (some) people's view about Rob's personality. Thereafter, the interaction develops in response to Vivian's comment, whilst Nancy's enquiry is simply 'lost'; it is not answered here or anywhere later throughout the mealtime conversation. Nancy has opportunities to ask again, for instance in line 31, where instead she gets caught up in the talk about which of them has met Rob. After this Nancy does not ask again about Rob's camera, nor is that mentioned at all during the rest of the conversation.

It is worth noting that Nancy's turn in line 18 is an enquiry or a question; hence when we say that this is 'lost' in the conversation, we mean that a response to her question – an answer – is relevantly absent (Sacks 1992). It was a turn for which there was some expectation that one of the recipients might respond; in Stivers and Rossano's terms, there was a "pressure to respond" (Stivers and Rossano 2010). Yet no response was forthcoming. Another feature of her turn that should be noted is that it was lost (or rather its sequential implicativeness was lost) through its having been interjected by Vivian's overlapping turn. Both Nancy's and Vivian's turns are somehow topically and sequentially connected to the prior talk; but in different ways; as it happens, subsequent talk – which does not fragment into the kind of schism reported by Egbert (1997) – focuses on Vivian's remark, to the exclusion of Nancy's question.

In the following extract (taken from the German version of the TV reality show 'Big Brother', first season) a remark by Sabrina is similarly 'lost' in the subsequent talk about boyfriends; then another remark of hers, very shortly after, suffers the same fate.

(2)   [BB I 76, 3] (about boyfriends)

```
1   Ver:  ja aber du, ich ich könnt,
          yes but listen I I could

2         das hatt ich noch nie dass ich äh echt dass ich dem
          it's never been like this before that I uhm really that I could

          (-) ich (-) ich küss dem (sogar) seine füße
          I I (even) kiss his feet

3   Jrg:  a=haha

4   Ver:  ja wirklich weißte,
          yes really you know

5         so, ich hab die füße,
          like this I have his feet

6         so so an meinem köpfchen,
          like like close to my little head

7         so weißte, so,
          like this you know like this

8         ich <<laughing>bin die füße am küssen so>
          I'm kissing his feet like this
```

```
 ->   9  Sbr: komischerweise,
                strangely enough

 ->  10       mit dem ich so lang zusammen war,
                (the one) I was together with for so long

 ->  11       den hab ich am anfang gar',
                in the beginning I didn't (( )) him

 ->  12       war so (-)
                was like

     13 Jrg: warum SAGST du dem das nicht,
                why don't you tell him that

     14       dass du den so liebst?
                that you love him so much?

     15 Ver: <<p>neh:>
                no

     16 Jrg: das sag ich meiner freundin jeden zweiten tag,
                I say that to my girlfriend every second day

     17       dass ich sie so liebe.
                that I love her so much

     18 Ver: jah: aber aber nach drei monaten?
                yes but but after three months?

 ->  19 Sbr: nee, mein freund hat mir das aber auch nicht immer,
                no, my boyfriend also didn't (( )) me that always

 ->  20       aber ich wusste dass=er'
                but I knew that he

     21 Ver: nach drei monaten
                after three month

     22 Jrg: da is noch nich das vertrauen so da oder
                at that time you don't have that much confidence or

     23 Ver: ja und das is ja noch dieses-=weißte
                yes and it's not yet this you know

     24 Sbr: ja n bissel unsicher und so
                yes a bit insecure and so on

     25 Ver: jaha und (-) und ich will mir ganz SICHer sein
              weißte
                yes and and I want to be totally sure
                you know
```

Although it is difficult to understand precisely where Sabrina's first remark in this excerpt is going (lines 9–12), it is clear enough from the left-dislocated (clefted) *mit dem ich so lang zusammen war* ('(the one) I was together with for so long', line 10) and the transitive frame *den hab ich am anfang gar* ('in the beginning I didn't (( )) him', line 11) that the subject of this remark is herself and that the object is her former boyfriend; perhaps she was going to say something like "den hab ich am Anfang gar nicht geliebt" ('in the beginning I didn't love him at all'). At any rate, her remark is interjected by Jürgen, in lines 13–14, who responds to Verena's enthusiastic report about her present boy-friend and argues that she should tell him how much she loves him. Sabrina then attempts to make another remark (lines 19–20), this time focusing not on herself but on her boyfriend (presumably: 'my boyfriend in the beginning also didn't tell me all the time that he loved me'). Once again this is interjected, this time by Verena's re-peated enquiry whether it would be right to tell a newly acquired boyfriend that she loves him (see lines 18 and then 21), and Sabrina's second attempt to contribute to the conversation between Verena and Jürgen, too, is 'lost' interactionally. There is no evi-dence that in lines 19–20 Sabrina is trying to say the same thing as she attempted ear-lier in lines 9–12; as far as one can tell, these are two independent remarks – the only connection between them being that they fail to be taken up interactionally. Neither of Sabrina's incomplete remarks is addressed by any of the other participants, and Sabrina does not subsequently return to them either. They were simply swallowed up by the ongoing conversation – they were attempted contributions that were 'lost'.

These are, as far as we can tell, not common events in conversation, but they are ones with which we can all, perhaps, empathise; we say something, or begin to say something, in an attempt to make a point, ask a question, state an opinion, whatever – and what we said or started to say is simply 'lost' in the ongoing talk. We did not get the opportunity we had hoped for or expected. It's not so much that our remark was ignored by our co-participants; it was apparently never salient in the conversation – it simply vanished. (It is quite likely that children, especially, suffer this difficulty of find-ing the moment to say something; they say it, or try to say it, and the talk engulfs them, going off in a different direction.)

But such instances of turns being 'lost' in the unfolding interaction are uncom-mon because, generally, a speaker whose turn or attempted contribution to the conver-sation is similarly intercepted by another speaker's turn, *tries again*. Whilst the losses in (1) and (2) are permanent (they never return to Nancy's question, or to whatever Sabrina was going to tell about her and a previous boyfriend), more usually this is only temporary because speakers try again and succeed in 're-launching' the turn that was initially attempted but interjected.

When a speaker's attempted turn is intercepted by another's, as is illustrated in these first two examples, that speaker may re-launch or re-initiate their turn – doing again what they first attempted; that is, they may produce what is recognisably the 'same' turn or object. They may do so – and hence attempt to re-launch their turn that was somehow intercepted by another – in broadly one of three positions.

They may *retrieve* their intercepted turn at a first opportunity after their first at-tempt. In this example, for instance, the host of a radio phone-in programme tries again to deliver his appreciation of what the caller (Dot) has just told listeners.

(3)   [VEGTALK-BBCR4.02.01.04 683s]

    1 Dot: .hh and it's fantastic

    2   (.)

-> 3 Host: [Dot that-]

    4 Cha: [w o n d e] r ful (.)

-> 5 Host: Dot that's lovely (.) I for one am going to get a tape

He recognisably re-launches his appreciative remark through lexical repetition (lines 3 and 5–6) (we will discuss other linguistic, particularly phonetic, features of such repetitions as our analysis proceeds); and he does so at an earliest opportunity, when another's 'interjecting' turn (line 4) is complete. Note that although Charles's turn in line 4 has the effect of 'interjecting' the host's turn in line 4, they began speaking simultaneously, at a point where it was entirely legitimate for either to speak, and moreover each of their turns is doing the same thing – appreciating Dot's contribution. And note also that the Host's repetition of the turn-initial address term *Dot* in line 5 displays that he is 'trying this again'; he is not continuing his initial attempt, but is re-launching it.

The host's re-initiation of his appreciation in (3) is done through repeating the start of his first attempt, immediately when the overlap is resolved. By contrast, in the second position in which speakers retrieve their intercepted turns, speakers defer 'trying again' until they have responded to the other's interjection – after which they *re-do* what they had been going to say but which was interjected. Here is an example.

(4)   [CH4247–433]

    1   Bob: how long have you been there by the way

    2   Sal: over here uh it'll be three years in November

    3   Bob: .pt wow (0.5) so you really are out of touch aren't yo(h)u

    4   hun hun (0.6) .hhhh[h

    5   Sal: [we(hh)ll I like to think I'm not totally

    6   out of touch hih .h[eh

-> 7   Bob: [well y- I [know what i]t's [like

    8   Sal: [h h   ] I [was never

    9   very in touch even when I was still in Americahh though huh

   10   uh

   11 Bob: oh okay you're that type I got you huh huh [huh huh [huh huh

   12 Sal: [heh heh [hI was

   13   always away in my own world anyway [so

   14 Bob: [huh

   15   (0.3)

-> 16 Bob: huh huh .hhhhhhhh well I know what it's like because I've

   17   wor- having lived over in Korea for almost three years uhm

   18   (0.3) it's (0.7) you know when you come back all of a sudden

   19   (0.3) the- you know the society's changed a little bit you

   20   know

Bob begins to say something that continues his observation about Sal being out of touch, and in response to Sal's defensive reply (*not totally out of touch*, lines 5–6) – a reply that she continues in lines 8–10, interjecting Bob's turn. Bob then responds (humorously) to Sal's reply, which generates some laughter (lines 11–14); after which in line 16 he re-launches what he had begun to say in line 7 (compare the highlighted sections). Again, as in (3), the lexical repetition displays that Bob is trying again, is making another attempt to tell what he had embarked on telling in line 7. Note that the character of Bob's turn in line 16 as re-launching what he attempted in line 7 is en-hanced by his repeating the turn-initial *well*, an object which is typically *not* repeated when a speaker is continuing by picking up from where they left off, but repeating just a word or two to frame their continuation. So, as in (3), Bob's repeating from the very start, i.e. from the *well*-preface, displays that he is doing this again.

A third position in which a speaker may try again to launch something they had attempted to introduce earlier in the talk, but which was abandoned when interjected by another's turn, is at the end of the topic launched by the interjecting turn. For ex-ample, in (5) Gordon re-launches the turn in which he attempted to tell Susan about his driving (lines 10 and 12), only after Susan's topic has come to an end.

(5)   [Holt:SO88:1:5:1–3]
      (Gordon and Susan are teenagers; Susan has called to tell Gordon that she failed her driving test the day before)

```
       1    Gor:   .hh.t.hhhhh hehm .mp (0.7) .mp that's really sad
       2           that's a real shame
       3                  (0.3)
       4    Sus:   tis [isn'it]
       5    Gor:       [ .t .k].t .h
       6                  (0.2)
       7    Gor:   yea[h
       8    Sus:      [hh-hh you got yours booked up
       9           (0.4)
      10    Gor:   .pt have I got mine no .hh not as of yet .hh[h I
      11    Sus:                                              [.hhh
 -> 12    Gor:   [was driving]
      13    Sus:   [what about] Fra[nce are you going to Fr] a ]nce
      14    Gor:                   [the   other   n i g h t ].t ]am I going
      15           to Fra-nce .hh[h
      16    Sus:                 [(( )
      17    Gor:                     [ehm .t.hh hu- I her- had a reply
      18           from the- (.) the woman I sent u- the .hhhhhh huhm
      19           hhh whatever it's called to you know the thing your dad
      20           wrote mh
      21           (0.3)
```

```
        22  Sus:  mhm

        ...

        ((discussion about Gordon possibly spending a year in France – 35 lines, 55
        seconds, elapse))

        ...

        54  Gor:  .ts.khhh they can s- all speak about (.) five
        55         languages .hhh[hh
        56  Sus:              [(yeanh)
        57         (0.2)
        58  Gor:  .k ff Dutch origin hhhhh the husband's English
        59         and they're living in France (0.3) .hhh .hhhhhhhhhh
        60  Sus:  blimey
        61         (1.1)
   ->   62  Gor:  great stuff uhm (0.2) I was driving last night
        63         (0.5)
        64  Gor:  .ptch ah (.) me dad brought the Land Rover home .plk got
        65         this massive great Land Rover it's it's (b)really (.)
        66         brilliant
```

In response to Susan's enquiry about whether he has booked his driving test (line 8), Gordon begins to tell her about some driving experience of his, *I was driving* (lines 10 and 12). However, almost simultaneously with that, Susan asks something else (whether Gordon is going to France, line 13), a simultaneous start that – just as happened in (3) – has the consequence of interjecting Gordon's initiation. The talk proceeds for a further minute about Gordon's plans to spend the summer in France (most of this not shown – see lines 14–62), after which he tries again, *resuscitating* what he had first said in lines 10 and 12. This time he is successful in telling Susan about a driving experience *last night* (line 62).

The focus of this study is the repeated attempts speakers make to re-launch a turn that was attempted before, but – because it was interjected by another speaker's turn – was temporarily 'lost' in the interaction. In these circumstances a speaker may try again, repeating what they had initially said. They may do so in three positions; in *retrieval* out of overlap, as illustrated in (3); by *re-doing* the turn after responding (usually briefly) to the other's interjecting turn, as in (4); or by 'resuscitating' the (temporarily) lost turn, after the topic of the interjecting turn has come to an end, as in (5). We show that 'trying again' has distinctive features in each of these three positions. Part of the distinctiveness of each lies in the variations of phonetic designs described in this report. We describe these three types of 'trying again' using English and German data. At the level of analysis we are concerned with, no systematic differences between the two languages emerge. Rather, the basic distinction is the same although the structural means by which the three types of re-launching an earlier attempt are distinguished are of course subject to the phonetic and prosodic regularities of the two languages.

We should note that our enquiry here has connections with Couper-Kuhlen's account of how prosody is deployed to cue the (topical) status of what the speaker is saying. Couper-Kuhlen (2001, 2004) focuses particularly on the prosodic cues through which speakers indicate that the upcoming turn is a new topic. In this report we are investigating the phonetics, not of new topics, but of another kind of 'newness' – doing something for another first time (as opposed to doing it another time).[2]

2.   Position 1 – Retrievals

A speaker may retrieve an intercepted turn at some earliest opportunity, usually immediately after the interception is completed, and before any other talk ensues. Let's look again at Example (3).

(3′)   [VEGTALK-BBCR4.02.01.04 683s]

	1	Dot:	.hh and it's fantastic
	2		(.)
->	3	Host:	[Dot that-]
	4	Cha:	[w o n d e] r ful (.)
->	5	Host:	Dot that's lovely (.) I for one am going to get a tape

The radio call-in host repeats what he started, and what was lost in overlap, after Charles's intercepting turn is complete, and without any further intervening talk (lines 3 and 5). Of course in this case it would have been unlikely that any further intervening talk would have developed out of Charles's turn (line 4), since that is plainly a single appreciative remark – although of course it is conceivable that the host might have decided to reiterate and somehow follow up Charles's sentiment, instead of pursuing his remark. In other cases, however, it is perhaps clearer that a speaker either eschews responding to or following up an interjecting/intercepting remark before retrieving and continuing with his/her own; or only minimally acknowledges that interjecting turn, before retrieving their own aborted turn.

(6)   [Frankel]

->	1	Rich:	I think if [you-
	2	Car:	[am I right
	3		(.)
->	4	Rich:	if you bring it into them

(7)   Heritage.III.1.14:4

	1	Jan:	alright u-yes I'll look into that u-and uh s[ee if we=
	2	Edg:	[yuh

---

2.   "This paper ... inquired what *linguistic* signs allow speakers to signal – and recipients to infer – that something new is beginning. The argument here is that one cue may be *prosodic* in nature: at points in talk where a sequence could possibly close down, a discontinuity in timing and/or a sudden, extreme shift of pitch and volume – typically upwards – at the beginning of a next turn is argued to be a cue that the turn underway is launching a new course of action or a new activity." (Couper-Kuhlen 2004: 336)

```
       3   Jan:   =can got one=
       4   Edg:   =[yes
       5   Jan:   =[eh but you're hap[py with the fir]rst   one]
  ->   6   Edg:                    [I I am n o t   ]making ] a I am not
  ->   7          making a very big issue of it=
       8   Edg:   =[(            )
       9   Jan:   =[no well it's right that we should know especially eh-
      10          you know uh
```

(8)   [SBL 3.5.11]

```
       1   Gin:   uh (.) kind of keep it in mind for next Wednesday
       2   Mil:   °m:: ° kh[hh
       3   Gin:            [and uh
       4                   (0.7)
       5   Gin:   wi[i'll see how the]t u works o[ u t   ]
  ->   6   Mil:     [I wouldn't hold]            [yeah I] wouldn't hold you
       7          to it because I: never ca:- am sure either
```

(9)   [NBIV.3.2]

```
       1   Lot:   you you walked ho:me hu:[h
       2   Emm:                          [oh: yeah it's delightful
       3          [b u t   a   l o t   o f   ] people out
  ->   4   Lot:   [did you go down to the]
       5                 (.)
  ->   6   Lot:   yeah did you go down the dime store
       7   Emm:   yeah I got my peds
```

(10) [Pumuckls]

```
       1   F:   JA; (.) GUT;
            yes (.) o.k.
       2   M:   GUT mein mÄusc[hen;
            Ok my sweetheart
       3   F:                 [JA; (-) JA;
                               yes     yes
       4   M:   also; (.) dEnn
            ok        then
       5   F:   ja; (.) GUT; (.)
            yes       all right
       6   M:   viele KÜSSch[en (-) ja;
            many  kisses          ok
       7   F:               [ja (.) ja;
                             yes     yes
       8   auch; (-)
            also
```

```
    9   M:  nich?=
            right?
->  10  F:  =i(k)  [(nehm)  heut   die`]
            I'll          take   today  the
    11  M:         [(              so,) ]
                    (   like     this)
    12         ich ruf heut noch[mal AN. (-) ja?
               I'll call you back today           ok?
->  13  F:                     [JA:; (-) ick
                                yes       I'll
->  14         nehm heut die PUmuckls mit;
               take today the munchkins with me
```

Such cases as these in which a speaker recovers his/her turn out of overlap retrieving their aborted turns in immediate proximate position after the interjections are by now quite familiar (e.g. Jefferson 2004, Schegloff 1987). In (6) and (7), overlapped speakers retrieve their turns immediately, whilst in Examples (8)–(10) the retrievals follow minimal acknowledgements of the others' interjecting turns (*yeah*, line 6 and *ja::* in line 13, respectively).

So in cases of such first position retrievals, speakers whose turn is intersected and temporarily halted elide the intersecting turn, and then retrieve their turn at a first opportunity by recycling the aborted turn, through lexical repetition.

These first opportunity retrievals share a variety of phonetic characteristics. Their retrieved parts are typically (though not always) shorter than the first production in overlap; they maintain the overall design of the pitch contour of their first production and its accentual pattern; their overall pitch height is the same as or lower than the first production, their pitch range is typically not greater than the first production and they are not noticeably louder than the first production. So for instance in fragment (3) the comparable parts of the first two words of host's retrieval at line 5 (*dot that*) are some 67 milliseconds shorter (16%) than his first (cut off) production, the overall pitch is lower and the pitch range is 2.2 semitones narrower (Figure 1).

Similarly in fragment (7) the duration of Edgerton's second version of *I am not making a* is 100 milliseconds (some 10%) shorter than the first, the overall pitch contour is similar (highest peak associated with *not*, with the pitch dropping thereafter) and has the same accentual pattern; the second version is noticeably lower overall in pitch. It has a marginally narrower pitch range (1.2 semitones) and is quieter than the first production (Figure 2).

Figure 3 provides an annotated pitch trace and indication of relative intensity (indicated by the dotted trace) of Millie's first and second versions of *I wouldn't hold* in fragment (8). Again we can observe the relatively lower pitch of the second production (the pitch range is only marginally narrower in the second production – 0.5 ST), the duration of the second production is 11% shorter than the first. We can think of such

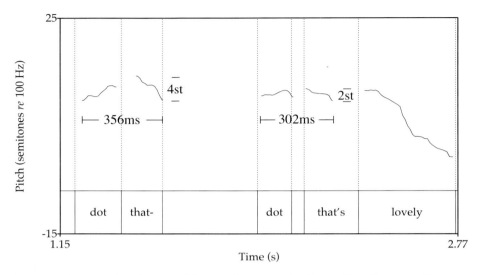

Figure 1. Annotated pitch trace of first production and redone talk in Fragment (3)
VEGTALK-BBCR4.02.01.04 683s

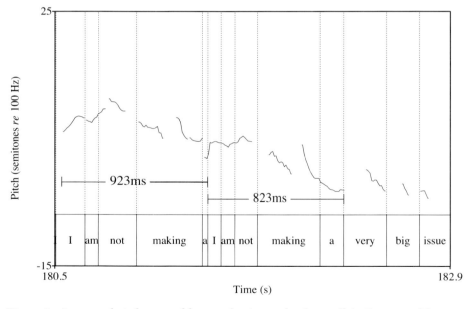

Figure 2. Annotated pitch trace of first production and redone talk in Fragment (7)
Heritage.III.1.14:4

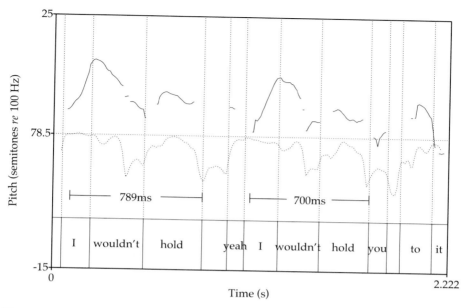

Figure 3. Annotated pitch and amplitude traces of first production and redone talk in Fragment (8) SBL 3.5.11

constellations of characteristics as a kind of phonetic 'downgrading' or subordination.[3] The downgrading is, so we claim, a reference to the first attempt. There is a systematic contrast between the first and the second launching of the activity which turns the second version into a *hearably* second version, one whose production can proceed undisturbed and without concurring or competing talk by the co-participant.

3.   Position 2 – Redoings

In the second position in which speakers try again to launch something which was interjected and aborted, they re-do what they tried to do earlier (cf. Rauniomaa 2008 for a recent account restricted to the verbal level). *Redoings* differ from retrievals both interactionally and phonetically. As with retrievals, we find participants redoing talk and pursuing actions that they have begun previously but in these cases the redone talk may either have been intercepted by overlapping talk or may not have received appropriate uptake in next position where a co-participant pursues a different line of action. Unlike retrievals, redoings are not undertaken at a first possible opportunity. As we

---

3.   Recent work by Barrow (2009) suggests that where a speaker immediately recycles talk out of overlap following a co-ordinate start-up of talk by two participants, the recycle will be produced with 'upgraded' phonetic features.

have already seen in fragment (4), the co-participant produces talk which is responded to (often minimally) before the subsequent attempt is launched. Redoings regularly redo materials that have been disattended or not aligned with by participants who are pursuing their own lines of talk – to this extent redoings may on occasion come off as 'persistence' in the face of problems with getting talk done. Phonetically, in redoings speakers do *not* 'downgrade' the design of their second attempts relative to their first attempts. Indeed we regularly find some kind of upgrading – phonetic and/or lexico-syntactic. Fragments (4) and (11)–(13) provide exemplification:

(11)   [NB:IV:10:26]

```
        1    Lot:    so he says here take this so he e-she got that and i
        2            and it's never bothered her
        3                    (0.2)
        4    Emm:    .t.hha[hhhhhhhh
        5    Lot:           [.t.hhhh a[nd get]    that] in the tube Emma
        6    Emm:                    [ oh  ]    gah-]hh
        7    Emm:    alright dea[r
        8    Lot:               [get the tube and now tonight I I took a
        9            toothpick and I .hh and I put the[th-ih s]tuff] down in my
       10    Emm:                                    [m m ]h m ]
       11    Lot:    uh- and my nails yo[u k n o w]
       12    Emm:                       [isn't  this] funny you and I would
       13            have it.h
       14                    (0.4)
       15    Emm:    this is ri[dicul ] ous ]
  ->   16    Lot:              [e v ry]body]'s got it .hh isn't that funny we
  ->   17            were in a p-uh[:
       18    Emm:                  [oh god it's terrible Lottie my toenails
       19            .hehh they just look so sick those big toenails it just u-
       20            makes me sick you know they're just (.) u-dead (.)
       21            everything's dead I d- I sat out (.) today and I said my
       22            God am I just (.) dying it's (.) like I'm ossified
  ->   23    Lot:    no I- we were in some [place uh don't know if it was
       24    Emm:                          [((sniff))
       25    Lot:    Bullock's or someplace (0.4) I guess it was Bullock's
       27            and somebody was talking about it and I bet there were
       28            .hhh ten people around there and they all started say
       29            well they had the same thing en I know like Doctor Compton
       30            says it's from the damn .p detergent
```

In fragment (11) Emma and Lottie, though orienting to the same topical material, pursue rather different tacks. As we join this fragment, Emma and Lottie have been talking about a treatment ("Vioform") for a fungal foot infection which has been troubling Emma – a topic which has arisen earlier in the call. Here Lottie is reporting that an acquaintance has benefitted from its use and at line 8 exhorts Emma to buy some soon (*tonight*). Lottie then begins to relate how she's applied the same cream to her nails using a toothpick. As she gets to the end of this telling Emma comes in overlap and rather than, for instance, pursuing an enquiry about Lottie's use of the product and its effect on her condition, comments on the oddness of the fact (*isn't this funny...*) that both suffer from the same condition. This gets no uptake from Lottie and following a (0.4) gap Emma pursues her line with an assessment *this is ridiculous*. Just as she has begun to produce the adjectival part of this assessment Lottie starts in overlap with what looks like the beginning of a counter-version – they are not alone or unusual in having the infection, it is widespread – *everybody's got it*. She then embarks on a telling *we were in a p=uh* which gets overlapped by Emma, whose talk displays no attentiveness to where Lottie's turn might be headed but gives instead an over-the-top version of her own reactions to the condition. After a terse initial rejection of Emma's formulation (*no*), Lottie's turn at line 23 redoes her earlier talk from 16–17 (slightly altered: *a* changed to *some*) and goes on to produce evidence to support her claim that she and Emma are by no means the only individuals suffering from this condition.

Fragment (12) is again drawn from recordings of the German Big Brother programme mentioned earlier. Here, Verena is about to leave the house after having been voted out. The other participants in this fragment, Sabrina and Jürgen, have been acting out being in a relationship during their stay in the Big Brother house.

(12)   [BB80:Kartoffeln]

```
      1   Ver:   nee aber ich hab ja nich mehr LANG.  (-)
                 no, but I don't have much longer you know

      2          ich muss ZWEI SCHEIne schreiben. (0.3)
                 I have to take two exams

      3          ZWEI SCHEIne.
                 two exams

      4          (0.5)

      5          ich hab bis? ich hab neun scheine schon geschrieben.
                 I have until I've already done nine of them

      6          (1.5)

      7   Sbr:   da wärst ja DOOF.
                 you'd be such an idiot {not to take them}

      8   Ver:   ja wenn ich die zwei scheine nich mehr schrei[ben
                 würde
                 yeah if I didn't do these two exams {I'd be a fool}

 ->   9   Jrg:   ((enters through the kitchen door))        [die
                 Kartoffeln, (-)

                                                            the
          potatoes
```

```
->  10        sollen die in WÜRfeln geschnitten [werden?]
              should they be cut in cubes?

    11 Ver:                                     [uh hh ]hh

    12        (0.3)

    13 Sbr:  [hallo sch]atz
               hi darling

    15 Ver:  [.h h h h ]

    14        (0.6)

    16 Sbr:  was denn hier (0.3) was IS mit DIR?
              what's here           what's wrong with you?

    17        (0.2)

    18 Jrg:  <<p, whispering voice>kannste gleich mitgehen am
              sonntach?>
              you can join (her) on Sunday

    19 Sbr:  ich war doch DRAUSsen bei dem [(        schlafen)]
              I did go outside                        sleep

    20 Jrg:                                [JA NIX, is doch nix
                                                       mehr] LOS
                                           yes nothing there's
                                           nothing on any longer

    21        hängst nur noch hier im zimmer (-) LANGweilig.
              you only hang around in your room (-) boring

->  22        sollen die kartoffeln in würfel [geschnitten werden
              should the potatoes be cut into cubes

    23 Sbr:                                   [((laughing      ))

    24        (0.2)

    25 Jrg:  JA oder NEIN.
             yes or no

    26        (0.2)

    27 Jrg:  ↑JA.
             yes

    28        (0.5)

    29       ÄTZend.
             that sucks
```

At the beginning of the fragment Verena and Sabrina are alone in the bedroom and
Verena is talking to Sabrina about her university exams. She says she wants to continue her university studies because she has completed almost all of her tests, and it
would be stupid not to take the final two. At this point Jürgen comes to the door of the
bedroom from the kitchen where he is busy preparing dinner and asks whether the

potatoes should be cut into cubes (*soll = n die kartoffeln in würfeln geschnitten werden*). Neither Verena nor Sabrina respond directly to his question: Verena giggles, Sabrina first greets him ('hi darling', line 13) and then asks him what's the matter. Jürgen now plays the guy who is cross with his 'girl-friend' because she neglects him. Instead of responding to Sabrina's greeting he suggest that she joins Verena when she leaves the house as their 'relationship' has ground into tedium (*ja nix, is doch nix mehr hängst nur noch hier im zimmer (-) langweilig*). Following this at line 22, he redoes his earlier talk, reorganising the word order (the first version starts with the topicalised/prolep-tic noun phrase *die kartoffeln*, while the second version integrates the subject NP into a verb-first question: *soll = n die kartoffeln in würfel...*), and, after a 0.2-second gap, adds *ja oder nein* thus emphasising that he is seeking a direct (type conforming) re-sponse (Raymond 2003, this volume). But even now the answer is not forthcoming (the *ja* in line 27 refers back to lines 20–21 and reaffirms his point, and so does the evaluation in line 29).

In fragment (13) we again find a turn being disattended by its intended recipient. Here a family around the dinner table is chatting and bickering. Present are Mom, older brother Wesley, his girlfriend Pru, and the sisters Beth, who is taping the video for her college course, and Virginia. The turns of interest here are those of Wesley at lines 11 and 14. Beth and Virginia (along with their brother Wesley and Mom) are ar-guing about what a boy (Paul) called, or did not call, them. At line 7, Virginia asserts that whatever she was called so was her sister Beth – a claim which Beth rejects at line 8 and Virginia reasserts at line 9. At this point the bickering abates and their brother Wesley comes in at line 11 and asks Beth what the boy called her. He doesn't get an answer; Virginia, rather than Beth, speaks next in terminal overlap with his turn. She addresses her talk to Beth (rather than Wesley), re-asserting her earlier claim from line 7 and rejecting Beth's denial. Immediately on completion of Virginia's turn Wesley launches his question again and at line 15 gets a response (albeit one which deflects his question) from Beth.

(13)   Virginia: 30:18:54

```
       1    BET:    Paul didn't like you anyway
       2    VIR:    ew(h)ellh hhow do [you know he always ([          )]
       3    WES:                      [ehh huh huh
       4    BET:                                      [umcause what he ca]ll
       5            you
       6            (.)
       7    VIR:    well he called you the same thing
       8    BET:    he did not [(        ) that]
       9    VIR:               [yes he did he did] so he did so
      10            (0.7)
  ->  11    WES:    what did he call [you
      12    VIR:                     [I'm sorry Beth he did say that about
```

```
        13              you y(h)ou can't tell me he didn't cause he told me
->      14  WES:        what did he call you Beth
        15  BET:        that's none of anybody el[se's business] (you all talk)=
        16  VIR:                                [I k n o w   ]
        17  BET:        =(like that and you sit there and [you-)
        18  WES:                                          [(he) call you honey
        19              (0.5)
        20  BET:        no
```

The phonetic characteristics of these second attempts are noticeably different from those found in retrievals. The comparable parts of the second versions of redoings are 'upgraded' lexically and/or prosodically and display combinations of some or all of the following: unlike retrievals they are not shorter than the first versions (they may display longer durations), they routinely exhibit increased loudness and have higher pitch than their first productions. They may, as is the case with fragments (11)–(13) also display differences in their lexico-syntactic formatting, which is rare in the case of retrievals.

In fragment (4), the first production (line 7) and the redoing (line 16) have the same accentual pattern (\I know \what it's \like – where backslashes indicate the stressed syllables of the metrical feet). The comparable parts of the redoing have a somewhat greater duration than the first version (first version 745ms, second version 786ms). However, while the two versions have similar overall pitch contours the second is audibly (and visibly) higher in the speaker's range than the first (e.g. the pitch peaks associated with *I know* portion is 2 ST higher in the second than the first).[4] The second version is also audibly louder overall than the first. This is illustrated in Figure 4 where the continuous trace represents pitch and the dotted trace represents relative intensity.

As Figure 4 shows, the duration, pitch and loudness characteristics of the comparable part (*we were in*) of the redoing in fragment (11) are upgraded relative to the first production. The redoing is some 10% longer than the first version, and the pitch of the redoing is overall higher than the first production even though its pitch range is slightly wider (first production 4.6 ST, redoing 5.4 ST); the maximum pitch of the redoing is noticeably higher (3.5 ST) than that of the first version.

In Fragment (13) the second attempt (in which the intended recipient is specifically named) is again noticeably louder than the first. Insofar as it is possible to tell (with the overlapping talk) the durations of the comparable parts *what did he call you* are not noticeably different. Certainly the second is not shorter than the first. The pitch of *what did he* is higher in the redoing than the first version. Fragment (13) also illustrates a property of redoings that is not found in retrievals: accentual patterns of second versions may be different from those in their first production. Where this happens

---

4.   We note here that there appears to be a difference in the alignment of the rising pitch/pitch peak associated with the *I know* portion of the utterance.

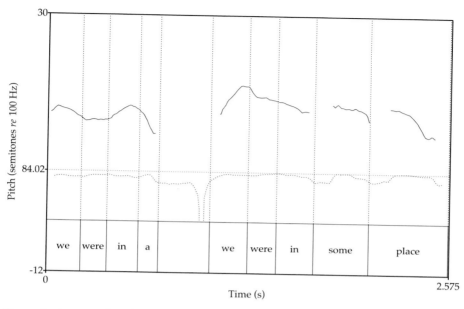

Figure 4. Annotated pitch and amplitude traces of first production and redone talk in Fragment (11) NB:IV:10:26

the second version typically exhibits a greater number of pitch accents than the first production. In the first production of *what did he call you* (line 11), the main accent of the turn occurs with *call* (*/what did he/call/you* – where underlining indicates the locus of the main pitch accent and backslashes indicate the stressed syllables of the metrical feet). In the second it occurs with *you* (*/what did he/call/you/Beth*) with *Beth* occupying a separate intonation phrase.[5]

Fragment (12), from the German corpus, is somewhat different and illustrates a version of upgrading that we do not have represented elsewhere in our English redoings data. Talk immediately after the first doing in line 18 is characterised by a striking change in phonation type (whispery-voiced). This taken-back articulation occurs on a TCU which is intended as a strong attack on Sabrina (he wants her to leave the container which is tantamount to 'splitting up'). In the following lines, Jürgen resumes modal phonation, but his voice remains in a low pitch and intensity register. There is no prosodic break between his lines 20–21, designed as a complaint directed to Sabrina, and his redoing in line 22, which returns to the issue of chopping the potatoes. A long period of friction at the end of *langweilig* begins with palatal resonance and changes at around two thirds of its duration to alveolar as it moves into *soll*. The redoing itself is characterised by a noticeable overall *lowering* of pitch when compared to

---

5.   The intensity peak associated with *you* in the first production is the consequence of Virginia's overlapping *I'm* in line 12.

the first version, as can be seen by comparing Figures 5 and 6. In addition, the range of the pitch movement is strongly reduced; while in the first version, we observe a major pitch movement in the nucleus with a L-tone on the accented syllable *WÜR-* and a subsequent H-tone which reaches its phonetic peak only late on *schnit-*, and then sharply falls,[6] the LH tone sequence in the redoing is so flat that it is hardly recognisable in the pitch extraction; the very minor peak is already reached on *-fel*, and the remainder of the intonational phrase remains almost level, which makes the whole pitch movement sound subdued. In its sequential embedding, this prosodic re-contextualisation encodes anger of someone 'about to explode', and even 'restrained agressivity' (as evidenced by the apodictic *yes or no* in line 25); this interactional upgrading is paradoxically achieved by phonetic reduction. The significance of this is that in none of the cases of retrievals (in English or German) do we find similar differences.

As in retrievals, speakers who format redoings in the way described (i.e., by upgrading them) establish a contrast between the first and the second doing, thus making the second a hearably second doing. But since the second doing is upgraded rather than downgraded, as in the retrievals, this format of 'trying again' often conveys a speaker's insistence on getting his or her turn. Apart from prosody, expansions of the utterance such as Jürgen's *yes or no* in Fragment (12) or Wesley's *Beth* in (11) also play a role in signalling this insistence.

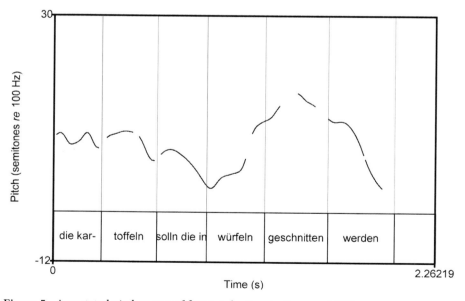

Figure 5. Annotated pitch traces of first production in Fragment (12)

---

6.   The LH-tone is typical of the Cologne accent (cf. Bergmann 2008) and highly marked among the other accents of German.

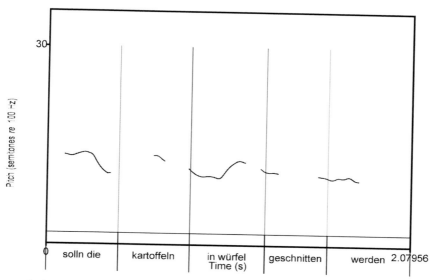

Figure 6. Annotated pitch traces of the redoing in Fragment (12)

4.   Position 3 – Resuscitations

Whereas retrievals exhibit downgrading, and redoings exhibit upgrading, careful examination of resuscitations – exemplified by fragments (5) and (14)–(16) – suggests that they do not appear to have a particular cluster of phonetic characteristics associated with their production. Rather, their phonetic design appears to be related to the sequential and interactional position in which they occur.

Thus, in fragment (5) Gordon's first, intercepted, attempt at lines 10–11 to tell Susan about his driving comes off phonetically as an afterthought to/ continuation of his self-querying response to her question as to whether he has booked a driving test. Immediately following the final word of his response to Susan (*yet*), Gordon produces a 0.3 second inbreath which is followed immediately without a break by the *I* of *I was driving*. *I was driving* itself is produced quickly (four syllables in 540 ms). As with the *not as of yet*, which precedes it, it has a relatively narrow pitch span and is centered below the middle of his pitch range; it is not noticeably louder than his preceding talk. That is, it has none of the characteristics routinely associated with 'new beginnings' (Couper-Kuhlen 2001, 2004), which we found in the redoings discussed in the last section.

By comparison, when Gordon resuscitates this topic telling at line 62, he does so disjunctively, as a clear announcement of news following joint sequence closing. His turn begins with a loud, relatively high pitched *uhm* which is centered some 4 ST higher than his immediately preceding talk (*great stuff*), itself around mid in his range.

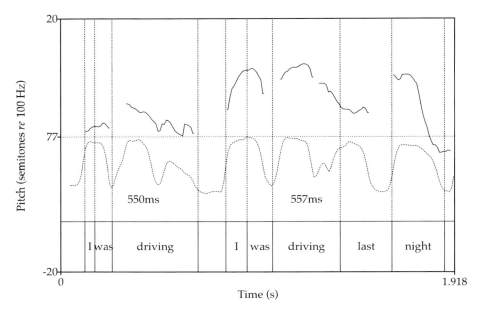

Figure 7. Annotated pitch and amplitude traces of first production and redone talk in Fragment (5) Holt:SO88:1:5:1–3

The first three syllables of *I was driving last night* are stepped up in pitch again to just under 200Hz (just over half an octave above the middle of Gordon's pitch range), while the remainder stays high in his range only falling to low at the very end of the diphthong in *night* (this results in an audibly wide pitch range for this talk (13.9 ST) – noticeably different from that of the first version (5 ST)). Some of these differences are pictured in Figure 7.

In fragment (14) at line 2, John's *die is* is anaphorically tied to, and hearable as the beginning of some kind of an assessment of *die marmelade* which he has just topicalised at line 1. Adriana's turn at line 3, which is produced as a response to John's question at line 1, along with Jürgen and Sabrina's teasing accusations at lines 4, 9 and 6 and John's response to and rejection of them (*was? nee nee*, lines 7–8), means that he does not redo his assessment at a first, next opportunity. But at line 22 John produces a sequentially disjunctive *nee* which serves to indicate that (a) subsequent talk is not to be taken as connected to his immediate prior, and (b) it will link to some earlier material (cf. Local 2004); and at line 24 he resuscitates his earlier intercepted assessment: *die = s lecker die marmelade.*

(14)   BB80 – 230–276sec

```
  -> 2 Jhn:   hast du schon DIE: (-) die sie mitjebracht hat
              probiert, die marmelade?
              have you already tried the one: (-) which she brought us, the jam?
```

```
-> 3  Jhn: [di[e is
             it is

   4  Adr: [nee
             no

   5  Jrg:    [hast das HALbe glas gegessen wa?]
              you've eaten up half of the jar right?

   6  Sbr:    [wo du schon reingefallen bist? ] ((laughs))
              which you plunged into?

   7  Jhn: was? (-)
           what?

   8       [nee=nee                              ]
            no no

   9  Jrg: [da haste ja das HALbe glas gegessen wa?]
            so you ate half the jar then?

  10  Jhn: HIE:R (-) HALLO: (-),
           here (-) listen

  11       verONa hat heut morjen da:jehang (-),
           Verona spent the morning

  12       inne WOHNstube und brötchen jegessen.
           in the lounge eating bread buns

  13  Jrg: ach so.
           ah I see

  14  Sbr: ach so?
           really?

  15  Jhn: hm=hm.
           hm hm

  16       ((cut, Verona cleaning her teeth, 14 secs))

  17       ((cut back))

  18  Adr: ja da hat se richtig geFUTTERT ne?
           yes she really stuffed herself then?

  19  Jhn: schön LANGsam,
           really slowly

  20       (-) aber auch immer so (1.0) [VIEL marmelade?]
           but she always took loads of jam like this

  21  Adr:                              [((laughs))    ]

  22  Jhn: nee ick hatte jestern aber auch schon von der
           marmeLADE jekostet? (-)
           no but I'd tried this jam already yesterday
```

```
      23        als sie DIE jebracht hat hab ich mir die hier inn joghurt
                rin=jemacht.
                when she brought this one I put some of it in my yoghurt

  ->  24        (0.3) .ptth (0.3) die=s LECker die marmelade.
                  ((sucks))            it's delicious this jam
```

John's first production of *die ist* is temporally contiguous with his prior talk and rhythmically and prosodically integrated as a continuation of his turn at line 1. The overall pitch of this turn is just above mid in his range, and the highest pitch is coincident with the penultimate (lexically stressed) syllable of *marmelade* which ends in a fall to relatively low in his range. The pitch of *die is* begins a little below the end of this fall and rises slightly before becoming inaudible in the overlapping talk. Insofar as it is audible, *die is* sounds slightly less loud than the preceding talk.

Although John's resuscitation at line 24 is separated by some 0.7 seconds from the end of his immediately prior talk (*joghurt rin jemacht*), it too is designed to come off as non-disjunctive in relation to that prior. Between the end of his turn at line 23 and the beginning of his resuscitation, John's making a sucking noise in appreciation of the jam. His verbal assessment follows. The pitch at the beginning of *die = s lecker* matches that at the end of *jemacht* and comes off as designed to be prosodically related to it rather than disjunctive: it is lower in John's pitch range and narrower in pitch range than his prior talk. Figures 8 and 9 provide graphical representations of the relationships in the two instances:

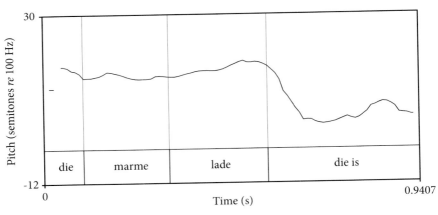

Figure 8. Annotated pitch trace of lines 2–3 (*die marmelade die ist*) of Fragment (14) BB80 – 230–276sec

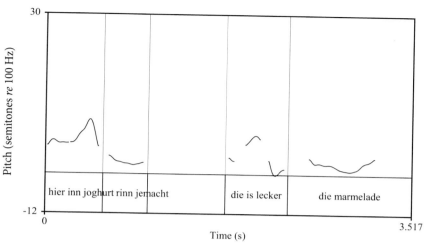

Figure 9. Annotated pitch trace of line 23 (*in joghurt rin jemacht die = s lecker die marmelade*) of Fragment (14) BB80 – 230–276sec

The design of the resuscitation in fragment (15), and its relationship to its first attempt, are somewhat different.

(15)   [NB:II:2:1–2]

```
        1    Emm:  [.hhhhh] Bud just left ]to play golf he's got to go to Riverside
        3    Nan:  [ (0.4)  ]  y e h   a h ]
        4    Nan:  [o h    ]
        5    Emm:  [in a compan]y deal so .t.h[hhhhh
        6    Nan:                            [oh
  ->    7    Emm:  God [i t  rih- ]
        8    Nan:      [to River]side today
        9    Emm:  .hhh yeah they they're going tee off at twelve it's a company
       10          deal so (.) the couple was supposed to come down to (.)
       11          last night and you know k-Harry and Katherine they're uh
       12          keh cause Harry was going play k-
       13    Nan:  oh[:
       14    Emm:    [and company and then .hhh there was a death in their
       15          family so (.) [.hhh
       16    Nan:               [aw
       17               (.)
  ->   18    Emm:  hey God uh this has really been a week hasn't it=
       19    Nan:  =oh it really has
       20    Emm:  i[t's r e a ]
       21    Nan:  [gee it rea]lly it really ha[s
       22    Emm:                             [I won't even turn the tee vee on
```

Here both the first production and the resuscitation are done as disjunctive news tell-ings. Following Emma's informing at line 1, Nancy produces a news receipt *oh* and at line 5 Emma increments her own turn with a construction which ends with a turn-yielding trail-off conjunctional (Local and Kelly 1986) produced with creaky voice at the bottom of her pitch range (*so*), followed by a long inbreath. In overlap with this in-breath, Nancy produces another *oh*-token. Emma's next turn at line 7 is phonetically very different from that which she produced at line 5. It comes off as an exclamation which prospectively opens up a new topic: *God it rih-*. This utterance has the phonetic characteristics of new topic starts: specifically, it is strikingly louder and higher in pitch than Emma's preceding talk. The highest pitch of *God* is 8 ST higher than *Bud* (the highest part of Emma's preceding talk) and over two octaves (27 ST) higher than the highest part of *so*. Figure 10 provides a graphical representation of these differences.

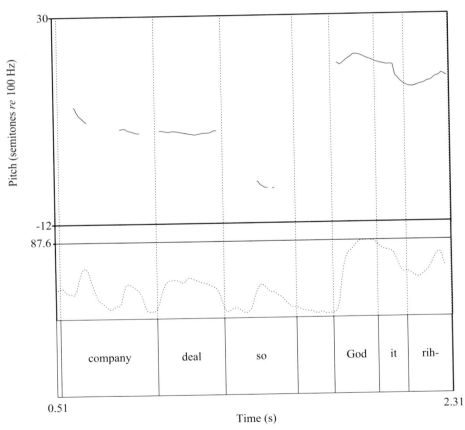

Figure 10. Annotated pitch and amplitude traces of line 5 (*company deal so*) and line 7 (*God it rih-*) of Fragment (15) NB:II:2:1–2

However, Emma's attempted 'new' (touched off) topic launch in line 7 is intercepted by Nancy's seeking some kind of clarification about Emma's announcement in line 1 concerning Bud (her husband). Emma cuts off midword, then responds to Nancy's enquiry, bringing it to a close with another trail-off *so* (lines 9–15). Following Nancy's sequence closing appreciation at line 16 and a brief gap, Emma embarks on what is recognisable as a second attempt at her earlier turn, *hey God uh this has really been a week hasn't it* (line 18). Again this turn has a disjunctive phonetic design that sets it off from the prior talk. It is noticeably louder overall than Emma's immediately prior talk and noticeably higher in pitch. *Death in their family so* is on average 5 ST below Emma's mean pitch while *Hey God uh this has really* is on average 5 ST above her mean. The resuscitation begins 17.4 ST higher than the prior talk ends, and the highest part of the resuscitation (*hey*) is over half an octave (8.4 ST) higher than the highest part of Emma's immediately prior talk (*death*). In its sequential context, this phonetic design brings off Emma's talk as a new beginning.

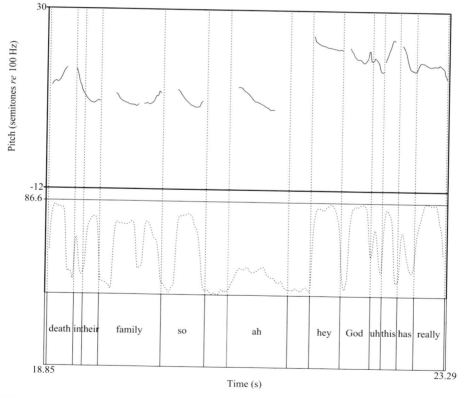

Figure 11. Annotated pitch and amplitude traces of lines 14–15 (*death in their family so*) and line 18 (*hey God uh this has real*) of Fragment (15) NB:II:2:1–2

In sum, there is no general phonetic pattern which can be systematically linked to resuscitations. If a speaker 'tries again' at a considerable temporal and sequential distance from his or her first attempt, the prosodic packaging of the resuscitation seems to be entirely dependent on its immediately prior sequential context. There is then, in this case, no reference to the first attempt. The second attempt is displayed as a second *first* attempt.

5.   Conclusion

In this paper, we have considered some of the ways in which co-participants can re-launch activities which failed to be successful at first try, either because they had to be broken off or because they did not receive adequate uptake. By relaunching their activities, co-participants can (and often do) prevent these failed first attempts from getting 'lost' in conversation. On the basis of English and German data, we were able to identify three types of such relaunchings in different sequential positions and characterised by different sets of formal – mostly prosodic – features, termed retrievals, redoings and resuscitations here. All of them are formally marked by the fact that some of the lexico-syntactic materials of the first attempt are also used for the second attempt. In the case of retrievals out of simultaneous talk, speakers deal with their potentially lost activity immediately after its occurrence, with no or only minimal response to the overlapping participant's talk. Compared to the overlapped first version, the retrieval version is formally downgraded, i.e. it may be delivered faster, with less loudness or at a lower pitch level. The pitch make-up of the first attempt is usually re-used but sometimes attenuated (less pitch range, etc.). In redoings, the speaker's first attempt is not regularly intercepted by prolonged stretches of simultaneous talk; rather the speaker drops out immediately and cedes to the co-participant's turn which can be properly dealt with before the re-doing occurs. Formally, the opposite from retrievals can be observed: while the pitch contour of the first attempt is also regularly reused, redoings are upgraded, giving them a touch of insistence. But note that both retrievals and redoings establish a formal relationship, and therefore a link, between the first and the second try. They are produced so that they can be heard as second attempts. This is different in the third case: in resuscitations, no systematic relationship between the form of the first attempt and that of the second attempt was found. Resuscitation is done in whatever prosodic format seems appropriate in the immediate sequential context in which the activity is resuscitated. We have noted that resuscitations sometimes occur at a considerable distance from the first attempts. It may be argued that they were simply forgotten by co-participants. Our analysis suggests a different interpretation. Instead of seeing the speakers' non-orientation at the first attempt in this third type of relaunching as a 'natural' consequence of these first attempts having been forgotten, we suggest that re-launching co-participants *construe conversational memory*: the time-depth of a conversation as it unfolds in time is made interactionally real by participants' (non-)orientation to prior events. Resuscitated (failed) first activities are treated as something beyond conversational memory; therefore, they are second attempts only for the analysts, working with a transcript and therefore free from memory constraints. For the participants, they are second *first* attempts.

References

Barrow, Christopher 2009. Phonetics of talk-in-interaction: Recycled talk out of overlap. Dissertation submitted for MA by Research. Department of Language and Linguistic Science, University of York.

Bergmann, Pia 2008. Regionalspezifische Intonationsverläufe im Kölnischen. Tübingen: Niemeyer.

Couper-Kuhlen, Elizabeth 2001. "Interactional prosody: High onsets in reason-for-the-call turns." *Language in Society* 30: 29–53.

Couper-Kuhlen, Elizabeth 2004. "Prosody and sequence organization: The case of new beginnings." In: *Sound patterns in interaction*, Elizabeth Couper-Kuhlen and Cecilia E. Ford (eds.), 335–376. Amsterdam: Benjamins.

Egbert, Maria M. 1997. "Schisming: the collaborative transformation from a single conversation to multiple conversations." *Research on Language and Social Interaction* 30 (1): 1–52.

Jefferson, Gail 2004. "A sketch of some orderly aspects of overlap in natural conversation." In: Conversation analysis: Studies from the first generation, Gene Lerner (ed.), 43–59. Amsterdam: Benjamins.

Local, John 2004. "Getting back to prior talk: and-uh(m) as a back-connecting device." In: *Sound patterns in interaction*, Elizabeth Couper-Kuhlen and Cecilia E. Ford (eds.), 377–400. Amsterdam: Benjamins.

Local, John and Kelly, John 1986. "Projection and 'silences': Notes on phonetic and conversational structure." *Human Studies* 9: 185–204.

Rauniomaa, Mirka 2008. *Recovery through repetition. Returning to prior talk and taking a stance in American-English and Finnish conversations.* Acta Universitatis Ouluensis B85. Oulu: Oulu University Press [http://herkules.oulu.fi/isbn9789514289248/ isbn9789514289248.pdf].

Raymond, Geoffrey 2003. "Grammar and social organization: Yes/No interrogatives and the structure of responding." *American Sociological Review* 68: 939–967.

Sacks, Harvey 1992. *Lectures on conversation* Vol. 1 (Fall 1964-Spring 1968). Oxford: Blackwell: 292–299 (Spring 1966, lecture 4b).

Schegloff, Emanuel A. 1987. "Recycled turn beginnings: A precise repair mechanism in conversation's turn-taking organisation." In: *Talk and Social Organization*, Graham Button and John R. E. Lee (eds.), 70–85. Clevedon: Multilingual Matters.

Stivers, Tanya and Rossano, Federico 2010. "Mobilizing response." *Research on Language and Social Interaction* 41 (1): 3–31.

Doing confirmation with *ja/nee hoor*

Sequential and prosodic characteristics of a Dutch discourse particle*

Harrie Mazeland and Leendert Plug
University of Groningen, The Netherlands
and University of Leeds, United Kingdom

This paper offers sequential-interactional and prosodic observations on the confirmation forms *ja hoor/nee hoor* ('yes'+ particle *hoor*/ 'no' + *hoor*) in Dutch talk-in-interaction, as part of a larger analysis of the form and function of the particle *hoor*. We show that *ja/nee hoor* is used as a marked confirmation in sequentially specifiable context-types. When used as a response to queries, the speaker marks doing confirmation as programmatically motivated. When used in environments that further sequence expansion, *ja/nee hoor* resists such expansion. Thus, the use of *ja/nee hoor* is motivated by an orientation to multiple levels of discourse organization. *Ja/nee hoor* is associated with recurrent pitch contours which are systematically distributed across environments of use. We discuss our findings in relation to previous findings on the use of *hoor* in Dutch.

1. Introduction

Participants in Dutch talk in interaction routinely use a number of discourse particles to articulate or fine-tune the discursive status of the ongoing turn. Several of these particles occur in clause-final, or tag-position, and have a fairly straightforward response-eliciting function; *hè* is a particularly common example (see Jefferson 1981). But Dutch also has a final particle that does not appear to elicit a particular type of response: the particle *hoor* (literally 'hear', but native speakers of Dutch do not link its meaning to 'hearing'). Its general function has been described as retro-actively reinforcing or emphasizing an aspect of the preceding utterance (Kirsner 2000, 2003, Wenzel 2002: 228), but depending on its specific environment of use and the kind of action implemented by the utterance it is attached to, *hoor* may be said to fulfill such heterogeneous functions

---

* We thank the editors, two anonymous reviewers, and Bob Kirsner, Tanya Stivers and Trevor Benjamin for their comments on drafts of this paper.

as mitigating the action (ten Have 2007: 126–128), signaling the speaker's sincerity (Berenst 1978), downtoning the assertion that the speaker is making (Kirsner 2000), or articulating the action's reassuring character (Kirsner 2003).

Kirsner and colleagues (Kirsner and Deen 1990, Kirsner et al. 1994, Kirsner and van Heuven 1996, Kirsner 2000, 2003) have attempted to account for the various functions of *hoor* in terms of a contextually-governed interplay between four semantic parameters: 'no-question status', 'recipient involvement', 'dominance' and 'friendliness'. While their work offers an elegant model for dealing with the variation in function associated with *hoor*, their notion of 'context' is rather abstract, and their analysis based mainly on isolated utterances. An important question is whether a similar characterization of function would be arrived at if the starting point of analysis were a detailed consideration of instances of the particle in actual use.

Mazeland (2010) proposes a description of the use of *hoor* that is based on an analysis of real, specifiable sequential environments in which the particle is used. In this paper we elaborate on a subset of Mazeland's data: about 30 cases in which *hoor* is used for doing confirmation as part of responses of the type *ja hoor* ('yes'+*hoor*) and *nee hoor* ('no'+*hoor*).[1] We focus on these because we have observed some interesting correlations between the sequential-interactional functions of *ja/nee hoor* and its prosodic characteristics; in particular, its associated pitch contours.

Kirsner and colleagues have presented the prosody of *hoor* as somewhat problematic: Kirsner et al. (1994) suggest that as a discourse particle which tries to actively engage the recipient, *hoor* should be highly compatible with a final rising contour, which in their model of intonational meaning serves to signal an 'appeal' to the listener. On the other hand, since *hoor* does not function to elicit a response, it should also be compatible with a final falling contour: part of the function of *hoor* is to signal 'finality'. In a subsequent listening experiment, Kirsner and Van Heuven (1996) find that listeners generally judge utterances ending in discourse particles including *hoor* to be most "natural" with a rising contour; however, in the case of *hoor*, utterances with a falling contour are acceptable too. Of course, these findings warrant a systematic study of the prosodic patterns *hoor* is associated with in actual usage. In this paper we offer preliminary observations on *ja/nee hoor*, which suggest, firstly, that *hoor* is associated with a number of recurrent pitch patterns, and, secondly, that a sequential-interactional approach to describing its function may help us understand the variation.

After sketching a general framework for the analysis of *ja/nee hoor* (Section 2), we will offer a sequential analysis of specific contexts in which *ja/nee hoor* responses occur (Section 3), and a description of their associated pitch contours (Section 4). Section 5 concludes.

---

1.   All instances are taken from a set of 28 phone calls of about 120 minutes in total. 6 calls from this set are calls within an institutional or professional setting, most of them calls with an employee of a travel agency (5 calls, in total 30 minutes).

2. "Marked" and "unmarked" confirmation forms

The main site of occurrence of *ja/nee hoor* in our data is the 'second pair-part' turn. As is well known, participants in talk in interaction organize communicative projects in ordered sequences of actions, and the basic format for organizing sequences is the *adjacency pair* (see Schegloff 2007). When a speaker shapes a turn at talk as the *first pair-part* (FPP) of a specific type of adjacency pair, for example by asking a question or making a request, s/he puts the delivery of an appropriate second pair-part (SPP) in next turn on the interactional agenda. *Ja hoor* and *nee hoor* are regularly used for doing confirmation in a SPP turn, as illustrated in extract 1.[2] Mrs. L has called the travel-agency desk to change her holiday booking. In discussing an alternative destination, she inquires as to whether one of the places she is considering is 'pleasantly crowded' (line 1). The desk employee confirms with *jah hoor:*.

(1) **Travel-agency call 1** (cf. sound file [MP-1-Travel agency call 1.wav])

```
 1      MsL:    maar u    weet zeker    dat   't ook
                but  you know surely   that  it also
                but you know for sure that it is also

 2              gezellige   drukteh=ehuh[ihs:.
                pleasantly   crowded         is
                pleasantly crowded.

 3→     Dk1:                          [jah hoor:.
                                       yes hoor
                                       yes  hoor.
```

Confirmation with *ja/nee hoor* can be called 'marked' in the sense that confirmation can also – and is more commonly – be done with *ja/nee* alone (see Stivers forthc.). Extract 2 shows both forms of confirmation. Here a mother calls her son, who is in a boarding school and has returned there after a weekend at home, to ask how he is. In line 4, the son confirms his mother's interpretative elaboration of his answer to her opening question with *ja hoor*. In line 7, he confirms her subsequent comment with *jah:* alone:

(2) **Phone call mother and son** (cf. sound file [MP-2-Mother and son.wav])

```
 1    mth:    hoe is 't:?
              how is it
              how are things?
```

---

2. Note that in Dutch, an agreeing response token's polarity has to match that of the statement it agrees with (Mazeland 1990, Jefferson 2002). Thus, in the context of a negative statement an agreeing response can be done with *nee* ('no') (see extract 10). This is why we label the confirmation format *ja/nee hoor*.

```
    2    son:    GOED hè
                 good TAG
                 good hè

    3    mth:    zo: van  je  bent  wel  goed  aangekO:m['n?
                 so   like you are   PRT  well  arrived
                 well like you've arrived safely indeed?

    4→   son:                                    [ja   hoor.
                                                  yes  hoor
                                                  yes  hoor.

    5    mth:    j:a:h  (weer   binne.  and'rs)   zulle  we 't wel-
                 yes    again inside otherwise)   will   we it PRT
                 yes (in there again. otherwise) we will indeed-

    6            anders       hadden  we het  wel gehoord  h[è?
                 otherwise    had     we it   PRT  heard   TAG
                 otherwise we'd surely have heard it, right?

    7→   son:                                    [jah:!
                                                  yes
                                                  yes!

    8            (0.4)

    9    mth:    zo:. hoe was ('t) vandaag  weer  op schoo:l
                 so   how was (it) today    again at school
                 so. how was your day today at school.
```

It would seem reasonable to assume that the particle *hoor* performs some secondary operation on what is being done by *ja/nee*; the question is, of course, how we can characterize this operation. As a first observation, we can note that both 'unmarked' *ja/nee* and 'marked' *ja/nee hoor* responses are mostly used for doing preferred seconds – that is, SPPs that do agreement with the FPP. In other words, preference organization does not appear to play a role in conditioning the variation between *ja/nee* and *ja/nee hoor*. More likely, doing confirmation with *ja/nee hoor* is used for managing other aspects of the interaction. What other aspects is the question we will try to answer in the following section.

3.   Doing confirmation with an eye on the encompassing activity

Most confirmations with *ja/nee hoor* in our corpus are responses to queries and requests of various kinds. Three types can be discerned in terms of the action done in the FPP turn and the line of development the sequence is furthering. In the first type, *ja/nee hoor* confirms a query which has a recognizable purpose in a more encompassing course of action. In the second type, *ja/nee hoor* is used in response to questions that implement requests. In the third type, the format is used in response to topic proffers. We discuss these three types in turn.

3.1   Type 1: Casting confirmation as fashioned for the larger course of action

The first type of use of *ja/nee hoor* occurs in responses to requests for confirmation which are part of a larger course of action and which test a contingency for the progression of this course. Extract 3 provides an example. It occurs 1.5 minute earlier in the travel-agency call from which extract 1 was taken. Mrs. L wants to change her holiday booking and is considering an alternative destination. She inquires after its touristy qualities by first reporting an assessment of it (lines 1–2), then asking whether it is a crowded place (line 7). Both queries are confirmed with *ja/nee hoor* (lines 4, 9):

(3)   **Travel-agency call 2** (cf. sound file [MP-3-Travel agency call 2.wav])

```
  1     MsL:    (en) dat >zegge ze< dat 't ook heel e:h
                (and) that say they that it too very
                (and) this one they say that it must be very u:h

  2             leuk moet we:zeh
                nice must be
                nice as well

  3             (.)

  4     Dk1:    ja hoor. da's op zich ook best
                yes hoor that-is in itself also rather
                yes hoor. that's in principle also

  5             wel leuk. e:h (is) ook wel 'n vrij e:h
                PRT nice        is also PRT a rather
                quite nice indeed, u:h is also a pretty u:h

  6             (1.1) vrij    groot plaatsje.
                      rather big   place
                (1.1) pretty big village.

  7     MsL:    ook druk?
                also crowded
                also crowded?

  8             (0.2)

  9→    Dk1:    'n beetje- ja hoor:.
                a bit yes hoor
                a bit- yes hoor.

 10             (1.6)

 11             °hm.°
```

The caller's queries occur in an epistemically non-neutral context. Each incorporates a claim that must be confirmed for the course of action of which the query is part – settling on an alternative holiday destination – to be furthered. Moreover, the formulation of each query articulates the alternative that is most likely to advance the larger course of action in a direction that matches the speaker's concerns (cf. Pomerantz 1988): the first inquiry invites confirmation that the holiday resort *is* nice; the second one that the resort is indeed crowded. For each of the caller's queries, the desk's use of *ja/nee hoor* provides a preferred response – that is, the kind of response that is articulated as preferred in the design of the customer's question turns, and which furthers the decision-making activity in the direction in which the customer is recognizably heading.

It may be noted that in both sequences the desk displays that the basis for doing confirmation is far from strong. Her response to the first query, *ja̲ hoor* is followed by a downgraded assessment: the customer's *heel leuk* ('very nice', lines 1–2) becomes *op zich ook best wel leuk* ('in principle rather nice indeed', lines 4–5). That is, after confirming the customer's query, the desk modifies the terms of the query: she does not agree with it without restraint (see Raymond 2003: 166–211). In the next sequence, the desk's response moves from partial to full confirmation. Before expressing confirmation with *ja̲ hoor:*, the desk offers a response in which the terms of the question are modified: *'n beetje-* ('a bit-', line 9). This response asserts a state of affairs rather than complying with the *yes/no*-choice set by the form of the customer's question. Such 'non-type-conforming' answers often signal the speaker's resistance to the terms of the question (Raymond 2003, also this volume). In this particular case, the desk does not complete the nonconforming response, but restarts with *ja̲ hoor:* – an answer design that is not only type-conforming, but also an upgrade: the desk now expresses a full confirmation of the query. The speaker moves in an interactionally traceable way from partial to full confirmation. This may undermine the reliability of the basis for doing confirmation: the self-repair shows doing full confirmation as a second choice (cf. Jefferson 1974). Note that the desk does no further work to remedy the full confirmation's endangered trustability, although this might be what the caller is waiting for in the 1.6 seconds silence following the response in line 10.

Extract 3 shows that doing what would appear to be full confirmation with *ja/nee hoor* does not preclude that the basis for confirmation is tentative and open to moderation. In both sequences in extract 3, the desk delivers the response turn in ways that allow the recipient to observe a divergence between the full confirmation done with *ja/ nee hoor* and weaker forms of confirmation perspiring in cues provided in the same turn. The desk observably tilts her response towards doing full confirmation. She is showing that she "chooses" (see Schegloff 2007: 172) to confirm the customer's query, rather than to provide a more balanced response that would reflect the facts. The reasons for this seem obvious. Full confirmation advances the course of action the customer's queries are implementing, while weaker forms of confirmation might thwart its advancement.

Extract 4 provides a similar example. Real estate developer Willem has called his contact in the city administration at home in the evening to informally discuss the administration's modification of a zoning plan that threatens to undermine arrangements Willem's company has made for building a row of houses. Adriaan has advised Willem to initiate legal proceedings against the administration, but Willem prefers to solve the matter in the meeting he will have the next day. In extract 4 he inquires – for the second time in the call – as to whether the arrangements with his company are laid down well within the administration (lines 1–2):

(4) **Willem**

(Phone call real estate developer (Willem) with his personal contact in the city administration (Adriaan))

```
 1   Wil:   •h en   intern      ligt dat  toch ook   goed
                and internally lays that  PRT  also  well
             and you're sure this is also laid down well

 2          vast [Adriaan.
            down
            internally ((name))?

 3→  Adr:        [ja!
                  yes
                  yes

 4          (.)

 5   Adr:   dat [is  ook   zo:,]
            this is  also  that-way
            that's that way indeed,

 6   Wil:       [dat  gesprek ] van- •h van: e:h •h ik  denk
                 that talk       like      like     I   think
                 that talk like-like u:h I think

 7          dat    dathh (0.2)  eind mei of begin:-   dat  we
            that   that         end  May or beginning that we
            that at the end of May or the beginning- that we

 8          dat eh: toen 'n keer: (.)
            that    then a  time
            that uh then a time

 9→  Adr:   JA:h hoor!
            yes  hoor
            yes hoor!

10          (0.8)

11   Wil:   dat ligt toch int[ern      hebbe]n jullie toch
            that lays PRT internally have      you    PRT
            that is laid (down) internally- you do

12   Adr:                    [°absoluut.° ]
                              absolutely
                              absolutely.
```

```
13  Wil:   ook    [notities   (o[ver?)
           also    notes         about
           have minutes about this don't you?

14  Adr:          [hrnghm.      [JAwE:l:
                                 yes+PRT
                  ((scrapes))    yes we do

15             we hebben daar toch- we hebben daar  toch
               we have there PRT     we have    there PRT
               we do have indeed- we do have indeed

16             gespre:ksnotities van enneh,
               meeting-notes         of and
               meeting notes of this don't we and uh
```

Willem ignores Adriaan's first attempt to respond with *ja* ('yes', line 3) and extends his query in a third-turn repair (Schegloff 1997) in which he specifies the approximate period of the talks he is inquiring about (lines 6–8). Adriaan then responds with *JA:h hoor* (line 9). His response turn has several features that show his eagerness to close the sequence and to ward off more talk on the issue Willem is pursuing. First, he pre-emptively cuts off further articulation of the query by responding before Willem has finished his turn. Second, by not elaborating his response, allowing for the emergence of a noticeable silence after *JA:h hoor*, he proposes that the latter should suffice as a full confirmation of Willem's query. This silence is comparable to that in line 10 in extract 3. In both cases, the speaker negotiates – in fact, attempts to enforce – sequence closure by not elaborating on the *ja/nee hoor* response.

We may now begin to account for the contribution of *hoor* in doing confirmation. The sequences considered so far suggest that *hoor* retro-actively highlights the programmatic character of the speaker's confirmation. Although the terms set by the co-participant's query may not be met with respect to every possibly relevant detail, the use of the tag shows the speaker chooses to provide the unconditioned, sequentially preferred type of response 'for all practical purposes'. The speaker protects his response against elaboration with details and particulars that may lead to sequence expansion and a less preferred sequence outcome. Instead, he shapes the response as a preferred SPP that promotes sequence closure (Schegloff 2007) and that will push the interaction over the sequence boundary.

Note that in neither case the recipient of the *ja/nee hoor* response immediately embraces the proposal to close the sequence: the subsequent silence is also the result of the recipient delaying to take a next turn. This may be an indication of the recipient's understanding of *ja/nee hoor* as a programmatic confirmation. In extract 4, Willem pursues an alternative response by redoing his query (see Pomerantz 1984). In particular, he revises the query's terms from *goed vastliggen* ('laid down', lines 1–2) to *notities over hebben* ('having notes', line 13), forcing Adriaan to commit himself to a more specific state of affairs. As in the case of extract 3, then, there are features in the interaction which suggest that confirmation with *ja/nee hoor* is used to propose sequence closure although the speaker's response might be open to moderation. By using the marked confirmation format, the speaker displays his response as motivated by contingencies above the local sequence level and this is what the recipient seems to worry about in both cases.

In conclusion, in response to queries testing contingencies that are relevant for the advancement of the larger course of action, *ja/nee hoor* responses not only accomplish confirmation, but also cast doing confirmation as – programmatically – fashioned by considerations with respect to the progression of the more encompassing activity.

3.2   Type 2: Confirming questions implementing requests

The second environment in which *ja/nee hoor* occurs in our corpus is similar to that described above in that it can be said to involve orientation to the progression of a more encompassing course of action. In this case *ja/nee hoor* is used in response to requests. Consider extract 5. Joop is calling for Hetty's husband, Hans.

(5)   **Phone call to family phone 1** (cf. sound file [MP-5-Family phone 1.wav])

```
1    Het:   Hetty Driebergen
              ((name))
              ((name))

2    Jop:   da:↑g,   met    Joop Jansen,
              hi      with   ((name))
              hi:, this is ((name))

3             (.)

4    Het:   HAllo[↓:.
              hello.
              hello.

5    Jop:         [hallo.  >is Hans      ook<  thui↑:s?
                   hello  is   ((name))  too   home
                   hello is ((name)) also home?

6→   Het:   ja   hoor.  ik  zal    'm   ev'n    roep'n.
              yes  hoor   I   shall  him  briefly  call
              yes hoor. I'll call him right away.

7             mom[ent   hoor!
              moment    hoor
              just a moment hoor!

8    Jop:         [ja!  (.) bedankt
                   yes       thanks
                   yes!      thanks

9             (38.0)
```

Joop's question in line 4 as to whether Hans is at home does *double duty* (Schegloff 2007: 73–78): it functions as a practice for making the *request* to get Hans on the phone. The relevancies mobilized by such double-layer first pair parts may be responded to in a response turn that is parsed into distinct slots: (i) the response-to-the-interrogative slot, and the (ii) the response-to-the-action slot (see Raymond 2000: 196–208, and this volume). The basic order of these slots reflects the asymmetric action-logic dependency of the response to action upon the response to the question. In her response turn (lines 6–7), Hetty first answers Joop's question with *ja hoor* and then grants the request that the question is implementing *ik zal 'm even roepen* ('I'll call him right away', line 6). Notice that *hoor* is part of the TCU in the response-to-the-interrogative slot rather than the response-to-action slot.

As in extracts 3 and 4, *ja/nee hoor* in extract 5 occurs in an environment in which the speaker enables progression of the course of action initiated by the recipient. Our corpus does not contain any instances of *ja/nee hoor* in responses to questions implementing requests which block progression. In the latter context, we find *ja/nee* alone. Extract 6 is a case in point. The caller's question as to whether her friend is at home is answered negatively, with the single-word TCU *neeh!* (line 3). While in extract 5, *ja hoor* is followed immediately by a TCU in which the speaker delivers the response-to-the-action, in extract 6 the call taker expands the response-to-the-interrogative slot with two more TCUs in which the whereabouts of the non-available person are explained (lines 4–7).

(6)   **Phone call to family phone 2** (cf. sound file [MP-6-Family phone 2.wav])

```
1    MvH:   met     Van Hoof?
            with    ((name))
            ((name)) speaking?

2    Mar:   met     Marieke  Oudenhoven.   is  Nynke    er     oo:k?,
            with    ((name))               is  ((name)) there  also
            ((name)) speaking. is ((name)) there?

3           (0.3)

4→   MvH:   neeh!  die  is  op-  schoolreisje.   die  e:h
            no     she  is  on   school-trip     she  er
            no! she's on a school trip. she er

5           (0.8)

6    Mar:   o[:h.
            oh
            oh.

7    MvH:     [(komt)  na    zes   uur.
               comes   after six   o'clock
               (will be home) after six o'clock.

8           (0.5)
```

```
9   Mar:  oh. (.)   dan  eh
          oh         then er
          oh. (.) then er

10        >probeer   ik 't dan   nog  wel  'n keer.<
           try       I  it then  PRT       a  time
          I'll try again then.

11        (0.2)

12  MvH:  ja!  okay  hoor?
          yes  okay  hoor
          yes! okay hoor?

13  Mar:  okay[:.
          okay
          okay.

14  MvH:      [do[ei::.
               bye
               bye

15  Mar:          [doei.
                   bye
                   bye
```

Extracts 7 and 8 allow for further comparison between *ja/nee* and *ja/nee hoor* responses, and provide evidence that the addition of *hoor* to *ja/nee* displays an orientation on the speaker's part to progression within the more encompassing activity. In line 8 of extract 7, the customer responds with *ja hoor* to the desk's request for permission to call her back, and the desk initiates the follow-up sequence that is made possible by the customer's confirmation.

(7)   **Travel agency call 3** (cf. sound file [MP-7-Travel agency call 3.wav])

```
1   Dk2:  ik  moet  namelijk   de  aanbetaling eh  binnen
           I   must  namely     the down-payment    within
          you see, I have to receive the down payment

2         vijf  dagen  binnen he[bben.
          five  days   in     have
          within five days

3   MsW:                       [oh maar da's    geen
                                oh but  that's no
                               oh but that's no

4         probleem.  dan  kan ik zelf  wel  even  brengen dan.=
          problem    then can I  self  PRT  just  bring   then
          problem. then I can bring (it) myself then.

5   Dk2:  =nou   dan  is  't verder    geen  pun:t.
           well  then is  it further   no    problem.
          well then it's not a problem any longer.
```

```
6              >maar  kan  ik  je   dan   toch   bellen   om<  te:h
               but    can  I   you  then  still  call     to
               but can I still call you in order to

7              d[oor te geven] of  't gelukt      is?=
               pass-on             if  it succeeded  is
               pass on if it's worked?

8→   MsW:      [ja  hoor. ]
               yes  hoor
               yes hoor.

9    MsW:      =(j[ah.)
               yes
               yes.

10   Dk2:      [en  je   telefoonnummer  i:s?
               and  your phone-number    is?
               and your phone number is?
```

Two minutes earlier in the same call, the desk made the same request after receiving the specifications of the holiday Mrs. W. wants to book. At that point, the customer confirmed the desk's question with *j:a̲h!*

(8)   **Travel agency call 4** (cf. sound file [MP-8-Travel agency call 4.wav])
      (2 minutes earlier in the same call as extract 7)

```
1    Dk2:  mja[:h en  >kan ik (je) daarover terug     bel↑len?<
           yes      and  can I  you there-about back    call
           m-yes and can I call you back about this?

2    MsW:      [(°en dan°)
               and then
               and then

3              (0.9)

4→             °eh° j:a̲h! >maar ik ↑had eigenlijk< 'n: vraa:gjeh?=
               yes!  but  I   had actually      a  question-DIM
               uh yes. but I did have a question actually?

5    Dk2:  =j:a̲:h?
           yes
           yes?

6              (.)

7    MsW:  a̲ls 't  nog   vrij is,
           if   it  still free is,
           if it's still vacant,

8              (0.3)

9    Dk2:  ja̲:h,
           yes,
           yes,
```

```
10   MsW:  wilde   ik e:h  als  't   kan  morgenavond- (.)   komen
           wanted  I       if   it   can  tomorrow-evening   come
           I wanted if it's possible to drop by to

12         bespreken.  kan je   't   vasthouden  dan?
           discuss     can you  it   retain      then
           talk about it tomorrow evening. can you put it aside then?
```

Notice that unlike *ja hoor* in extract 7, *j:ah!* in extract 8 is immediately followed by a
pre-pre (Schegloff 1980), and the subsequent proposal of settling the booking in person (lines 7–12). Asking for permission to call back is the kind of making arrangements that is typical for moving towards call closure (Schegloff and Sacks 1973). In
extract 8, the customer does not align with the course of action that is prefigured in the
desk's question, and blocks the movement to call closure in the second TCU of her
turn. This strongly suggests that by adding *hoor* to an otherwise unmarked confirmation by *ja/nee*, the speaker displays an orientation to the larger course of action in
which the FPP is embedded, and signals that the way is free to advance in that course
of action.

3.3   Type 3: Doing alignment without affiliation

In the preceding two sections, we have described how *ja/nee hoor* is used as an SPP
that provides confirmation in a way that marks the speaker's orientation to the FPP's
purpose within a larger course of action. Here we show that, particularly in the environment of double-duty FPPs, doing confirmation with *ja/nee hoor* is used to align
with prior turn without really collaborating with the action the prior speaker proposes.
We focus on two specific environments: responses to assessments inviting agreement,
and responses to topic-proffering questions.

Starting with responses to assessments inviting agreement, consider extract 9. It is
taken from a call of two middle-aged sisters, Hetty and Ella. Their disabled sister, who
lives in a home, is staying at Ella's place for the weekend, and Hetty calls on the first
morning of her visit. The day before, Ella had called Hetty about the visit and inquired
about the new clothes Hetty had bought for their sister. In extract 9, Hetty returns to
this issue by inviting agreement with the assessment that the new clothes suit their
sister well (line 1). Ella confirms Hetty's assessment with *jA:h hoor:* (line 2):

(9)   **Return call sisters** (cf. sound file [MP-9-Sisters.wav])

```
1   Het:  maar  dat   stiet  haar  wel  lEU:K  hÈ:?
          but   that  suits  her   PRT  nice   TAG
          but this looks pretty nice on her, doesn't it?

2   Ell:  jA:h   °hoor[:°
          yes    hoor
          yes hoor
```

```
 3  Het:               [passe ('s:) [de::h-  schOenen=
                        fit            the    shoes
                    do the shoes fit

 4  Ell:                           [(°m-°)

 5  Het:   =ook an:?=
            too on
           well too?

 6  Ell:   =jahh!
            yes
           yes!

 7         (0.3)

 8  Het:   no[u↓:h
            so
           so:

 9  Ell:     [ja:h, ziet 'r goed   ui:t!
              yes, looks     good   PREP
             yes, looks great!

10  Het:   jah die     bin'n  <ook  wel  mooi:>      [toch?
           yes these   are    too   PRT  beautiful    PRT
           yes these are rather beautiful too, don't you think?

11  Ell:                                            [jah. ja.
                                                     yes yes
                                                    yes. yes.

12         zeker        we:t['n.
           certainly    know
           certainly.

13  Het:                        [ja:h
                                 yes
                                yes

14         (0.3)

15         nou: gelukkig:.
           so   fortunately
           well I'm glad about this.
```

Ella's expression of agreement in line 2 is minimal, and by marking the confirmation as motivated by programmatic considerations, she signals possible resistance to the terms of agreement. This resistance becomes clear in the continuation of the interaction. After Ella's *ja hoor*, Hetty posits an evaluatively more neutral question about another detail of their sister's outfit (lines 3–5). When this question is also receipted with a minimal response (line 6), she prompts for elaboration with *nou* (line 8),[3] and Ella then responds (line 9) with an upgrade of the assessment in line 1. Hetty treats this upgrade as an appropriate response by overtly agreeing with it (line 10).

While Ella aligns with her sister's initial assessment by confirming it with *ja hoor*, she does not comply with the action that is implemented in it. There are two aspects of Hetty's assessment that Ella may resist. First, Hetty herself has bought the new outfit that is the object of her assessment. In other words, Hetty can be heard as fishing for a compliment when she assesses the new clothes positively. By merely confirming the assessment with *ja hoor*, Ella at first passes on making a compliment. Second, first assessments evaluating issues both participants have access to constitute a context in which participants may do subtle negotiations about who has more or better rights to assess the matter at hand (Heritage and Raymond 2005). By making herself the first speaker to assess their mutual sister's clothes, Hetty may claim epistemic primacy regarding the clothes she has bought. Moreover, by tagging the assessment with the confirmation-soliciting prompt *hè?*, she displays the assumption that Ella will agree with the position presented in the assessment.[4] By confirming her sister's assessment with *ja hoor*, Ella not only withholds a compliment; she is also working on "the terms of agreement", resisting the claim of epistemic primacy implicated in her sister's assessment. With *ja hoor*, she formally aligns with the format of prior speaker's turn while exploiting its closure-implicativeness to avoid collaborating with the situated particulars that are co-implicated with it.

We find a similar type of use of *ja/nee hoor* in the environment of responses to topic-proffering questions. In this context, *ja/nee hoor* is used to confirm an action that promotes the opposite of sequence closure: while in most sequence types, the delivery of a preferred response is closure-relevant, following a topic-proffering question the preferred response furthers elaboration (Schegloff 2007: 169–180). Extract 2, partially repeated below, is a case in point. The mother's question in line 1 launches the first topic of the call. When the son responds in a minimal fashion only, the mother formulates a more specific inquiry (line 3). This inquiry is receipted with *ja hoor* (line 4):

---

3.   The use of the particle *nou* (lit. 'now') in line 8 is very similar to the use of stand-alone *so* in English as described by Raymond (2004). Like stand-alone *so*, stand-alone *nou* prompts a responsive action that the recipient has not yet appropriately delivered. The understanding documented in Ella's response to *nou* shows that she hears it prompting for a less pro forma type of assessment of their sister's new outfit.

4.   Heritage and Raymond (2005) describe how English tag questions like *isn't it?* are used to downgrade epistemic claims associated with first-position assessments. The Dutch tag *hè* rather seems to underline the speaker's claim with respect to epistemic primacy. Instead of inviting the recipient's agreement, it presumes agreement as a mutually shared perspective.

(2′)   **Phone call mother and son (Detail from extract 2)** (cf. sound file [MP-2-Mother and son.wav])

```
1    mth:  hoe  is  't:?
           how  is  it
           how are things?

2    son:  GOED  hè
           good  TAG
           good hè

3    mth:  zo: van  je  bent  wel  goed  aangekO:m['n?
           so  like you  are   PRT  well  arrived
           well like you've arrived safely indeed?

4→   son:                                     [ja  hoor.
                                              yes  hoor
                                              yes  hoor.

5    mth:  j:a:h  (weer   binne.) (...)
           yes          again  inside
           yes (in there again.)
```

The son's *ja hoor* is again a minimal response to his mother's topic-proffering inquiry, and is treated as not furthering elaboration: the mother continues by elaborating on the topic herself (line 5). As in the case of *ja/nee hoor* confirmations of assessments inviting agreement, *ja/nee hoor* confirmations of topic-proffering inquiries express alignment with the prior turn, but at the same time signal that the recipient is not going to comply with the invitation to elaborate on the topic that has been made relevant by the inquiry. Doing confirmation with *ja hoor* functions in this context as a 'no elaboration' response (cf. Raymond 2000: 185–195). The *hoor* tag provides a shield against the sequential implications that are also made relevant in the first pair part. It may be noted that this use of *ja/nee hoor* is therefore different from the uses discussed in previous sections with regard to preference organization. While responses to queries and requests are cast as preferred continuations that enable progression within the larger course of action, aligning responses to assessments or topic proffers do so without complying with the line of action that is proposed in the FPP-turn.

4.   Prosodic characteristics of *ja/nee hoor*

We will now turn to the phonetics of *ja/nee hoor*. All instances were subjected to impressionistic auditory and acoustic analysis. Particular attention was paid to the pitch contour associated with *ja/nee hoor*, and four recurrent contours were distinguished.[5] In what follows we describe these in terms of their distribution across the sequential-interactional contexts we have distinguished so far.[6]

4.1   Type 1 and 2 uses of *ja/nee hoor*

In fragments in which *ja/nee hoor* is used to confirm a course-of-action-furthering query (Type 1) or to confirm a question implementing a request (Type 2), we find two recurrent contours, which we label FALL and RISE. Instances with a FALL contour typically start impressionistically high in the speaker's range and fall early in the form, leveling mid-range. Instances with a RISE start impressionistically low in the speaker's range and rise to mid or high, either gradually through the phrase as a whole or, more commonly, towards its end. We will also discuss instances with FALL-RISE, a pitch contour we consider as a variant of FINAL-RISE contours. Instances with FALL-RISE start impressionistically high in the speaker's range and early in the form. However, rather than ending level, they end with a rise to mid or high.

The FALL contour is most frequent in our collection. As an illustration of this contour we can revisit extract 3; it is repeated here in part as extract 3'.

(3')   **Travel-agency call (Detail from extract 3)** (cf. sound file [MP-3-Travel agency call 2.wav])

```
1    MsL:   (en) dat >zegge ze< dat 't ook heel e:h leuk
            (and) this one they say that it must be very u:h nice

2           moet we:zeh
            as well

3           (.)

4→   Dk1:   jah hoor. da's op zich ook best wel leuk.
            yes hoor. that's in principle also rather nice indeed,
```

Figure 1 shows a pitch trace and waveform of the end of the caller's inquiry, and the desks response including *ja hoor*. It can be seen that in terms of pitch, *ja hoor* starts high and falls quickly and dramatically: from about 425 Hz to 210 Hz, or 12 Semitones.

---

5.   It is worth pointing out that *ja hoor* and *nee hoor* are commonly 'contracted' into a single prosodic word, and many of our instances are hearable as monosyllabic. It therefore makes sense to consider the pitch contour of *ja/nee hoor* as a whole, rather than attempting to isolate *hoor* in each case.

6.   The FPPs to which instances of *ja/nee hoor* respond form a heterogeneous set prosodically. In Dutch, declarative statements interpreted as questions – so-called 'declarative questions' – and *yes/no* interrogatives have been shown to have predominantly rising contours in experimental and Map-Task speech (Haan 2001, van Heuven and van Zanten 2005, Lickley et al. 2005). In our collection, we find both rising and falling contours (cf. Englert forthc. on Dutch, and Selting 1995 and Kügler 2007 on German), but we do not discuss these contours in detail here.

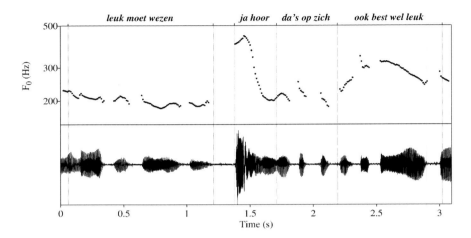

Figure 1. Segmented pitch trace and waveform for lines 1–3 of extract 3, illustrating FALL

The subsequent TCU, *da's op zich ook best wel leuk* ('in principle also rather nice indeed, line 4) starts at the latter level, rising to a peak on *best wel*. Notice that the pitch at the start of *ja hoor* is substantially higher than the pitch throughout the latter part of the prior turn, *leuk moet wezen*. That is, the onset of *ja hoor* is *noticeably high* in the immediate context.

As a further illustration, consider extract 4'. As explained above, *ja hoor* (line 9) here does a programmatic full-confirmation of the prior query, which is testing a contingency that is relevant for the negotiations Adriaan is talking about with Willem:

(4')   **Willem**

(Phone call real estate developer (Willem) with his personal contact in the city administration (Adriaan). Detail from extract 4.)

```
6    Wil:  [dat gesprek ] van- •h van: e:h •h ik
            that talk like-like u:h I

7          denk dat dathh (0.2) eind mei of begin:- dat we
            think that at the end of May or the beginning- that we

8          dat eh: toen 'n keer: (.)
            that uh then a time

9→   Adr:  JA:h hoor!
            yes hoor!
```

Figure 2 shows the falling contour of *ja hoor*, which again starts noticeably high in the immediate context. In this case the fall is from about 175 Hz to 130 Hz, which corresponds to 5 Semitones.

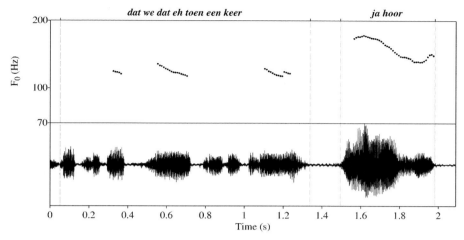

Figure 2. Segmented pitch trace and waveform for lines 7–9 of extract 4, illustrating FALL

As an illustration of the RISE contour we can consider extract 10, which has not been discussed in Section 3. This fragment contains one instance of *ja hoor* and two instances of *nee hoor*, all of which convey the message that the caller, who is worried that the holiday destination under consideration is not very bustling, is worrying needlessly.

(10)   **Travel-agency call** (cf. sound file [MP-10-Travel agency call 5.wav])

```
1     MsL:   maar  u     weet   zeker   dat   't   ook
             but   you   know   surely  that  it   also
             but you know for sure that it is also

2            gezellige   drukteh=ehuh[ihs:.
             pleasantly  crowded          is
             pleasantly crowded.

3→  Dk1:                            [jah hoor:.
                                     yes hoor
                                     yes  hoor.

4     MsL:   ik [hou van    drukte       hoor.
             I   love       crowdedness  hoor
             I do love crowdiness hoor.

5     Dk1:       [hihuh

6     MsL:   niet da   'k e[:h   met   z'n tweeën
             not  that I         with  the two-of-us
             not that I u:h am sitting alone on an isle

7     Dk1:                       [•hh huhuh •hih.

8     MsL:   heemaal    op  'n eilandje  alleen  zit.
             entirely   on  an isle      alone   sit
             with just the two of us.
```

```
 9              want die [tijd hebbe w[e gehad. ]
                because that time  have  we had.
                because that time was over long ago.

10→  Dk1:              [hhh          [nee hoor,] dat  is
                                      no  hoor    that is
                                      no hoor, that's

11              echt    niet  zo:.
                really  not   so
                really not the case.

12              (0.3)

13   MsL:  nee:h?
           no
           no?

14 →  Dk1:  nee  hoor,
            no   hoor
            no hoor,

15              (.)

16   MsL:  o:kay.  nouh-,  •h  moet ik dus  per se     eve
           okay    well        must I  so   necessarily just
           okay. well so do I have to

17              langskome  om te  laten   annuleren?
                come-by    to     let     cancel
                come by to make cancellations?
```

Figure 3 shows that *jah hoor:* (line 3) has the FALL contour illustrated above. As seen in Figure 4, however, the two instances of *nee hoor* have a rising contour. The rise is slight on the first instance, although impressionistically clearly hearable as different from level.[7] The second instance of *nee hoor*, which functions as a separate TCU, shows a more obvious rising contour with a final rise from about 200 to about 290 Hz (6 Semitones).

A relevant question at this point is, of course, whether the FALL and RISE contours can be associated with distinct functionalities. We propose that the FALL contour is the normal, unmarked contour for doing confirmation with *ja/nee hoor* in the environment of queries testing speaker concerns with respect to the progression of the larger course of action. Instances with a RISE contour occur in a more specific context: namely, in responses to queries that indicate that the speaker is not able to fully accommodate

---

7.   Part of the reason for this may be that *nee hoor dat is echt niet zo* ('no *hoor* that's really not the case', lines 10–11 in extract 10) is formatted as a single prosodic phrase, without any significant discontinuity in terms of pitch, amplitude or temporal organization between *nee hoor* and *dat is echt niet zo* – despite the fact that on grammatical and pragmatic grounds, the two phrases constitute separate TCUs. The prosodic phrase as a whole shows a gradual rise to the main accented item *echt*, of which *nee hoor* forms the onset.

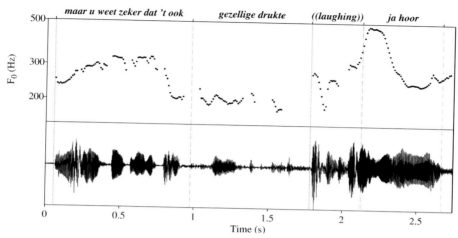

Figure 3. Segmented pitch trace and waveform of lines 1–3 in extract 10, illustrating FALL

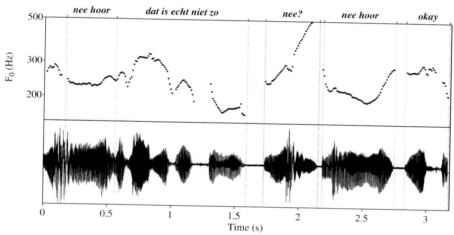

Figure 4. Segmented pitch trace and waveform of lines 10–16 in extract 10, illustrating RISE

the information or action in prior turn – for example by challenging or checking some aspect of it. The instances of *nee hoor* in extract 10 are a case in point. The first *nee hoor* (line 10) confirms what *ja hoor* has earlier confirmed: that the holiday destination is bustling. When the customer further challenges the desk's reassurance in line 7 with the polarity repeat *no?* (line 13) (Englert 2008), the desk re-asserts her position with a second *nee hoor* – this time produced in the clear, with a RISE contour which marks it out as different from the earlier *ja hoor*. We suggest that the marked prosody may be used as a technique for prompting the recipient to take a stand on the action that is re-asserted in it. This is exactly what the recipient does in next turn: she accepts the assurance with *okay* (line 16).

Our analysis suggests that the FALL-RISE contour is comparable to the RISE in terms of its contextual distribution. That is, it seems useful to distinguish between 'unmarked' FALL and 'marked' FINAL-RISE contours, where the marked contours index the reinstallment of sequential relevancies deferred by the prior inquiry.

4.2   Type 3 uses of *ja/nee hoor*

While Type 1 and 2 instances of *ja/nee hoor* are very similar in terms of observed pitch contours, the no-elaboration use of *ja/nee hoor* illustrated in Section 3.3 are markedly different in our collection. Among these, we find no instances of the FALL and RISE contours described above. Rather, we find two recurrent contours: FALL-RISE and a contour we label LOW LEVEL. Instances with this contour start impressionistically low in the speaker's range and do not change significantly.[8]

As an illustration of the FALL-RISE contour used for doing non-affiliating confirmation, we can revisit extract (9). As explained above, Ella's *ja hoor* (line 7) here constitutes a reserved response to Hetty's assessment.

(9′)   **Return call sisters (Detail from Extract 9)** (cf. sound file [MP-9-Sisters.wav])

```
1   Het:   maar dat stiet haar wel lEU:K hÈ:?
           but this looks pretty nice on her, doesn't it?

2   Ell:   jA:h °hoor[:°
           yes hoor
```

Figure 5 shows that *ja hoor* starts high, rising quickly to 500 Hz, then falls to around 200 Hz, and rises again towards 400 Hz in the latter part of the phrase. Notice that the start of *ja hoor* matches the final pitch of the prior question closely. This is the case with the FALL-RISE instances in this context more generally: while in the Type 1 and 2 fragments discussed above, *ja/nee hoor* invariably starts noticeably high or low in relation to the immediately prior turn, the non-affiliating instances with a FALL-RISE do not involve a pitch upstep or downstep at the onset.

Finally, as an illustration of the LOW-LEVEL contour we can again revisit extract 2. As explained above, the son's *ja hoor* (line 4) constitutes a minimal response to his mother's immediately prior elaboration of his similarly minimal answer to her initial question. Figure 6 shows that *ja hoor* is realised with level pitch around 120 Hz. As such it constitutes a marked downstep from the immediately prior question, which is realized with a final rise.

---

8.   Together, the FALL-RISE and LOW LEVEL contours account for all seven Type 3 fragments in our collection.

(2″) **Phone call mother and son (Detail from extract 2)** (cf. sound file [MP-2-Mother and son.wav])

```
1   mth:   hoe is 't:?
            how are things?

2   son:   GOED hè
            good hè

3   mth:   zo: van je bent wel goed aangekO:m['n?
            well like you've arrived safely indeed?

4   son:                                    [ja hoor.
                                             yes hoor
```

Again, a relevant question is whether the FALL-RISE and LOW-LEVEL contours can be associated with distinct functionalities. At this point we do not have a clear answer to this question. In particular, it does not seem to be the case that instances of *ja/nee hoor* that do confirmation of an assessment have different prosodic characteristics from instances that confirm a topic-proffering question – but our collection is small. What does seem clear is that an analysis in which a FALL-RISE contour is taken to project continuation by the same speaker (see Gardner 2001 and Szczepek Reed 2004 for references) is not applicable here: in the context under consideration, *ja/nee hoor* is typically *not* followed by same-speaker talk. The occurrence of LOW-LEVEL contours in the context under consideration is perhaps more easily accounted for, with reference to our analysis of Type 3 instances of *ja/nee hoor* as marking non-affiliation in the course of action initiated by prior turn. Low pitch and monotony have been found to be associated with non-affiliation in previous work: see for example Müller's (1996) analysis of 'continuers' in English and Italian. Still, this leaves the differentiation of the two attested pitch contours unexplained.

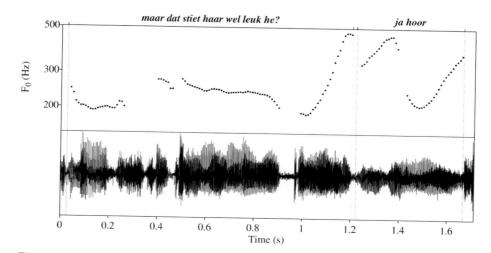

Figure 5. Segmented pitch trace and waveform of lines 1–2 of extract 9, illustrating FALL-RISE

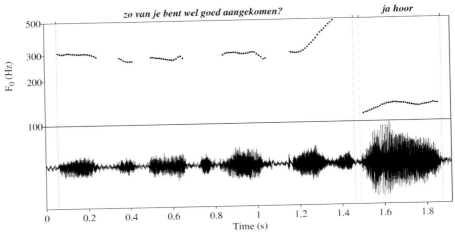

Figure 6. Segmented pitch trace and waveform of lines 3–4 of extract 2, illustrating
LOW-LEVEL

5. Summary and discussion

In this article we have offered observations on the sequential-interactional and prosodic characteristics of the confirmation form *ja/nee hoor* in a corpus of Dutch talk in
interaction, as part of a larger effort to account for the form and function of the discourse particle *hoor*. We have shown that *ja/nee hoor* is used as a marked confirmation
form in sequentially specifiable context types. When it is used as a response to queries
and requests, the speaker marks doing confirmation as programmatically motivated
with an eye on the larger course of action in which the ongoing sequence recognizably
participates. The speaker links multiple levels of interactional organization. He does
not just do confirmation as a response to prior turn, but he displays doing confirmation as directed towards contingencies above the sequence level.

Since doing confirmation is a preferred type of response that makes sequence closure relevant, the *ja/nee hoor* format may be used in environments that further sequence expansion, as a device for resisting such expansion. For example, while a *ja/nee
hoor* response to a topic-proffering query does confirm prior speaker's question, it is
heard as declining doing more talk about the topic. Contrary to responses to queries
and request that show the speaker's orientation towards advancement and progression
within some more encompassing activity, the speaker's orientation to relevancies above
the sequence level here does not result in advancing the project of prior speaker, but
rather indicates the speaker's reservation against social relevancies that are co-implicated in the design and the action of prior turn. Again the format is used for doing

multiple tasking on different levels of interactional organization, but its use engenders different consequences.

Thus, *ja/nee hoor* combines local relevancies with more global orientations in a relatively small number of sequential-interactional contexts. This confirms that doing confirmation in a sequence is usually not an action in its own right, but contributes to some more encompassing activity in which the local sequence takes part (Raymond 2004: 192–199). With reference to Kirsner et al's work on *hoor* (Kirsner and Deen 1990, Kirsner et al. 1994, Kirsner 2000, 2003), our analysis confirms that detailed contextual analysis is necessary if we are to make progress in understanding the particle's meaning and function. In fact, it highlights the importance of considering the sequential-interactional context of individual instances of use: it is arguably this context that informs our intuitive interpretations of the particle as 'doing reassurance' or 'doing emphasizing'.

Moreover, we have shown that the sequential-interactional analysis also provides insights into the prosodic variation associated with *ja/nee hoor*. Our observations suggest that prosodic design is sensitive to both the local relevancies and more global orientations engendered by *hoor*. We have shown that the particle *hoor* is associated with more recurrent pitch contours than a reading of previous literature might suggest, which are distributed systematically across the three contexts of occurrence we have distinguished. It is worth noting the frequent association of *ja/nee hoor* with the FALL contour, which does not sit easily with Kirsner and Van Heuven's (1996) finding that utterances with *hoor* sound most "natural" with a high boundary tone. It is of course possible that *ja/nee hoor* is distinct from 'clause + *hoor*' in this respect, and we hope to address this issue in further research.

As it stands, our findings are more in line with those of Caspers (2003, 2004), who reports that as a response to a *yes/no* question, *ja* is commonly realized with a falling contour, although listeners judge a range of contours as acceptable in this context. Caspers does not consider the functionality of this range of acceptable contours, and we have arguably made little progress on this front: we have so far been unable to come up with clear definitions of the functionalities of the pitch contours associated with *ja/ nee hoor*. But perhaps this is an unrealistic goal in work on prosody in interaction (cf. Schegloff 1998, Sczcepek Reed 2004): given the sensitivity of prosodic patterns to levels of organization in addition to that of turn-taking, abstracting 'core meanings' of the type proposed by Kirsner and colleagues almost inevitably involves glossing over complexities at some of these levels.

References

Berenst, Jan 1978. "Partikels als illocutieve indicatoren." In: *Taalbeheersing 1978*. VIOT/Department of Applied Linguistics, University Twente.

Caspers, Janneke 2003. "Local speech melody as a limiting factor in the turn-taking system in Dutch." *Journal of Phonetics* 31: 251–276.

Caspers, Janneke 2004. "On the role of the lvaate rise and the early fall in the turn-taking system of Dutch." In: *On speech and language: Studies for Sieb G. Nooteboom*, Hugo Quené and Vincent J. van Heuven (eds.), 27–35. Utrecht: Landelijke Onderzoekschool Taalwetenschap.

Englert, Christina 2008. *Polarity repeats.* Master thesis Research Master Linguistics, University of Groningen.

Englert, Christina in press, 2010. "Questions and responses in Dutch conversation." In: *Question-response sequences in 10 languages* [Special Issue]. *Journal of Pragmatics*, Tanya Stivers, Nick J. Enfield and Stephen C. Levinson (eds.).

Gardner, Rod 2001. *When listeners talk: Response tokens and listener stance.* Amsterdam: Benjamins.

Haan, Judith 2001. *Speaking of questions: An exploration of Dutch question intonation.* [LOT Dissertation Series 52] Utrecht: Landelijke Onderzoekschool Taalwetenschap.

Have, Paul ten 2007. *Doing conversation analysis.* Second edition. London: Sage.

Heritage, John and Raymond, Geoffrey 2005. "The terms of agreement: Indexing epistemic authority and subordination in talk-in-interaction." *Social Psychology Quarterly* 68 (1): 15–38.

Heuven, Vincent J. van, and Zanten, Ellen van 2005. "Speech rate as a secondary prosodic characteristic of polarity questions in three languages." *Speech Communication* 47: 87–99.

Jefferson, Gail 1974. "Error correction as an interactional resource." *Language and Society* 2: 181–199.

Jefferson, Gail 1981. "The abominable "ne?". An exploration of post-response pursuit of response." In: *Dialogforschung*, Peter Schröder and Hugo Steger (eds.), 53–87. Düsseldorf: Pädagogischer Verlag Schwann.

Jefferson, Gail 2002. "Is "no" an acknowledgment token? Comparing American and British uses of (+)/(-) tokens." *Journal of Pragmatics* 34: 1345–1383.

Kirsner, Robert S. 2000. "Empirical pragmatics: Downtoning and predictability in a Dutch final particle." In: *The Berkeley conference on Dutch linguistics*, Thomas F. Shannon and Johan P. Snapper (eds.), 5–62. Lanham, MD: University Press of America.

Kirsner, Robert S. 2003. "On the interaction of the Dutch pragmatic particles *hoor* and *hè* with the imperative and infinitivus pro imperativo." In: *Usage-based approaches to Dutch*, Arie Verhagen and Jeroen van de Weijer (eds.), 27–56. Utrecht: LOT.

Kirsner, Robert S. and Deen, Jeanine 1990. "Het mes snijdt aan twee kanten: on the semantics and pragmatics of the Dutch sentence-final particle *hoor*." In: *The low countries: Multidisciplinary studies*, Margriet Bruijn Lacy (ed.), 1–12. Lanham: University of America Press.

Kirsner, Robert S. and Heuven, Vincent J. van 1996. "Boundary tones and the semantics of the Dutch final particles *hè, hoor, zeg* and *joh*." In: *Linguistics in the Netherlands 1996*, Crit Cremers and Marcel den Dikken (eds.), 133–146. Amsterdam: Benjamins.

Kirsner, Robert S.; Heuven, Vincent J. van and Bezooijen, Renée van 1994. "Interaction of particle and prosody in the interpretation of factual Dutch sentences." In: *Linguistics in the Netherlands 1994*, Reineke Bok-Bennema and Crit Cremers (eds.), 107–118. Amsterdam: Benjamins.

Kügler, Frank 2007. *The intonational phonology of Swabian and Upper Saxon.* Tübingen: Niemeyer.

Lickley, Robin J.; Schepman, Astrid and Ladd, Robert D. 2005. "Alignment of 'phrase accent' lows in Dutch falling rising questions: Theoretical and methodological implications." *Language and Speech* 48: 157–183.

Mazeland, Harrie 1990. ""Yes", "no", "mhm": Varations in acknowledgment choices." In: *Les formes de la conversation*, Vol. 1, Bernard Conein, Michel de Fornel and Louis Quéré (eds.), 251–282. Issy les Moulineaux: Reseaux.

Mazeland, Harrie 2010. "*HOOR* als tag: Een beroep op sequentie-overstijgende relevanties." In: *Studies in taalbeheersing 3*, Wilbert Spooren, Margreet Onrust and José Sanders (eds.), 271–284. Assen: Van Gorcum.

Müller, Frank E. 1996. "Affiliating and disaffiliating with continuers: Prosodic aspects of recipiency." In: *Prosody in conversation. Interactional studies*, Elisabeth Couper-Kuhlen and Margret Selting (eds.), 131–176. Cambridge: Cambridge University Press.

Pomerantz, Anita 1984. "Agreeing and disagreeing with assessments: Some features of preferred/dispreferred turn-shapes." In: *Structures of social action*, John. M. Atkinson and John Heritage (eds.), 57–101. Cambridge: Cambridge University Press.

Pomerantz, Anita 1988. "Offering a candidate answer: an information seeking strategy." *Communication Monographs* 55: 360–373.

Raymond, Geoffrey 2000. *The structure of responding: Type-conforming and nonconforming responses to YNIs*. Ph.D. dissertation, UCLA.

Raymond, Geoffrey 2003. "Grammar and social organization: Yes/no interrogatives and the structure of responding." *American Sociological Review* 68: 939–967.

Raymond, Geoffrey 2004. "Prompting action: The stand-alone "so" in ordinary conversation." *Research on Language and Social Interaction* 37: 185–218.

Schegloff, Emanuel A. 1980. "Preliminaries to preliminaries: "Can I ask you a question?"" *Sociological Inquiry* 50 (2): 104–152.

Schegloff, Emanuel A. 1997. "Practices and actions. Boundary cases of other-initiated repair." *Discourse Processes* 23 (3): 499–547.

Schegloff, Emanuel A. 1998. "Reflections on studying prosody in talk-in-interaction." *Language and Speech* 41: 235–263.

Schegloff, Emanuel A. 2007. *Sequence organization in interaction. A primer in conversation analysis*, Vol. 1. Cambridge: Cambridge University Press.

Schegloff, Emanuel A. and Sacks, Harvey. 1973. "Opening up closings." *Semiotica* 7: 289–327.

Selting, Margret 1995. *Prosodie im Gespräch*. Tübingen: Niemeyer.

Stivers, Tanya in press. "Moral responsibility and question design. 'Of course' as contesting a presup of askability." In: *The morality of knowledge in conversation*, Tanya Stivers, Lorenza Mondada and Jacob Steensig (eds.). Cambridge: Cambridge University Press.

Szczepek Reed, Beatrice 2004. "Turn-final intonation in English." In: *Sound patterns in interaction*, Elisabeth Couper-Kuhlen and Cecilia E. Ford (eds.), 63–96. Amsterdam: Benjamins.

Wenzel, Veronika 2002. *Relationelle Strategien in der Fremdsprache. Pragmatische und interkulturelle Aspekte der Niederländischen Lernersprache von Deutschen*. Münster: Agenda Verlag.

Appendix. Main transcription conventions

Sequential relations

sp[eaker-1	left-hand brackets mark the onset of simultaneous talk of a
[spr-2	second speaker
sp[eake]r1	right-hand brackets indicate where a speaker's utterance stops
[yes]	relative to the talk of another speaker
(0.7)	length of a silence in tenths of a second
(.)	a silence less than 0.2 seconds
text=	latching of turns by two speakers
=text2	

Pitch movement

.	final pitch fall
,	slight final pitch rise
?	strong final pitch rise
↑	noticeable local pitch rise in the syllable (part) after the arrow
↓	local pitch fall

Other sound production features

accent	an underlined segment is noticeably accented
goo:d	noticeable sound stretch
•hh	hearable inbreath (each *h* indicates a duration of roughly 0.2 seconds)
hhh	hearable outbreath (each *h* indicates a length of roughly 0.2 seconds)
cut off-	cut-off production
lhaughihngh	laughter
CAPitals	a capitalized segment is noticeably louder than surrounding talk
°quieter°	a segment between degree signs is noticeably more quiet than surrounding talk
>faster<	the pace of a segment between carats is noticeably faster than surrounding talk
(guess)	an utterance part in brackets is an uncertain hearing

PART II

Prosodic units as a structuring device in interaction

Intonation phrases in natural conversation

A participants' category?

Beatrice Szczepek Reed
University of York, UK

This chapter tests the usefulness of the category *intonation phrase* for the analysis of natural conversation. It asks whether the intonation phrase is a relevant unit for participants, and if so, whether it is a prosodic, or indeed an interactional category. The data show that while participants do divide their speech into intonation phrase-like chunks, these chunks are not defined by intonation alone. Instead, participants draw on a variety of interactional modes in their production of speech chunks, which are defined here as building blocks for turns and Turn Constructional Units. Chunks are shown to be employed as interactional units below the turn, and potentially below the Turn Constructional Unit; therefore the term *Turn Constructional Phrase* is suggested.

1. Introduction

Research on intonation traditionally draws on the notion of a phonological unit that is defined by a coherent pitch movement and/or accentual pattern. This unit has been referred to as tone unit (Crystal 1969, Brazil 1997), tone group (Halliday 1967, Brown et al. 1980), intonation-group (Cruttenden 1997), intonation phrase (Wells 2006), intonation unit (Du Bois 1991, Chafe 1993, Barth-Weingarten 2007a), rhythm unit (Pike 1945), breath group (Liebermann 1967) and speech bar (*sprechtakt*, Klinghardt and Klemm 1920, Klinghardt 1923). While some of these terms, such as *rhythm group*, emphasise a perspective on the phenomenon as a collection of smaller prosodic events connected together, others, such as *intonation unit*, stress the concept of a single holistic entity. However, all terms refer to the basic notion of a linguistic unit defined by suprasegmental aspects of speech. To give a general idea of the intonation phrase, we could say that it is a stretch of talk delivered as one recognisable overall pitch movement. In a standard textbook scenario, this pitch movement would contain a pitch accent near the beginning, and another, typically more prominent pitch accent on the final stressed syllable; it would start with a comparatively high pitch onset, which would be followed by gradual declination in overall pitch register and loudness; the last syllable would be lengthened; and the whole phrase would be followed by a brief pause (for a more detailed discussion of intonation phrase structure see Section 2).

The following extract from a lecture on Martin Luther shows some typical examples of intonation phrases as they are traditionally defined. The speaker is reading from a book, a context in which clear boundaries between intonation phrases are common. The example is taken from the Santa Barbara Corpus of Spoken American English. All data for this study have been transcribed according to an adapted version of the GAT transcription system devised by Selting et al. (1998); all relevant transcription conventions can be found in the Appendix.

(1) **The Egg which Luther Hatched** (SBC025) (cf. sound file [SZC-1-the-egg-which-Luther-hatched.wav])

```
1    Lecturer:    for ↑HOW can a ↑PERson;
2                 (0.41)
3                 be re↑SPONsible for his ↑DEE:DS;
4                 (0.08)
5                 if he po↑SSEsses no free ↑WILL.
6                 (0.62)
```

The utterance *for how can a person be responsible for his deeds if he possesses no free will* is divided here into three chunks of speech. Each chunk contains two pitch accents, one near the beginning, and one very near, or at, the end. In each chunk, pitch is higher at the beginning than at the end; and each chunk is followed by a pause. Figure 1 shows a F0 analysis of the entire utterance.[1]

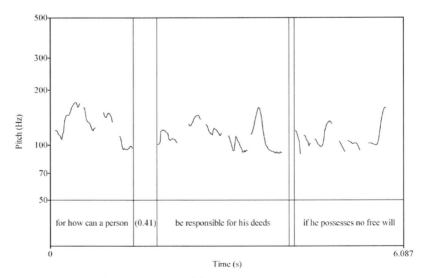

Figure 1. Intonation phrases in excerpt (1)

---

1.   This frequency analysis has been created in Praat 5.1. (www.fon.hum.uva.nl/praat/).

This chapter represents an attempt to test the usefulness of the category of the intonation phrase for the analysis of natural conversation. Before this issue is addressed, the phenomenon itself is introduced below with reference to some previous literature.

2.   The intonation phrase: An introduction

As noted above, among the many distinctions that can be made between different definitions of the intonation phrase, one is that between the notion of a holistic intonational phenomenon, and that of a collection of smaller phonological events, such as pitch accents. The first is the perspective adopted by the so-called British school of intonation; the second is that employed in the field of autosegmental-metrical phonology. In this chapter we are mainly interested in the first approach, although our main conclusions hold for both. For reviews of the intonation phrase in autosegmental-metrical phonology see, for example, Ladd (1996: 235–251) and Grice (2006).

As many publications that follow the British school of intonation are aimed not only at linguists, but also at learners of English, a rather prescriptive approach is prevalent in the majority of them (cf. Wells 2006). One of several exceptions is the work of Cruttenden (1997), whose definition of the *intonation-group* is therefore a good place to start. His internal criteria for defining a stretch of speech as an intonation-group include, firstly, the existence of at least one stressed syllable; and secondly, pitch movement on, to, or from that stressed syllable. Thus, minimally, an intonation-group could consist of a monosyllabic word which is delivered, for example, as a fall from a high pitch onset. External criteria for identifying intonation-groups are those that define potential boundaries. According to Cruttenden, one such criterion is a potential pause following an intonation-group; however, according to Cruttenden, pauses are not obligatory boundary markers and may also occur within a group. Other external criteria include anacrusis, that is, fast delivery of unstressed syllables before the first pitch accent; lengthening of the final syllable; and a potential change in the pitch direction of any unstressed syllables from one intonation-group to the next. Cruttenden concedes, however, that cases remain in which it is difficult to decide where one intonation-group ends, and another one begins, particularly in the analysis of natural conversation (1997: 29).

Another influential definition of the intonation phrase is Crystal's (1969). His emphasis is on the internal structure of the *tone-unit*. It comprises minimally the *nucleus*, that is, the main tone-carrying syllable, and maximally a structure of pre-head, head, nucleus and tail. Combinations of these structural elements are also possible (1969: 207–209). At the heart of Crystal's tone unit analysis – and generally at the heart of the British approach to intonation phrases – is a detailed classification of types of nuclear tones, such as falling, rising, level, rising-falling, falling-rising, etc., and their possible realisations in the structure. Crystal asserts that "every tone unit contains one and only one nucleus, or peak of prominence" (1969: 209). In contrast to Cruttenden, Crystal claims tone unit identification is unambiguous, provided the speech sample under analysis is "normal" and "not too hurried" (1969: 205).

One of the most recent publications on intonation in the British tradition is Wells (2006). The book follows Halliday (1967, 1970) in its description of intonation according to *tonality* – that is, where are the intonation phrase boundaries; *tonicity* – that is, which syllable carries the nucleus; and *tone* – that is, which intonation pattern do the nucleus and other accents receive. Intonation phrases are presented as well-defined phonological entities, and a large variety of rules and possibilities are introduced for the three issues mentioned above.[2]

Students of naturally occurring conversation have been concerned with intonation phrases primarily from a perspective of transcription, rather than from one of phonological structure. Du Bois (1991) and Du Bois et al. (1993) put forward the transcript notation known as Discourse Transcription (DT), with the *intonation unit* as one of its central categories. Du Bois et al. (1993: 47) define it as "a stretch of speech uttered under a single coherent intonation contour", with potential initial cues of pausing and an upward shift in overall pitch, and a potential final cue of syllable lengthening. Similar to the phonological literature, where form and placement of the main accent – the nucleus – take centre stage, researchers of natural talk have focused primarily on the pitch movement at the end of the intonation phrase. However, discourse analysts who directly address the intonation phrase typically have an interest in discourse function, rather than phonological form. The final pitch movement of an intonation phrase is interpreted in terms of whether it projects *completion* or *continuation* (of a sentence, an idea, or a turn-at-talk). Du Bois et al. (1993: 52–53) call this *transitional continuity*. It is marked by transcript notations that refer to functional categories such as *continuing, final,* and *appeal*. No prosodic characteristics are specified for these categories. While the authors go on to say that "each category is more or less consistently realized by a specific form" (Du Bois et al. 1993: 53), they give preference to a purely functional approach in order to be able to generalise across languages. Defining the transcription process, Du Bois (1991) describes the relation between linguistic theory and data material:

> "The process of discourse transcription is never mechanical, but crucially relies on interpretation within a theoretical frame of reference to arrive at functionally significant categories, rather than raw acoustic facts." (Du Bois 1991: 72)

Chafe (1980, 1987, 1988, 1993), too, is interested in intonation phrases from a functional perspective, with a focus on information flow. However, his approach claims a closer relation between phonetic form and discourse function:

---

2.   More in-depth explorations of intonation phrase structure can be found in some of the most prominent contributors to the British school of intonation analysis, notably Palmer (1922), Armstrong and Ward (1926), Schubiger (1935, 1958), Kingdon (1958), O'Connor and Arnold (1961/1973) and Halliday (1963/1973, 1967, 1970).
Reviews of the British school of intonation can be found in Gibbon (1976), Crystal (1969) and Couper-Kuhlen (1986).

"Even in listening to an unfamiliar language one can hear that every so often an idea unit ends with that distinctive falling intonation contour which we naturally associate with "the end of a sentence". To us English speakers, certainly, and probably to the speakers of most or all languages, this sentence-final intonation communicates an impression of completeness: the impression that the speaker has come to the end of something which has some kind of significant closure. This impression contrasts with the impression of incompleteness given by the intonation contours at the end of other idea units, marked in our transcripts with commas." (Chafe 1980: 20)

Here, a universalist claim is made for the function of intonation contours, vaguely defined as falling or non-falling, to signal completion or incompletion.[3] Similarly, Gumperz (1993) favors a "basically functional perspective" on transcription, "so that, in transcribing a feature such as pausing, for example, we are less interested in *absolute duration* and more in the *interpretive evaluation*" (Gumperz 1993: 92, emphasis in the original). His prosodically defined *informational phrases* are delimited by boundary markers such as pauses and certain unit-final pitch movements, all of which are characterized from the outset as fulfilling certain pragmatic functions, such as signaling definiteness, or uncertainty.

In their outline of a transcription system for conversation analysis (Gesprächsanalytisches Transkriptionssystem, GAT), Selting et al. (1998) employ the notion of *phrasing units* (*Phrasierungseinheiten*), the boundaries of which are defined by prosodic, syntactic and semantic closure (1998: 101); however, the main criterion is a prosodic one. As in the above approaches, phrase-final punctuation marks are used which, in contrast to the approaches described above, refer to pitch movements, rather than functional categories.

All discourse related approaches have in common a primary interest in how intonation phrases *end*. This interest is due to the role ascribed to prosody for turn-taking (cf. Local et al. 1985, Local et al. 1986, Selting 1996, Wells and Peppè 1996, Schegloff 1998, Wells and Macfarlane 1998, Fox 2001, Caspers 2003, Szczepek Reed 2004) and narrative structure (cf. Chafe (1980, 1987, 1988, 1993). Investigations of these relationships routinely link the prosodic form of phrase endings to notions of continuation and closure.[4] It is therefore possible to argue that for most, if not all

---

3.   In contrast, Szczepek Reed (2004) shows that almost any pitch contour which is part of the overall intonational repertoire of English may co-occur with turn-finality, depending on the interactional context.

4.   Cf. Schegloff (1998) and Fox (2001), who both argue that a pitch peak on the final stressed syllable of a TCU foreshadows an upcoming transition relevance place (TRP), and allows other participants to anticipate an opportunity for speaker change. Wells and Macfarlane (1998) show that in West Midlands English the last accent does not involve a peak but a valley, arguing "that it is the occurrence of the final major accent itself that projects an upcoming TRP, and not just the phonetic characteristics of the postaccentual syllables" (1998: 288).

discourse-related approaches, an interest in intonation phrases as a holistic category, while expressed, takes second place behind a primary interest in phrase *boundaries*, and their prosodic form.

This priority is also present in the most recent investigation into intonation phrases from an interactional linguistic perspective, and the only one not motivated primarily by an interest in transcription. Barth-Weingarten (2007a) asks, much like this chapter does, whether *intonation units* are an aspect of everyday interaction. Barth-Weingarten starts from the assumption that if intonation units exist in natural talk, then the way in which participants design intonation unit endings prosodically is likely to bear similarities to the prosodic design of turn endings. She finds that prosodic strategies that mark turn endings, such as final pitch peaks or valleys, final syllable lengthening and final diminuendo, also occur at the end of potential turn-internal intonation units, albeit in a reduced form. This significant finding is potential first evidence that participants do indeed structure their talk by orienting to a speech unit of intonation phrase-like length and design.

As this section has outlined, research from two very different fields of language study employs the notion of a prosodically defined unit. While phonological definitions of the intonation phrase go into extensive detail regarding its phonological structure, discourse oriented definitions are more interested in the forms and functions of its boundaries, and its advantages for transcription. In both approaches, the intonation phrase is very much an analyst's category. With the exception of Barth-Weingarten (2007a, but see also Selting 1995), no attempts have been made so far to verify that it is also a relevant category for conversational participants. The following sections represent one step towards such an attempt. The questions raised and the potential answers suggested are in no way intended to provide final solutions for the problematic interface between prosodic and sequential boundaries, and/or units. Instead, by attempting to present natural language from within a purely descriptive and observational framework, they are intended simply to raise awareness of the issues arising from applying theoretically defined categories to talk-in-interaction with its continuously unfolding clusters of inter-reliant features.

With this in mind, the sections below address the following questions: Is the intonation phrase a relevant category for conversational participants themselves; that is, can we find empirical evidence of participant orientation to intonation phrases, both in terms of turn production and turn receipt? If so, is it useful from a conversation-analytic perspective to regard intonation phrases as an independently prosodic unit? Or are they part of a broader chunking mechanism that delimitates not only prosodic units, but also, among others, interactional, sequential and syntactic ones?

3.   Participant orientation to intonation phrases

The vast majority of research on intonation phrases to date involves linguistic introspection, or, if spoken data are used, is based on read-aloud sentences such as those presented in extract (1). It is therefore legitimate to ask whether intonation phrases actually exist in spontaneous talk. However, while participants in naturally-occurring talk may well deliver their speech in intonation phrase-like bursts of speech, it cannot be assumed from the outset that those bursts (a) comply with phonological rules of intonation phrase structure, and (b) are best described in terms of intonation at all. For these reasons, we initially refer to any short bursts of talk below as *chunks,* thus avoiding their immediate classification in terms of prosody (by using the term *intonation phrase*) or indeed syntax (by using the terms *phrase, clause* or *sentence*).

In the analyses of extracts from naturally-occurring talk below, we first look for evidence that participants orient to speech chunks as holistic entities, and subsequently ask whether those chunks are indeed oriented to as intonation phrases. In approaching this issue we must keep in mind two participant perspectives: that of *production,* i.e. currently speaking participants' use of chunks and intonation phrases as elements of their turns; and that of *receipt,* that is, next speakers' treatment of previous stretches of talk as chunks and intonation phrases. In the following we will look at these two perspectives in turn.

3.1   Orientation to speech chunks by currently speaking participants

The first perspective involves a close look at how utterances in naturally-occurring talk are structured by currently speaking participants. Listening to spontaneous speech soon reveals that speakers produce talk on a chunk-by-chunk basis, even if determining where these chunks begin and end is not always straightforward. See, for example, extract (2) below, from the Santa Barbara Corpus. The conversation is a face-to-face interaction between Lajuan and Cam.[5] Each line in the transcript refers to one holistic chunk.

(2)   **He Knows** (SBC044) (cf. sound files [SZC-2-he-knows.wav])

```
1   Lajuan:   i lIstened to my sIster when my nEphew;
2             (0.3)
3             .h started COLLege how she was sAY:ing;
4             .hh SHE filled out all o' his applicAtions for
              where he was gO:ing: an';
5             .hh SHE did All of these THINGS when hE applied
              for a SCHOlarship or whatEver -
6             .hh SHE filled out Everything and I'm lI:ke;
```

---

5.   The lack of video recordings restricts our analysis to the verbal and prosodic domains. Hence this paper cannot explore the visual cues for participants' phrasing of discourse, which remain a significant topic for future research.

```
 7              (0.39)
 8              hh. I did it by my↑SE:LF;
 9              (0.34)
10              .hh you READ the fOrm;
11              (0.14)
12              And you fIll it OUT.
13              (0.41)
14  Cam:        [well -
15  Lajuan:     [N:O one dId it for ME:,
16              (0.51)
17              .hh you knOw an' I was vEry,
18              (0.47)
19              mUch -
20              (0.39)
21              whatEver i NEEDed;
22              (0.53)
23              .hh i i gOt my mOney from my FA:ther,
24              (0.12)
25              he paid for ↑SCHOO:L,
26              (0.47)
27              .hh but -
28              (0.13)
29              I did everything on my ↑OWN.
```

In this extract Lajuan can be observed to produce one chunk of speech at a time. Speech chunks are divided either by pauses (lines 11, 13, 18, 20, 24, 28), in-breaths (lines 4, 5, 6) or both (lines 2–3, 7–10, 16–17, 22–23, 26–27). In some cases, boundaries between chunks may not be what our expectations of individual interactional modes would suggest. For example, the chunk at line 3, *started college how she was saying* is not a syntactic construction; indeed, it spans the end of one construction, *my nephew started college*, and the beginning of another, *how she was saying she filled out all of his applications*.

More interestingly for us, not all chunks comply with established phonological rules for intonation phrases. In the first chunk, *i listened to my sister when my nephew* (line 1), there is no single pitch accent that stands out as dominant. It is therefore not possible to determine a nucleus. Similarly, lines 5 and 15 contain several pitch accents of the same prominence.[6] Furthermore, the chunk at line 19, *much*, separated from the preceding chunk by a pause (lines 17–18), could be heard by a phonologically trained analyst as continuing a previous intonation phrase: *you know an' i was very (0.47) much*. The final word of the chunk at line 17, *very*, contains slightly rising pitch, whereas *much* remains at the pitch level reached by this rising movement. Thus, *much* carries no independent pitch movement. With regard to phonological intonation phrase

---

6.   This is inconsistent only with the British school. Most autosegmental-metrical approaches do not stipulate the primacy of one pitch accent.

structure it is therefore not a candidate for an independent intonation phrase. It is, however, observably separated from the previous chunk by a pause, which is not defined by glottal closure (see below). This shows that the speaker himself is content to implement some degree of separation between the two chunks.[7] While pauses and in-breaths are observable physical actions performed by the speaking participant, the integration of one pitch level into a previous pitch pattern can only be analysed as such in terms of a separate phonological theory. It is therefore an interpretation of the data, rather than an empirical observation. Keeping in mind the conversation analytic aim of a participant perspective and an empirical description of participant actions, it is therefore possible to argue that activities such as pausing and breathing are more suitable indicators of speech chunk boundaries than theoretical concepts such as integration and non-integration of pitch movements.

However, as the above example shows, the most frequent resource for chunking is simultaneous patterning of co-occurring interactional modes. Most speech chunks are units in more mode than one: they may be words, clauses, semantico-pragmatic concepts, gestures, gazes, and, of course, intonation phrases, to name only the most obvious. It may be that only in cases where one or more of these modes are not clearly recognizable as a single pattern, as in the case of syntactically incomplete clauses, that pauses and in-breaths (and possibly other physical actions) become predominantly relevant as cues for participants' chunking practices. In answer to our question regarding speaking participants' orientation to chunking and intonation phrases, we can say that participants appear to regularly divide their talk into shorter chunks. However, a phonological definition of those chunks as intonation phrases is not always successful.

3.2   Orientation to speech chunks by next participants

Next participants' treatment of previously speaking participants' chunks as chunks can be explored by looking for next actions, such as recipient responses, next turn onsets, repair initiations and non-linguistic activities such as coughs and in-breaths at places of potential boundaries. Their treatment of chunks as intonation phrases is much more difficult to show, as we will see below.

The following extract from a radio program broadcast on KSTP Minneapolis and recorded at the Minnesota State Fair during the 1980-ies, shows next speaker actions placed after chunks produced by a first speaker. In (3), interviewee Cathy has won the prize for 'Best Pickle', and is explaining to radio host Joe what makes a winning pickle.

---

7.   *much* is of course also syntactically integrated into the previous chunk. However, this is not necessarily a valid criterion for intonation phrase boundaries, as individual words can form independent intonation phrases.

(3)   **KSTP Minnesota state fare** (cf. sound file [SZC-3-KSTP Minnesota state fair. wav])

```
 1  Cathy:   a wInning pIckle is one that is CRI:SP,
 2  Joe:     RIGHT,
 3  Cathy:   VERy flAvourful:,
 4  Joe:     alRIGHT,
 5  Cathy:   .hh and SNAPS when you to-
 6           (0.28)
 7           bIte INto it?
 8  Joe:     uHU,
 9           (0.25)
10  Cathy:   .hh and is ↑JU:ST EXcellent.
```

Joe's recipiency displays at lines 2 and 4 occur after chunks from Cathy that show some features of intonation phrases (final lengthening, coherent overall pitch contour), alongside syntactic and semantico-pragmatic boundaries. In addition, Cathy's suspension of turn-continuation after each chunk shows her to be designing them as separate entities. However, lines 5–8 show that suspension of immediate continuation is not always treated by Joe as a location for recipiency display: as Cathy aborts her talk at line 5 by breaking off mid-word and keeping her glottis closed, the resulting pause is treated by both participants as an opportunity for self-repair (Schegloff et al. 1977). Following Local and Kelly (1986), who differentiate between pauses with or without glottal closure, one could argue in this case that the talk at lines 5–7 is treated by both participants as one chunk, which is being repaired in the production process: Cathy's glottal closure shows ongoing phonetic activity rather than 'pausing' from speaking, while Joe's withholding of response tokens during a turn in which he regularly produces them shows his possible orientation to the lack of a chunk-boundary. Regarding intonation phrase structure, Cathy's talk at line 7 could stand alone as an independent intonation phrase, whereas her talk at line 5 could be classed as an aborted one. However, an interpretation of the whole utterance as one intonation phrase is not possible due to the presence of nuclear accents in each part (*snaps*, line 5; *in-*, line 7).

While an observation of next participants' treatment of chunks as chunks can be relatively straightforward, their treatment of chunks as intonation phrases is much more difficult to investigate. In order to show that a next participant treats a chunk specifically as an intonation phrase, we would require examples in which next actions are placed after bursts of talk that are not characterised by any linguistic or kinesic units and boundaries other than those postulated for intonation phrases. Proof of such independence would be notoriously elusive, as kinesic boundary markers such as for example hand or foot gestures may escape the camera, and thus the analyst's view. The closest research has come to proving the existence of intonation phrases as an independent prosodic category is in experiments on listeners' agreement on intonation phrase boundaries in de-lexicalised (i.e. unintelligible) spoken language data (de Pijper and Sanderman 1995, Sanderman 1996). Interestingly, this research seems to suggest that inter-listener agreement is most strongly influenced by the presence and length of pauses; other influences being different kinds of pitch discontinuities. However, in contrast to experimental methods, research on naturally-occurring talk would find it impossible to control all relevant parameters, and it is unlikely that these results could be verified for language and language perception during spontaneous conversation.[8]

3.3   Speech chunks as trouble sources

The previous two sections have shown rather straightforward instances of currently speaking participants' production of speech chunks; and next participants' recipient responses to them. In both instances, participants appeared to agree on boundary locations, or at least showed no overt disagreement. In the case of an aborted chunk (see (3), line 5), both participants oriented to the necessity of self-repair. However, the following data sample provides evidence for the negotiable nature of the forms that chunks take, and the location of their boundaries, as one participants' chunking practice is treated as unsuccessful by a repair-initiating next participant. The recording comes from the Santa Barbara Corpus. At line 1, Angela, aged 90, begins a new sequence in which she describes a type of community service she is looking for. The intonational packaging we are interested in occurs at lines 1–7; it is followed by two repair initiations from co-participant Doris (lines 11–21, 54–56).

(4)   **This retirement bit** (SBC011) (cf. sound file [SZC-4-this retirement bit.wav])

```
 1 Angela:   I STILL haven't found Anybody that wAnts to -
 2            (1.41)
 3            lEt me pay a little FEE and then;
 4            (1.87)
 5            CALL them Every mOrning -
 6            (0.99)
 7            that i'm
 8            (0.25)
 9            UP and aROUND.
10            (0.54)
11 Doris:     <<all> what what what - >
12            (0.42)
13            bAck UP a minute.
14            (.)
15            DO WHAT,
16            (0.35)
17 Sam:       hh.
18            (0.67)
19 Doris:     [YOU'LL PAY -
```

---

8.   Cf. Hughes and Szczepek Reed (forthcoming) for an evaluation of experimental methods for research on naturally-occurring talk.

```
20  Angela:  [.hh I've I've
21  Doris:    [<<p> to be CALLED ->
22  Angela:   [been lOOking for SOMEbody who will sIt by the
             PHONE in the MORning,
23           (1.02)
24           and-
25           (0.73)
26           and CLIENTS will cAll in and say good ↑MORning
             I'm ↑UP -
27           (0.65)
28           hehe
29           (0.79)
30           and so that-
31           (0.31)
32           they're THROUGH for the DAY then.
33           (0.58)
34           I'm UP.
35           (0.46)
36           If I DON'T call in by say: NINE o'CLOCK;
37           (1.1)
38           [then-
39  Doris:   [well I'll be GLAD to do that for a FEE,
40           (0.55)
41  Angela:  you WILL?
42           (0.34)
43           [how mUch is the F[EE thOUgh;
44  Doris:   [ehhhh           [hehehehehehehe
45  Angela:  he[hehehehe
46  Sam:       [ehehe
47           (0.78)
48  Doris:   (Angela) does thAt-
49           (0.2)
50           does it really BOTHer you,
51           (0.91)
52  Angela:  .h I'D like to have somebody i can call into
             EVery MORning.
53           (0.55)
54  Doris:   YOU cAll In -
55           (.)
56           or I cAll In.
```

In Angela's first turn (lines 1–9) not all chunks coincide with conventional syntactic boundaries. However, most chunks are produced as coherent intonation contours, and are followed by pauses. All except line 7 start with high onset syllables, and contain stressed syllables somewhere near their end. They are therefore designed by Angela as prosodically holistic entities, without necessarily being syntactic constructions at the same time. The first boundary between *I still haven't found anybody that wants to* and *let me pay a little fee and then* (lines 1–3) splits a *that*-clause in the middle of a verb phrase. A more expectable syntactic division may have been:[9]

> *I still haven't found anybody*
> *that wants to let me pay a little fee*

Similarly, the next boundary between *let me pay a little fee and then* and *call them every morning* divides a syntactic construction dependent on the verb *let*:

> *Let me pay a little fee and then (let me) call them every morning.*

In the emergent context of natural talk, the end of the first phrase *and then* could have been designed as 'dangling' final particles, similar to what has been shown for *but* and other connectors at certain locations (Barth-Weingarten 2007b, Mulder and Thompson 2008). Such a construction would then be followed by a new main clause. However, Angela's continuation shows that this interpretation is not valid here; her second phrase is indeed syntactically dependent on the first.

Returning for a moment to the question concerning the intonation phrase as an independent prosodic category, we could interpret this kind of mismatch between prosodic and syntactic patterns (see also extract (2)) as evidence for the potential independence of intonation. However, in the above example, a next participant's treatment of Angela's turn reveals that there are limits to which such discrepancies between interactional modes are treated as acceptable.

Doris' repair initiation (lines 11–21) *what what what back up a minute you'll pay to be called* locates a trouble source in Angela's lines 3–5 which contain the items *pay* and *call*: *let me pay a little fee and then call them every morning*. Six turn exchanges later, the issue is still not resolved, as Doris initiates further repair over the same question when she asks: *you call in or I call in* (lines 54–56). Doris' repair is aimed at the two verbal items *pay* and *call*, divided by Angela's chunking of syntactic material: the pause dividing the phrases *let me pay a little fee and then* and *call them every morning* is almost 2 seconds long. As noted above, this allows a co-participant and listener to interpret the final part of the previous intonation unit *and then* as a 'dangling' new beginning, raising the expectation of a new main clause. However, according to this expectation, the next phrase *call them every morning* is lacking a subject. Thus, while Angela's chunking strategies show on the one hand what locations she treats as potential places for chunking boundaries, her co-participant's repair initiations show on the other hand that these chunking strategies render her turn a trouble source for others.

While the above example shows a lack of alignment between intonation and traditional syntactic boundaries, which may suggest that this participant treats the two as separate systems, it also shows that other participants may treat this lack of alignment

---

9.   However, see Steedman (1991, 2000) for an account of intonational phrasing and syntactic surface structure.

as a trouble source. Thus, in answer to our second research question, which asked whether intonation phrases should be regarded as independent prosodic categories, we can conclude that this is most probably not useful. Instead, the practice of chunking seems to be oriented to by participants as an interactional strategy, employed for the structuring and sequencing of turns. If patterns of co-occurring interactional modes overstep the limit of intelligibility, this appears to present potential problems for next participants. This is consistent with a perspective on the interactional and emergent reality of natural talk in situ. If we take seriously the notion of talk as a multimodal activity, it is unlikely that we will find individual modes handled by participants independently of others, as interactants continuously produce and receive clusters of interactional practices for their accomplishment of conversational actions.

3.4   Chunks, turns and TCUs

Orientation by next participants to boundary locations shows in the first instance that some sort of *sequential* boundary has been reached, rather than a specifically prosodic, syntactic, or pragmatic one. And since that sequential boundary is not always treated as a potential turn completion point, we can say that in those cases participants orient to boundaries other than transition relevance places (TRPs). Following on from this, we can ask whether these boundaries actually delimit some form of interactional *unit*. If so, that unit would have to be described as one below the turn-at-talk, as clearly some of the stretches of talk designed and treated as chunks by participants do not have the potential to be stand-alone turns (e.g. *I listened to my sister when my nephew*, (2), line 1). Furthermore, if chunks are units, they may even have to be described as units below the TCU, depending on our definition of TCUs. For Schegloff (1996), TCUs are potentially turns, and are always followed by TRPs:

> "These units *can* constitute possibly complete turns; on their possible completion, transition to a next speaker becomes *relevant* (although not necessarily accomplished)." (Schegloff 1996: 55, emphasis in the original)

In contrast, Selting (2000) argues that only some TCUs make turn transition relevant. Her analysis of syntactic and prosodic resources for turn construction leads her to distinguish between TCUs that are followed by a transition relevance place (TRP), and those that are not. It is not entirely clear whether Selting's notion of turn-internal TCUs overlaps entirely with the chunks of speech we encounter in the example above, or whether they are indeed more global units. However, in making this distinction, Selting is able to retain a definition of the TCU as the smallest interactional unit:

> "TCUs must be conceived of as the smallest interactionally relevant complete linguistic units in their given context. They end in TRPs, unless particular linguistic and interactional resources are used in order to project and postpone TRPs to the end of larger turns." (Selting 2000: 512)

Selting's argument is closely related to the suggestion made by Lerner (1991, 1996), who introduces the notion of *compound turn constructional unit formats*. They are two-fold structures consisting of a preliminary and a final component, as in the case of an *if X then Y* format. TRPs are located only at the completion of final components, while preliminary component completions allow recipients to project an upcoming final component, and thus an upcoming TRP. Thus, Lerner's preliminary TCU components are interactional units below the turn, which are not delimited by TRPs.

Data such as those above show that the boundaries participants design through the use of various interactional resources, and which next participants may orient to through recipient responses, are clearly boundaries other than TRPs. Whether they delimitate some kind of 'unit'; and whether those units are TCUs, or smaller units, is open to discussion.

However, what is most relevant from a conversation analytic perspective is participants' chunking of talk, rather than their phrasing in the phonological domain. Rather than using a term such as *intonation phrase*, it is therefore more appropriate to use a term such as *chunk*, *stretch of talk*, or, given the possibility that chunks may be used as building blocks for turns and potentially even TCUs, a term such as *turn constructional phrase* (TCP).

4.   Conclusion

As talk-in-interaction unfolds on a moment-by-moment basis, participants routinely divide their own speech into chunks, and orient to others' chunks as entities with beginnings and ends. As a result, emerging turns-at-talk are produced step by step, chunk by chunk. However, defining chunks in terms of any single linguistic category is not straightforward. Firstly, chunks may well be intonation phrases, as well as syntactic clauses, as well as sequential increments, etc. Secondly, the data frequently show instances of unconventional chunking in separate modes (incomplete or ill-formed syntactic constructions; aborted intonation phrases; intonation phrases with more than one primary pitch accent). Thus, the thought process presented here leads us to conclude that it is not helpful to define speech chunks as intonation phrases, if one is interested in the analysis of talk-in-interaction. While from a phonological perspective it may be appropriate to analyse isolated stretches of spoken language, and identify patterns along the lines of tonality, tonicity and tone, in naturally-occurring conversation these patterns interact with such a wide variety of other interactional modes that a separate analysis of them as *intonation phrases* does not reflect the reality of language produced for talk-in-interaction.[10]

---

10.   From a phonological perspective, the fact that an intonation phrase is also characterised by non-prosodic features is not necessarily problematic. Many phonological approaches consider intonation in close relation with other linguistic systems, typically syntax, focus and information structure (Halliday 1970, Heusinger 1999, Gussenhoven 1984, Rooth 1992, Selkirk 1984, 1995, Wells 2006). The problem from an empirical perspective arises from the clearly defined structure of intonation phrases; and the clearly defined form of their alignment with non-prosodic features.

Furthermore, a transcription practice which divides talk into *intonation phrases* is problematic, because the kinds of chunks that are oriented to by participants are not defined purely on intonational, or even prosodic grounds; and because established definitions of the intonation phrase may stand in the way of a conversation analytic investigation into their defining features in naturally-occurring talk. Instead, participants produce and treat chunks as multi-layered interactional events.

This concept of chunks as interactional, rather than intonational units is in line with those discourse analysts who have used intonation phrases as functional categories in their transcript notations. Their primary interest in discourse functions, particularly their focus on what the end of an intonation phrase signifies in terms of speaker continuity, is at the heart of talk-in-interaction, and prosody-in-interaction research. Furthermore, an approach to chunks as interactional, rather than purely phonological phenomena allows analysts to focus on the prosodic design of chunks without having to reconcile them with a pre-supposed intonation phrase structure.

Based on the above suggestions that a) participants divide their talk into chunks smaller than turns, and possibly smaller than TCUs; and b) intonation is not the only feature oriented to in the production of these chunks, I suggest the term *turn constructional phrase* (TCP) as one that denotes the nature of speech chunks as an interactional, rather than a purely prosodic category. A tentative definition of a TCP could be as a 'building block' for turns and TCUs, if we agree that the TCU is defined as a potential turn. The main interactional feature of a TCP is that it is designed by its speaker, and treated by other participants as a separate, but potentially turn-internal entity. From a perspective of speech production, the most typical way of designing TCPs as separate entities is simultaneous patterning of interactional modes (action-, sequence-, syntax-related, etc.) in combination with released pauses, that is, pauses that are not the result of glottal closure (Local and Kelly 1986), and/or in-breaths. From a recipient perspective, the most obvious ways of treating another participant's TCP as a separate entity, particularly while a turn is in progress, is display of recipiency at TCP completion points, including refraining from uptake, placement of minimal response tokens, and non-linguistic actions such as breaths and coughs; and onset of turn-competitive talk or overlap. These are only first suggestions, and are likely to be more clearly defined in the future.

However, the same claim made by Schegloff (1996) for TCUs below possibly holds for the chunks of talk I refer to here as TCPs:

> "What sorts of entities (described in grammatical or other terms) will be used and treated as turn-constructional units is determined by those who *use* the language (broadly understood – that is, to include gesture, facial expression, when/where relevant), not those who study it academically. Calls for formal definitions of a TCU – beyond their status as units which can constitute possibly complete turns as above – are therefore bound to be disappointed, but empirical inquiries to explore such issues should be expected to yield interesting results." (Schegloff 1996: 115, emphasis in the original)

An interaction-based definition such as the one we propose here avoids the numerous difficulties analysts have faced over the issue of intonation phrase boundaries: if participants are not clearly demarcating boundaries, we as analysts should be careful to assume their existence. The definition also allows for the wide variety of internal structures of TCPs in terms of syntax, information structure, pragmatic concepts, action and prosody. Focusing on what participants treat as unproblematic units, rather than on pre-established definitions on what those units should be, can guard against analytical dangers identified by Ford (2004):

> "While working toward a precise account for units, interactionally oriented linguists run the risk of foregrounding the discreteness of units and backgrounding their constant and functionally crucial malleability." (Ford 2004: 29–30)

And:

> "The drive to define units may cause us to miss systematic practices that make conversation work for participants in real contexts of use." (Ford 2004: 38)

Ford (2004) argues that rigid definitions of units and their boundary features have little use for an analysis of talk-in-interaction. While a practice of defining the exact characteristics of units is the norm in approaches to linguistics where language is studied as a system outside the interactional context, analysts of language in conversation "need to hold loosely (their) conceptions of structure, rule, and unit" (Ford 2004: 48), and keep in mind the flexibility of language as a resource for dealing with constantly emerging contingencies:

> "(Interactants') skill in the production of (a) turn unit lies not in an ability to unilaterally plan and execute it, without a hitch, but rather in (their) artful production of a unit on the fly. (Their) skill is in producing a coherent unit through resources and practices that are systematically adapted for the management of contingencies." (Ford 2004: 30)

An analytical mindset that identifies boundaries only where participants orient to them must include instances in which the potential for boundaries is made interactionally relevant. Past research has identified a number of practices in which participants exploit the notion of boundaries by producing talk that is noticeably designed as suppressing them, such as the rush-through mentioned in Schegloff (1982, 1998) and the abrupt-join described by Local and Walker (2004). The interactional work invested into suppressing these boundaries clearly shows participant orientation to their potential relevance and occurrence.

In the description and analysis of conversation we have so far worked with the turn constructional unit as the smallest interactional unit. And indeed, TCUs are designed and treated by participants as separate entities of talk, frequently held together by a complete syntactic structure, an overarching prosodic pattern, a coherent semantico-pragmatic concept, and a clearly identifiable social action. However, in many cases, TCUs are made up of two or more shorter chunks of talk which in themselves are not potential turns, and which are clearly parts of a larger unfolding pattern. These chunks of talk can be oriented to by participants as entities in their own right. As the term *intonation phrase* neither describes the multi-layered nature of these smaller entities, nor their role for turn construction, one option is to refer to them as *turn constructional phrases*. Defined as building blocks for turns and TCUs, and identified by participant orientation to their boundaries, they facilitate a deeper understanding of the structure of conversation without imposed restrictions on their nature and characteristics. Future research into the structure of turns will show how participants employ these smaller entities, what role they play in the accomplishment of conversational actions, and what they tell us about participants' perspectives on boundaries and unit-formation in interaction.

References

Armstrong, Lilias E. and Ward, Ida C. 1926. *Handbook of English intonation*. Leipzig and Berlin: Teubner. Second edition (1931). Cambridge: Heffer.

Barth-Weingarten, Dagmar 2007a. "Intonation units and actions – evidence from everyday interaction." Paper presented at IPrA, Göteborg, 8–13 July, 2007.

Barth-Weingarten, Dagmar 2007b. "Prosody, construction grammar and language change." In: *Anglistentag 2006 Halle. Proceedings*, Sabine Volk-Birke and Julia Lippert (eds.), 421–433, Trier: Wissenschaftlicher Verlag.

Brazil, David 1997. *The communicative value of intonation in English*. Cambridge: Cambridge University Press.

Brown, Gillian; Currie, Karen L. and Kenworthy, Joanne 1980. *Questions of intonation*. London: Croom Helm.

Caspers, Johanneke 2003. "Local speech melody as a limiting factor in the turn-taking system in Dutch." *Journal of Phonetics* 31: 251–276.

Chafe, Wallace L. 1980. "The deployment of consciousness in the production of a narrative." In: *The pear stories. Cognitive, cultural and linguistic aspects of narrative production*, Wallace L. Chafe (ed.), 9–50. Norwood, New Jersey: Ablex.

Chafe, Wallace L. 1987. "Cognitive constraints on information flow." In: *Coherence and grounding in discourse*, Russell S. Tomlin (ed.), 21–55. Amsterdam: Benjamins.

Chafe, Wallace L. 1988. "Linking intonation units in spoken English." In: *Clause combining in grammar and discourse*, John Haiman and Sandra Thompson (eds.), 1–27. Amsterdam: Benjamins.

Chafe, Wallace L. 1993. "Prosodic and functional units of language." In: *Talking data. Transcription and coding in discourse research,* Jane A. Edwards and Martin D. Lampert (eds.), 33–43. Hillsdale: Lawrence Erlbaum.

Couper-Kuhlen, Elizabeth 1986. *An introduction to English prosody*. London: Edward Arnold.

Cruttenden, Alan 1997. *Intonation*. Cambridge: Cambridge University Press.

Crystal, David 1969. *Prosodic systems and intonation in English*. Cambridge: Cambridge University Press.

du Bois, John W. 1991. "Transcription design principles for spoken discourse research." *Prag-matics* 1: 71–106.

du Bois, John W.; Schuetze-Coburn, Stephan; Cumming, Susanna and Paolino, Danae 1993. "Out-line of discourse transcription." In: *Talking data. Transcription and coding in discourse re-search*, Jane A. Edwards and Martin D. Lampert (eds.), 45–89. Hillsdale: Lawrence Erlbaum.

Ford, Cecilia E. 2004. "Contingency and units in interaction." *Discourse Studies* 6: 27–52.

Fox, Barbara A. 2001. "An exploration of prosody and turn projection in English conversation." In: *Studies in interactional linguistics*, Margret Selting and Elizabeth Couper-Kuhlen (eds.), 287–315. Amsterdam: Benjamins.

Gibbon, Dafydd 1976. *Perspectives of intonation analysis*. Frankfurt am Main: Peter Lang.

Grice, Martine 2006. "Intonation." In: *Encyclopedia of language and linguistics*, Keith Brown (ed.), 778–788. Second Edition, Vol. 5. Oxford: Elsevier.

Gumperz, John 1993. "Transcribing conversational exchanges." In: *Talking Data. Transcription and coding in discourse research*, Jane A. Edwards and Martin D. Lampert (eds.), 91–121. Hillsdale: Lawrence Erlbaum.

Gussenhoven, Carlos 1984. *On the grammar and semantics of sentence accents*. Dordrecht: Foris.

Halliday, Michael A. K. 1963. "The tones of English." *Archivum Linguisticum* 15, 1–28. Reprinted in *Phonetics in linguistics. A book of readings*, W.E. Jones and John Laver (eds.) (1973), 103–126. London: Longman.

Halliday, Michael A. K. 1967. *Intonation and grammar in British English*. The Hague: Mouton.

Halliday, Michael A. K. 1970. *A course in spoken English: Intonation*. Oxford: Oxford University Press.

Heusinger, Klaus von 1999. *Intonation and information structure*. Habilitationsschrift, Univer-sity of Konstanz (http://elib.uni-stuttgart.de/opus/volltexte/2003/1396/pdf/heusinger.pdf).

Hughes, Rebecca and Szczepek Reed, Beatrice forthcoming. "Learning about speech by experi-ment: Issues in the investigation of spontaneous talk within the experimental research paradigm." *Applied Linguistics*.

Kingdon, Roger 1958. *The groundwork of English intonation*. London: Longman.

Klinghardt, Hermann 1923. *Sprechmelodie und Sprechtakt*. Marburg: Elwert.

Klinghardt, Hermann and Klemm, Gertrude 1920. *Übungen im englischen Tonfall für Lehrer und Studierende*. Cöthen: Otto Schulze Verlag.

Ladd, D. Robert 1996. *Intonational phonology*. Cambridge: Cambridge University Press.

Lerner, Gene H. 1991. "On the syntax of sentences in progress." *Language in Society* 20: 441–458.

Lerner, Gene H. 1996. "On the 'semi-permeable' character of grammatical units in conversation: Conditional entry into the turn space of another speaker." In: *Interaction and grammar*, Elinor Ochs, Emanuel A. Schegloff and Sandra A. Thompson (eds.), 238–276, Cambridge: Cambridge University Press.

Lieberman, Philip 1967. *Intonation, perception and language*. Cambridge, Mass: MIT Press.

Local, John; Wells, Bill and Sebba, M. 1985. "Phonology for conversation. Phonetic aspects of turn delimitation in London Jamaican." *Journal of Pragmatics* 9: 309–330.

Local, John and Kelly, John 1986. "Projection and 'silences': notes on phonetic and conversa-tional structure." *Human Studies* 9: 185–204.

Local, John; Kelly, John and Wells, Bill, 1986. "Towards a phonology of conversation: Turn-taking in Tyneside English." *Journal of Linguistics* 22: 411–437.

Local, John and Walker, Gareth 2004. "Abrupt-joins as a resource for the production of multi-unit, multi-action turns." *Journal of Pragmatics* 36: 1375–1403.

Mulder, Jean and Thompson, Sandra A. 2008. "The grammaticization of *but* as a final particle in English conversation." In: *Crosslinguistic studies of clause combining*, Ritva Laury (ed.), 179–204, Amsterdam: Benjamins.

O'Connor, Joseph D. and Arnold, Gordon F. 1961/1973. *Intonation of colloquial English*. London: Longman.

Palmer, Harold E. 1922. *English intonation, with systematic exercises*. Cambridge: Heffer.

de Pijper, Jan R. and Sanderman, Aaltjen A. 1995. "On the perceptual strength of prosodic boundaries and its relation to suprasegmental cues." *Journal of the Acoustical Society of America* 96: 2037–2047.

Pike, Kenneth L. 1945. *Intonation of American English*. Ann Arbor: University of Michigan Press.

Rooth, Mats 1992. "A theory of focus interpretation." *Natural Language Semantics* 1: 75–116.

Sanderman, Aaltjen A. 1996. *Prosodic phrasing. Production, perception, acceptability and comprehension*. Technische Universiteit Eindhoven.

Schegloff, Emanuel A. 1982. "Discourse as an interactional achievement: Some uses of 'uh huh' and other things that come between sentences." In: *Georgetown University Round Table on Linguistics 1981. Analysing Discourse: Text and Talk*, Deborah Tannen (ed.), 71–93. Washington: Georgetown University Press.

Schegloff, Emanuel A. 1996. "Turn organization: One intersection of grammar and interaction." In: *Interaction and grammar*, Elinor Ochs, Emanuel A. Schegloff and Sandra A. Thompson (eds.), 52–133. Cambridge: Cambridge University Press.

Schegloff, Emanuel A. 1998. "Reflections on studying prosody in talk-in-interaction." *Language and Speech* 41: 235–263.

Schegloff, Emanuel A.; Jefferson, Gail and Sacks, Harvey 1977. "The preference for self-correction in the organization of repair in conversation." *Language* 53: 361–382.

Schubiger, Maria 1935. *The role of intonation in spoken English*. Cambridge: Heffer.

Schubiger, Maria 1958. *English intonation: its form and function*. Tübingen: Niemeyer.

Selkirk, Elisabeth 1984. *Phonology and syntax. The relation between sound and structure*. Cambridge/MA: MIT Press.

Selkirk, Elisabeth 1995. "Sentence prosody: Intonation, stress, and phrasing." In: *The Handbook of phonological theory*, John A. Goldsmith (ed.), 550–569. Oxford: Blackwell.

Selting, Margret 1995. *Prosodie im Gespräch. Aspekte einer interaktionalen Phonologie der Konversation*. Tübingen: Niemeyer.

Selting, Margret 1996. "On the interplay of syntax and prosody in the constitution of turn-constructional units and turns in conversation." *Pragmatics* 6: 357–388.

Selting, Margret 2000. "The construction of units in conversational talk." Language in Society 29: 477–517.

Selting, Margret; Auer, Peter; Barden, Birgit; Bergmann, Jörg R.; Couper-Kuhlen, Elizabeth; Günthner, Susanne; Meier, Christoph; Quasthoff, Uta; Schobinski, Peter and Uhmann, Susanne 1998. "Gesprächsanalytisches Transkriptionssystem (GAT)." *Linguistische Berichte* 173: 91–122.

Steedman, Mark 1991. "Structure and intonation." *Language* 68: 260–296.

Steedman, Mark 2000. "Information structure and the syntax phonology interface." *Linguistic Inquiry* 31: 649–689.

Szczepek Reed, Beatrice B. 2004. "Turn-final intonation in English." In: *Sound patterns in interaction. Cross-linguistic studies from conversation*, Elizabeth Couper-Kuhlen and Cecilia E. Ford (eds.), 97–118. Amsterdam: Benjamins.

Wells, Bill and Peppè, Sue 1996. "Ending up in Ulster: Prosody and turn-taking in English dialects." In: *Prosody in conversation*, Elizabeth Couper-Kuhlen and Margret Selting (eds.), 101–130. Cambridge: Cambridge University Press.

Wells, Bill and Macfarlane, Sarah 1998. "Prosody as an interactional resource: Turn-projection and overlap." *Language and Speech* 41: 265–294.

Wells, John C. 2006. *English intonation. An introduction.* Cambridge: Cambridge University Press.

Appendix

Transcription Conventions (adapted from Selting *et al.* 1998)

Pauses and lengthening

(2.85)	measured pause
:::	lengthening

Accents

ACcent	primary pitch accent
Accent	secondary pitch accent

Phrase-final pitch movements

?	rise-to-high
,	rise-to-mid
-	level
;	fall-to-mid
.	fall-to-low

Pitch step-up/step down

↑	pitch step-up
↓	pitch step-down

Change of pitch register

<<l> >	low pitch register
<<h> >	high pitch register

Volume and tempo changes

<<f> >	forte
<<ff> >	fortissimo
<<p> >	piano
<<pp> >	pianissimo
<<all> >	allegro
<<len> >	lento

Breathing
.h, .hh, .hhh   in-breath
h, hh, hhh   out-breath
Other conventions
[overlapping talk
[

Making units

Comments on Beatrice Szczepek Reed "Intonation phrases in natural conversation: A participants' category?"

Jan Anward
University of Linköping, Sweden

1. Strange chunks?

In Beatrice Szczepek Reed's stimulating paper, she convincingly demonstrates that conversationalists chunk their turns into smaller units, and that such units are typically designed as intonation phrases. Let me start this comment on her paper, though, by taking issue with her analysis of her Example (4), the first 18 lines of which are reproduced below.

(4) **This retirement bit** (SBC011)

```
 1   Angela:   I STILL haven't found Anybody that wAnts
               to -
 2             (1.41)
 3             lEt me pay a little FEE and then;
 4             (1.87)
 5             CALL them Every mOrning -
 6             (0.99)
 7             that i'm
 8             (0.25)
 9             UP and aROUND.
10             (0.54)
11   Doris:    <<all> what what what - >
12             (0.42)
13             bAck UP a minute.
14             (.)
15             DO WHAT,
16             (0.35)
17   Sam:      hh.
18             (0.67)
```

Szczepek Reed locates the source of Doris's trouble in lines 11–15 in the way Angela articulates her turn in lines 1–9 in smaller chunks. However, Doris's trouble seems rather to have to do with the unusualness of what Angela is saying: that she wants to pay some people so that she can call them every morning and tell them that she is fine. Normally, if you pay people, you want them to do something. This reading is strengthened by the fact that Doris is still confused in the very last lines (54–56) of Szczepek Reed's Example (4), even though Angela produces a couple of syntactically impeccable chunks, in lines 50 and 52, just before that turn (cf. the following excerpt):

(4)   **This retirement bit** (SBC011) (ctd.)

```
47              (0.78)
48  Doris:      (Angela) does thAt-
49              (0.2)
50              does it really BOTHer you,
51              (0.91)
52  Angela:     .h I'D like to have somebody i can call
                into EVery MORning.
53              (0.55)
54  Doris:      YOU cAll In -
55              (.)
56              or I cAll In.
```

2.   Open and closed units

In contrast to the contents of Angela's first turn in (4) (lines 1–9), there is in fact nothing unusual in the syntactic chunking of that turn. Angela constructs the turn from five consecutive units. The first four of these units are prosodically non-final units, ending on a level or mid pitch. Three of them are also syntactically open, i.e. projecting, units. The fifth and final unit provides both a prosodic and a syntactic closure: a low pitch, and no further projections.

This is a common enough turn pattern in conversation – at least in Swedish conversations, I should perhaps add (see Anward 2003) – where a combination of continuating prosody and syntactic non-closure serves as an effective turn-holding device. Notice that this turn-holding function is eminently evident in Szczepek Reed's Examples (2), (3), and (4), where all feedback items are produced only after units that are both prosodically and syntactically closed. It is mostly in monologic sequences, such as Szczepek Reed's Example (1), that a speaker can afford to use both prosodically and syntactically closed units in mid-turn.

There is thus nothing "wrong" with syntactically open and prosodically demarcated units. On the contrary, Szczepek Reed's paper provides excellent evidence that such units are one of the chunking options available to conversationalists.

And in any reasonable syntactic framework, such as Steedman's online version of Categorial Grammar (Steedman 2000; see also Auer 2009 and O'Grady 2005), syntactically open units are easily characterized. For example, the fourth unit in Angela's first turn in Example (4), *that i'm*, is an S\(S/AP), a unit which – combined with a preceding sentence (S) – makes up a unit which – combined with a following adjective phrase (AP) – makes up a sentence. All in all, and simplifying somewhat, Angela can be heard to use the following syntactic units in constructing her first turn in Example (4): S/S, S/S, S, S\(S/AP), AP.

3.   Whither chunking

From the evidence mustered by Szczepek Reed and from the discussion above, I think it is fair to conclude that conversationalists indeed chunk their turns into smaller units, that such units are typically designed as intonation phrases, and that conversationalists can choose whether to design such units as turn-holding, often syntactically open, units or as turn-yielding units.

Whether we generalize the notion of TCU to both kinds of units or use turn-constructional phrase (TCP) as a general category, as suggested by Szczepek Reed, is another matter, which I will take no stand on here.

Instead, I would like to end this comment by pointing to something which is in need of further investigation. Chafe (e.g. 1998) has argued that an intonation phrase typically corresponds to one idea. Thus, he holds that the rhythm of conversation is basically an informational rhythm. Alternatively, one could conjecture that chunk size in conversation is basically determined by constraints on efficient processing (see e.g. Hawkins 2004). However, such things need to be studied empirically.

For example, look at the beginning of Szczepek Reed's Example (2):

(2)   **He Knows** (SBC044)

```
 1   Lajuan:   i lIstened to my sIster when my nEphew;
 2             (0.3)
 3             .h started COLLege how she was sAY:ing;
 4             .hh SHE filled out all o' his
               applicAtions for where he was gO:ing:
               an';
 5             .hh SHE did All of these THINGS when hE
               applied for a SCHOlarship or whatEver –
 6             .hh SHE filled out Everything and I'm
               lI:ke;
 7             (0.39)
 8             hh. I did it by my↑SE:LF;
 9             (0.34)
10             .hh you READ the fOrm;
```

```
11              (0.14)
12              And you fIll it OUT.
13              (0.41)
```

Lajuan constructs his first turn in several steps. In line 1, he presents the actors involved, and then in line 4, he constructs a format which is then recycled in lines 5, 6,
8, and 12 (for this method of turn construction, see Anward 2004).

This observation makes a couple of further observations relevant. First, there can
indeed be said to be an informational rhythm in Lajuan's turn, but it does not rest on
any a priori foundation. Instead, it is one crucially constructed by Lajuan himself,
through the recycling of the format of line 4. Secondly, while there may well be an upper bound for how complex a chunk may be, in this example, complexity can be seen
to interact with the emergent informational rhythm and thus be context-dependent.
Note that the most complex chunk in Lajuan's turn (line 5), in terms of number of
words or phrases, is a rather close repeat of line 4, and that complexity is reduced in
lines 8, 10 and 12, when Lajuan uses the recycled format to introduce his own values,
as opposed to those of his sister and nephew.

As Szczepek Reed shows in her stimulating paper, chunking is an achievement.
What is achieved, though, above and beyond the chunks themselves, remains to a large
extent to be investigated.

References

Anward, Jan 2003. "Samhällets syntaktiska sida." In: *Grammatik och samtal*, Bengt Nordberg,
    Leelo Keevallik Eriksson, Kerstin Thelander and Mats Thelander (eds.), 135–148. Uppsala:
    Institutionen för nordiska språk.
Anward, Jan 2004. "Lexeme recycled. How categories emerge from interaction." *Logos and lan-
    guage* V: 31–46.
Auer, Peter 2009. "On-line syntax: Thoughts on the temporality of spoken language." *Language
    Sciences* 31: 1–13.
Chafe, Wallace L. 1998. "Language and the flow of thought." In: *The new psychology of language*,
    Michael Tomasello (ed.), 93–111. Mahwah, NJ: Lawrence Erlbaum.
Hawkins, John A. 2004. *Efficiency and complexity in grammars*. New York: Oxford University
    Press.
O'Grady, William 2005. *Syntactic carpentry*. Mahwah, NJ: Lawrence Erlbaum.
Steedman, Mark 2000. *The syntactic process*. Cambridge, Mass.: MIT Press.

Speaking dramatically

The prosody of live radio commentary of football matches*

Friederike Kern
University of Potsdam, Germany

Live commentaries of football matches provide a rich source for the analysis of verbal constructions of drama and suspense. In this paper, I will show how radio reporters construct and employ the different speech styles "building up suspense" and "presenting a climax" for the contextualization of specific verbal actions. Both speech styles are used for dramatic descriptions of events on the soccer field but they feature different sets of prosodic characteristics. Whereas "building up suspense" displays a continuous rise of fundamental frequency across units, relatively narrow pitch range within units, and an absence of pauses within and between units as the most relevant features, "presenting a climax" exhibits a considerable deceleration of articulation rate, with extremely lengthened nuclear syllables. Furthermore, it will be argued that both types of dramatic speech style differ significantly from speech styles used for the presentation of background information on the match.

1. Introduction

People listening to football matches consider it the radio commentators' job to present events in as lively a manner as possible to their unknown audience. Although the drama and increasing suspense that is communicated throughout the commentary is to a certain extent defined by the progression of the match itself, it is also created by the commentators, with their voices as virtually the only resource they have.[1]

---

* I would like to thank Dagmar Barth-Weingarten, Elisabeth Reber, Beatrice Szczepek Reed and an anonymous reviewer especially for their valuable comments to earlier versions of this paper. Also, thanks is due to Alexandra Imrie for checking my English.

1. There is, of course, background noise from the stadium that can be used in live transmissions for the creation of suspense as well. However, in the present paper I will not deal with this aspect.

Live radio commentary of football matches thus provides a rich source for the analysis of speakers' linguistic construction of drama and suspense. I use the terms "drama" and "suspense" as an audience-oriented interpretative category instead of "excitement" or "high emotional involvement" that in my view constitute speaker-oriented categories. This choice was made because I do not intend to make statements about the reporters' possible emotional states but about the potential effects of their speech on the audience. In this paper, I aim to show how radio reporters construct a "dramatic speech style[2]" by employing specific linguistic, i.e. syntactic and prosodic, means.[3]

In order to do so, I will first investigate how radio reporters contextualize different verbal actions in their commentaries through the use of different styles of speaking that exhibit two sets of co-occurring syntactic and prosodic features respectively. In contrast to previous research on live radio commentaries (cf. e.g. Simmler 2000, Siehr 2006, Müller 2007a), I will show that the reporters not only make a difference between what was named "describing events on the soccer field" and "summarizing and evaluating the match so far" (cf. e.g. Müller 2007a) but that the "descriptions of actions" have to be differentiated further: using different sets of prosodic characteristics, the reporters additionally distinguish between the building-up of suspense and the presentation of an event on the soccer field as a highlight of the match.

In my analysis, I will concentrate on the comparison of these two actions but I will also contrast them with a third action, namely "summarizing and evaluating the match so far", which belongs to what is known as elaborations (cf. e.g. Müller 2007a, 2007b, also Section 3.1) that also take place during live commentaries. My aim is to describe relevant prosodic and syntactic features employed to present some events on the soccer field as more dramatic to the audience than others. The focus will be on the interplay of these means and in particular I will demonstrate how the gestalts of prosodic units differ with respect to specific prosodic parameters – articulation rate, intonation, and pitch range – which operate as contextualization cues for dramatization. Furthermore, I will take a look at how the speakers organize the transition between the dramatic description of events and other verbal actions.

2.   Methodology

Contrary to everyday conversations, radio commentaries do not constitute what is commonly called "talk-in-interaction" (cf. Schegloff 2007), i.e. they are not part of what is considered the main area of research interest in conversation analysis, nor interactional linguistics nor phonetics-in-conversation (cf. Couper-Kuhlen and Selting

---

2.   For the notion of speech style see e.g. Sandig and Selting (1997).

3.   I will not deal with lexico-semantics here, see e.g. Simmler (2000) for a description of typical lexemes used in "descriptions of events on the soccer field", albeit with no reference to suspense.

2001, Local 2007, Schegloff 2007). Instead, radio commentary is, as mass media communication in general, clearly non-interactive and an anonymous and monologic one-to-many form of communication (cf. Habscheid 2005). Reporters usually have no more than a rough picture of the audience, and they use this picture when they produce their commentary (cf. Burger 2001). In this particular way, there is interaction between speaker and listeners albeit not in a direct way. These characteristics of radio commentaries bear methodological consequences: the recipients' orientations to analytical categories cannot be used as evidence for the accuracy of the researcher's interpretations, as it is usually the case in interactional linguistics or in other CA-oriented work. Instead, the researchers have to rely on their own knowledge as a competent member of their speech community about the desired effects of the reporters' use of linguistic resources. Furthermore, other types of evidence can be used, namely the relation of sequences of speech to prior sequences in terms of the discriminability of the linguistic features used (cf. Couper-Kuhlen and Selting 2001).

Another problem concerns the unequal access to visual information about the soccer match: while the reporter can actually see the match, the researcher cannot. This, however, puts the researcher in the same position as other members of the audience who exclusively rely on the reporters' verbal representations of the match (see Section 4 below for a further discussion).

There is, however, one major characteristic of radio talk that proves to be of advantage for the investigation of the linguistic construction of drama from a methodological standpoint: the exclusive use of the vocal channel to create drama and suspense. Especially in live commentaries, the reporters have to exploit their verbal and vocal resources fully to meet the expectations of the audience; that is, to draw a lively and authentic picture of the events on the soccer field. In fact, it is regarded as one of the reporters' key tasks to design live commentaries of football matches to be as dramatic as possible, and to convey the atmosphere in the stadium to the audience at home. Radio language, to sum up, can only use resources that are derived from its phonic realization.

Another methodological benefit deriving from the restriction on the auditory channel is that both the natural audience and the linguist have access to the same linguistic, i.e. verbal and paraverbal, signals; visual cues are irrelevant in radio talk.

Another feature of radio language often mentioned is its "secondary orality", a phrase coined by Ong (1982[2]: 134). In contrast to primary orality, secondary orality is based on written preparations and uses style features of written language (cf. Holly 1995). However, even though secondary orality may differ from the orality of everyday conversations, it still has to use the same resources, which are grounded in its verbal and phonetic realisation. Besides, contrary to other occurrences of secondary orality, the language used in the live commentary of football matches is for the most part not based on text that was written before the match, but text that is spontaneously produced in the course of the match.

3. Previous linguistic studies of radio sports commentaries

3.1 Verbal actions and their linguistic features in live commentaries of football matches

Research on the language used in live football commentaries on the radio commonly differentiates between at least two verbal actions: the description of actions and events happening on the soccer field, and elaborations providing background information about players, tactical issues etc. or evaluating the status of the match so far (cf. Rosenbaum 1978, Brandt 1979, Simmler 2000, and Siehr 2006 for an overview). It is the descriptions of actions and events that accomplish the main function of radio live commentaries because they make the soccer field "visible" and thus experienceable for the audience.

For commentaries of football matches on British radio, Delin (2000) differentiates between no less than four different verbal actions, i.e. narrating, evaluating, elaborating, and summarizing. Narrating, which corresponds to the above mentioned "descriptions of actions", is – in contrast to the other actions – composed of "time-critical" utterances, which occur simultaneously with the play and describe it. "Narrations" or "descriptions" as I would like to call them with reference to Rosenbaum (1978), Brandt (1979) and Siehr (2006) (see below) thus serve the primary purpose of live commentary.

Major differences between descriptions and other verbal actions are found in their syntactic and morpho-syntactic structures. According to Delin (2000), descriptions consist of utterances with little syntactic complexity and they are provided in the present tense, whereas other verbal actions exhibit syntactically complex structures and are realized in the past tense. Delin's observations concerning the prosodic features of live commentary are relatively vague: she mentions higher pitch range and a flat, list-like intonation, which other researchers (cf. Tench 1997) have already suggested to be typical of sports commentary. She also lists high speech rate as an important feature of horse race commentaries and suggests that it can be found in descriptions in live football commentaries as well. Little information is provided about her methods of analysis, though.

Studies on German football commentaries argue that descriptions of actions ("Aktionsbeschreibungen") differ from background comments ("Hintergrundkommentare") with respect to syntactic complexity and speech rate: descriptions exhibit syntactically less complex constructions than elaborations and are produced with a faster speech rate (cf. Rosenbaum 1978, Brandt 1979, Siehr 2006). This is particularly the case in situations with goal-scoring potential. Siehr (2006) mentions increased volume as another feature of descriptions of actions.

Most of these observations were confirmed by a recent study on football commentaries which adds a contrastive perspective to the investigation: Müller (2007a) compares German and English radio football commentaries. He distinguishes between "descriptions" and "elaborations" as the two main verbal actions in live commentary. "Elaborations" in his definition contain everything that is not a description of an event on the soccer field event. Additionally, Müller uses video material to further differentiate the descriptive actions between references to soccer field events made at the same time as the event is happening (*online-references*), references made after the event has happened (*offline-references*), and references made even before the event happens (*anticipations*). He finds that theses verbal actions can be distinguished from one another, among other things, in terms of morpho-syntactic marking of time reference (cf. Müller 2007b for more details).

In another study, Müller (2007c) concentrates on the measurement of speech rate (measured as syllables per Unit of Analysis, see below) and fundamental frequency (f0) on the one hand, and the complexity of syntactic structures on the other hand in the three verbal actions "online-reference", "offline-reference" and "elaboration". According to his observations, both online-references, and elaborations are characterized by a significantly higher speech rate than offline-references. These results hold for two of the three commentators investigated in his data.

The increasing speech rate is ascribed to the time-criticality of some utterances: the faster the events on the soccer field are happening, the faster the speech rate has to be. This, however, only holds for utterances with high syntactic complexity. Here, Müller finds an important difference between German and English commentators: in his view English commentators avoid syntactically complex structures to neutralize the effect of time pressure, whereas German commentators compensate the time pressure by using a higher speech rate while still using syntactically complex utterances.

Another of Müller's observation concerns the fundamental frequency in the different verbal actions. His results show that both offline und online-references are characterized by higher fundamental frequency than elaborations. Müller argues that the increased pitch rate reflects the reporters' increasing suspense and their evaluation of the described events as extremely important.

Even though Müller's (2007a) study allows interesting insights into the syntax and prosody of "descriptions" as compared to "elaborations", there are some problems with his approach to and derivation of analytical categories. Müller's (2007a) analysis is not based on the phonological category "intonation phrase" (cf. e.g. Ladefoged 2006) or "prosodic unit"; instead he segments speech into units bounded by clearly noticeable pauses. These units are called Units of Analysis; they constitute his basic categories for the measurement of speech rate. This may be problematic because, as Dankovičová (2001) points out, it is not clear at all what kind of unit the interpause stretch is, especially because pauses may fulfill several different functions at the same time (cf. Dankovičová 2001: 6 and 26–27). Furthermore, Müller focused on average f0 over these units of analysis only and was explicitly not interested in single intonation contours within such units of analysis. Within his approach it thus remains open whether the specific design of prosodic units plays an important role in the construction of drama and suspense.

3.2   The prosody of horse race commentaries

Trouvain and Barry (2000) carried out a study on the acoustic properties of horse race commentaries broadcast on British television. With their study they intended to acoustically verify the following auditory observations: a steady increase in pitch level, tempo, and intensity from one series of intonation units to the next and a decrease in pitch range. The authors believe these parameters to signal the increasing suspense communicated by the speakers.

Their measurements confirmed most of the auditory observations: fundamental frequency level and intensity clearly increased and fundamental frequency range narrowed at least for one of the three speakers investigated. Furthermore, an increased breathing rate was regarded as another parameter reflecting rising suspense.

Against all expectations, however, the increase in tempo could be verified neither by measurements of speech rate or articulation rate[4], nor could they confirm a reduction of pauses, which was assumed to be responsible for the auditory perception of increasing tempo. The factors responsible for the impression of acceleration thus remain open.

3.3   Summary: Current state of research on prosodic characteristics of live radio commentaries

The state of research on live football commentaries presented reveals at least two desiderata. The first concerns the adequacy of the prosodic categories: the choice of "Units of Analysis" (cf. Müller 2007a) as the basic unit seems somewhat arbitrary and not in compliance with interactional-linguistic theory (cf. Selting and Couper-Kuhlen 2001), which is the approach chosen as a basis for this investigation. Hence, in this case study I will make use of the category "prosodic unit" that is characterized, among other things, by a coherent pitch contour (cf. e.g. Selting 1995). A prosodic unit may contain a single syntactic phrase (such as a nominal or prepositional phrase), or a complex syntactic structure. The use of prosodic units as basic analytical units allows us to focus on the make-up of local and global contours within and across units. I believe that the latter, in particular, is one of the major prosodic resources for the constitution of a "dramatic speech style".

The second desideratum concerns the identification of the different verbal actions. In previous research, this was mainly grounded on semantic properties and their temporal relation to the events on the soccer field. More precisely, not all time-critical descriptions of actions exhibit the above mentioned prosodic and syntactic features. Instead, commentators use them locally to present selected events on the soccer field

---

4.   For the measurement of speech rate (production of phonological syllables with pauses), syllables per second were calculated; the same was done for measurements of articulation rate (production of phonological syllables without pauses).

as extremely dramatic. After introducing the data in Section 4, I will present some first observations on the linguistic differences between elaborations and descriptions, the latter being characterized by "dramatic speech style" (Section 5.1). I will then show how the commentators, when "speaking dramatically", make further distinctions between the presentation of dramatic events to build up suspense and the presentation of a dramatic event (i.e. a goal) as a climax (Sections 5.2 and 5.3). In the next section, the linguistic features of elaborations are further established (Section 5.4). In the final part of Section 5, the transition between two different speech styles will be looked at in particular (Section 5.5).

4. Data and methods of analysis

This paper gives first insights into the linguistic construction of drama and suspense in football commentaries. The results are thus preliminary and should be confirmed on the basis of a larger sample.

Recordings of three football matches with 3 male speakers were used for analysis. All of them were broadcast on major German radio stations. One commentary covers an UEFA-Cup game in December 2007 (Bayern München – Aris Thessaloniki), the other two originate from the 2008 European Championship, with Germany playing against Poland and Austria respectively. Ten examples of dramatic speech style and their context were analysed in detail. As a first step of analysis, instances of what was intuitively recognized as "dramatic speech" were selected and then transcribed along with the sequences before and after the dramatic speech. Thus, in contrast to the studies mentioned above, the analysis did not begin with a collection of different verbal actions to describe their prosodic characteristics but with utterances that are perceived to signal increasing drama and suspense.

Even though the distinction between time-critical descriptions of events on the pitch and other verbal actions such as summarizing or delivering background information is useful, I started off from the linguistic constructions of verbal actions describing events of the match, regardless of their temporal relation to the current events on the soccer field. This approach is in compliance with interactional-linguistic and contextualization theory, according to which language is used to construct verbal actions by way of creating the relevant context.

Articulation rate was calculated for each prosodic unit as the number of syllables per second excluding silent pauses longer than 0.10 seconds (cf. Trouvain and Barry 2000).

The intonation contours of the selected stretches of speech were then carefully described. The auditory description was backed up by acoustic analysis conducted with the help of PRAAT (cf. Boersma and Weenink 2010). Special attention was paid to the make-up of intonation contours within and across prosodic units, and to their internal structuring, with pauses and syllable lengthening as relevant criteria.

5.   The linguistic construction of drama and suspense: speaking dramatically

I will now turn to the question of how reporters use linguistic resources to construct drama and suspense and how they contextualize different verbal actions by employing different speech styles. Contrary to former research, the analysis will reveal at least two different time-critical "descriptive" verbal actions subsumable under the heading of "speaking dramatically": The reporters differentiate – mainly by prosodic means – between the "building up of suspense" on the one hand, and the "presentation of a highlight" on the other hand. The following extract contains instances of these two verbal actions (lines 1–4 and 5–9 respectively), and, additionally, exemplifies the verbal action of elaboration. The extract is used as a showcase example as it displays characteristic linguistic features of the verbal actions under investigation. For practical reasons, I will present the entire extract first (cf. sound file [KER-1-complete excerpt]).

(1)   Example 1

```
1   also  diese  ↑AUFgehitzte   phase; (.)
    PTCL  this   charged        phase
    well this charged phase

2   die   wir  noch  in  der  ersten   viertelstunde: (.)
    that  we   PTCL  in  the  first    15 minutes
    geSEHN             haben-
    PST PART see       AUX-1
    that we have seen in the first fifteen minutes

3   und  die   manfred  breukmann  HIER  geschildert   hat- .h
    and  that  manfred  breukmann  here  describe      AUX-3
    and that was described by manfred breukmann

4   <<steigend>  könn  wir  nur   beSTÄtigen,=
                 can   we   only  confirm-INF
    <<rising>         we can only confirm

5   =und  sehn  jetzt  die  CHANCE-
     and  see   now    the  chance
    and now see the chance

6   .h für   KlOse-
       for   KLOse
       for klose

7   <<all> auf  dem  weg  zum      ersten tor  des turNIERS,=
           on   the  way  to the   first goal  of the tournament
           on the way to the first goal of the tournament

8   spielt  ab      zu poDOLSki-=
    pass    PREFIX  to podolski
    passes to podolski
```

```
9  =und  dann  das  (.)   EI:NS  zu  NU:LL;>
   and  then  the      one   to  zero
   and then the         one to zero
```

5.1   Elaborations vs. descriptions: First observations

Semantically, the extract can be divided into two parts. In the first part (lines 1–4), the commentator delivers a longer evaluative remark on the course of the match so far. The second part (lines 5–9) refers directly to the events on the soccer field. Hence, the first part is an "elaboration" whereas the second part is a "description of actions".

According to previous research, the descriptions of actions should be produced with faster articulation rate than the elaborations. Yet, upon close analysis, even though an increase in articulation rate can be perceived auditorily, it could not be verified by measurements of phonological syllables per second (without pauses). The results are thus in agreement with Trouvain and Barry's (2000) measurements of articulation rate in horse race commentaries.

(1) a.   Example 1: Articulation rate measurements

```
1  also diese ↑AUFgehitzte phase,
   Well this charged phase
   5.9 syll./sec
```

```
2  die wir noch in der ersten viertelstunde (.) geSEHN
   haben;
   that we have seen in the first fifteen minutes        7.5 sylls/sec
```

```
3  und die manfred breukmann hier geschildert hat; .h
   and that was described by manfred breukmann
   8 sylls/ sec
```

```
4  <u> können wir nur beSTÄtigen,=
   we can only confirm
   8 sylls/sec
```

```
5  =und sehn jetzt die ↑CHANCE- (.)
   and now see the chance
   5 sylls/sec
```

```
6  für ↑KlOse-
   for   klose
   6.2 sylls/sec
```

```
7  <h, all> auf dem weg zum ersten tor des tur↑NIERS,=
            on the way to the first goal of the tournament
   6.2 sylls/sec
```

```
8  spielt ab zu poDOLSki;=
   passes to podolski
   7 sylls/sec
```

9 und dann das (.) <h, rufend> EI:NS zu NU:LL;>[5]
and then the one to zero
2.09 syll./sec

Articulation rate varies significantly over this stretch of talk. The only noticeable irregularity, however, concerns the last utterance (line 9), where the speaker slows down considerably. I will return to this phenomenon later (Section 5.3).

What can be noted is that the prosodic units become increasingly smaller in the course of the extract. At the beginning, they correspond to larger syntactic structures, such as the relative clauses in lines 2 and 3. From line 5 onwards (cf. sound files [KER-excerpt line5.wav], [KER-excerpt line6.wav], [KER-excerpt line7.wav], [KER-excerpt line8.wav]), i.e. with the beginning of the description of actions, the prosodic units become considerably shorter; small syntactic phrases that are part of larger syntactic units – compare the short prepositional phrase in line 6 and the extended phrase in line 7, both part of the same larger syntactic phrase – or with elliptical structures in line 8 and 9. Moreover, after line 4, the prosodic units are often latched onto each other with no pauses between them, and the accented syllables in lines 4–8 exhibit only little lengthening compared to the accented syllables before and after these lines.[6]

To conclude, a combination of features, namely reduced syntactic complexity and latched prosodic units, seems to be responsible for the auditory impression of gradual acceleration. These findings hold across other examples of action descriptions as well.

Even though measurements of articulation rate do not support the claim of different verbal actions in football commentaries in a straightforward way, there seem to be differences concerning the structure of prosodic units in elaborations and descriptions of actions. I would like to follow up on this observation and now turn to a more elaborate discussion of what I call "speaking dramatically". All ten examples show that the speakers make a clear difference between the description of potentially dramatic events and the description of a dramatic event, as, e.g. a goal, by choosing different speech styles. In what follows, I will use "dramatic" as an umbrella term and distinguish further between descriptions that build up suspense and therefore contextualize the described events as dramatic, and descriptions of highlights that are presented as most dramatic events.

5.2   Dramatic descriptions (1): Building up suspense

In the showcase example, drama and suspense are audibly constructed from the utterance *und sehn jetzt die chance* ('and now see the chance', line 5) onwards. What is most perceivable is the increase in pitch across several units, which, according to Müller

---

5.   The last part of the utterance, 'one to zero', was not included in the measurements because it already produced in a new style, with different linguistic features, of which speech rate is one (see Section 5.3 below).

6.   This comparison is based on auditory analysis only.

(2007a) and Trouvain and Barry (2000), is one of the prosodic features to signal suspense. In contrast to the measurements of articulation rate, the increase in pitch can be
acoustically verified.

An acoustic analysis of the units of lines 5–9 reveals an overall increase in pitch
rate, with fundamental frequency ending at almost 400 Hz in the utterance *eins zu null*
('one to zero', line 9). In what follows I will present a unit-to-unit-analysis, describing
the main prosodic characteristics of each unit.

The first time-critical utterance to indicate rising suspense and drama (line 5: *und
sehen jetzt die chance* 'and now see the chance') shows an increase of fundamental frequency from 203 Hz at its beginning to approximately 260 Hz at its end, as is shown in
Figure (1).

Two intonational features are noteworthy: first, the rise in pitch at the beginning
of the utterance (*und sehen jetzt die* 'and now see the') that is perceived as steep, and
second, the flat pitch movements on the nucleus /CHAN/. Because of the steep rise,
the overall pitch range comprises 5.01 semitones which is considerable compared to
the following units.

The next unit (line 6) consists of a short prepositional phrase with a full contour.
See Figure (2) for details.

The unit starts with a very high onset (nearly 300 Hz), which is followed by an
immediate decrease in fundamental frequency. At the end of the unit, another slight
decrease can be observed. In contrast to the previous unit, the pitch range is relatively
narrow; it covers 23 Hertz instead of almost 70 Hertz in line 5. The contour is thus
relatively flat, with the pitch range covering 1.36 semitones.

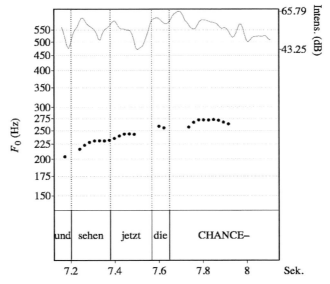

Figure 1. Pitch trace of line 05 (cf. sound file [KER-excerpt line5.wav])

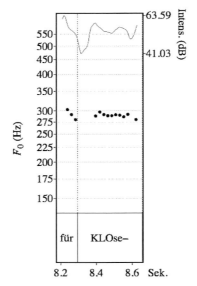

Figure 2. Pitch trace of line 06 (cf. sound file [KER-excerpt line6.wav])

The subsequent unit (line 7) begins on approximately the same pitch level as the previous one ended; a slight rise and fall can be observed on the nucleus /NIER/, reaching 337 Hz. Even though the pitch range is less narrow than in the previous unit, the contour is still relatively flat (2.68 semitones), as can be seen in Figure (3).

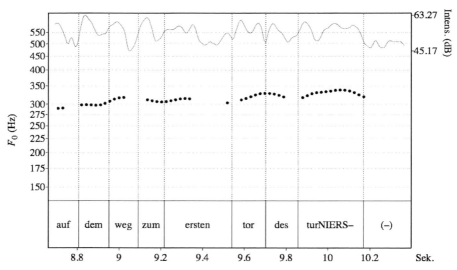

Figure 3. PRAAT-Picture of line 07 (cf. sound file [KER-excerpt line7.wav])

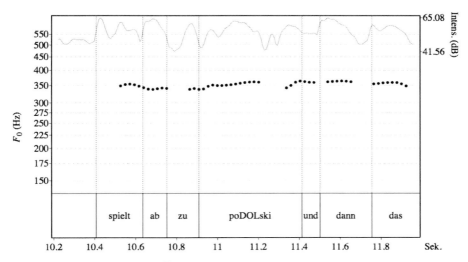

Figure 4.   Pitch trace of line 08[7]

The next utterance (line 8) starts at 350 Hz and stays on more or less the same high level. Again, the contour is relatively flat, with hardly any pitch movement. The pitch range covers 2.68 semitones (cf. Figure 4).

The analysis of pitch contours supports the findings of Müller (2007a) and Trouvain and Barry (2000): increasing pitch that is produced systematically over a series of prosodic units can be found in descriptions of events, and it signals that something important is going on. Rising suspense seems to be an important effect of increasing pitch level. There are, however, other prosodic features that co-occur with rising pitch and that may also signal rising suspense.

The following features which are also found in all other examples of dramatic speech analysed are used to signal rising suspense and thus contextualize the time-critical description of specific events on the soccer field as dramatic:

- high-rising intonation, with a steep rise in the first unit and gradual increase in the following units,
- narrow pitch range within single units, which is due to the minimal peaks on accented syllables,
- final level intonation: most units exhibit no or only little pitch movements on their last syllables (if they are not the nucleus). Together with the narrow pitch range, this leads to a list-like, stylized intonation contour in many of the prosodic units,
- unclear boundaries between prosodic units: many units are tied together closely by latching (lines 4–5, 7–8, 8–9) and there are only few pauses between units or within units,
- absence of lengthening on accented syllables.

---

7.   The figure also shows part of line 9 because both units cannot be separated auditorily.

Features (4) and (5) may contribute to the auditory impression of an ongoing acceleration of articulation rate that could, however, not be verified by measurements. Yet this
is not the only way in which time-critical descriptions can be presented to the audience, as will be discussed in the next section.

5.3   Dramatic descriptions (2): The presentation of a climax

In comparison to the prosodic units that describe a series of events on the pitch as dramatic, the unit that describes the most exciting event in a match, i.e. a goal, usually displays a different set of prosodic features. In the case of Example (1), the analysis of the
utterance *eins zu null* ('one to zero', line 9) reveals the following typical characteristics:

First, the speaker reaches the highest pitch level in this extract, with fundamental
frequency arriving at nearly 400 Hertz. Second, even though the speaker rushes into
the unit, he slows down considerably after a short break. This auditory impression is
paralleled by measurements: in contrast to the units before, here the reporter produces
only 2.09 syllables per second. The deceleration is mainly achieved through an extreme lengthening of accented syllables in the second part of the unit (*eins zu null* 'one
to zero').

As a third feature, a deep drop in pitch on the last syllable can be observed. This is
visualized in Figure (5):

The commentator creates a contrast between the description of a series of events
on the pitch as dramatic (such as seen in lines 4–8) and the presentation of the most
dramatic event, i.e. the goal. This contrast is achieved by the use of a specific set of
prosodic features that are as follows:

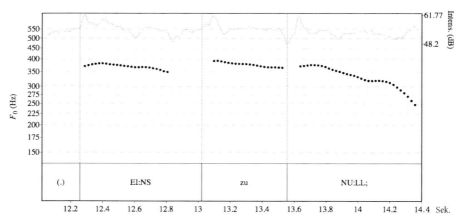

Figure 5. Pitch trace of line 9 (cf. sound file [KER-excerpt line9.wav])

- the pitch level reaches a maximum height,
- the articulation rate is slowed down considerably, with lengthened syllables
- many pauses occur within the prosodic unit
- a deep drop in pitch occurs on the last syllable of the utterance.

In sum, the analysis of linguistic resources in the commentaries at hand clearly shows that the reporters use different prosodic resources for the description of different kinds of events. Other examples of dramatic speech support the claim that, apart from the basic distinction between the verbal actions of "descriptions" and "elaborations" on the grounds of their respective time-criticality, we have to distinguish further between descriptions which build up suspense and descriptions of the highlights of the match, usually the goals. Different ways of speaking dramatically are used for the constitution of the two types of descriptions. It is thus argued that speaking dramatically consists of at least two subtypes, namely "building up suspense" and "presenting a climax".

5.4   Elaborations: Summarizing and evaluating

Finally I would like to discuss an instance of an elaboration sequence to be found at the beginning of Example (1) which is again representative of the data. Once more, the reporter uses syntactic and prosodic means to constitute the verbal action of "elaborating". In the case of Example (1), the elaboration sequence contains evaluative information about the match so far. See Example (1c) for the relevant extract (cf. sound file [KER-1c-excerpt lines 1–4.wav]).

(1) c.   Example 1: Summarizing and evaluation

```
1 also diese ↑AUFgehitzte phase; (.)
  PTCL this  charged      phase
  well this charged phase

2 die wir noch in der ersten viertelstunde: (.)
  that we  PTCL in the first   15 minutes
  geSEHN   haben-
  PST PART see AUX-1
  that we have seen in the first fifteen minutes

3 und die manfred breukmann HIER geschildert hat- .h
  and that manfred breukmann here describe    AUX-3
  and that was described by manfred breukmann

4 <<steigend> könn wir nur  beSTÄtigen,=
          can  we  only confirm-INF
  <<rising> we can only confirm
```

Apart from the syntactic features mentioned above (Section 5.1), the units also differ in terms of prosodic features from the verbal actions of "building up suspense" and "presenting a climax".

In the first prosodic unit (line 1, cf. sound file KER-excerpt line1.wav]), the speaker produces a high pitch peak on the accented syllable; indeed, this is often found in utterances providing background information, evaluations or other information that is not time-critical. The following units also exhibit considerably more pitch movements than observed during the dramatic speech style. As a result, the pitch range in this unit is rather wide but the overall pitch rate does not exceed 250 Hz on the accented syllable. Figure (6) visualizes the acoustic properties of line 1.

The high pitch peak on the nuclear syllable and the pitch movement on the last syllable of the unit are immediately observable as features contrasting with the prosodic characteristics of the units analysed previously (lines 5–8). Furthermore, the pitch range is much larger, comprising 7.60 semitones altogether.

The subsequent units (lines 2–3) coincide with a long relative clause, which is the syntactic continuation of line 1, and again they feature distinct pitch peaks on nuclear syllables. The unit in line 2, in addition, includes both a lengthened syllable and a short pause following immediately after. The pitch range in both units is slightly narrower than in the previous unit, covering 4.68 semitones and 3.93 semitones respectively. See Figures 7 and 8 for details.

To sum up, verbal actions of elaboration exhibit the following prosodic characteristics:

– unmarked pitch register,
– wider pitch range, especially on accented syllables,
– distinctive pitch movements on nuclear syllables,
– frequent pauses in and between units,
– lengthened syllables within units.

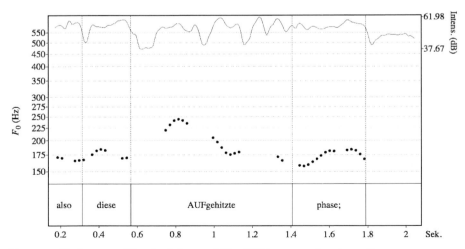

Figure 6. Pitch trace of line 01 (cf. sound files [KER-excerpt line 1.wav])

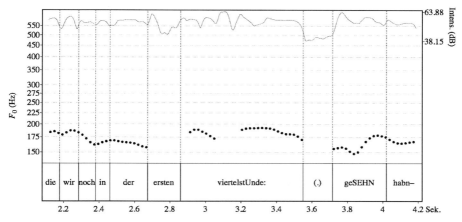

Figure 7. Pitch trace of line 02 (cf. sound files [KER-excerpt line 2.wav])

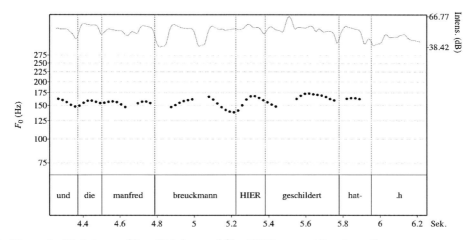

Figure 8. Pitch trace of line 03 (cf. sound files [KER-excerpt line 3.wav])

This list of features is also characteristic of other examples of elaborations in the data. These features are in stark contrast to the prosodic characteristics of the types of dramatic descriptions discussed above, and when these feature co-occur they play a major role in the constitution of the verbal action of elaborating as opposed to speaking dramatically.[8]

That prosody indeed plays an important part in signalling drama and suspense is moreover confirmed by looking at the utterance which presents the "switch point" between "elaborating" on the one hand, and "speaking dramatically" on the other hand.

---

8.   The syntactic features were mentioned in Section 5.1.

5.5   Transition between "summarizing" and "speaking dramatically"

In Example (1), it is the utterance *können wir nur beSTÄtigen* ('we can only confirm', line 4) that constitutes, as I will argue, the transition space or "switch point" between elaborating and speaking dramatically.

Semantically, the utterance contains a confirmation that is still part of the evaluative recapitulation of the last few minutes of the match. However, it can already be auditorily perceived as signalling rising suspense and thus gives the hearer an indication that something interesting is happening in the match. This is mainly achieved by the use of specific prosodic features.

The most notable acoustic difference to the previous unit (line 3) is the high step-up in pitch at the beginning: the previous unit ended at approximately 160 Hz whereas this unit starts at 225 Hz. This up-step is auditorily clearly perceivable and possibly part of the reason why this unit can already be heard as more dramatic than the previous ones. Other prosodic features are a relatively flat pitch range compared to the previous units (2.18 semitones) and an absence of pauses and lengthened syllables within the prosodic unit. Moreover, the speaker rushes into the next unit where he produces a steep rise in pitch, as mentioned above. See Figure (9) for a visualization of the characteristics described.

With this speech style, the reporters do not only contextualize their verbal actions as "describing events on the football pitch" but present the events described as particularly dramatic and exciting.

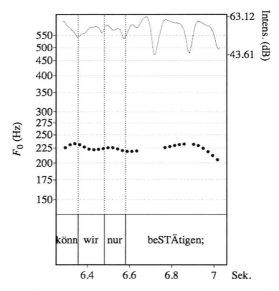

Figure 9. Pitch trace of line 4 (cf. sound files [KER-excerpt line 4.wav])

To sum up, the reporter uses prosodic features to construct drama and suspense for the hearer even before he starts talking about the exciting events on the pitch. Prosody here works as an anticipatory device to prepare the audience for exciting events that may be happening on the pitch soon (see also Klewitz and Couper-Kuhlen 1999 for the use of prosody to signal upcoming reported speech).

6.   Conclusion: Unit production in dramatic speech style

Following up on the distinction between time-critical descriptions of events on the soccer field and non-time-critical elaborations that provide the audience with background information, this paper argued that reporters in live commentaries of football matches use linguistic resources for the construction of drama and suspense. On the basis of a showcase example, it was demonstrated that the reporters make a clear distinction between the description of events that are potentially dramatic by signalling rising suspense and the presentation of the most dramatic event that can happen on the pitch – a goal – by using different speech styles that can be described as sets of co-occurring prosodic features. "Building up suspense" features a continuous rise of fundamental frequency across units and a relatively narrow pitch range within units as the most relevant features. The prosodic units correspond to short syntactic phrases, with blurred prosodic unit boundaries between them. Furthermore, the absence of lengthened accented syllables and of pauses within and between units are possibly at least partly responsible for the perception of an increase in articulation rate. With this speech style, the reporters do not only contextualize their verbal actions as "describing events on the soccer field" but present the described events as particularly dramatic and exciting.

However, reporters use a different speech style when presenting a climax. This style features a considerable deceleration of articulation rate, with extremely lengthened syllables, and a particularly high pitch register. Often, a deep drop in pitch can be found on the last syllable.

The analysis thus shows that drama and suspense are not simply triggered by the events happening in the real world but are constructed via the use of specific linguistic resources in the context of spontaneously produced speech. Indeed, other examples of dramatic speech style show that suspense is often built up without a goal being scored subsequently. However, in such cases the prosodic delivery is the same and thus gives a foreshadowing of the dramatic events that may follow.

In contrast, reporters employ different prosodic cues in other verbal actions such as summarizing or evaluating the match so far. Prosodic units then display many pauses and lengthened syllables between and within units. In addition, unmarked pitch register and pitch range are used, with high steps on accented syllables occurring regularly.

To conclude, the observations show that it is not sufficient to distinguish between time-critical descriptions on the one hand and utterances that do not deliver time-critical information on the other hand. An analysis that uses the prosodic and syntactic features of different speech styles as a starting point should be able to reveal many more verbal actions taking place in live commentaries of football matches. Another future topic of research should explore the function of prosody as an anticipatory device to foreshadow specific verbal actions in more detail and in different contexts.

References

Boersma, Paul and Weenink, David 2010. "Praat: doing phonetics by computer" (Version 5.1.23) [Computer program]. Last access: January 1, 2010, from http://www.praat.org.

Brandt, Wolfgang 1979. "Zur Sprache der Sportberichterstattung in den Massenmedien". *Muttersprache* 89: 160–178.

Burger, Harald 2001. "Textsorten in den Massenmedien." In: *Text- und Gesprächslinguistik: Ein internationales Handbuch zeitgenössischer Forschung.* vol. 1, Klaus Brinker, Gerd Antos, Wolfgang Heinemann and Sven Sager (eds.), 614–628. Berlin: de Gruyter.

Couper-Kuhlen, Elizabeth and Selting, Margret 2001. "Introducing Interactional Linguistics". In: *Studies in Interactional Linguistics*, Margret Selting and Elizabeth Couper-Kuhlen (eds.), 1–22. Amsterdam: Benjamins.

Dankovičová, Jana 2001. *The linguistic basis of articulation rate variation in Czech.* Frankfurt/ Main: Hector.

Delin, Judy 2000. *The language of everyday life.* London: Sage Publications.

Habscheid, Stephan 2005. "Das Internet – ein Massenmedium?" In: *Websprache.net*, Torsten Siever, Peter Schlobinski and Jens Runkehl (eds.), 46–66. Berlin: de Gruyter.

Holly, Werner 1995. "Secondary orality in the electronic media". In: *Aspects of oral communication,* Uta Quasthoff (ed.), 340–363. Berlin: de Gruyter.

Klewitz, Gabriele and Couper-Kuhlen, Elizabeth 1999. "Quote – unquote". The role of prosody in the contextualization of reported speech sequences." *Pragmatics* 9 (4): 459–485.

Ladefoged, Peter 2006. *A course in phonetics.* Boston: Thomson Wadsworth.

Local, John 2007. "Phonetic detail and the organization of talk-in-interaction." In: *Proceedings of the 16th International Congress of Phonetic Sciences*, 115–118. Saarbrücken. (http://www. icphs2007.de/?/conference/)

Müller, Torsten 2007a. *Football, language and linguistics.* Tübingen: Narr.

Müller, Torsten 2007b. "Grammatical past time reference in spontaneously produced language". In: *Spoken language pragmatics. An analysis of form-function relations*, Regina Weinert (ed.), 29–59. London: Continuum.

Müller, Torsten 2007c. "Speech rate, time pressure and emotion in English and German football commentary". In: *Spoken language pragmatics. An analysis of form-function relations*, Regina Weinert (ed.), 160–181. London: Continuum.

Ong, Walter 1982[2]. *Orality and literacy.* London: Routledge.

Rosenbaum, Dieter 1978. "Gesprochen: 'Ein-Wort-Sätze' im Aktionstext." In: *Sport- und Massenmedien*, Josef Hackforth and Siegfried Weißenberg (eds.), 142–157. Bad Homburg: Limpert.

Sandig, Barbara and Selting, Margret 1997. "Einleitung." In: *Sprech- und Gesprächsstile*, Margret Selting and Barbara Sandig (eds.), 1–8. Berlin: de Gruyter.

Schegloff, Emanuel 2007. *Sequence organization in interaction. A primer in conversation analysis.* Cambridge: Cambridge University Press.

Selting 1995. *Prosodie im Gespräch. Aspekte einer interaktionalen Phonologie der Konversation.* Tübingen: Niemeyer

Siehr, Karl-Heinz 2006. "Lucio kommt zu spät und ....TOR TOR! Zur sprachlichen Analyse des Spannungsgehaltes von Livereportagen." *Praxis Deutsch* 196: 31–37.

Simmler, Franz 2000. "Textsorten im Bereich des Sport". In: *Text- und Gesprächslinguistik,* vol. 1, Klaus Brinker, Gerd Antos, Wolfgang Heinemann and Sven Sager (eds.), 718–731. Berlin: de Gruyter.

Tench, Judith 1997. "The fall and rise of the level tone in English." *Functions of Language* 4 (1): 1–22.

Trouvain, Jürgen and Barry, William J. 2000. "The prosody of excitement in horse race commentaries." *Speech Emotion 2000*: 86–91.

Commentating fictive and real sports

Comments on Friederike Kern "Speaking dramatically: The prosody of radio live commentary of football matches"

Johannes Wagner
University of Southern Denmark

And it's Johnson – Johnson with the Quaffle (...) and she´s ducked Warrington, she´s passed Montague, she´s – ouch – been hit from behind by a Bludger from Crabbe ... Montague catches the Quaffle, Montague heading back up the pitch and – nice Bludger there from George Weasley, that's a Bludger to the head of Montague, he drops the Quaffle, caught by Katie Bell, Katie Bell of Griffindor reverse-passes to Alicia Spinnet and Spinnet's away – (...) dodges Warrington, avoids a Bludger – close call Alicia – and the crowds are loving this, just listen to them

(Rowling 2003: 360)

The introductory quote is taken from an unscripted online commentary of a match of Quidditch – an airborne game on broomsticks with three different balls. The "transcription" by Rowling, although it might be inadequate, captures features typical of online commentaries on fast sport events: short syntactic units, frequent references to players and actions and inserted comments, but first and foremost an indication of the talk trying to keep up with the action on the playground. The talk is built with short syntactic units ("Johnson with the Quaffle") which at times even get shorter ("dodges Warrington, avoids a Bludger") and hereby builds suspense. The transcription uses symbols that read as indication of pauses ("-", "...") or of changes between descriptive and evaluative parts ("she's – ouch – been hit from behind by a Bludger").

Although the example is taken from a book of fiction and illustrates something as odd as an online stadium commentary of ongoing actions – odd since the game is visually available for the spectators for whom the commentary is delivered –, the example catches the experience of radio transmitted sports commentaries where features of the delivery of the commentary signal tension and drama on the pitch which may result in the listeners paying special attention.

In a case study, Friederike Kern's paper describes the prosody of radio football commentaries – which are different from comments of televised games. Here the audience has visual access to the game and the commentators can stay silent for spates of time and often – especially in uneventful games – deliver evaluations and analyses instead of an online narration of the game. In radio commentaries, the speaker needs to deliver all the details through the talk and build the suspense which is the main attraction of sport events.

The main surprise in Kern's careful description of live radio soccer commentaries is that the impression of increased speech rate is actually not produced by an increased number of syllables per second. The resources used by the commentators to build up suspense towards a climax are short prosodic units that are latched onto each other and exhibit rising fundamental frequency. Suspense is built up by a rise of fundamental frequency to a very high register (in the example examined from about 200 Hz to nearly 400 Hz for a male voice) as well as by narrowing the pitch range. Kern argues convincingly that local and global prosodic contours are a major resource in the construction of dramatic speech style.

Contrary to most research in this area, Kern starts her analysis with prosodic characteristics and not with an analysis of the verbal actions in the commentary. So the analysis is based on what is perceived as specific dramatic speech style, and the challenge is to describe how the specific prosodic production cues that style.

Since commentators – as Kern rightly remarks – have no access to their recipients' responses, analysts have no proof of next turn procedure, that is, analysts cannot build their arguments on what participants do. Analyzing mass media interaction needs to build on careful description of the phenomenon as well as the analyst's membership knowledge. The careful description in this case produces specific prosodic contours and stylization of talk that is recognizable as a dramatic narration of an ongoing event for somebody who does not have any visual access to the event.

Now, this begs the question whether all sports commentaries use the same pool of prosodic resources, i.e. whether Kern's description may be generalized to other types of sports? What does her study tell us about ways of dramatizing the ongoing activity on the field in other sport events?

The answer may be found in research on other sports. Kuiper (1996), for example, has analyzed online commentaries of horse racing in data from the UK and New Zealand. Kuiper's analysis is methodologically quite different from Kern's. He is mainly interested in formulae and their role in fluent talk, i.e. the problems of fast speech processing and the resources that enable speakers to speak fast and smoothly. Yet, he makes some interesting comments on the prosody of the race "callers". The "archetypical" prosodic pattern is rising in semitones in regular intervals. In the course of the commentary of a single race, the caller's pitch rises a full octave. The callers speak monotonously in a 'droned' intonation, defined as "a speaker consistently speaks in a monotone with little or no normal speech intonation" (1996: 19). As in Kern's findings, there is rising pitch until a climax (which in horse racing is the finish, in football a situation which may lead to a goal). In football commentaries the pitch range is narrowed, in horse race calls the pitch range is extremely minimal. So, although both sports commentators use comparable resources, the ways in which they are used are different.

Kuiper compares what he found in horse racing calls to the commentary of "slow" sports as e.g. cricket. Cricket commentaries, apart from rare spurts of high activity, do not seem to show features of stylization. This might indicate that prosodic patterns might be different in sports with fast pacing where the commentator's talk displays the fast actions on the field as compared to slow sports where commentators have a leeway for other forms of talk due to the slowly moving actions on the field. Kern's results may therefore form grounds for a hypothesis that stylized features of prosody would be found in all types of fast sports and there may even be a common pool of prosodic resources for different types of sport commentaries.

Kern's study is a contribution to the study of stylized intonation. It describes membership knowledge about the ways certain actions are prosodically recognizable even when the words of the talk, i.e. the segmental information, might become inaccessible for the listeners due to background noise in the stadium or atmospheric conditions. The prosodic resources for building suspense and drama in the narration of a football game are probably found as well in the ways speakers build up suspense and drama in mundane talk. However, this has to be shown in further studies.

References

Rowling, Joanne K. 2003. *Harry Potter and the order of the Phoenix.* London: Bloomsbury.
Kuiper, Koenraad 1996. *Smooth talkers. The linguistic performance of auctioneers and sportscasters.* Mahwah, N.J.: Lawrence Erlbaum.

Tonal repetition and tonal contrast in English carer-child interaction*

Bill Wells
University of Sheffield, United Kingdom

Research has so far failed to demonstrate how, or even that, young children progressively acquire a set of tones or pitch accents that have distinct meanings or functions. From recent work in the phonetics of conversation, there is some evidence that a speaker's choice of tone can be accounted for by reference to the tone used in the previous speaker's turn rather than by reference to an intonational lexicon. This view is supported by analysis of interactions between Robin, aged 19–21 months, and his mother. Robin systematically uses a repeat of his mother's tone to display alignment with the ongoing activity, while using a different, contrasting tone when initiating a new action or sequence. It is suggested that such tonal repetition and contrast are fundamental to children's learning of English intonation.

1. Introduction

Talk between young children and their caregivers brings into sharp focus the role of prosodic features in interaction, not least because it is the principal arena in which intonational and interactional competences are shaped. This chapter reports on a new direction in a wider research programme investigating children's development of intonation from the perspective of talk-in-interaction. Hitherto, the focus of attention has been on the delimitative and cohesive roles of accentual prominence (Corrin et al. 2001) and how these can be learnt or accessed by the young child in the course of turn-taking with carers, taking as primary evidence the design and placement of overlapping talk and participants' orientation to overlap (Wells and Corrin 2004).

---

* This analysis was first presented at the conference 'Prosody and Interaction', University of Potsdam, September 15–17, 2008. I am grateful to the participants at that meeting for their suggestions and to the following for comments on earlier versions of the chapter: Dagmar Barth-Weingarten, Jan Gorisch, Friederike Kern, Sue Peppé, Elisabeth Reber, Gareth Walker. Special thanks are due to Juliette Corrin, for access to the recordings of Robin and his mother, and for many fruitful discussions about the data.

The topic of the present chapter is the emergence of the system of tone, which is widely viewed as central to the communication of meaning through intonation. This chapter presents an analysis of interactions between Robin, aged 19–21 months, and his mother, in which Robin systematically uses a repeat of his mother's tone to display alignment with the ongoing activity, while using a different, contrasting tone when initiating a new action or sequence. It is argued that tonal repetition and contrast may be important for Robin in learning how tone works in English intonation. Following a review of relevant issues in the adult and child intonation research, an extended fragment of interaction is presented which illustrates the interplay of different aspects of English intonation in the course of interaction between Robin and his mother. This is followed by shorter data fragments which specifically illustrate the interactional roles of tonal repetition and tonal contrast.

1.1   Tone: Form and function

Most researchers in English intonation have taken as axiomatic the notion that English, in most if not all its varieties, has a repertoire of distinct tones, sometimes subdivided into pitch accents and boundary tones (cf. Gussenhoven 2004: 124). This can be understood by analogy with lexical tone systems in a language such as Mandarin Chinese. Formally, tones can be differentiated along a number of parameters, including: pitch direction (rise vs. fall vs. level); relative complexity of pitch movement (rise vs. fall-rise, fall vs. rise-fall); start and /or end point within the speaker's range, e.g. low fall (from mid to low) vs. high fall (from high to low). Different notations have been adopted in attempts to capture the range of patterns found within a language variety, across language varieties, and across languages (Cruttenden 1997: 55).

Functionally, there has been an assumption that the distinct tones or pitch accents are associated with distinct meanings or sets of meanings, just as tones in a lexical tone language are associated with non-overlapping sets of lexical items. In studies of intonation languages such as English, the meanings of the tones have most often been derived from the impressionistic judgement of the analyst, e.g. Halliday (1967). More recently Gussenhoven (2004: 297) has described the tone system of English using this approach, as has Cruttenden (1997), who describes two falling tones of English as follows:

> "Both falling tones involve a sense of finality, completeness, definiteness and separateness when used with declaratives....The low-fall is generally more uninterested, unexcited and dispassionate, whereas the high-fall is more interested, more excited, more involved...."   (Cruttenden 1997: 91).

This view of tone meaning implies a speech production model like that of Levelt (1989) whereby the speaker generates a message with a syntactic structure, semantic content and a pragmatic function, the tone being selected from the language's repertoire of tones in order to convey the pragmatic function of the utterance.

According to Levelt, the melody of an intonational phrase "is, through its nuclear tone, an important instrument for expressing the utterance's illocutionary force." (Levelt 1989: 398)

In an effort to free intonation analysis from reliance on the analyst's intuitive interpretation of intonational meanings, numerous studies of prosody in naturalistic conversation have been published since the 1980's, in which claims about prosodic meaning are systematically warranted from the behaviour of the conversational participants themselves (e.g. Couper-Kuhlen and Selting 1996, Couper-Kuhlen and Ford 2004). Much of this research has been concerned with the speaker turn, its continuation and the projection of its end, in which pitch features have been shown to be implicated. For this function, a critical opposition seems to be between the presence of a major accent, projecting turn delimitation, vs. its absence, projecting further talk by the current speaker (cf. Wells and Macfarlane 1998). The extent of pitch movement apparently plays a critical role, in conjunction with other non-pitch features, in determining whether a response is expectable and if so, what type of response (Barth-Weingarten 2009). The child's control over the amount of pitch movement deployed on the different elements of the utterance has also been shown to be central to the early development of young children's turn-construction abilities (Corrin et al. 2001).

As for the direction and shape of the terminal pitch contour, though it is often thought that this is the determining factor in conveying pragmatic meaning (cf. Cruttenden 1997), Szczepek Reed (2004) has suggested that in naturally occurring talk-in-interaction this may vary in rather unsystematic ways, in relation to pragmatic function. In fact, within the 'prosody and conversation' literature, there has been rather little engagement with tonal contrastivity and its possible functions. An exception is the systematic investigation of the potential opposition between tones at the same place in interactional structure that was carried out by Walker (2004). Walker examined the phonetic characteristics of adjacency pairs in a corpus of naturally occurring conversational data. The first pair parts included invitations, enquiries, offers, assessments and requests. Syntactically, both interrogative and declarative forms were found and two distinct pitch contours were also found, one falling and the other rising. However, there was no evidence of any relationship between the syntactic form of the first pair part and its pitch contour; nor between pitch contour and the type of first pair part, for example whether it was a request or an assessment. Thus neither syntactic nor pragmatic accounts of the meaning of English tones were supported.

In sum, it is hard to find robust evidence from studies of naturally occurring talk that speakers and listeners actually make use of tonal contrast to convey meanings in the way that many intonation researchers have suggested. Much recent intonation research has put to one side the question of how intonational form, including that of tones or pitch accents, relates to meaning and has instead focussed on formal aspects of pitch modelling. However, this does not mean that tone is interactionally irrelevant.

Walker (2004: 119–122) demonstrates that, when granting a first speaker's request, one resource that second speakers use is to match the pitch contour of the request itself, whereas when a request is declined such pitch matching is absent. This finding contributes to a growing body of research demonstrating the interactional relevance of prosodic repetition by a next speaker (e.g. Couper-Kuhlen 1996, Szczepek Reed 2006). This line of research, focussing on the idea that a speaker's choice of tone may on many occasions be accounted for by reference to the previous speaker's turn rather than by reference to an intonational lexicon, informs the research into a young child's use of tone that is described in the present report.

1.2   Tone in child language development

While the belief lingers that different tones or pitch accents will eventually be shown to have distinct and inherent meanings, there is virtually no recent research on how children might come to acquire such a system. The most recent studies of children's development of tone have, like adult intonation studies, concentrated on formal aspects. For example, Balog and Snow (2007), having identified an end point in terms of the tonal or contour inventory of adult American English, studied children's productions at different ages (12–17 vs. 18–23 months) to see (a) which adult contours they already use (b) which adult contours they do not yet use and (c) what non-adult contours they use. The authors were unable to demonstrate an age-related shift towards the adult inventory and distribution of tones. This result indicates that, whatever is going on in terms of intonation at this crucial early stage in the development of communicative skills, it cannot be interpreted as a progressive acquisition of adult tones. Moreover, such an approach has nothing to say with regard to how a child's ability to accurately reproduce the intonation contours of the community relates to the child's ability to use these contours in conversation. This issue is starkly highlighted in the often reported phenomenon of echolalia in cases of severe (low-functioning) autism, in which the child may produce perfectly formed, adult-like prosodic contours but with very limited ability to use them as an interactional resource (Local and Wootton 1995). Such cases suggest a potential dissociation between form and content with respect to tones and their development.

As discussed above, researchers investigating the functions of tone in intonation languages typically assign a distinct meaning or set of (normally, related) meanings to each member of the tone system identified for that language. On this view, the young child's task is, formally, to learn a system of tones along with their phonetic exponents, and, functionally, to learn what the meanings of each tone are. However, the studies that have taken this approach have produced problematic results.

The most comprehensive description of intonation development in functional terms is Halliday's study of his son Nigel (Halliday 1975). This description is situated within a functional approach to adult language. Up to around a chronological age of eighteen months (C.A. 1;06), Nigel used high level tones on proper names, and otherwise a variety of falling tones. Then at C.A. 1;07, Nigel within one week "introduced a systematic opposition between rising and falling tone" (Halliday 1975: 52). He retained this with complete consistency from C.A. 1;07 – 2;0. In general, rising pitch was used for utterances demanding a response – Halliday calls these Pragmatic; while falling pitch was used for utterances not demanding a response, which Halliday calls Mathetic. These led into Interpersonal and Ideational functions respectively, in the next phase of development, which is close to the adult functional system as conceived by Halliday.

According to Halliday (1975: 53), this use of intonation to express Mathetic vs. Pragmatic may be specific to Nigel – other children will not necessarily follow the same path. Moreover,

> "...Nigel is *not* using intonation as it is used in adult English, since the contrasts in meaning that are expressed by intonation in English are still outside his functional potential. He is adapting the elementary opposition between rising and falling, which he knows to be significant, to a functional system that is within his own limitations."
>
> (Halliday 1975: 53).

In fact, Halliday later claims that "Nigel's use does reflect the basic meaning that the opposition between falling and rising has in English" (1975: 136), suggesting that there is a smooth progression that leads Nigel from the contrastive use of rise vs. fall for the emergent functional categories Pragmatic vs. Mathetic, to the adult system of tones, which can take on a variety of functions within the grammar of English (cf. Halliday 1967).

From the perspective of subsequent research, one important methodological drawback to Halliday's study is that the data derive from field observations without the use of audio or video recordings. This raises the issue of the replicability of the analysis, which later studies have sought to address. With the aim, similar to Halliday's, of tracking the developmental relationship between pitch variables and communicative functions, Flax et al. (1991) recorded three mother – child pairs at three time points throughout the second year of life. F0 properties of all utterances were measured, leading to a classification of each utterance as either rise or non-rise. A set of functional (communicative) categories, including four types of request, three kinds of comment and so on, was derived from Halliday (1975) and other similar studies.

Flax and colleagues found no change over time for any child, in the relation between communicative function and tone (rise vs. non-rise). This does not tally with Halliday's account of important intonational changes in Nigel's language over the same period. Moreover, there were considerable differences among the children regarding the proportion of rise vs. non-rise tones used. Finally, although rises tended to be used for requesting functions (rather than other functions), non-rises too were used for requesting functions (as well as for non-requesting functions). Since their results did not present a clear developmental picture, Flax and colleagues recommended more detailed research on caregivers' input, suggesting that a child's choice of pitch direction (rise vs. non-rise) might be influenced by local contextual factors. This resonates with the research on prosody in talk-in-interaction described earlier, which emphasizes the importance of the sequential position of a turn at talk in determining its prosodic characteristics.

2.   Method

In the present study, local sequential factors are given analytic primacy, in order to shed light on the use of tones by a young child learning English. Naturalistic recordings (described below) were analysed without reference to pre-defined sets of communicative categories on the one hand or of tones on the other. Instead, evidence was sought from the orientation of the participants as to whether tone choice was relevant to their attempts to make sense to one another, and if so, how.

Material is taken from eight interactions, each of between 20 to 30 minutes, between Robin (male) C.A. 1;07–1;09, and his mother. The home language was Southern Standard British English. The family dog (Elsa) was also present. The participants were engaged in play activities, mainly with a jigsaw puzzle board into which pieces had to be fitted. Video and audio recordings were made, with a researcher present. Intonation and other prosodic features were first transcribed impressionistically, as were the segmental aspects of Robin's talk. A suggested gloss of Robin's utterance is presented in italics, on the right of the phonetic transcription. Where no gloss has been attempted, this is indicated by "?". Key portions were later subjected to acoustic analysis, though because of the quality of the original recordings and characteristics of the child's vocal productions, it was not always possible to obtain a reliable acoustic record. The transcripts of extracts presented here represent the convergence of results from both these procedures, with the aim of keeping them readable. For this reason, details of nonverbal activity have been kept to a minimum. Pitch features of Robin's talk are presented iconically between staves representing what is taken to be his habitual pitch range, which reached as high as 800 Hz on occasion, the base being in the region of 250 Hz. The same procedure is used for those of his mother's turns which are most relevant for the details of the present analysis. Her pitch in these interactions ranged from around 180 Hz to 500 Hz. In the interests of space and readability, the intonation of the mother's remaining utterances is presented using a systematic notation derived from Halliday (1967). This is taken to represent intonation patterns that form part of the linguistic resources of mature speakers of Southern British English, such as Robin's mother. In line with one of the practices of Conversation Analysis, examples are presented that illustrate the main findings of detailed sequential and phonetic analysis of a larger number of individual cases.

3.   Accentuation and tone

Researchers in English intonation have found it useful to identify at least three subsystems: a system for marking boundaries between intonational phrases (or tone units), a system of accentuation and a system of tone. These subsystems are closely connected: the accentual system is the principal means for marking intonational boundaries, and an accent is realised principally by means of a tone. Though these systems can be separated out in theory, in practice they are implemented simultaneously by speakers. In order to prepare the ground for a more detailed analysis of the tonal system, the interconnections between these three systems, as manifested in carer-child interaction, will be illustrated first, with reference to Extract 1. Although the pitch behaviours that Robin and his mother produce are very diverse, it is nevertheless evident that the prosodic design of their turns is shaped by sequential factors. These include: (a) projecting completion of the turn in progress; (b) orientation to what has been presented as the topic of the prior turn; (c) alignment with the action in which the other participant is currently engaged.

(1)   RB 8 'teddy' (cf. video file [WEL-1-teddy.wmv])

```
   1    M:    whos `this ((holding soldier piece))


   2    R:    ?a səuʃə                              a soldier
               {f}

   3    M:    a ˇsoldier (.) and 'whos `this one ((holding teddy piece))


   4    R:    ?a dɪdi                               a teddy


   5    M:    a `teddy thats `right


   6    R:    ?ɪ dɛ ((placing duck piece))          it there


   7    M:    yes but push his `head in (.) 'first and then its `easier


   8    R:    dɪs                                   this


   9    M:    thats 'right (.) thats 'it


  10    R:    ?əŋa=                                 in there


  11    M:    =so where does the `teddy go

               (2.0)


  12    R:    ?au dɛ= ((placing teddy piece))       on there


  13    M:    ='goes in `there d'you 'think


  14    R:    ?a dʲɵ                                on there
               {p}
```

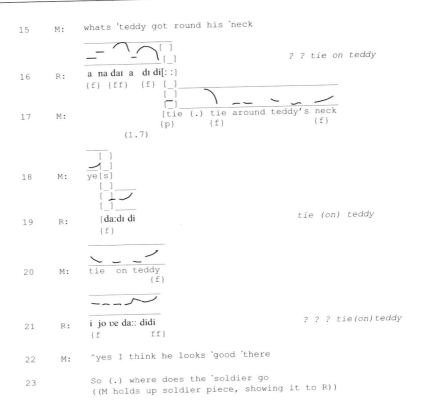

```
15    M:     whats 'teddy got round his `neck

                                    [ ]
                                    [_]                    ? ? tie on teddy
16    R:     a  na daɪ a   dɪ di[: :]
             {f} {ff}   {f} [_]
                                [ ]
                                [ ]
                                [tie (.)  tie around teddy's neck
                                {p}        {f}              {f}
17    M:
                    (1.7)

                       [ ]
                       [_]
18    M:     ye[s]
                [_]
                [ ]
                [_]
                                                    tie (on) teddy
19    R:     [da:dɪ di
             {f}

20    M:     tie   on teddy
                      {f}

                                                    ? ? ? tie(on) teddy
21    R:     i  jo ʋe da:: didi
             {f            ff}

22    M:     ^yes I think he looks `good 'there

23           So (.) where does the `soldier go
             ((M holds up soldier piece, showing it to R))
```

Robin (R) is seated on the floor, fitting pieces into a form board. He is looking at the board throughout and does not have eye contact with his mother. His mother (M) is sitting on the floor close to the form board and to Robin, watching him as he places the pieces onto the board. Each piece depicts something different; in this extract, pieces depicting a soldier, a duck and a teddy bear are involved.

In general, talk about the piece in question may precede, accompany and/or follow the placing of the piece, while on some occasions talk about a piece may be separated from the action of placing the piece. This is the case in (1): at line 3, Mother does not wait for Robin to place the soldier piece before eliciting the labelling of a new piece, the teddy. Thus in lines 1–5 there are two typical three-part labelling sequences, in which Mother requests the name of the piece. Robin responds with the name, delivered with a falling pitch contour to the base of his range. This is treated as a completed turn by Mother, who follows up immediately with a repeat. The ability of Robin and other children at a similar developmental stage to use prosodic means to signal completion of the turn is described by Corrin et al. (2001).

Although in line 6, instead of placing the teddy piece, Robin engages in placing a duck piece (cf. lines 7–10), there is evidence of an expectation, at least on the part of his mother, that the labelling of a piece will at some point be followed by Robin placing the piece: in line 11, she reintroduces the teddy, both by connecting back (using *so*) to the earlier talk about the teddy and by locating the main accent on *teddy*, thereby retopicalising it. After a pause, this topic is taken up by Robin in line 12. It forms the basis for further talk from Mother in line 13, but now there is no direct mention of the teddy, it is implicit in the omitted subject of *goes in there*; and in line 15, where *teddy* is again mentioned, it no longer carries the main accent. Mother's treatment of the lexical item *teddy* in this sequence conforms to usual descriptions of how new and old/given items are handled in terms of accentuation and anaphora in English (e.g. Cruttenden 1997: 73).

In line 15, where *teddy* is not accented, the main accent is located on *neck*, again with a fall. However, in line 16, Robin's turn has two clear points of intonational prominence. The first is on *[daɪ]*, which is the expected focus in response to Mother's preceding question; then there is a further prominence on *[dɪdi]*, at the end. Both accents have rising-falling pitch as well as intensity peaks, the first being more prominent on both counts. In line 17, following a brief overlap and self-repair, Mother appears to recast and expand Robin's turn: the main accent is a rise-fall on *tie*, reaching high in her range and mirroring the accent on *[daɪ]*, that Robin used. At the lexical level, Mother expands Robin's *[dɪdi]*, to *around teddy's neck*, realising this with an accent that has rising pitch from low to mid in the range, subordinate to the accent on *tie* but nevertheless prominent compared to the rest of the utterance. Thus Mother's turn can be seen as a partial recast of Robin's turn in accentual terms, involving both pitch copying (the accent on *tie*) and modification – of Robin's final rise-fall accent to a low rise. As mentioned above, according to standard accounts of English accentual placement, this reflects the status of *teddy's neck* as already given. Thus from the perspective of accentuation, the sequence from line 11 to line 17 illustrates how accent placement shifts to reflect the shifting topical status of semantic elements. Discussing a similar example from the same data set, Wells and Corrin (2004) proposed that such sequences, involving overlap and repair, provide rich opportunities for the child to learn about accent placement and prominence as resources for handling topic.

It is against this background of prosodic development, whereby Robin can be seen to project turn completion and to be engaged in learning about accentuation in relation to topic, that the emergence of the tone system will now be considered. The focus will be on sequences similar to the one that now follows in Extract 1, from lines 18–23. The pitch pattern in Robin's line 19 echoes not only line 18 but also the final part of Mother's line 17, with its terminal rise. Mother seems to treat Robin's line 19 as a truncated version of line 17: in line 20, her recast *tie on teddy* is more succinct than in line 17, *tie around teddy's neck*. However, she now mirrors the final rise of Robin's line 19. Thus lines 18, 19 and 20 are each analysable as having a final rising tone. There is no evidence that any of them is being designed or treated as a request – one function traditionally associated with a high rising tone: there is no eye contact, and throughout

Robin continues to focus on fitting the piece into the puzzle. Rather, the rising tones appear to be the product of the current speaker copying or repeating the tone used by the other speaker in the preceding turn.

Why should the participants copy each other's tone? One possibility is that, following the temporary disruptions of overlap, repair and pause in lines 16–18, tonal repetition contributes to a mutual display of alignment between the speakers, who are orienting to a shared understanding and appreciation of the activity in progress. In line 21, Robin provides his own expansion, adding *[ijo ve]* prior to *[da:: didi]* the latter hearable as *tie (on) teddy*. This latter portion preserves the pitch pattern of the preceding two lines, as does Mother's turn in line 22: she has been looking at Robin as he places the teddy piece in the board, and offers her confirmation and approval: *yes I think he looks good there.* Mother's more explicit orientation, in line 22, to Robin's action in line 21 may reflect the phonetic 'upgrading' that is evident in Robin's turn: while he retains the rising pitch pattern of the preceding turns, his turn is stepped up in the pitch range and produced with increased volume. In line 23, Mother breaks the cycle of tone repetition, with a fall on *soldier*, as Mother shifts the topic back to a puzzle piece originally introduced in line 1.

To summarise, sequential factors that appear to influence the distribution of accent and tone in this extract include:

a. Turn projection: turn exchange happens immediately or shortly after the production of a tone by current speaker (e.g. lines 1–15).
b. Topic: this is evident in the problematic distribution of tonal accents in lines 16–17.
c. Alignment with the action in which the co-participant is engaged. This is evident in the tonal repetition of lines 18–22.

4.   What is tonal repetition?

In the remainder of this chapter, we will explore the relevance of repetition and alignment for the child's development of tone usage. Observations of sequences like lines 18–22 of (1) suggest that one key issue for a young child when producing a turn at talk is whether or not to repeat the tone of the prior turn, in the light of local considerations regarding alignment with an action in progress. This leads to the hypothesis that opportunities to repeat adults' turns can provide the child with access to the functional use of tone. It has been long noted that in interactions between young children and their carers, instances of repetition are common – carer repeating child, and child repeating carer (Keenan 1983). In talk-in-interaction, one fundamental choice that participants, including young children, have each time it is their turn to talk, is: shall I repeat what the previous speaker said, or shall I do something else? Repetition can be at various levels (Schegloff 1996), one of which is prosodic. Within interactional analysis of adult talk, and to a lesser extent of adult-child talk, there has been much careful analysis of different types of repetition, elucidating both formal and functional aspects. This provides a basis for exploring child repeats of adult turns, in relation to intonation development.

From the phonetic perspective, there are a number of parameters that can be repeated, including parameters relating to individual syllables (pitch height, direction, loudness) and to longer phrases/utterances (e.g. pitch register, rate) (Szczepek Reed 2006). From a formal point of view, both verbal and prosodic repetitions are on a continuum:

> "in both cases it is useful to conceptualise repetition not as a binary, plus-or-minus feature but as a cline, extending roughly from a 'perfect copy' at one extreme through a 'near copy' at some intermediate stage to a mere 'copy for all practical purposes' at the other extreme" (Couper-Kuhlen 1996: 368).

Formally, the issue for the child is to work out what counts as a copy for all practical purposes, i.e. repetition of the prior speaker's tone; as opposed to what will be heard and treated as something else and therefore potentially have different functional implications. The latter will be referred to here as tonal contrast. To work out whether a particular turn constitutes tonal repetition or tonal contrast is a tricky task, for the analyst and possibly for the child too:

> "As far as pitch is concerned, the possibilities for repetition are more complex, due to the interaction of stress and pitch. It is customary to identify simple or complex pitch movements on or initiating on stressed syllables, which I shall refer to as *tones*. The stressed syllables of two utterances may have the same or a similar tone, with the same or similar amount of pitch excursion. Moreover the pitch of unstressed syllables in a copy may have varying degrees of resemblance to those of the original." (Couper-Kuhlen 1996: 370)

Part of the challenge for the child is to learn to produce versions of adult tones that are recognisable as that tone and not another one. Some of these issues can be illustrated from Extract 1, lines 19–21, reproduced here as (1a):

(1)   a.   **RB 8 'tie on teddy'** (cf. video file [WEL-1-teddy.wmv])

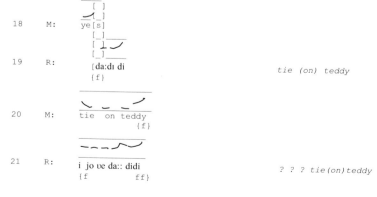

In Robin's turn in line 19, there is a rise of nine semitones from the (level) first syllable (c. 330 Hz) to the end of the turn. Mother's turn in line 20 is set relatively high in her own pitch range, but nevertheless is slightly lower in absolute terms than Robin's in line 19. There is a drop of two semitones from the initial *on* to *tie* and a rise of seven semitones from *on* to *teddy*. In line 21 the pitch shape after the first three syllables is very similar to that of line 20. The first three syllables themselves can be heard as a head that Robin has added before the tonic segment. In line 21, the syllables *[da:]* and the final *[di]* are about the same height, with a dip in between. The relative height of the *[da:]* syllable compared to what follows is comparable to the higher pitch on *tie* in Mother's line 20, the preceding turn, though line 21 differs slightly from line 20 in that the F0 of this initial accent is just as high as that of the final syllable, and also has an intensity peak. In line 21, the rise from dip to end is ten semitones. The overall pitch setting in register is considerably higher than line 19 (and line 20), at around 430 Hz for the portion immediately preceding the rise.

So what does this suggest for a definition of tonal repetition? Our proposal is that the perception of two accents per line, separated by a dip in pitch, with a rise on the final accent of at least four semitones (cf. Balog and Snow 2007) is sufficient to render lines 20 and 21 hearable as tonal repeats. This is not undermined by the addition of a 'head' in line 11, since it is subordinated in terms of pitch height. Nor is it undermined by the difference in overall F0, which may prevent a hearing of mimicry that could have resulted from absolute register matching (Couper-Kuhlen 1996). It is suggested that tonal repetition involves the copying of the tonic segment, with or without additions in the form of a head; and without absolute register matching.

This still leaves open the question: what are the limits to treating a tonic segment as 'the same' as the preceding one? For example, can a fall-rise be treated as a repeat of a rise, and vice versa? Can a low fall be treated as a repeat of a high fall, and vice versa? In what follows, the issue of what can count as tonal repetition is explored by focussing in the first instance on interactional analysis, the hypothesis being that: if a turn *functions* in the unfolding interaction as a repeat of the prior turn, then there is a prima facie case for treating the tone of the second turn as 'the same' as that of the first turn.

While prosodic aspects of adult repeats of child turns have already been the subject of detailed interactional analysis (Tarplee 1996), the focus here is on child repeats of adults, in order to explore the child's use of tones. All instances were identified in the data where there appeared to be exact, or almost exact *verbal* repetition by Robin of the end of his mother's prior turn. Verbal repetitions were examined in the first instance, since they present prima facie evidence that repetition is relevant for participants at that point in the interaction. There is the possibility that some verbal repetitions will also involve tonal repetition, whereas other verbal repetitions may be produced with a different tone, i.e. contrasting with the tone of the prior turn. This permits the exploration of the specific role of *tonal* repetition. The collection of verbal repetitions was then subdivided into groups according to their most salient interactional features.

5.   Tonal repetition following other-initiated other-repair

There is at least one environment where repetition of the immediately prior word produced by Mother is relevant and indeed expected in the child's next turn: that is, following an explicit request by Mother for repetition, as in (2).

(2)   **RB5 'tractor'** (cf. video file [WEL-2-tractor.wmv])

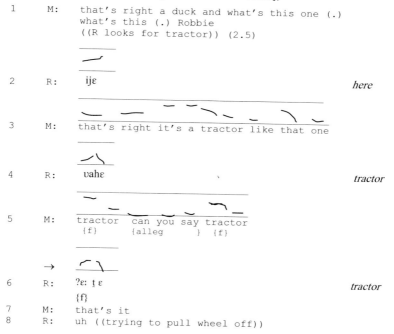

```
1       M:      that's right a duck and what's this one (.)
                what's this (.) Robbie
                ((R looks for tractor))  (2.5)


2       R:      ijɛ                                              here


3       M:      that's right it's a tractor like that one


4       R:      ʋahɛ                            ˎ              tractor


5       M:      tractor    can you say tractor
                {f}            {alleg    }  {f}


   →
6       R:      ʔɛ: ʈɛ                                          tractor
                {f}
7       M:      that's it
8       R:      uh ((trying to pull wheel off))
```

Robin's turn in line 6 matches the end of the preceding turn: The final words of line 5
and line 6 both have a stepped variant of a falling contour. Measurement of F0 is ham-
pered by the phonotactic structure of *tractor*, where all the consonants are voiceless.
With that proviso, the step down in line 5 seems to be around seven semitones, and in
line 6, also seven semitones. In both versions, there is an intensity peak on the first but
not the second syllable; the durational ratio of the two syllables appears similar, at
around 2:1, creating a similar rhythmic pattern. Thus not only the pitch patterns but
also the overall prosodic shapes of the two versions of tractor resemble each other. Following Robin's repeat in line 6, Mother closes the topic in line 7, and in line 8 Robin
moves to further play.

In such cases, both Mother and Robin orient to Robin's verbal and tonal repeat of
the word just pronounced by Mother, as a sequentially fitted move: it serves to close
the sequence, without further work. This suggests that Mother is content that Robin
understands what this word means and even with how it is pronounced, although at
the segmental level there are considerable phonetic divergences between her version

and his (cf. Tarplee 1996). Explicit requests for repetition like the one in line 5 invariably come at the end of an extended repair sequence that has focussed on articulatory aspects of pronunciation. The request invariably follows Mother having named the item herself. These examples suggest that repair sequences may be one environment that is fruitful for learning about tone: here, that matching the tone of the model is part of producing an acceptable version of the word that caused trouble, thereby enabling the repair sequence to be closed (cf. Corrin 2010 for a more extensive account of repair in the talk of Robin and his mother).

6.   Tonal repetition in other-initiated self-repair

Repair can provide a less explicit opportunity for a child repeat: this is following an adult correction of the child, in an other-repair sequence initiated by the adult. The adult supplies the correct form and the child immediately repeats it, along with its tone, as in lines 3 and 4 of (3). In line 5, Mother treats Robin's turn as an acceptable version of the word, with *that's right*, following which she moves the topic on.

(3)   **RB8 'funnel'** (cf. video file [WEL-3-funnel.wmv])

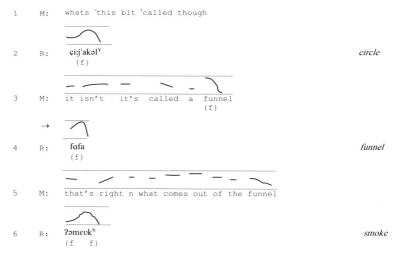

In the last phrase of line 3, *a funnel*, there is a 1.5 semitone step up from *a*, to the first syllable of *funnel*, then a fall of eight semitones on the second syllable. Intensity is higher on the first syllable. In Robin's turn in line 4, there is a three-semitone rise on the first syllable, descending ten semitones to the final syllable. There are intensity peaks on both syllables, the higher being on the first. Their tonal shape as just described is similar, even though the alignment of the rise-fall pitch contour differs between the two speakers' versions of the phrase, as does their segmental content. This illustrates one of the methodological issues in describing tonal repetition: tones that the co-participant (and the analyst) may perceive and respond to as 'the same' may not be identical in terms of their F0 contour, because of the effect of segmental differences (cf. Gussenhoven 2004: 7–10).

In Extracts (2), and (3), illustrating repair environments, the tone repeated by Robin is a fall of some kind, but this is not always so: in Extract (4) the repeated tone is a rise. Although it is again an other-initiated repair sequence, the issue in (4) is not that of producing the correct label, as in the earlier examples, since Robin produces an accurate version of *cheese* without repair at line 3. The trouble arises with regard to the location of the cheese.

(4)   **RB6 'cheese'** (cf. video file [WEL-4-cheese.wmv])

```
 1  M:   can you see any ´cheese (2.2)
         is there any `cheese in this ´picture
 2       (1.1)
 3  R:   ((sitting in M's lap, looks at book))


         ‿
         ──
         ʧis                                        cheese
 4       (0.6)
 5  M:   |where's some `cheese
 6       (.)
         ((looks at book; finger scans page, head lifts, points across
 7  R:   room))

         ─  ── ── ── ╱
         ─  ─
         ────────
         ɔ ge  di: ɒ dis                             ?
             {f      f}
 8       (0.6)

         ╱
         ──
 9  M:   hm
10       (.)
11  R:   ((repeats action of pointing across room))

         ‿  ╲
         ────
12       nʌ dis                                     no cheese
13       (0.5)

         ‿  ╱
         ────
14  M:   no cheese
15       (2.0)
16  R:   ((looks back to book, turns to next page))


  →      ‿  ‿
         ────
         nɔʊ |dis
                                                    no cheese
```

```
17          (.)
            _____

                ___
18    M:    no cheese
            {f}
19          (2.0)
20          what are `these (.) whats `that
```

The problem for Mother arises from line 7, where Robin develops the topic, animatedly but unintelligibly. Mother's open class repair initiator in line 9 gives rise to Robin's repair in line 12, with what appears to be a truncated verbal reformulation, accompanied by a repeat of the point action (line 11), with falling pitch. In line 14, Mother produces a candidate interpretation of Robin's turn, including embedded correction of the onset consonant of *cheese*, with a rising, i.e. contrasting, tone (seven semitones). Although, as will be shown in the next section, tonal contrast has the potential to initiate a new course of action in the talk, there is no evidence from Robin's response in line 16 to indicate whether he regards Mother's turn as initiating a new action, and if so, what kind of new action. In line 16, Robin produces a verbal repetition with a rise of six semitones, i.e. a repetition of Mother's step rise. There is no evidence that either Robin or his mother are treating his repeat at line 16 as an understanding check, or any other action that actively seeks a response from M: his attention is back on the book, not out in the room where it was when he produced the trouble source (lines 7 and 11) and he is progressing the joint activity by turning to the next page. Thus, Extract (4) demonstrates that a rise can be repeated too: Robin's tonal repetition in repair sequences is not restricted to falls. A comparable repeat of a rising contour was described in Extract (1a), lines 20–21.

7. Tonal contrast to initiate repair

Although Robin's verbal repeats are most often accompanied by tonal repetition, this is not always the case. Extract (5) is another labelling sequence where Mother initiates a repair from Robin (line 4).

(5)   **RB5 'man'** (cf. video file [WEL-5-man.wmv])

```
        1      M:    mhm (.) a `what (.) `what's `this
        2            (4.9)
               _____

                 ↘   ↘    ⌒
        3      R:    ma: (.) wiə dɛ                              man   ?   there
                     {f}
               _____

                  ⌣  ⌒  ─
                 ╱
```

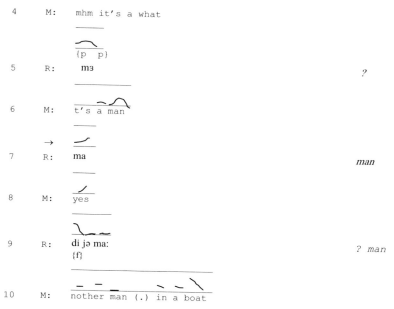

```
    4    M:    mhm it's a what

    5    R:    mз                                           ?
                {p  p}

    6    M:    t's a man

    7    R:    ma                                          man
         →

    8    M:    yes

    9    R:    di jə ma:                                 ? man
               {f}

    10   M:    nother man (.) in a boat
```

The sequence is similar to earlier extracts as far as line 6. However, in line 7, Robin does not do a tonal repeat to accompany the verbal repeat: whereas in line 6 Mother has used a rise-fall contour over the phrase, Robin produces a rise of five semitones.

Mother's *yes* response in the next turn (line 8) suggests that she is treating Robin's verbal repeat with tonal contrast as an understanding check that requested confirmation. None of the cases of verbal plus tonal repetition by Robin in the earlier extracts was treated by Mother as a request for confirmation, whether the tone in question was rising or falling. This suggests that it is the tonal contrast that constitutes the verbal repeat as an understanding check. Following Mother's confirmation, which closes the repair sequence, Robin immediately develops the topic further, in line 9.

8.   Tonal contrast and development of topic

In Extract (5), which showed that tonal contrast by Robin can initiate a new action, the tonal contrast took the form of a rise contrasting with the mother's fall. The new action was an understanding check, in the course of an other-initiated repair sequence. In Extract (6), there is again tonal contrast but this time Robin produces a fall, contrasting with Mother's rise. His new action is to shift the topic of attention and of the talk from one object to another. The two objects in question are both 'balls' – one an actual ball, the other a jigsaw piece depicting a ball. For both participants there is an issue of clarifying which of the two balls they are talking about. In lines 1–2, Mother makes clear that she is talking about the jigsaw piece. In lines 4–6, the direction of Robin's gaze makes it clear that his reference is to the real ball, which Mother confirms in line 6. However, in line 7 Robin refers to the ball jigsaw piece, which he has just picked up again.

(6)   **RB4 'two balls'** (cf. video file [WEL-6-two balls.wmv])

```
 1    M:   you got the ˋball
 2         ˈwhere does the ˈball ˋgo(.) from the ˋjigsaw
 3         (3.0)
           ((R, holding jigsaw ball, walks from jigsaw to near M))

                 ∧
 4    R:   bɔ ((looking at real ball on floor, drops jigsaw ball))      ball
           {p}

                 __∧
 5         ɛ jə dɔkʰ ((R picks up real ball with lh , transfers it to rh))    ?

            ⌣    ⌣   ⌡
 6 →  M:   there's  your  ball

                ∧
 7 →  R:   bɔ ((R picks up jigsaw ball with lh))                      ball
           {f}
            ⌣    ⌣
 8    M:   two  balls
 9    R:   heh
           ((R turns round, walks back to jigsaw holding real ball and jigsaw ball))
10    R:   ʔɛ i (.) jɛ ((attempting to put real ball in jigsaw))          ?
11    M:   it doesn't ˋfit so well ˋdoes [it]
12    R:                              [jɛ]((fitting jigsaw ball in jigsaw))
13    M:   that's right (1.3) that one goes in there
```

In line 6, the main prominence is on *ball*, as it has the main pitch movement and is relatively loud. The F0 rises by c. 11 semitones. By contrast, in line 7, Robin uses a wide rise-fall on *ball*. Although the falling component is not captured by the pitch tracker, it is clearly audible over the last part of the utterance, accompanied by diminution in energy.

Though it is lexically a repetition of Mother's final word in line 6, the referent of Robin's turn in line 7 is different: Robin was previously referring to the real ball, but now he is referring to the jigsaw piece, which he picks up. This topic shift gets taken up by Mother in line 8, where the tonic is on *two*. The topic of two competing balls is then animatedly pursued by Robin, who tries to fit both into the jigsaw. This extract thus indicates that tonal contrast can be deployed by Robin for topic development. On the other hand, it was shown in earlier examples that Robin's tonal repeats left the onus of topic development on his mother or else led to sequence closure. Thus the system available to Robin, of either repeating or not repeating the final tone from his mother's prior turn, provides him with a resource for managing topic development and sequence closure.

9. Conclusion

Occasions on which Robin repeats his mother's talk suggest how the sequential environment may be implicated in his choice of pitch contour in relation to her immediately prior turn. The study has been restricted to one child-adult pair and the number of interactional environments examined in detail is as yet quite small, with the particular limitation that only cases where the child's turn involves verbal repetition have been analysed. With these caveats, it is claimed that some important aspects of tonal usage are revealed if the starting point is taken to be the relationship of the child's turn to the immediately prior turn of the carer, rather than the illocutionary force of the turn in question as has been traditional. The analysis so far suggests that the child's tone may take one of two forms with respect to the prior, each of which has distinct interactional implications. It may be a tonal repeat, aligning the child with the course of action in progress. Alternatively, it may be a tonal contrast, which initiates a new course of action by the child.

According to this view of English intonation, the speaker's choice of tone in a turn does not necessarily require access to a lexicon of tonal meanings of the kind that is often assumed in intonation research. Instead, it can be locally determined by considerations of producing a tone that is recognisably the same or different from the one that the prior speaker has just produced. In this respect tone, like accent placement, is a resource for the local management of interactional meaning: choice of tone, like choice of accent placement, is a resource that the speaker can employ to display how the current turn relates to its proximate context. If this is indeed the case, it goes some way to explaining why studies of children's tone development have been inconclusive: the distribution of tones in the child's talk at different developmental points will be determined not primarily by processes of internal maturation, nor by progressively learning to associate a tone with a range of context-free pragmatic meanings, but by the unfolding detail of the interactions that they have with their carer on the particular occasions on which they are recorded. Changes in child-carer interactions over time may in part be determined by maturational factors, the carer adjusting to the child in terms of language and activity as the child gets older, but the basic procedures of aligning with a current action or initiating a new one, will remain relevant whatever the age of the participants in the talk.

References

Balog, Heather and Snow, David 2007. "Application of relational and independent analyses for intonation production in young children." *Journal of Phonetics* 35 (1): 118–133.

Barth-Weingarten, Dagmar 2009. "When to say something – some observations on prosodic-phonetic cues to the placement and types of responses in multi-unit turns." In: *Where prosody meets pragmatics,* Dagmar Barth-Weingarten, Nicole Dehé and Anne Wichmann (eds.), 143–182. Bingley: Emerald.

Corrin, Juliette; Tarplee, Clare and Wells, Bill 2001. "Interactional linguistics and language development: a conversation analytic perspective on emergent syntax." In: *Studies in interactional linguistics,* Margret Selting and Elizabeth Couper-Kuhlen (eds.), 199–255. Amsterdam: Benjamins.

Corrin, Juliette 2010. "Hm? What? Maternal repair and early child talk." In: *Analysing interactions in childhood: Insights from conversation analysis,* Hilary Gardner and Michael Forrester (eds.), 23–41. Wiley Blackwell.

Couper-Kuhlen, Elizabeth 1996. "The prosody of repetition: on quoting and mimicry." In: *Prosody in conversation: Interactional studies,* Elizabeth Couper-Kuhlen and Margret Selting (eds.), 366–405. Cambridge: Cambridge University Press.

Couper-Kuhlen, Elizabeth and Ford, Cecilia E. (eds.) 2004. *Sound patterns in interaction.* Amsterdam: Benjamins.

Couper-Kuhlen, Elizabeth and Selting, Margret (eds.) 1996. *Prosody in conversation: Interactional studies.* Cambridge: Cambridge University Press.

Cruttenden, Alan 1997. *Intonation, (2nd edition).* Cambridge: Cambridge University Press.

Flax, Judy; Lahey, Margaret; Harris, Katherine and Boothroyd, Arthur 1991. "Relations between prosodic variables and communicative functions." *Journal of Child Language* 18: 3–19.

Gussenhoven, Carlos 2004. *The phonology of tone and intonation.* Cambridge: Cambridge University Press.

Halliday, Michael A. 1967. *Intonation and grammar in British English.* The Hague: Mouton.

Halliday, Michael A. 1975. *Learning how to mean: Explorations in the development of language.* London: Edward Arnold.

Keenan, Elinor Ochs 1983. "Making it last: Repetition in children's discourse." In: *Acquiring conversational competence,* Elinor Ochs and Bambi B. Schieffelin (eds.), 26–39. London: Routledge Kegan Paul.

Levelt, Willem J. M. 1989. *Speaking: From intention to articulation.* Cambridge, Mass.: MIT Press.

Local, John and Wootton, Tony 1995. "Interactional and phonetic aspects of immediate echolalia in autism: A case study." *Clinical Linguistics and Phonetics* 9: 155–184.

Schegloff, Emanuel A. 1996. "Confirming allusions: Towards an empirical account of action." *American Journal of Sociology* 104: 161–216.

Szczepek Reed, Beatrice 2004. "Turn-final intonation in English." In: *Sound patterns in Interaction,* Elizabeth Couper-Kuhlen and Cecilia E. Ford (eds.), 97–118. Amsterdam: Benjamins.

Szczepek Reed, Beatrice 2006. *Prosodic orientation in English conversation.* Basingstoke: Palgrave Macmillan.

Tarplee, Clare 1996. "Working on young children's utterances: Prosodic aspects of repetition during picture labelling." In: *Prosody in conversation: Interactional studies,* Elizabeth Couper-Kuhlen and Margret Selting (eds.), 406–435. Cambridge: Cambridge University Press.

Walker, Gareth 2004. *The phonetic design of turn endings, beginnings and continuations in conversation; PhD Thesis.* York, UK: University of York.

Wells, Bill and Corrin, Juliette 2004. "Prosodic resources, turn-taking and overlap in children's talk-in-interaction." In: *Sound patterns in interaction,* Elizabeth Couper-Kuhlen and Cecilia E. Ford (eds.), 119–143. Amsterdam: Benjamins.

Wells, Bill and Macfarlane, Sarah 1998. "Prosody as an interactional resource: turn-projection and overlap." *Language and Speech* 41: 265–298.

Repetition and contrast across action sequences

Comments on Bill Wells "Tonal repetition and tonal contrast in English carer-child interaction"

Traci Walker
University of York, United Kingdom

Wells' chapter, focusing on the acquisition of English tone by examining the unfolding of talk in naturally-occurring sequences between children and their carers, raises several interesting questions relating to linguistic repetition vs. linguistic contrast, and how the terms *repetition* and *contrast*, or same and different, are (or can be) defined. In what follows, I explicate three of the questions Wells' findings raise for researchers in phonetics and sequential analysis alike, including the notion of a *tonal inventory* with tone-meaning associations. Given the constraints of space, however, it is left to future research to address these questions.

1. Repetition and contrast of other phonetic parameters

Although Wells' chapter is explicitly concerned with children's acquisition of the adult inventory of tones, his findings invite the exploration of whether the salience of contrast vs. repetition relates to the manipulation of other linguistic parameters, for instance duration, rhythm and loudness, not to mention the (mis)match of articulatory targets. Since every utterance is produced with some constellation of pitch, duration, loudness, etc., the question is whether speakers can vary or repeat only some of them to achieve the same outcome or meaning ascribed in that instance to "same" or "different". Wells' work suggests that the answer is *yes*, given that the caregiver accepts lexical repetitions from the child that are quite different in segmental structure from those she herself produces, treating them as performing different actions not based on closeness of fit with her pronunciation but on how the child varies the tone (see also Tarplee 1996). A definitive answer, however, awaits empirical investigation.

2.   Differentiating 'repetitions' in adult's talk

Some extant research combining interactional and phonetic analysis of adult self-repetitions also bears on the question of what counts as repetition or contrast, and what activities repetition or contrast may be employed to do. Obviously, self-repetitions occur in a different sequential location to those that Wells investigates, and they can be used to accomplish different kinds of work. However, the questions about what counts as same or different when compared to a prior turn are similarly valid and interesting.

Traci Walker (2009) looked at the phonetic composition of adult self-repetitions in other-initiated repair sequences. Two distinct phonetic patterns are described, which I shall for now call patterns A and B, rather than adopting the terms used in Walker (2009), for reasons which will become obvious. Pattern A has an expanded pitch range, is louder, longer, and has an altered vocal tract setting when compared to the trouble source turn (the utterance which engenders the repair initiation); Pattern B has the same or a compressed pitch range, is quieter, shorter, and is very similar in articulatory detail when compared to the trouble source turn. These different phonetic patterns correlate with a difference in the sequential fittedness of the trouble source turn. In other words, the use of a particular phonetic pattern on a repetition repair shows the speaker's realization or acceptance of the fact that the first saying (the turn which has repair initiated on it) either was, or was not, ill-suited to the sequence at the time it was produced.

One possible way to interpret this phonetic description is that pattern A is maximally different, whilst pattern B is maximally the same, phonetically, as the trouble source turn. The fact remains, however, that in many ways the phonetic patterns are *equally* different: expanding the pitch range of the utterance makes it just as different as compressing or lowering it; saying something more loudly is just as different as saying it more quietly. Only for articulatory detail can it clearly be said that one pattern emphasizes difference while the other emphasizes sameness. Thus, here we do not have a case of (phonetic) repetition vs. contrast, but a division of labour within a phonetically contrastive lexical repetition.

By setting this work alongside that of Wells, we can begin to see the nuanced contribution of phonetic composition to the unfolding of an interaction. In Walker (2009), pattern A – there called upgraded – is used for repairs of fitted trouble source turns, and pattern B – downgraded – for repairs of disjunct trouble source turns. One way of interpreting this is that upgraded repetitions pursue completion of the sequence that was interrupted by the repair initiation, whilst downgraded repetitions accept the blame for a sequential disruption (rather than placing blame on the repair initiator). Wells, on the other hand, shows how tonal repetitions display alignment with the ongoing sequence, whilst tonal contrast initiates a new sequence.

There is no way, and no need to, meld the two analyses. We ought not to expect all uses of phonetic contrastivity or phonetic similarity to have the same interactional functions. Tonal repetition and tonal contrast are locally motivated, locally employed devices (and there may even be, as Wells suggests, a developmental aspect to the use of tonal repetition and contrast). We must instead rely on speakers' displayed orientations to and treatments of utterances we as analysts might see as phonetically the 'same' or 'different'. Any difference, no matter how small, might seem to an analyst like a functionally implicated difference; what is important is not that a difference can be heard or measured, but how speakers *treat* the difference.

3. Tone and "meaning"

Finally, Wells' paper ought to lead researchers interested in prosody to question the seemingly universal drive to attach meanings to intonation patterns. What is of interest in Wells' findings is the *interactive* construction of meaning through the contrast with, or repetition of, the prior tone; not the idea that a rising tone means X, and a falling tone means Y. Many if not all of the leading intonation researchers – save Couper-Kuhlen (1986) – take for granted the idea that particular tones have given, intrinsic meanings (e.g., Cruttenden 1997, Gussenhoven 2004, Ladd 1987); however, they expend a good deal of energy explaining the various other influences (e.g., syntax, lexis, 'discoursal' setting) that can override or enhance a given tone's meaning. I believe this ought to make us question very seriously the idea of a tonal inventory as it is generally presented. While few if any linguists would accept the idea that a phoneme, or a phonetic realization of a phoneme, has an intrinsic meaning (however abstract or however locally-conditioned), most seem to accept without question the claim that tones have inherent meanings. The "proof" that this is so comes either from the authors' intuitions as native speakers, or from carefully controlled experiments where participants are instructed to assign meanings to tones. Following an instruction to assign meaning is surely different from reacting to or treating an utterance as having a particular meaning in a naturally-occurring environment.

I suggest that trying to associate "a tone" with "a pragmatic function", no matter how widely defined, is no different than a claim that [b] or a [p] has an inherent meaning. Though accepted as phonologically contrastive in English, there is no drive to associate any meaning such as interest or excitement with [b], and boredom or lack of interest with [p]. The claim that humans are conditioned by "biological codes" (Gussenhoven 2004: 71) to respond to high or low tones in the ways we do might have put the cart before the horse. Consider the following alternative view of the language faculty, one taking interpersonal human communication as its starting point.[1]

Most intuitive descriptions of high tones claim that they sound (i.e., "mean") excited or interested. This intuition is then given a possible biological explanation: when we are interested or aroused our muscles are more tense, thus producing higher pitch. However, as shown in Couper-Kuhlen((2001) high pitch is regularly used in telephone

---

1.   I am indebted to Richard Ogden for this suggestion.

calls to signal the reason-for-calling, with the absence of a high pitch onset also being oriented to as marking out a turn as not being the reason for the call. Given that it is through language use that we come to understand how to use our language, it is possible (if not probable) that the distribution of prosody and other phonetic cues within interactions gave rise to the "feeling" or idea that a particular prosodic configuration means something outside of any environment of use. In other words, I am suggesting that it may be the ways that intonation is deployed in interaction that colors our perception of what tones "mean", rather than a biological response. As Wells notes in the conclusion of his paper, it is as children attending to the "unfolding detail of the interactions [we] have" that we learn what tones "mean" – or more appropriately, what they can be used to do.

References

Couper-Kuhlen, Elizabeth 1986. *An introduction to English prosody*. London: Edward Arnold.
Couper-Kuhlen, Elizabeth 2001. "Interactional prosody: High onsets in reason-for-the call turns." *Language in Society* 30: 29–53.
Cruttenden, Alan 1997. *Intonation (2nd edition)*. Cambridge: Cambridge University Press.
Gussenhoven, Carlos 2004. *The phonology of tone and intonation*. Cambridge: Cambridge University Press.
Ladd, D. Robert 1987. *Intonational phonology*. Cambridge: Cambridge University Press.
Tarplee, Clare 1996. "Working on young children's utterances: Prosodic aspects of repetition during picture labelling." In: *Prosody in conversation: Interactional studies*, Elizabeth Couper-Kuhlen and Margret Selting (eds.), 406–435. Cambridge: Cambridge University Press.
Walker, Traci 2009. *The phonetics of sequence organization: an investigation of lexical repetition in other-initiated repair sequences in American English*. Saarbrücken: VDM Verlag Dr. Mueller.

PART III

Prosody and other semiotic resources in interaction

Communicating emotion
in doctor-patient interaction
A multidimensional single-case analysis

Elisabeth Gülich and Katrin Lindemann
University of Bielefeld, Germany and University of Zurich, Switzerland

We present a multidimensional single-case analysis of a research interview between a doctor and a patient in an epilepsy centre, focusing on two sequences which illustrate the complex process involved in the conversational treatment of fear. The patient talks about extremely painful/frightening events in her life without explicitly naming emotions. However, closer examination shows that a connection between past emotions and reconstructed events can be indicated without relying on explicit naming of emotions. In the case at hand the interplay of different communicative resources allows the doctor to connect the patient's communicative behaviour to fear. Through their joint effort, doctor and patient come to understand that the emotion is part of the depicted events.

1. Introduction[1]

In this paper we show how a patient's feelings of fear are expressed through diverse communicative resources and how this expression develops in the conversational process. The patient in question is a woman suffering from various types of epileptic seizures. Her case being a complicated one, she has received several different diagnoses over a long period of treatment. In the context of her seizures, fear plays a prominent, although clinically still undefined role.

---

1. We would like to thank the editors Dagmar Barth-Weingarten and Elisabeth Reber, as well as our anonymous reviewers, for their comments on earlier drafts of this paper, which contributed to sharpening our analysis.

1.1   Research context

The analysis presented here is embedded in the larger framework of the interdisciplinary research project "Communicative description and clinical representation of fear", carried out in 2004 by a specialist group comprising linguists, sociologists, psychiatrists, neurologists and psychotherapists at the Centre for Interdisciplinary Research at the University of Bielefeld.[2] The main focus of this project was on the accounts patients give of their fear or panic attacks, the assumption being that the frequent lack of diagnostic information and the unsatisfactory treatment of patients suffering from fear or anxiety disorders are to a large extent due to a lack of knowledge about the communicative means patients use in describing their subjective feelings of fear (cf. Gülich and Schöndienst 2005).

Two groups of patients were studied: patients with epileptic fear and patients with panic attacks. For both of these groups, an exact diagnosis tends to be very difficult, and they are often confused with each other (cf. Schmitz and Schöndienst 2006: 146). The main purpose of the project was to find out what resources patients use to communicate fear and to see whether certain types of description can be linked to certain types of fear. Thus the motivation for a detailed study of patients' descriptions of symptoms was the assumption that it might provide useful information for diagnostic processes.[3]

1.2   Data

Two hospitals were involved in this study: a facility specialising in epilepsy and a psychiatric hospital. In order to obtain spontaneous descriptions of the illness, the interview was to be the first encounter between patient and doctor. Each patient was therefore interviewed by a doctor from the other facility. The interviews were conducted following certain guidelines, the most important among them being that the interviewer should start with an open question, thereby encouraging the patient to report what seemed important or relevant to her/him and to give exhaustive descriptions of these topics.[4] Based on the medical history, each patient interviewed was expected to

---

2.   For further information see www.uni-bielefeld.de/ZIF/KG/2004Angst/index.html

3.   The idea that linguistic analyses might contribute to medical diagnoses arose from a previous project which was concerned with the conversational "methods" patients suffering from epilepsy or other kinds of seizures use in describing their seizures. It has been shown that there are conversational patterns typical of one or the other type of seizure. For general information on this project see http://www.uni-bielefeld.de/lili/forschung/projekte/archiv/epiling/; for results concerning linguistic contributions to differential diagnosis see e.g. Schöndienst (2002), Schwabe et al. (2008), Surmann (2005). The same type of research but with English patients is conducted by Marcus Reuber (Sheffield), see Plug et al. (2009), Schwabe et al. (2007).

4.   The technique of asking an open question at the beginning of a medical interview and the different ways in which patients use this 'open space' are explained in more detail in Gülich et al. (2003), Plug et al. (2009), Schöndienst (2002).

suffer from fear or panic attacks, however, the interviewer did not mention this at the outset; the idea was to see whether or not the patient would spontaneously bring up the topic. If the aspect of fear did not occur in the patient's description within about 20 or 30 minutes, it was then mentioned by the interviewer. Describing and processing the highly subjective sensation and perception of fear often proved to be a difficult task for both doctors and patients participating in the encounters.

The interview presented here is conducted by a doctor from a psychiatric hospital who talks to an in-patient of an epilepsy centre. The patient with the pseudonym "Ms. Korte" is a 58-year-old woman from Poland who has been living in Germany for a long time and is used to speaking German in the context of her illness. She speaks German fluently, but her use of grammar and lexis sometimes differs from that of native speakers; she also has a strong Polish accent. The interviewer at times displays some difficulties in understanding Ms. Korte by using numerous reformulations, repair initiations, etc.

1.3   Previous research on fear

In previous research on fear and panic attacks, little attention has been paid to the communicative resources used for the description of these emotions. One exception is the elaborate case analysis by Capps and Ochs (1995a, 1995b) of an agoraphobic woman's communicative representation of her panic attacks.[5] However, the analysis of multi-modal aspects, which are crucial for the communication of emotion, is still at its beginnings, even if their importance has been generally recognised (cf. Fiehler 2001). Thus Drescher (2003) emphasizes "[d]ie herausragende Bedeutung der Stimme in ihren paraverbalen und konventionalisierten Facetten für den Ausdruck von Emotionen" ('the outstanding importance of the speaker's voice in its paraverbal and conventionalised aspects for the expression of emotion', 2003: 91, our translation). In describing the expression of reproach in everyday communication, Günthner (2000: 88, 91, 97, 128–153) presents detailed analyses of the "reproachful voice" (*vorwurfsvolle Stimme*). For the expression of fear, an analysis of multi-modal resources including prosodic aspects was first attempted by Streeck and Streeck (2002) and by Gülich and Couper-Kuhlen (2007).

At the centre of our analysis is the interplay of different communicative resources used to express fear. Research on emotion often deals with the emotion present in the actual conversation. In our analysis we do not examine current fear which is described or expressed but the narrative reconstruction of past fear which is interactively made relevant by the participants. We thus take the verbal dimension as a starting point, to then go and look at other resources involved. Prosody, though it is an important element of emotional expression, we will not study in any detail; not only because we do not specialise in this field but particularly, because we do not want to consider each

---

5.   Recent research on German data shows the importance of linguistic means and the variety of techniques in the description of fear and panic, e.g. Gülich and Couper-Kuhlen (2007), Günthner (2006), Lindemann (2009), Schwabe (2006: 252–280), Surmann (2005: 325–330).

level of expression individually: Our aim is to describe the *interplay* of resources. We therefore consider prosodic elements as an integral part of a multi-modal gestalt (Dausendschön-Gay and Krafft 2002).

1.4   Method

In this article, we use the method of single-case analysis in the framework of conversation analysis (cf. Schegloff 1987, Whalen et al. 1988). In order to analyse the gradual process of expressing fear, we will present a sequential analysis of two extended sequences from the same interview. We have chosen these examples because they are impressive illustrations of the difficulty, length and complexity which the process of conversational treatment of fear can hold.[6] The narrative reconstruction of a particular episode (the patient runs out of the house during a seizure) plays an important part in the expression of fear in this conversation. Our analysis therefore focuses on the sequences relating this particular episode, and we ask: How does this particular patient express fear? By what conversational devices is fear expressed even while not being named? And how does the expression of fear develop in the course of the conversation?

We analyse the two sequences in the order of their occurrence in the interview. For reasons of clarity, we present them divided into five excerpts (two excerpts for the first sequence, three for the second). In the first sequence, which is taken from the first few minutes of the interview, the episode of the patient running out of the house is mentioned for the first time. After a brief summary of the results of this first analysis, we pass on to the second sequence, much later in the interview, where the episode is retold in a different context. Finally, we compare the two versions of the episode, summarise the main differences and then show the development in the expression of fear during the conversational process. As the data are in German, we have added an interlinear translation to the transcripts.[7]

2.   Analysis

2.1   The first sequence: Narrative reconstruction of a seizure episode ("running-out-of-the-house")

In this section we show how the patient builds a reconstruction of situations that seem to be closely connected with certain emotions, without, however, making explicit mention of the emotions concerned.

---

6.   These excerpts are also presented in Gülich et al. (2010) with emphasis on the process of establishing and refining knowledge in interaction.

7.   For reasons of correctness the relevant non-vocal phenomena with their beginning and ending are noted (in English) below the original German verbalisations, not below the English translation.

The doctor begins the thematic part of the interview by an open question (not shown here) to encourage the patient to talk freely, in order to be able to establish the nature of her problem. By doing so, the doctor builds a conditional relevance for Ms. Korte to produce a multi-unit turn (cf. Schegloff 1982: 75).

Ms. Korte answers hesitantly. By saying <<len> *DA:S einfach is so (.) HARMlos ANgefangen* ('it began harmlessly enough', not shown here), she opens a frame for describing her illness. She continues by a narrative reconstruction of typical seizure episodes, using an iterative form of reconstruction (*immer*, 'always', *meistens*, 'usually', not shown here).

She then refers back to the frame and comes to speak about an aggravation of her illness. Here she switches to another narrative technique, namely to the reconstruction of an episode:[8]

(1)   **Aggravation of symptoms and first narration** (Korte I, lines 61–75)

```
61   K:  <<len, ausatmend> u:nd=äh> <<len> da=war MEHR,>
         <<exhaling> and uh there was more>

62       (---) nachHER,
         afterwards

63       (-) (und) da:: (---)
         and then/there

64       <<all> i hab> den: glaub=ich schon=ge schon geSAGT,=
         I think I've already said

65       =dass ich hatten (2.5) auch so=was dass ich aus dem HAUS
         laufe;                              _____
```

\
abruptly lifts her head to the
right, directly looks at I.

that I also had something like such that I run out of
the house

```
67       (--)
         \_/
          \
```
I: nods at the end of the pause

```
68   K:  i war schon: (.) i=der in der nacht bei BAUerHOF,
         _____
```
\
shifts gaze to the left, stops looking at I.
I even was at a farm at night

---

8.   See Appendix I for the transcription notations. They are based on the GAT notations established by Selting et al. (1998).

```
69        .hh das war (---) knapp (.) zwölf UHR,
                                        \__/
                                         \
```

                                        lifts head (less pronounced than line 65),
                                        shifts gaze to I.

```
          that was nearly twelve o'clock
70        (2.0) weil=ich=s a´ (.) alleine (war=i´) in in der
71        WOHnung,
          because I was a alone in the
          flat
72        mein sohn war in ausTRAlien,=
          my son was in Australia
73        =da hat=er stuDIERT,
          he was studying there
74        (-) .hh ((leicht seufzendes Ausatmen))
                 ((exhales slightly sighing))
75        (1.5) u::nd jetzt is=er da/\/
          and now he is here
```

In contrast to the 'harmless' beginning that she claimed earlier, Ms. Korte now focuses on a different situation: *da = war MEHR, (–) nachHER* ('there was more afterwards'). She uses a typical narrative connector *und da::* ('and then/there'), as if she were continuing a previous narration (line 63), however, by lengthening it and by the use of an adjacent pause she shows hesitation. She then interrupts herself in order to mark the subsequent utterances as having been mentioned before (lines 63–64). She starts a reconstruction in an iterative way (lines 65–66: use of present tense, generalisation by *so = was*, 'something like that'). When she says that she runs out of the house, she quickly raises her head to the right and clearly looks at the doctor. She seems to wait for a reaction and continues only after the doctor nods and subsequently shifts her gaze away from the doctor.

    Then she focuses on the particular episode of running out of the house, in its temporal and spatial setting. She specially stresses the time aspect: *in der nacht* ('at night', line 68) is reformulated by a more precise indication (line 69: *das war (–) knapp (.) zwölf UHR*, 'that was nearly twelve o'clock', and this reformulation is highlighted by the same technique as before (lines 65–66), a raising of her head and change of gaze direction, but in a less pronounced way.

    Ms. Korte then presents a supplementary reason for her behaviour, interpreting her running to the farmhouse as seeking contact (lines 70–71.). This is followed by a brief, self-initiated side sequence (cf. Jefferson 1972), in which she explains that her son had been studying in Australia (lines 72–73), but has come back home now.

    After this side-sequence, Ms. Korte continues the narrative reconstruction of the episode of running out of the house:

(2) **Continuation of the first narration** (Korte I, lines 76–102)

```
76   K:   (2.5) u::n:d=äh::m (.)
          and uhm

77        JA;
          well

78        (1.5)
79   K:   hab=ich LICHT gesehn,=
          I saw light

80        =hab=ich geSCHELLT,
          I rang the doorbell

81        .hh dann: (2.0) ziemlich <<len> LA:Nge> (---)
                          \__/
                             \
                  K:pronounced facial expression that marks reflecting
                  I: shifts gaze to K
          then quite a long time

82   K:   ziemlich lange hat das geDAUert,=
          it took quite long

83        =bis ich mi erinnert habe wo i WOHne,=
                        _____
                                       \
                  gesture with right hand in breast height: marks
                  relevance of the verbal
          till I remembered where I live

84   K:   =und wie=i HEISS.
          _____/
                         \
          marked end of the gesture: right hand back to her lap
          and what I'm called

85        (3.0)
          \__/
             \
          I: presses lips together, nods repeatedly

86   I:   ((Schnalzlaut)) <<all> da wo sie geSCHELLT ham;>=
          ((clicking tongue)) where you rang the bell

87        =<<dim> an dem bauernhof.>
          at the farm

88        (-)
          \_/
             \
               K: nods

89   I:   <<p> m=HM,>
```

```
 90      (--)
 91  K:  <<pp> JA;>
                 \_/
                   \
              shifts gaze away from I.
         Yes
 92      (---)
 93  K:  <<p> wusste i GAR nix;>
         I didn't know anything
 94      (2.0)
 95  K:  <<len> u::n:d=äh:m (3.0) ab und zu> passiert(e) mi
 96      AUCH das:: äh DAS,=
                     \__/
                        \
                 lets right hand drop on her thigh
         and uhm now and then it also happened
         that uhm that
 97      =<<len> dass ich mit jemanden: REde,>
         that I'm talking to somebody
 98      (1.5) un=kann ich mich !I::!berhaupt nich erINnern;
         \__/                      \__/
            \                         \
         end of the pause:         K: lets right hand drop
         I. shifts ganze to K.     on her thigh
         and can't remember at all
100      (.)
101  K:  <<p> NE,>
         you know
102  I:  m=HM,
```

Ms. Korte resumes the narrative reconstruction, initially with clear hesitation, then more fluently (*hab = ich LICHT gesehn*, 'I saw a light', line 79, etc.). She begins to reconstruct the events step by step (seeing a light, ringing the doorbell) and then, without mentioning intermediate events, she goes straight to the end of the process giving a final characterisation of her condition during the seizure. Through emphasis (*ziemlich LA:Nge,* 'quite a long time', line 81), followed by a reformulation[9] with a different prosodic contour (*ziemlich lange,* 'quite long', line 82), she underlines the duration of the period of disorientation, which she presents in retrospect, viewed from the end of the event. Furthermore, through a pronounced facial expression that reflects her pondering the events (line 81) and a gesture at breast level (line 83), she underlines the relevance

---

9.   For a description of reformulation procedures see Gülich and Kotschi (1995).

of her verbal expression. During the pause in which Ms. Korte produces this facial expression, the doctor shifts her gaze towards her so that her visual attention as a listener becomes apparent (line 81). The end of Ms. Korte's evaluative turn is multi-modally marked by her letting her right hand, which she had used to form the gesture in front of her breast (line 83), fall back into her lap (line 84). The doctor nonverbally marks this turn as relevant by pressing her lips together and nodding repeatedly (line 85).

Subsequent to this pause, the doctor asks for confirmation of a particular point, to which Ms. Korte gives a non-verbal reply (she nods, line 88). The reply is ratified by the doctor and thus the sequence is potentially completed. After a short pause, Ms. Korte utters a quiet but prosodically emphasised JA; ('yes') with falling intonation (line 91) and terminates the eye contact with the doctor, thus multi-modally closing the question-answer sequence. After a silence, Ms. Korte reformulates and thereby underlines the relevance of the description of her condition, this time characterising the condition itself (*wusste i GAR nix*, 'didn't know anything', line 93). Here a change of vocal register can be observed: Ms. Korte now speaks in a low voice with less tension. By combining the change in volume and tension with the verbal technique of reformulation she underlines the relevance of her disorientation. Her utterance can be interpreted as an expression of resignation. Running out of the house while having a seizure at night ends up in a condition of disorientation which seems to cause her troubles.

She then starts a further iterative reconstruction of occurrences, initiated by hesitation markers: *u::nd = äh:m (0.3) ab und zu passiert(e) mi AUCH* ('and uhm now and then it also happened to me', lines 95–96.). This utterance is characterised by a change to present tense (*dass ich mit jemanden: REde*, 'that I'm talking to somebody', line 97). Again this description is multi-modally emphasised; simultaneously with stress on the word *das* ('that', line 96) she lets her right fist drop on her thigh; equally in line 98 on the word *!I::!berhaupt* ('at all') which is in addition prosodically marked by strong accentuation and prolongation of the vowel. The interactive attention is established by a rather long pause (line 95), which is terminated at the moment when the doctor shifts her gaze to Ms. Korte, who is already looking at her.

Subsequent to the extract cited above, Ms. Korte reports other episodes of a similar nature when, during a seizure, she clearly did not know what she was doing (contracting an insurance under her maiden name, giving the address where she used to live with her deceased husband; taking things from a supermarket without paying). After that she begins to speak about biographical details and then closes the frame that she had opened with the words <<len> DA:S einfach is so (.) HARMlos ANgefangen ('it began harmlessly enough', cf. beginning of this section) with *un = seitDEM (.) GEHT das den ganzen theater; ne,* ('and that is when the trouble started you know', not shown here).

In sum, the episode of running out of the house is the first episodic reconstruction in Ms. Korte's multi-unit account of what is important to her, given subsequently to a short iterative reconstruction (*immer, meistens*, 'always, usually') of her falling over. On a local level, it is triggered by her initial utterance about the worsening seizures (*da = war MEHR, (–) nachHER*, 'there was more afterwards', line 61), which sets up a contrast to the 'harmless' beginning. On a global level, it is embedded in a sequence initiated by the doctor's opening question. In the context of the adjacent examples of mistakes committed during seizures, the episode can be interpreted as yet another example of inappropriate behaviour. This, however, can only be concluded in retrospect.

A closer look at where Ms. Korte directs her gaze during this sequence shows that in general she does not try to keep eye contact with the doctor: She has a tendency to look down at her lap or towards the left (see Figure 1, upper screenshot below). At certain moments, however, she lifts her head and turns towards the doctor (see Figure 1, lower screenshot) thus clearly marking the points verbally addressed at these moments as particularly relevant.

With regard to her body posture, it is striking that Ms. Korte mostly remains in her original position – leaned backwards, elbows placed on the armrest, hands resting on her thighs – and hardly ever moves.

The episodic reconstruction shows a rather reduced narrative structure. For example, there is no reconstruction of interaction with others. The reduction can be observed at different levels, not only at the level of the narrative structure itself, but also with regard to information details and expressiveness.

Precisely because of this evidently reduced expressiveness, the few verbal and non-verbal means of accentuation that Ms. Korte does use show effect; the way she uses pauses and shifts her gaze to ensure the doctor's attention (see above); her mimics and gestures that are always accompanied by word accentuations; the prosodic stress of certain words (e.g. *!I::!berhaupt*, 'at all', line 98). It is obvious that the prosodic, mimical, gestural and verbal components in Ms. Korte's turns work together and build a multi-modal gestalt (Dausendschön-Gay and Krafft 2002). The doctor visibly reacts to these subtle means of accentuation by shifting her gaze at relevant points and by non-verbally marking the relevance of Ms. Korte's descriptions (e.g. line 85).

Subsequent to the narration of the farm episode and the mention of her disorientation during seizures, Ms. Korte describes her seizures in the context of her life story. She recounts a series of extremely stressful experiences – a business disaster due to fraud committed by an employee, the sudden death of her husband, the death of one of her sons, the protracted dying of her father, whom she took care of (not shown here). Nevertheless, while all of this could be expected to arouse very strong emotions, emotions are hardly ever mentioned during this part of the interview.

2.2   The second sequence: Fear of death as a central topic

There is a second sequence in the interview with Ms. Korte, which is essential with respect to communicating the relevance of fear as a factor pertaining to her illness. This sequence is noteworthy because it illustrates how lengthy and difficult the process of speaking about fear can be. It is initiated by the doctor after about 30 minutes of the interview, at a point where a different topic (the patient's headaches) has been finished.

Figure 1. Gaze directions; upper screenshot: home position[10], no eye contact; lower screenshot: marking relevance, establishing eye contact

There is a noticeable break in the conversation: Adjacent to a silence of 3.4 seconds, during which the doctor leafs through her papers, she introduces the new topic by asking what role fear plays for Ms. Korte. The question is asked according to the guidelines

---

10.   See Sacks and Schegloff (2002) for the concept of 'home position'.

for the interview: If the patient does not speak about fear by her/himself, the doctor is to raise the topic in a subsequent part of the conversation. In our case, after the doctor's question, the relevance of fear is interactively established in a long and complex conversational process and becomes the central topic of the second part of the interview. As, for reasons of spatial limitation, we cannot render this process in full detail, we will summarise the beginning (see 2.2.1) and then focus our attention on the reconstruction of the particular episode of running out of the house, which is retold in this sequence (see 2.2.2).

2.2.1   *The beginning of the topicalisation of fear*
The second part of the interview is opened by the doctor's question whether fear plays any part in Ms. Korte's life. This question is met by an unspecific repair initiator – *was?* ('what?', not shown here) – by which Ms. Korte displays a general problem of hearing and/or understanding.[11] Thereupon the doctor reformulates her question, but again Ms. Korte delays her answer with a repair initiator, echoing the word *angst* ('fear') in a thoughtful voice (not shown here). The doctor then reformulates her question again, now asking it for the third time. Ms. Korte produces several signals of delay, then finally denies the question. In reaction to this, the doctor gives a few examples of everyday fears – which are acknowledged by Ms. Korte – and then states that in contrast to these there can be other fears that are *ganz speZIEL[le]* ('very particular', not shown here). She then relates these fears to *andern beschwerden* ('other troubles') and finally asks Ms. Korte again if there is anything that frightens her, thus formulating her question for the fourth time. After a pause, Ms. Korte denies this question with a second pair-part of minimal length (not shown here). By this short answer she makes it clear that, as far as she is concerned, there is no need to treat "fear" as a relevant topic in the conversation.

2.2.2   *The continuation of the process of fear description*
During the further course of the conversation, concrete fears are named and analysed interactively: The doctor asks the patient about her fear of taking something from the supermarket without paying (which Ms. Korte had previously mentioned). This is followed by Ms. Korte taking the initiative and describing the worries that she has when her son does not come home at night (not shown here).

Having discussed fear related with concrete objects, the doctor then focuses on a particular kind of fear, namely fear experienced during a seizure, and asks a question with respect to this:

---

11.   See Drew (1997) for the concept of 'open class repair initiators' that indicate the speakers' "difficulty with the other's prior turn, but without locating specifically where or what that difficulty is." (Drew 1997: 71).

(3) **Fear of death during seizures** (Korte I, lines 913–952)

```
913 I: .HH IS das vielleicht schon mal gewesen dass sie auch
       was it perhaps the case already that you also
914    ähm (.) in nem !AN!fall (.) so=n angstgefühl HATten?
       erm felt afraid like that in a seizure
915    (2.2)
       \___/
          \
          K: stares into space, saying nothing
916 I: [können sie sich da dran eri]nnern?
       can you remember that
917 K: [(in ANfall,)                ]
        (during a seizure)
918    (4.8)
919 K: <<pp> hm;>
920    (---)
921 K: !JA!/\
       \___/
          \
          nods energetically
       yes
922    (1.3)
923 K: <<p> DAS hab=ich vergessen;>=
       that I had forgotten
924    =das IS- (1.1)
       that IS
925    krieg=ich ANGST,
       I get scared
926 K: (-) [ dass      ] GLEICH was pasSIERt,
       that something is going to happen now
927 I:     [<<p> m=HM,>]
928 K: musst du RAU:S/\/
       you've got to get out
929    weil du STERben kannst a=gleich;=NE,
       because you can die a=now you know
930    .hh und dann:=ä:h (1.4) ENTweder muss=ich AUFstehen,
       and then uh either I have to get up
931    (.) und schnell was NEHmen,
       and quickly take something
932 I: m=HM?
933 K: wenn (da da) (.) so (.) nich VIEl (.) von dem angst is,
       if there's not too much fear
934    .hh u::nd-
       and
```

```
935       oder WEGlaufen;
          or run away
936       (.) <<p> aus=em haus;>
          out of the house
937 I:    m=HM?
938       .h also <<len> sie MERken das geF:ÜH:L von
          so you do notice the feeling of
939 I:    ANG[ST?> ]
          fear
940 K:       [   M]HM\/
941 I:    <<len> und DENken dann (.) ich> (---) könnte STERben;
          and then you think maybe I'll die
942 K:    JA;=
          yes
943 I:    =also=s=is wie TOdes[angst;]
          so it's it's like fear of dying
944 K:                         [   GAN]Z geNAU.
                               that's exactly it
945 I:    m=HM?=
946 K:    =den TOdesangst das=is .hh vielleicht das
          to be afraid of dying maybe that's the
947       SCHRECK!lichste <<dim> was sein kann.>
          most awful thing that can happen
948 I:    das=is das SCHRECKlichste [was se]in kann;
          that's the most awful thing that can happen
949 K:                              [ mhm/\]
950 I:    m=HM,=
951       =dieses geFÜHL zu haben;
          to have this feeling
952 K:    mhm\/
```

The doctor's initial question (lines 913–914) is followed by a verbal pause during which Ms. Korte stares into space, saying nothing. Then the doctor expands her turn by approaching the topic from a different angle: she asks whether Ms. Korte is able to recall any such occurrence (line 916). At the same time Ms. Korte reformulates the task given to her by repeating *in ANfall* ('during a seizure'), the specific point the doctor has been asking about. This is followed by a further pause (line 918). Then there is a low, slightly downward *hm* from Ms. Korte, another pause, and a new start with a clearly emphasised *!JA!/* ('yes') with rising-falling intonation, accompanied by an energetic nodding of the head (line 921). After another short pause[12], Ms. Korte restarts in a low

---

12. A pause of 1.3 seconds might not seem 'short' in many types of conversation, however, it is rather short in this particular conversation and also in comparison with other interlocutions from our database that originated from the same context.

voice but with an emphatic *DAS* ('that') in reply to the doctor's last question about her ability to remember, saying *DAS hab = ich vergessen* ('that I had forgotten', line 923). In saying this, she accounts for the delay in talking about this type of fear (cf. Schegloff 1968: 1087). At first she seems to concentrate on something specific, which she begins to define by *das IS-* ('that is'), but she immediately breaks off and switches to a different syntactic construction with *ich* ('I') as the subject: *krieg = ich ANGST, (-) dass GLEICH was pasSIERT* ('I get scared that something's going to happen soon', lines 925–926.). This is the first time Ms. Korte uses a construction to describe fear as her own feeling; up to this point she has merely been agreeing with what was suggested by the doctor. What the fear is about, is expressed in a *that*-clause that follows but remains vague (*dass GLEICH was pasSIERT,* 'that something is going to happen soon').

After this, Ms. Korte becomes more specific, verbalising the feeling. At the same time she changes over to the second person as if she was speaking to herself: *musst du RAU:S/\/* ('you've got to get out', line 928), followed by a reason, *weil du STERben kannst a = gleich* ('because you can die a = now'). It is striking how quickly she mentions her running-out, once her fear during seizures has finally been established as a topic of the conversation; how she implicitly links these two aspects by placing them adjacent to each other. Thus the episode of running out of the house, which Ms. Korte has already told in the beginning of the interview, now appears in a new context, it is re-contextualised (cf. Günthner 2005) by being linked to the subject of fear. The turn is marked by significant emphasis on the words *GLEICH* ('soon'), *RAUS* ('out'), *STERben* ('die') (lines 926–929). This prosodic accentuation in short intonational units is accompanied by noticeable glances that switch between eye contact and withdrawal of gaze. Thus the central elements of the feeling of fear are underlined by various verbal, vocal and non-vocal means.

After a brief hesitation, Ms. Korte continues by describing alternative courses of action that she can take in this particular situation (*ENTweder – oder,* 'either' – 'or'). Whereas she describes the first possibility with relative fluency (lines 930–933), the second one is introduced by various hesitation markers (an audible gasp and a self-repair, initiated by a drawn-out *u::nd* 'and', lines 934–935). The second alternative is formulated in a way considerably shorter and simpler, consisting only of the word *WEGlaufen* ('run away'). After a micropause Ms. Korte adds, in a low voice, *aus = em HAUS* ('out of the house', line 936). The structural breaks in the whole complex utterance are met by the doctor's acknowledgment tokens.

Subsequently the doctor reformulates Ms. Korte's turn, summing up her description of fear. Ms. Korte confirms this reformulation at the relevant syntactic breaks and the doctor concludes with a self-reformulation, now classifying the feeling of fear as *TOdesangst* ('fear of dying', line 943). More precisely, she *compares* it to fear of dying (*wie,* 'like'). Even before the doctor has finished her turn, Ms. Korte confirms in terminal overlap in a noticeably lively manner with an emphasised *GANZ geNAU* ('that's exactly it', line 944). The doctor's *m = HM?,* produced with rising intonation, indicates that she intends to let Ms. Korte expand her turn.

Ms. Korte immediately continues with an explicit, strongly emphasised evaluation of the feeling of fear of death, thereby indicating a strong emotional involvement (lines 946–947). The doctor reformulates this evaluation by repeating and expanding on Ms. Korte's utterance, using the same emphasis. By confirming this, Ms. Korte marks the potential closing of the sequence (line 952).

In sum, Excerpt (3) is an impressive example of the difficulties with regard to speaking about a certain type of fear, namely fear during an epileptic seizure. The doctor's initial question about the role fear plays for Ms. Korte initiates a long, complex process of almost 4 minutes, during which the topic is developed in several steps, through the interactive categorisation and evaluation of the sensation of fear. The doctor guides this process by her questions that continually focus on different aspects of fear.

In the first step, Ms. Korte does not seem to understand the question and then negates the possibility of fear having any impact on her life. In the second step, with the doctor's encouragement and participation, she replies by giving examples of fear related to concrete matters (injury during seizures, unintentional stealing from the supermarket, worry about her son). It is only in the third step that the sense of fear during a seizure is established interactively as a topic of conversation and is categorised as fear of death. Starting out from an undefined fear *dass GLEICH was pasSIERT* ('that something is going to happen soon'), going on to a kind of flight reflex (*musst du RAU:S/\/*, 'you've got to get out') and eventually leading up to the fear of dying, Ms. Korte gradually arrives at an understanding of a feeling she had previously *vergessen* ('forgotten'). The term *TOdesangst* ('fear of dying') is introduced by the doctor, but Ms. Korte picks it up and marks it as suitable; this becomes evident both through her lively and emphatic confirmation and through her subsequent evaluation of this feeling. Therefore, even though the term comes up late in the conversation, it is clearly marked as being of central importance.

2.2.3 *Second narrative reconstruction of the seizure episode ("running-out-of-the-house")*
Following the mutual evaluation of the feeling of fear of death, Ms. Korte continues with the reconstruction of an event, using a drawn-out *u:n:d* ('and') as initiation:

(4)   **Second narration** (Korte I, lines 953–981)

```
953 K: u:n:d=ä:hm (-) ich hab mein NACHbar gegenüber die türn
       immer an::(-)geschellt,        _____
                                                  \
                                       long held gesture with
                                       left arm, then left index:
                                       pointing at direction of
                                       neighbour's door, then
                                       imitating ringing doorbell
       and I always rang the doorbells at my opposite
       neighbour's
```

```
955     .h und der war schon auch (-) paar ma in der NACH:T?,
        _____/
                  \
                end of gesture (see line 953) on "auch": hand back to lap
        and he was already a few times at night

956     (---) dann seitDEM: habe ich (im:/ihm:) (.)
        and since then I've (in/him)

957     da war (.) poliZEI zu hause,
        there's been police at home

958     .h da warn die ÄRZte,=
        there's been the doctors

959     =haben die mich MITgenommen,
        took me with them

960     (---) un=dann war=ich wieder nachher zu HAUse,=
        and then I was back home later

961     =weil=i WOLlte nich in krankenhaus bleiben,
        because I didn't want to stay in hospital

962     (1.0) u::nd=ä:hm (-) seitDEM hab=ich mein: (---) ein:
        and uhm since then I've got my a

963     (--) WOHnungsschlüssel bei dem NACHbarn.=
             _____/
                  \
                similar gesture as in line 953–954, less pronounced
        flat key at my neighbour's

964     =wenn was pasSIERT dann brauchen de (--) keine RUfen
        if anything happens then they need not call somebody

965     hab=i gesagt,
        I said

966     .hh der sollte mir einfach nur AUFmachen,=
        he should just open the door for me

967     =un ich lege <<dim> mich HIN.=ne,>
        and I'll just lie down you know

968     (1.7)
969  I: .hh das war IN nem ANfall;=
        that was in a seizure

970     =dass sie zu dem nachbarn geGANgen sind;
        that you went to your neighbour

971  K: NEIN;
        no

972     (--)
```

```
973 K: <<all> aHA/\>=
               \___/
                  \
            changes sitting position in marked manner
        oh
974     =bei dem ANfall,=JA;=
        during the seizure yes
975     =wenn (de) ich den TOdesangst hab;>
        when I'm scared to death
976 I: m=[HM?]
977 K:   [.hh] da hab=ich da geSCHELLT bei ihn,=
                _____/
                                      \
                        head "points" to the left,
                    indicating direction of neighbours
        door then I rang his doorbell
978 K: [weil ich] dachte wenn ich: irgendwo nich WEGlaufe,=
        because I thought if I somehow don't run away
979 I: [ m=HM,   ]
980 K: =dann gleich bin ich WEG;=ne,
        then I'll be gone right away you know
981 I: m=HM,
```

This is an example of the iterative reconstruction (*immer*, 'always', *paar ma*, 'a few times', lines 954–955) of a typical seizure. It is exactly the same type of episode related by Ms. Korte at the beginning of the interview. The main elements – her running out of the house at night and ringing someone's doorbell – are identical, but they are reconstructed here in more detail: At first Ms. Korte attempts to quickly get to the end of the episode (*dann seitDEM:*, 'and since then', line 956). However, she then breaks off and goes back to the situation already described, and she also reconstructs her interaction with others (the police, doctors, neighbours), before starting to produce a conclusion (lines 962–963). In this turn constructional unit she resumes her construction of events cut off in line 956 and finishes it: *seitDEM hab = ich mein: (–) ein: (–) WOHnungsschlüssel bei dem NACHbarn* ('and since then I've got my a flat key at my neighbour's'), etc.

Ms. Korte then associates this episode explicitly with fear of death, thereby replying to a question of the doctor (lines 969–970). Then she sums up the situation with the formulation *wenn ich: irgendwo nich WEGlaufe, dann gleich bin ich WEG* ' (if I somehow don't run away then I'll be gone right away', lines 978–980).

Thus the episode narrated during the first few minutes of the interview is put into an entirely new frame. While in the first narrative reconstruction the episode appeared in the context of the aggravation of the seizures and of examples of inappropriate behaviour resulting from loss of control, it here turns out to be an expression of fear of dying during a seizure.

The first version (excerpts 1 and 2) was marked by a reduced narrative structure. In the second one (excerpts 3 and 4), the narrative reconstruction is both more detailed and more dramatic. Ms. Korte also produces this dramatisation of the reconstructed episode(s) through non-verbal means by visually re-creating the spatial situation of the narrated time. Ringing the neighbour's doorbell is described verbally and by means of a distinct arm gesture (line 954; see Figure 2, upper screenshot): Starting with the word *NACHbar* ('neighbour', line 953), she raises her left arm up at face level, stretched to the left side, with her hand open, obviously pointing in the imagined direction of her neighbour's apartment. This gesture is held for a long time, until the word *geschellt* ('rang') where she modifies it by using her forefinger to imitate the ringing of the doorbell. The same applies to leaving a key with her neighbour (lines 962–963): Here she uses a very similar but less pronounced gesture to imitate the depositing of the key at her neighbour's (see Figure 2, middle screen shot). An even more reduced version of this gesture is used in line 977, in parallel to the words *da geSCHELLT bei ihn* ('rang his doorbell') where she uses her head to point in the imagined direction of the neighbour's apartment (see Figure 2, lower screenshot). It is striking that all these gestures – the only gestures she uses during the sequence – are employed to indicate the ringing at her neighbour's. In so doing, she emphasises this part of her description.

Another noteworthy moment occurs in lines 971–981: While answering one of the doctor's questions (lines 969–970), which she at first misunderstands[13], Ms. Korte changes her sitting position in a marked manner when speaking about her fear of dying during a seizure (lines 973–977). One cannot help wondering whether she is physically demonstrating the flight reflex.

There is another impressive example of a multidimensional description subsequent to the excerpt quoted above. It deals with the patient's motivation for running out of the house and ringing the neighbour's doorbell:

---

13.   Ms. Korte first replies in the negative and then self-repairs her turn (cf. Schegloff et al. 1977).

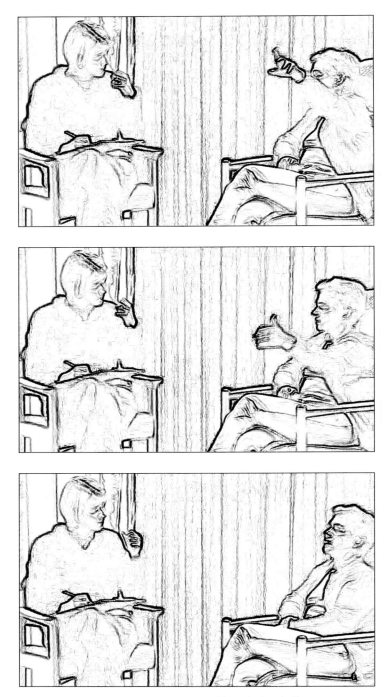

Figure 2. Gestures that indicate ringing the neighbour's doorbell

(5)   **Motivation for ringing the neighbour's doorbell** (Korte I, lines 982–1002)

```
982  I: un=da ham sie bei (.) IHM geSCHELLT;=
        and then you rang his doorbell

983  K: =JA;
        yes

984  I: m=HM,

985     und was: (1.3) (der hat n) (.)
        and what       (he  has a)

986     der HAT dann den ARZT gerufen?
        he called the doctor then

987     oder was WOLLten sie dann von ihm;
        or what did you want from him

988  K: <<cresc> he:[:::>      ]
989  I:             [was soll]te er machen;
                     what was he to do

990  K: IRgendwo (.)
        somewhere

991     WEIß ich nich was;
        I don't know what

992     (---)

993  K: vieLLEICH wenn'
        maybe if

994     dass jemand´ (.) sieht dass=ich !ST↑ER!be;=
        that somebody   sees  I'm dying

995  K: =das .hh das heiß [äh wen]n=i UMkippe [dann:] (.)
                          _____/
                              \
                   gesturing with left hand
        I mean uhm if I fall over then
996  I:                   [AH:/\ ]           [m=HM,]
                           oh                 m=HM,

997  K: die leute wissen be!SCHEID!/\ [nich; ] NE,
        people are informed you know

998  I:                             [AH=JA;]
                                     oh I see

999  I: sie wollten einfach dass jemand da=is der AUFpassen
        you just wanted somebody to be there who can take care
1000 I: ka[nn;]

1001 K:   [ J]A;
           yes

1002 I: m=HM,
```

In the closing section of this excerpt, the doctor shows that she tries to understand Ms. Korte's motivation for ringing at her neighbour's (line 985–987). In answering the doctor's question, Ms. Korte becomes unusually lively compared to her previous behaviour: although at first she states somewhat vaguely that she does not know the reason (*IRgendwo (.) WEIß ich nich was*, 'somewhere....don't know what', lines 990–991), her way of speaking is clearly louder and more intense than before, and thus she sounds more determined. She maintains these prosodic characteristics in her adjacent attempt at a possible explanation: *vielLEICH wenn' dass jemand' (.) sieht dass = ich !ST↑ER!be* ('maybe if somebody sees that I'm dying', line 993–994). The word *!ST↑ER!be* ('dying') is picked out and heavily stressed, with a strong upward pitch.

This particularly dramatic way of speaking is maintained by Ms. Korte in the subsequent detailed reformulation, as well as reinforced by her gesturing with her left hand while saying *das heiß* ('I mean', line 995). During the whole turn, she continuously shakes her head and her shoulder in a very slight way. Thus, the determination that is expressed prosodically is in clear contrast to the insecurity expressed non-verbally.

As the interview continues, the subject of fear of death takes on a central significance and the doctor asks several questions about the feeling of fear and running out of the house. The feeling of fear is intensely dealt with by both participants, thus becoming more precise and differentiated. It can be noticed that each new attempt at reformulation reveals new aspects and consequently new possibilities for explanations.

For reasons of space, we cannot describe the interactive work done on defining the feeling of fear of death in full length and detail here. However, we would like to point to the fact that, in the closing sequence of the interview, when asked what she would like to achieve through the treatment in the clinic, Ms. Korte replies without hesitation: *dass die ÄNGste weggehen* ('that the fears go away', not shown here). Against the background of her initial reaction to the doctor's question concerning fear, it again becomes clear that decisive changes have taken place during the conversational process.[14]

3. Conclusion

The two versions of the running-out-of-the-house episode show how the process of communicating the experience of fear in the course of the interviews progressively

---

14. This process is continued in a second interview, which took place some days after the first one because the doctor wanted to ask the patient some further questions. When the doctor mentions Ms. Korte's fear of death in this second conversation, Mrs. Korte replies quickly and spontaneously and then initiates another reconstruction of the act of running out of the house and ringing the neighbour's doorbell. Here she speaks in a very lively manner, and the combination of verbal, prosodic, gestural and facial means renders the narration more and more dramatic. The aspect of disorientation, which Ms. Korte already mentions in her first reconstructions of the episode, is interactively dealt with in great detail in this second interview (see Gülich et al. 2010).

provides new and different frames for one and the same type of event, an event characteristic of Ms. Korte's seizures, and how, as a result of this re-contextualisation (cf. Günthner 2005), the meaning of the episode gets altered.

If we look back to the first version of the episode (excerpts 1 and 2) from our present point of analysis, it is obvious that the central elements involved – namely, the running out of the house and the disorientation – are already present and have been focussed on, but with very reduced means. This episode has been told spontaneously, without hesitation, at the beginning of the conversation; the concept of fear is not mentioned in this context.

A longer period of time and intensive interactive work is required to reach the point where the feeling of fear of death is named. Then the patient says that this kind of fear is *das SCHRECKlichste was SEIN kann* ('the most awful thing that can be'), but before she had *vergessen* ('forgotten') to mention it. In the second version of the running-out-of-the-house episode the narration is more detailed, more lively and more dramatic on several levels.

Can we say that, in retrospect, in the light of the second version, the first one appears as a way to express fear of death just the same, only without naming the emotion explicitly? The expression of fear could be seen as being contained in the narration, that is, the patient spontaneously relates a typical episode of a fearful reaction/behaviour at the beginning of a seizure without verbally using the category 'fear' for this narration. Instead of establishing this category for her reaction/behaviour she chooses a different way of expression: by narrating certain events.

For the moment, the question to what extent fear of death is expressed when it is not named remains unanswered. A very fine prosodic analysis and extremely precise description of all types of resources used could perhaps enable us to detect a higher degree of emotional participation in the first version of the episode. Selting (this volume) points out that a description of voice qualities is a challenge for future research. We think that further findings in this domain might be very important for understanding descriptions – especially implicit representations – of emotional involvement, in particular of fear, anxiety and panic.

However, Couper-Kuhlen (forthc.) stresses in her "state of the art" that prosody rarely works alone. In a table at the end of her contribution she illustrates the "status of prosody" and lists a person's gaze, facial expression, gesture, body position and body movement as factors to be taken into account in a multidimensional analysis. For the case presented here, it is evident that all of these resources work together. The distinctions between the two versions of the episode are not to be found in the verbal procedures *and* voice *and* gaze *and* gesture, but in the gestalt (Dausendschön-Gay and Krafft 2002) formed by the interplay of all these resources. Thus, in our view, the description of such gestalts should be one central focus of future conversation analytic research on emotion.

References

Capps, Lisa and Ochs, Elinor 1995a. *Constructing panic: The discourse of agoraphobia.* Cambridge, Mass.: Harvard University Press.

Capps, Lisa and Ochs, Elinor 1995b. "Out of place – Narrative insights into agoraphobia." *Discourse Processes* 19: 407–439.

Couper-Kuhlen, Elizabeth (forthc.). "Pragmatics and prosody: Prosody as social action." In: *Foundations of pragmatics*, Wolfram Bublitz and Neal Norrick (eds.), Berlin: Mouton de Gruyter.

Dausendschön-Gay, Ulrich and Krafft, Ulrich 2002. "Text und Körpergesten. Beobachtungen zur holistischen Organisation der Kommunikation." *Psychotherapie und Sozialwissenschaft* 4 (1): 30–60.

Drescher, Martina 2003. *Sprachliche Affektivität. Darstellung emotionaler Beteiligung am Beispiel von Gesprächen aus dem Französischen.* Tübingen: Max Niemeyer.

Drew, Paul 1997. "'Open' class repair initiators in response to sequential sources of troubles in conversation". *Journal of Pragmatics* 28: 69–101.

Fiehler, Reinhard 2001. "Emotionalität im Gespräch." In: *Text- und Gesprächslinguistik. Ein internationales Handbuch zeitgenössischer Forschung*, vol. 2, Klaus Brinker, Gerd Antos, Wolfgang Heinemann and Sven F. Sager (eds.), 1425–1438. Berlin: de Gruyter.

Gülich, Elisabeth and Couper-Kuhlen, Elizabeth 2007. "Zur Entwicklung einer Differenzierung von Angstformen im Interaktionsverlauf: Verfahren der szenischen Darstellung." In: *Koordination: Beiträge zur Analyse multimodaler Interaktion*, Reinhold Schmitt (ed.), 293–337. Tübingen: Narr.

Gülich, Elisabeth and Kotschi, Thomas 1995. "Discourse production in oral communication. A study based on French." In: *Aspects of oral communication*, Uta M. Quasthoff (ed.), 30–66. Berlin: de Gruyter.

Gülich, Elisabeth; Lindemann, Katrin and Schöndienst, Martin 2010. "Interaktive Formulierung von Angsterlebnissen im Arzt-Patient-Gespräch. Eine Einzelfallstudie." In: *Wissen in (Inter-)Aktion. Verfahren der Wissensgenerierung in unterschiedlichen Praxisfeldern*, Ulrich Dausendschön-Gay, Christine Domke and Sören Ohlhus (eds.), 135–160. Berlin: de Gruyer.

Gülich, Elisabeth and Schöndienst, Martin 2005. "Kommunikative Darstellung und klinische Repräsentation von Angst. Exemplarische Untersuchungen zur Bedeutung von Affekten bei Patienten mit Anfallskrankheiten und/oder Angsterkrankungen. Abschlussbericht." *ZiF-Mitteilungen* 3: 4–9.

Gülich, Elisabeth; Schöndienst, Martin and Surmann, Volker 2003. "Schmerzen erzählen Geschichten – Geschichten erzählen Schmerzen." In: *Der erzählte Schmerz*. Themenheft von Psychotherapie und Sozialwissenschaft. Zeitschrift für Qualitative Forschung 5 (3), Elisabeth Gülich, Martin Schöndienst and Volker Surmann (eds.), 220–249. Göttingen: Vandenhoeck & Ruprecht.

Günthner, Susanne 2000. *Vorwurfsaktivitäten in der Alltagsinteraktion. Grammatische, prosodische, rhetorisch-stilistische und interaktive Verfahren bei der Konstitution kommunikativer Muster und Gattungen.* Tübingen: Niemeyer.

Günthner, Susanne 2005. "Narrative reconstruction of past experiences. Adjustments and modifications in the process of recontextualizing a past experience." In: *Narrative interaction*, Uta M. Quasthoff and Tabea Becker (eds.), 285–301. Amsterdam: Benjamins.

Günthner, Susanne 2006. "Rhetorische Verfahren bei der Vermittlung von Panikattacken. Zur Kommunikation von Angst in informellen Gesprächskontexten." *Gesprächsforschung – Online-Zeitschrift zur verbalen Interaktion* 7: 124–151 (http://www.gespraechsforschung-ozs.de/heft2006/heft2006.htm).

Jefferson, Gail 1972. "Side sequences." In: *Studies in social interaction*, David N. Sudnow (ed.), 294–338. New York: Free Press.

Lindemann, Katrin 2009. *Angst im Gespräch. Eine gesprächsanalytische Studie zur kommunikativen Darstellung von Angst*. Unpublished doctoral dissertation, University of Bielefeld.

Plug, Leendert; Sharrack, Basil and Reuber, Markus 2009. "Conversation analysis can help to distinguish between epilepsy and non-epileptic seizure disorders: A case comparison." *Seizure* 18: 43–50.

Sacks, Harvey and Schegloff, Emanuel A. 2002. "Home position." *Gesture* 2 (2): 133–146.

Schegloff, Emanuel A. 1968. "Sequencing in conversational openings." *American Anthropologist* 70 (6): 1075–1095.

Schegloff, Emanuel A. 1982. "Discourse as an interactional achievement: some uses of 'uh huh' and other things that come between sentences." In: *Analysing discourse: Text and talk*, Deborah Tannen (ed.), 71–139. Washington D.C.: Georgetown University Press.

Schegloff, Emanuel A. 1987. "Analyzing single episodes of interaction: An exercise in Conversation Analysis." *Social Psychology Quarterly* 50: 101–114.

Schegloff, Emanuel A.; Jefferson, Gail and Sacks, Harvey 1977. "The preference for self-correction in the organization of repair." *Language* 53 (2): 361–382.

Schmitz, Bettina and Schöndienst, Martin 2006. "Anfälle: Epilepsie und Dissoziation. Die Psychosomatik epileptischer und nicht-epileptischer Anfälle." In: *Neuro-Psychosomatik: Grundlagen und Klinik neurologischer Psychosomatik*, Peter Henningsen, Harald Gündel and Andreas Ceballos-Baumann (eds.), 131–175. Stuttgart: Schattauer.

Schöndienst, Martin 2002. "Von einer sprachtheoretischen Idee zu einer klinisch-linguistischen Methode. Einleitende Überlegungen." *Psychotherapie und Sozialwissenschaft* 4 (4): 253–270.

Schwabe, Meike 2006. *Kinder und Jugendliche als Patienten. Eine gesprächsanalytische Studie zum subjektiven Krankheitserleben junger Anfallspatienten in pädiatrischen Sprechstunden*. Göttingen: V & R unipress.

Schwabe, Meike; Howell, Stephen J. and Reuber, Markus 2007. "Differential diagnosis of seizure disorders: a conversation analytic approach." *Social Science and Medicine* 65: 712–724.

Schwabe, Meike; Reuber, Markus; Schöndienst, Martin and Gülich, Elisabeth 2008. "Listening to people with seizures: How can conversation analysis help in the differential diagnosis of seizure disorders." *Communication and Medicine* 5: 59–72.

Selting, Margret; Auer, Peter; Barden, Birgit; Bergmann, Jörg; Couper-Kuhlen, Elizabeth; Günthner, Susanne; Meier, Christoph; Quasthoff, Uta; Schlobinski, Peter and Uhmann, Susanne 1998. "Gesprächsanalytisches Transkriptionssystem GAT." *Linguistische Berichte* 173: 91–122.

Streeck, Jürgen and Streeck, Ulrich 2002. "Mikroanalyse sprachlichen und körperlichen Interaktionsverhaltens in psychotherapeutischen Beziehungen." *Psychotherapie und Sozialwissenschaft. Zeitschrift für Qualitative Forschung* 4 (1): 61–78.

Surmann, Volker 2005. *Anfallsbilder: Metaphorische Konzepte im Sprechen anfallskranker Menschen*. Würzburg: Königshausen & Neumann.

Whalen, Jack; Zimmerman, Don H. and Whalen, Marilyn R. 1988. "When words fail: a single case analysis." *Social Problems* 35: 333–362.

Appendix I: Transcript notations (GAT basic transcript)

[ ]	overlap and simultaneous speech
=	direct tying of two words
(.)	micro pause
(-)	short pause (app. 0.25 sec.)
(–)	medium pause (app. 0.50 sec.)
(–)	longer pause (app. 0.75 sec.)
(2.0)	measured pause in sec.
:; ::; …;	lengthening, depending on duration
´	cut off with glottal stop
beLIEVE	primary- resp. main stress
be!LIEVE!	extra strong stress
!	emphatic exclamation
?	high rising intonation, questioning intonation
,	medium rising intonation
;	medium falling intonation
.	falling intonation
-	level intonation
/\	rising-falling intonation
\/	falling-rising intonation
↑	noticeable jump in intonation upwards
↓	noticeable jump in intonation downwards
( )/ (there)	inaudible/suspected wording
(there/where)	possible alternatives
<<laughing> oh well>	interpretative commentaries, with given scope
((wheezing))	para- and non linguistic acts/events
.h; .hh; .hhh	audible inhale, depending on duration
h, hh, hhh	audible exhale, depending on duration
I: nobody at home	description of nonverbal/visible
_____/	aspects of communication
puts down receiver	

changes in volume and speed of talking with given scope:

<<f> >/<<ff> >	forte, loud/ fortissimo, very loud
<<p> >/<<pp> >	piano, quiet/low/soft/pianissimo, very quiet/low/soft
<<all> >/<<acc> >	allegro, quick/ accelerando, gradually becoming quicker
<<len> >/<<rall> >	lento, slow/ rallentando, gradually becoming slower
<<cresc> >	crescendo, gradually becoming louder
<<dim> >	diminuendo, gradually becoming quieter

Double function of prosody: Processes of meaning-making in narrative reconstructions of epileptic seizures*

Comments on Elisabeth Gülich and Katrin Lindemann "Communicating emotion in doctor-patient interaction. A multidimensional single-case analysis"

Elisabeth Reber
University of Erlangen-Nürnberg, Germany

1. Introduction

"Language has a heart" (Ochs and Schieffelin 1989). In accordance with this, interactional-linguistically informed emotion research has developed into a fast-growing field with work such as that by Elisabeth Gülich and Katrin Lindemann furthering our understanding of the interactional embodiment of emotion. In their single-case study the authors show how the patient reconstructs the highly negative experience of her epileptic seizures in so-called running-out-of-the-house episodes, deploying multimodal communicative resources (verbal, vocal, and visual). Gülich and Lindemann argue that these tellings are performed with increasing degrees of emotional intensity, which are reflected by an increasing expressiveness of the multimodal resources used. Furthermore, the authors observe that through their interactive work, doctor and patient jointly achieve an explicit labelling of the emotion associated with the seizures depicted, namely 'fear of death'.

Expanding on the analysis presented by Gülich and Lindemann, my comment will offer a more detailed analysis of the prosodic resources deployed in the story episodes

---

* I am indebted to Dagmar Barth-Weingarten and Margret Selting for their comments on earlier drafts of this paper. Thanks are also due to Laura McKee for checking my English.

(Excerpts 1–4).[1] In light of these findings, Gülich and Lindemann's suggestion that prosody contributes to the patient's multi-modal communication of fear will be further discussed. However, given that the patient is a non-native speaker of German and because of the lack of a larger comparable data set, be it in terms of published work or data material available, my analysis may raise more questions than answers.

In what follows, I will first outline some of the relevant literature on prosody in reconstructions of fear and panic and on story-telling in general. Providing a step-by-step analysis of the narrative sequences in Excerpts 1–4, I will then present the findings of the formal prosodic analysis: it will be proposed that the prosodic formatting of the running-out-of-the-house episodes is sequentially situated in the sense that versions of the episode performed in slots where the patient is allowed to self-initiate topical talk are formatted differently from that where topical talk is elicited by the doctor. The functional analysis suggests that the prosodic cues do both sequence-organising (i.e. structuring) work and serve as resources for emphasis and dramatisation in the interactional project of story-telling.

2.   Previous research on affectivity in story-telling

Similarly to Gülich and Lindemann, Fiehler (1990) observes that patients in German therapeutic interactions use narratives in order to recount past affect-laden events and experiences (ibid: 239). Moreover, he finds that it is a typical activity of the therapist to instigate an explicit labelling of the affective dimensions involved in the past experience narrated (ibid: 241). It is to note, however, that narrative structures are organised on more than one (affective) level: That is, on the one hand, the story-teller's affective stance towards a recounted event may be discordant with that of a character in the story: narrative reported speech, for instance, serves both to reconstruct the voice of the story character and to convey the story-teller's affective stance towards the quoted utterance (cf. Günthner 1997: 268, Couper-Kuhlen 1998: 21). In this way, the affectivity signalled in reported speech is enacted and dramatised for narrative purposes. On the other hand, what is heard as (affect-laden) prosody is at the same time deployed as a structuring device for single sequential moves in narrative sequences, e.g. "emphatic speech style" for the construction of story climaxes (cf. Selting 1994). In this sense, we can talk about a double function of prosody.

Turning to work specifically concerned with 'fear' and 'panic' in interaction, the scarce interactional work on its prosodic contextualisation available so far (cf. also the literature review by Gülich and Lindemann), seems to be exclusively concerned with the prosody of *reconstructed* experiences of panic and fear in narratives: Günthner (2006) on informal conversations about panic experiences in German, for instance,

---

1.   For reasons of space, the discussion will focus on the narrative sequences, thus excluding Excerpt 5.

observes that emphatic prosodic marking, i.e. dense accentuation and step-ups in pitch, together with hyperbolic formulations serve as contextualisation devices for the heightened relevance (*Relevanzhochstufung*) of the panic experiences described, that is, they are used in order to construct the panic experience as lying beyond usual everyday experiences (ibid: 133–134). In their single-case study on narrative stagings of fear in a single-case analysis of a doctor-patient interaction, Gülich and Couper-Kuhlen (2007) identify two "distinctive bundles" (*distinktive Bündel*, ibid: 303) of multimodal, i.e. verbal, vocal and visual resources to represent epileptic fear on the one hand and everyday fear on the other. In terms of prosody, representations of epileptic fear are mainly characterised by a 'whiny voice', glottal stops, and a recurrent, stylised pitch contour[2]. In contrast to Günthner (2006), the authors offer an iconic interpretation of the prosodic cues observed, treating e.g. the use of the stylised pitch contour accompanied by other multimodal cues as an indication of the patient's feeling helpless and rigid with fear in view of the potentially looming seizure (Gülich and Couper-Kuhlen 2007: 309).

Nevertheless, displays of affect in narratives are not necessarily to be taken as affect-laden displays in the here and now – one reason for this being that the conversational tasks in story-telling differ from those in other activities, which again requires different interactional work when performing affect-laden actions. So what could 'fear' sound like in situ? One of the rare studies of an affective dimension related to fear/panic in the here and now, Whalen and Zimmerman (1998) on 'hysteria' in American English emergency calls find that such displays are accompanied by extremely high volume, a 'distorted voice', sobbing or crying, gasping for breath, and exclamations (ibid: 146). This suggests that in situ displays are constructed through features that differ from those in *tellings about* affect-laden events.

3. The prosodic make-up of the running-out-of-the-house episodes

With respect to the several instantiations of the running-out-of-the-house episodes, Harrie Mazeland (p.c.) suggests that the patient "orients to different kinds of tellables and topical relevancies". In the excerpts examined, it will be shown that the prosodic make-up relates to these relevancies. Where the patient is allowed to self-initiate topical talk she will frame the episodes as tellings of what is relevant to her, whereas in the

---

2. The stylised contour is marked by a plateau at 8 semitones (195–200Hz) above the bottom of the speaker's voice range, which begins with the first syllable of the intonation unit, and a sharp down step to 2–3 semitones (141–146 Hz) above the bottom of the speaker's voice range right after the primary accent, a pitch level which is kept until the end of the unit (ibid: 308–309, 326). Representations of everyday fear include the following prosodic properties: intonationally parallel units and a 'more lively' way of speaking (more fluent, often fast speech tempo, fuller voice); reduced volume and 'conspirative' voice in reported thought (ibid: 327).

topical talk elicited by the doctor, issues on the medical agenda are addressed. Moreover, these different orientations influence the affective framing of the tellables.

3.1   Excerpts 1 and 2

The first episode (Excerpts 1 and 2; Gülich and Lindemann this volume: 273–276) is situated in response to the doctor's open question to bring up what the patient thinks is important (not shown in the extracts). Here the patient tells her about the symptoms connected with her seizures. The prosodic analysis shows that, following the story preface (Excerpt 1, lines 65–66), the elaboration is delivered in intonation phrases accompanied by a progredient intonation contour. The contour is first characterised by a plateau at about 219–229 Hz (i.e. in the middle of the speaker's voice range), with the tail rising to a pitch peak of 3–6 semitones (275–326 Hz) above that plateau. This kind of contour, which comes off as monotonous, is produced on the following lines[3]:

-    .hh das war (-) knApp (.) zwölf ´**UHR,** (Excerpt 1, line 69)
-    (2.0) weil=ich=s a´ (.) allEine (war=i´) in in der WOH´**nung,** (Excerpt 1, lines 70-71)
-    =da hat=er stu´**DIERT,** (Excerpt 1, line 73)
-    =hab=ich ge´**SCHELLT,** (Excerpt 2, line 80)

The intonation contour operates on the sequence-organisational and semantic levels of the activity: first, it serves as turn-holding device in that it secures the teller the floor and marks the ongoing telling as pre-climatic; secondly, it functions as a cohesive device (cf. Selting 2004 for a discussion of similar "staircase contours" and their functions in biographical tellings in the Berlin vernacular).

In Excerpt 2, the narrative comes to a first (potential) climax (lines 82–84): It is marked by an accelerated speech tempo, dense accentuation and rhythmic integration:[4]

```
K:  <<acc>ziemlich
    /lAnge hat das ge      /
    /DAUert,==bis ich mi er/
    /INnert habe wo i       /
    /WOHne,==und wie=i      /
    /↓heiß.>
```

This kind of "emphatic speech style" is a typical way of prosodic contextualisation for climaxes in German narratives (Selting 1994). However, the climax is further produced

---

3.   The syllables forming the tail and accompanied by rising pitch are marked in bold. Cf. Gülich and Lindemann (this volume) for further transcription conventions.

4.   Each line contains one foot. The slashes below one another indicate isochronous intervals. (Selting et al. 2009: 387)

within a declining, narrow pitch range of 4–5 ST (between 244 Hz and 188 Hz), which is heard as monotonous, and ends with a final pitch drop (to 83 Hz) on *heiß*. These features noticeably deviate from the bundle of prosodic cues usually found in "emphatic speech style" where high pitch peaks, i.e. a wide-ranging contour heard as a lively voice, are expectable. Content-wise, the wording of the climax suggests that the patient makes relevant her loss of self during the seizure as the point of her telling: *ziemlich lange hat das geDAUert,= =bis ich mi erinnert habe wo i wohne,==und wie = i heiß.* ('it took quite long till I remembered where I live and what I'm called', Extract 2, lines 82–84).

To conclude, the first instantiation of the story episode is cast as a story of loss of self: Prosodically, the progredient intonation constitutes a typical cohesive device. The climax bears features of "emphatic speech style". However, especially when compared to (the non-narrative) sequence in Excerpt 5, where the patient's speech is accompanied by a wide-ranging prosody, marked by high step-ups in pitch (Gülich and Lindemann this volume: 290), the lack of pitch peaks here make the climax come off as noticeably monotonous.

3.2   Excerpts 3 and 4

What is glossed as a single second story episode in Excerpts 3 and 4 by Gülich and Lindemann constitues both self-initiated and elicited topical talk and is, at least prosodically, performed as several instantiations of the episode: The first instantiation (Extract 3) is delivered as a doctor's topic, i.e. it is elicited by the doctor's question over whether the patient has had feelings of fear in a seizure before.[5] By introducing the emotion label and eliciting a verbalisation of the patient's feelings, the doctor constructs her category membership as the medical expert in the interaction. In this sense and in contrast to the local framing of the first episode, the doctor this time initiates topical talk about something relevant to *the medical agenda*. This kind of elicited talk about the patient's seizure is performed as a dramatic version of the story episode: lines 925 and 928 are delivered in short intonation phrases with the verb in first position (*Verbspitzenstellung*). This kind of construction, which results in a condensation of the action, is a resource typical of dramatisation in narratives in German (Auer 1993). The prosodic and syntactic marking is paralleled by the extreme contents, where the patient for the first time labels her feelings as fear in a story episode, specifying it as fear that she might die. The sequence reaches a preliminary, and notably non-narrative affective high point when the patient delivers an extremely negative assessment of the emotion label "fear of death", which was again proffered by the doctor (Extract 3, lines 938–952).

---

5.   This is confirmed by the patient. To proffer talk about feelings of fear was an item set on the doctor's interviewing agenda (Gülich and Lindemann this volume: 280)

After that, the patient *self-initiates* a further telling (Extract 4, lines 953–967), which is cast as an expansion of the running-out-of-the-house episode (cf. the discourse marker *u:n:d = ä:hm* (line 953) indicating the resumption of a suspended sequence, cf. Local 2004 for *and uhm*) and the chronological integration between the line where the first instantiation of the second story episode left off (Extract 3, line 935–936) and the second one begins (Extract 4, line 953). Prosodically, structurally and content-wise, it is framed as a move out of the affective involvement earlier shown by the negative assessment: it is accompanied by the same progredient intonation contour as in the first episode (Extract 1). Again it begins with a plateau at the middle of the speaker's pitch range with a final rising tail to 4–6 ST above the plateau (cf. Extract 4, lines 955, 957, 958, 959, 961). However, other than in the first episode, the telling does not work towards a climactic treatment of the patient's loss of self, but concludes with a solution of how to deal with her seizures (since this incident, her neighbour has a key to her flat) without noticeable prosodic marking (lines 962–963). In other words, in contrast to the first story episode, where the patient highlights her loss of self, as well as opposed to the display of terror displayed by the negative assessment *das SCHRECK-lichste was SEIN kann*, this instantiation of the episode constructs her as somebody in control of her condition.

To summarise, the second instantiation of the story episode, which is elicited as a doctor's topic, is performed in a dramatic way. Yet, its self-initiated expansion is produced with the same progredient intonation contour as in Excerpt 1 and is cast as a story of control.

4   Discussion

The analysis suggests that, at least as far as the prosodic cues are concerned, the different re-tellings of the story episode are not marked by continuously increasing degrees of emotional intensity. Rather, the affective framing is interactively managed, following local contingencies. In self-initiated topical talk, the narrative treatment of the seizures is accompanied by a noticeably monotonous, progredient intonation contour, which serves as a cohesive device in the pre-climactic phases (Excerpts 1–2 and 4). The climax of the first story episode has features of emphatic speech style, however, the narrow pitch movement and level pitch register make it again hearable as noticeably monotonous. In contrast to this, when prompted by the doctor in connection to fear, the narrative reconstruction of the seizure is produced in a more dramatic way (Excerpt 3). At the same time, these kinds of prosodic patterns serve a double function in that they are not functional in the management of cohesion or stance-taking alone; they also serve to structure the story under way, e.g. in contextualising the pre-climatic phases or the climax as such. Despite these observations, we must, however, not forget that prosody is only one of the multiple resources deployed in narrative meaning-making: It is for this reason that Gülich and Lindemann's work has an important share in our developing a multi-dimensional picture of social interaction.

References

Auer, Peter 1993. "Zur Verbspitzenstellung im gesprochenen Deutsch". *Deutsche Sprache* 3: 193–222.

Couper-Kuhlen, Elizabeth 1998. "Coherent voicing. On prosody in conversational reported speech." *InLiSt – Interaction and Linguistic Structures* 1 (http://www.ub.uni-konstanz.de/kops/volltexte/2000/453).

Fiehler, Reinhard 1990. *Kommunikation und Emotion. Theoretische und empirische Untersuchungen zur Rolle von Emotionen in der verbalen Interaktion*. Berlin, New York: de Gruyter.

Günthner, Susanne 1997. "The contextualisation of affect in reported dialogues." In: *The language of emotions. Conceptualisation, expression, and theoretical foundation*, Susanne Niemeier and René Dirven (eds.), 247–276. Amsterdam: Benjamins.

Günthner, Susanne 2006. "Rhetorische Verfahren bei der Vermittlung von Panikattacken. Zur Kommunikation von Angst in informellen Gesprächskontexten." *Gesprächsforschung – Online-Zeitschrift zur verbalen Interaktion* 7: 124–151.

Local, John 2004. "Getting back to prior talk: and-uh(m) as a back-connecting device." In: *Sound patterns in interaction. Cross-linguistic studies from conversation*, Elizabeth Couper-Kuhlen and Cecilia Ford (eds.), 377–400. Amsterdam: Benjamins.

Ochs, Elinor and Schieffelin, Bambi 1989. "Language has a heart." *Text* 9 (1): 7–25.

Selting, Margret 1994. "Emphatic speech style – with special focus on the prosodic signalling of heightened emotive involvement in conversation." *Journal of Pragmatics* 22: 375–408.

Selting, Margret 2004. "Regionalised intonation in its conversational context." In: *Regional variation in intonation*, Peter Gilles and Jörg Peters (eds.), 49–73. Tübingen: Niemeyer.

Selting, Margret; Auer, Peter; Barth-Weingarten, Dagmar; Bergmann, Jörg; Bergmann, Pia; Birkner, Karin; Couper-Kuhlen, Elizabeth; Deppermann, Arnulf; Gilles, Peter; Günthner, Susanne; Hartung, Martin; Kern, Friederike; Mertzlufft, Christine; Meyer, Christian; Morek, Miriam; Oberzaucher, Frank; Peters, Jörg; Quasthoff, Uta; Schütte, Wilfried; Stukenbrock, Anja and Uhmann, Susanne 2009. "Gesprächsanalytisches Transkriptionssystem 2 (GAT 2)." *Gesprächsforschung – Online-Zeitschrift zur verbalen Interaktion* 10: 353–402 (www.gespraechsforschung-ozs.de).

Whalen, Jack and Zimmerman, Don H. 1998. "Observations on the display and management of emotion in naturally occurring activities: The case of 'Hysteria' in calls to 9-1-1." *Social Psychological Quarterly* 61 (2): 141–59.

Multimodal expressivity of the Japanese response particle *Huun*

Displaying involvement without topical engagement

Hiroko Tanaka
University of Essex, UK

Of the half a dozen non-lexical response particles in Japanese sharing significant properties with *Oh* in English, this chapter focuses on a single feature of one such particle *Huun*, namely that of displaying involvement with ongoing talk without topical engagement, while making relevant a topic shift. A multimodal approach is taken to demonstrate that a free-standing *Huun* can be enlisted to withhold an explicit evaluative stand while simultaneously displaying attentiveness, if not profound affective alignment, with current talk, partly through harnessing its potentially rich expressivity. Participant reactions suggest the particle may even be treated "as if" a fully fledged, lexicalized turn. Furthermore, multimodal resources can be combined with the occasioning of *Huun* to gradually lead to topic attrition.[1]

1. Introduction

There is a considerable amount of linguistic research on Japanese conversation concerning the importance of listener response in Japanese in terms of its distributional qualities and interactional functions (e.g. Clancy et al. 1996, S. Maynard 1986, 1990, Iwasaki 1997, Okada 1996, Takubo and Kinsui 1997, Ward 1998, Ward and Okamoto

---

1.   Work on this chapter was partly supported through an Arts and Humanities Research Council grant. I would like to express my gratitude to the organisers and participants of the conference "Prosody and Interaction" held 15–17 September, 2008 at the University of Potsdam for their many useful comments and criticisms on an oral report of this chapter. A special thanks goes to Dagmar Barth-Weingarten for her very detailed and insightful co-presentation and the moral support she extended to me through many drafts. I would also like to thank Makoto Hayashi for reading and commenting on an early draft. I owe a great deal to the reviewers of this paper, who have pointed out major inaccuracies and offered many constructive criticisms. But I alone am responsible for the inadequacies that remain.

2003, White 1989, etc.). More recently, a number of conversation analytic studies have been appearing on the topic (e.g. Mori 2006, Hayashi 2009, Shimotani 2007).

In English, one of the most widely used non-lexical response particles is the 'change-of-state token' *Oh* (Heritage 1984: 300), which – among other things – has been characterized as a kind of 'response cry' (Goffman 1981). In Japanese conversation, there are at least six ubiquitous non-lexical response particles, *Aa*, ↑*Ee*, *Haa*, *Hoo*, *Hee* and *Huun*, each of which can be shown to have overlapping properties with the English *Oh*. They have multifunctional uses including newsmark, continuer and assessment (see Mori 2006 for *Hee*). While regularly occurring in similar environments (e.g. in response to informings) and sharing many common functions of response cries, each of the six particles also manifests distinctive semantic-pragmatic uses and prosodic patternings. The sheer multitude, variability and complexity of the contexualization cues which can accompany the respective particles, coupled with the abstractness of any apparent semantic core associated with them, renders the prospect of differentiating among the myriad uses of the particles – both individually and as a gestalt – a formidable task.

To make even a modest start on identifying and categorizing the manifold uses of even one of these particles is beyond the purview of this endeavor. Therefore, the present chapter, which forms part of a chapter of a book-in-progress (Tanaka in prep.) engages in a single-case study of a serial deployment of just one of these particles, namely *Huun*. In the instances discussed, it is used for displaying involvement in the main speaker's talk while progressively laying the groundwork for topic attrition, ultimately leading to a topic shift. In addition to investigating this crucial mode of operation for *Huun*, another aim is to undertake a methodological exercise in adopting a multimodal approach to shed light on the interactional salience of such items. It has been said that interactional linguists have mainly been concerned with evidence derived from lexical content, sequential placement and prosodic/phonetic realization in investigating the function and use of linguistic items (Dagmar Barth-Weingarten, p.c.). Indeed, past studies of response particles and reactive tokens have primarily focused on the examination of their semantic, sequential and pragmatic features, some incorporating, to a greater or lesser extent, the analysis of their prosodic patternings (e.g. Couper-Kuhlen 2009, Flowe 2002, Gardner 2001, Hayashi 2009, Local 1996, Mori 2006, Müller 1996, Sorjonen 2001, Wilkinson and Kitzinger 2006 among others). While building on insights from such studies, the purpose here is to explore how widening the enquiry to nonverbal aspects of the participants' conduct can potentially complement and extend the findings that can otherwise be obtained. Where indicated, please refer to this volume's website for sound clips (with extension .*wav*) and video clips (with extension .*mov*).

2.   Brief summary of the six response particles

At the risk of vastly simplifying the picture, presented below are some tentative observations made in Tanaka (in prep.) with respect to the six particles which are of relevance for the ensuing discussion. The database for the larger study consisted of approximately 15 hours of telephone and face-to-face conversations among participants speaking primarily the Kanto and Kansai dialects. As responses to informings, all six particles were found to occur either in free-standing form or followed by further components, such as those that advance an informing. Whereas *Aa* and ↑*Ee* both typically occur in these two forms, the remaining four *Haa, Hoo, Hee* and *Huun* occur predominantly in free-standing form. Also, the former two *Aa* and ↑*Ee* are found in either short or elongated versions, in contrast to the latter four, *Haa, Hoo, Hee* and *Huun*, which are almost always lengthened. Moreover, even though the six particles are somewhat interchangeable as newsmarks, continuers and assessments, a rough division of labor may be observed: *Aa* having the greatest resemblance to *Oh* in English as a 'change-of-state token' (Heritage 1984); ↑*Ee* as an 'open class repair initiator' (Drew 1997) to display a 'noticing of departure' from one's epistemic store (Hayashi 2009); *Hoo* and *Haa* for spontaneous affective displays; *Hee* for an appreciation of an informing as consistent with one's epistemic store; *Huun* as a display of going into thought, regularly used to exhibit the process of "taking in" an informing. Through the differential use of the range of particles, recipients of an informing can co-participate in an ongoing speaker's talk by positioning them at selected moments.

Huun occurs in many of the same kinds of environments as *Hee*, but there are subtle differences, which suggest that *Huun* may serve as a kind of placid, or subdued, version of a newsmark. This is evidenced in part by its regular deployment when a more enthusiastic or upbeat token such as *Hee* would be dispreferred, such as in the reception of bad news (e.g. illnesses, hardships and problems).[2] *Huun* also co-occurs with displays of a state of rumination about an informing. Finally, the particle is routinely featured toward the end of an informing sequence in an environment of pauses, as a "filler" for displaying a "residual appreciation" sometime after an informing has been produced, and often after other tokens such as *Aa* or *Hee* have already been produced.

3.   Brief summary of the prosodic patterns of *Huun*

Although normally written orthographically as *Huun*, according to Takubo and Kinsui (1997: 264) this particle is represented phonetically as [m̥mm] where [m̥] is the unvoiced bilabial nasal. The pitch contour of *Huun* is normally flat or rising, and very rarely simply falling. Exemplars of typical pitch contours are given in Figures 1 a–c, with the fundamental frequency F0 superposed on the sound pressure waveform.

---

2.   Nevertheless, it may be inappropriate to employ *Huun* to receipt bad news which has a grave or direct impact on a copresent participant (Makoto Hayashi, p.c.).

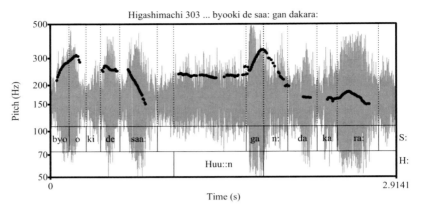

a. *Huun* with flat pitch

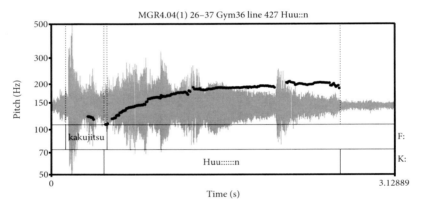

b. *Huun* with pitch beginning with a convex rise, ending in a plateau

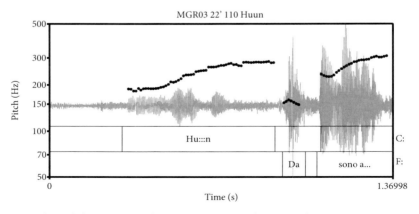

c. *Huun* with pitch beginning with a concave rise, ending in a plateau

Figure 1. Exemplars of typical pitch contours of *Huun*

The pitch tends to be relatively flat when employed to receipt bad news or in an environment of dispreference (cf. Figure 1a and sound clip [TAN-1-Figure1a.wav], where it is used to respond to news about the speaker's mother-in-law's illness).[3] When the pitch is rising, it may begin with a convex rise (cf. Figure 1b and sound clip [TAN-2-Figure1b.wav]) or alternatively with a relatively flat, concave rise (cf. Figure 1c and sound clip [TAN-3-Figure1c.wav]), though in either case, the contour tends to become rounded and flatter toward the end, forming a plateau (as can be observed in the F0 shapes of these two instances). As a dramatic variation of the latter type, the pitch can dip to a valley before rising, producing a singsong effect. The instances of *Huun* to be examined in this chapter broadly fall under this last type. In terms of the articulation, *Huun* is unique in being the only particle among the six that ends in a syllabic nasal [m] as a regular feature instead of terminating with a vowel. This chapter explores how some of the abovementioned prosodic characteristics may be consequential for the particular kinds of actions the token performs within the specific sequence of talk in which they are featured.

4. Huun for showing involvement while avoiding topical talk, leading to 'topic attrition'

A relatively long fragment containing four occurrences of the particle *Huun* is employed to demonstrate how a recipient can use the particle as a resource for exhibiting attentiveness and involvement with a main speaker's informing-in-progress while not engaging topically and paving the way toward an eventual topic shift. In particular, through a range of collateral multimodal displays, a recipient can maximize the expressivity of the token for showing appreciation of ongoing talk without a commitment to topical development (the first two instances). What is striking is that the particle in its highly embellished form – with elaborate prosodic features and nonverbal manifestations – may be capable of showing perhaps as much involvement as topical commentary. On the other hand, through a successive recalibration of its phonetic parameters coupled with nonverbal displays to create a stepped down effect, the particle may be instrumental for bringing a topic to closure while dealing with delicate interactional exigencies.

The deployment of *Huun* in four locations in the excerpt – in lines 6, 37, 44 and 48 – individually and cumulatively demonstrates the possible workings of the token for dealing with an ostensibly paradoxical exigency of showing appreciation for the speaker's talk while simultaneously withholding commitment to a development of the topic, thereby contributing towards 'topic attrition' and facilitating a transition to a different albeit related topic (Jefferson 1983, D. Maynard 1997, Gardner 1997). Jefferson (1983)

---

3. The F0 trace is slightly overlapped by the talk of a coparticipant, but it can be verified auditorily that the pitch contour is flat.

notes that minimal tokens (such as *Yah*) which may at first be used to display topical engagement and recipient alignment through an expressive intonational contour, may be redeployed subsequently in a flat contour as a pre-topic shift token for extinguishing the topic.

The fragment is taken from a conversation primarily between two women in their fifties, Chie and Mari, in which the former, the host, is engaging in an extended informing about the purportedly unconventional domestic arrangements of a close friend, Katsuyo. Chie had been going into considerable detail, noting that Katsuyo loses her temper unless her husband is at her beck and call, in contrast to the hardworking, self-effacing and dedicated husband. By way of illustration, Chie began reporting shortly before the segment reproduced below, that the husband does most of the cooking – including the evening meal.

From the camera angle, the participants are sitting on opposite sides of a rectangular dining room table, with Chie seated toward the left-hand side of the table with her son Yasu (denoted SON in the transcript) by her side. Mari is sitting to the right, facing Chie across the table with Mari's daughter Rika (DAU) beside her to the far right (see Figure 2) though she is only partly visible in the video recording. Selective descriptions of gaze and nonverbal conduct have been supplied where deemed especially critical for understanding the actions of participants, such as in line 4 where the main speaker (Chie) shifts gaze from the main recipient (Mari) to another participant (SON) in the middle of the turn, which explains why the latter nods in line 5. While for the discussion the excerpt is divided into shorter segments, the entire excerpt is given in the Appendix. Please also refer to the Appendix for the transcription conventions and for an explanation of the special symbols and abbreviations used in the transcripts.

Figure 2. Seating arrangement

(1) **Gossip, lines 1–14** (cf. video clip [TAN-4-(1) Gossip-lines_1–14.mov])

    1 Chie: De   atashi nanka no:,
               and me   like   GEN
               And for ((people)) like me

    2   shokuji- (1.2)
               meal

    3   gochisoo ni naru   toki wa,=
               invite.for.meal   *time* TOP
               when invited over for a meal,=

    4   ((shifts gaze from Mari to SON at * and nods))
               =.hh <u>hotondo</u>   *ga otto   da   yo ↑ne?
                  almost.always SUB *husband* COP FP FP
               =.hh ((it))'s <u>almost always</u> the husband ((who cooks)), right?

    5 SON: ((nodding)) °Un°.
                       °Mm°.

1st → 6 Mari: ↑**Huu**::::::::: ((creaky)) ↓↑:::::::::::::::**nn**
instance

    7   (0.6)

    8 Chie: >Zuibun   ii   deshoo<.
               quite   good COP
               Pretty good, isn't ((it))?

    9 Mari: <u>U::n.</u>
               <u>Mmm.</u>

   10   (1.0)

   11 Chie: >Soo   iu <u>uchi</u>   mo   aru   no yo<.
               that   say household ADVP   *exist* FP FP
               >There are <u>households</u> like that too. <

   12 Mari: ((creaky)) Hoo::::::::

   13 Chie: Sun- s[(   )] ((turns head to Mari at end of line13))
               DF   DF[4]

   14 Mari: [>Sor<u>ede</u>   oi]<u>shii</u> no.
                    and   tasty   FP
                  >And <u>is ((it)) tasty?</u>

The first instance of *Huun* (line 6) is used as a newsmark in response to Chie's informing that the husband almost always cooks when she is invited for a meal (lines 1–4). The particle is massively lengthened and appears to have a high degree of affective loading (see Goodwin and Goodwin 1987), as though to display surprise, amazement or wonderment, manifested particularly through a manipulation of pitch and loudness (cf. video

---

4. The turn-initial dysfluency was indiscernible.

clip [TAN-5-Huun 1st instance.mov] and sound clip [TAN-6-Huun 1st instance.wav]). The marked nature of the delivery of the token stands out in comparison to the relatively "matter-of-fact" prosodic qualities of Chie's description of Katsuyo's domestic situation as extraordinary (lines 1–4). Freese and D. Maynard (1998) observe:

> "Recipients' turns in news deliveries tend to employ more dramatic prosody than deliverers'. This difference may be attributed partially to differences in the shapes of the turns; deliverers' turns are constructed as sentential units that evaluate the news as it is reported, while recipients' turns are compact phrases (or even single words) that are more exclusively dedicated to the task of evaluating the news. Because deliverers are producing information-as-news, they have more complex turn-organizational tasks, whereas recipient turns can attend more narrowly to emotive displays." (: 213)

The prosodic features of this particle are rendered all the more dramatic, perhaps because the producer is vesting a free-standing token to respond single-handedly to what is being presented as a "juicy" piece of gossip.

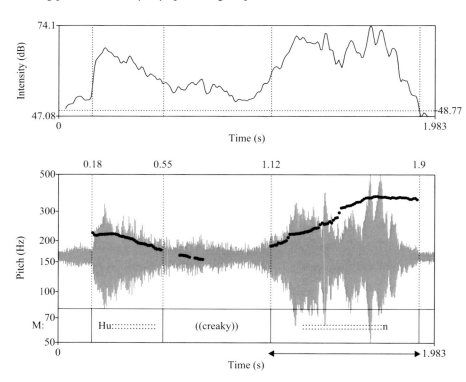

Figure 3. Pitch and intensity of the first instance of *Huun* (line 6)

As indicated in Figure 3 (cf. sound clip [TAN-6-Huun 1st instance.wav]), the F0 trace essentially shows a falling-rising contour which flattens to a plateau toward the end. The pitch tracker has apparently failed to detect the F0 trace in the mid portion where the phonation is non-modal (i.e. creaky), though the pitch contour can be verified independently as reaching a baseline in the mid portion. Moreover, the fluctuations in the F0 trace correlate quite closely with that of intensity. That is, the falling-rising F0 pattern (where recoverable) is matched by a falling-rising intensity pattern. Auditorily, this creates an impression of an undulating effect. By taking this particle to its expressive limits through a marked manipulation of its pitch and loudness, Mari registers her strong endorsement of Chie's characterization of Katsuyo's domestic situation as extremely unusual, without having uttered a single lexical item on the topic.

The dramatic prosody aligns with Chie's portrayal of Katsuyo's domestic arrangements as highly unusual, as is also played out through the nonverbal "matching" (see Couper-Kuhlen 1996) while Mari is producing this particle (cf. video clip [TAN-5-Huun 1st instance.mov]). That is, Mari nods deliberatively in tandem with the movement of the pitch to the baseline; at this point, Chie nods in unison, in ratification of Mari's appreciation of the informing; as the particle comes to an end, they both gradually bring their heads back to an upright position (see Figure 4).

Although difficult to see, it appears that Mari's visual behaviour is also coordinated with the prosodic pattern: Mari is directing her gaze toward Chie's son and Chie throughout the articulation of the particle, but as the pitch approaches the baseline, Mari starts to close her eyes, blinking deeply at the moment the pitch reaches the baseline, and opening her eyes as the particle comes to an end. In this way, Mari musters an arsenal of multimodal displays to enact the process of "taking in" Chie's informing.

It is worthy of note that Mari did not receipt the informing with a stronger, more forthright, and unquestioning token such as *Aa* or *Hee* but opted instead for the potentially weaker, if not more ruminative *Huun*. It has been suggested that *Huun* is routinely occasioned in environments where there is some problem in proffering a straightforwardly enthusiastic token (Tanaka in prep.). A case can be made that *Huun* may be used as one device (among potentially many others) for displaying recipient alignment while simultaneously avoiding topical involvement with an informing, whether it be due to lack of knowledge concerning the subject of the telling, lack of interest, or in order to distance oneself from the possible moral implications of actively joining in the talk, as in gossiping (see Bergmann 1993).

As one piece of evidence, this use of *Huun* appears to relinquish to the speaker any initiative in developing the topic-in-progress. Mari's post-token declination to produce further commentary or invite elaboration from Chie does little to contribute to topic expansion. Indeed the dramatic prosody of this token notwithstanding, Mari does not go on to respond topically to Chie's original informing (given in lines 1–4), and later even actively endeavors to shift the topical focus. To begin with, a gap can be observed in line 7, where commentary from Mari would have been relevant, which ends up being filled by Chie herself. Chie's ensuing pursuit of further response through

a. Near beginning of 1st instance of *Huun*: Mari and Chie's heads in upright position

b. Middle of 1st instance of *Huun*: Mari and Chie nod in unison

c. Near end of 1st instance of *Huun*: Mari and Chie bring their heads back to upright position

Figure 4. Screenshots of 1st instance of *Huun*

a tag question in line 8, >*Zuibun ii deshoo.*< ('Pretty good, isn't ((it))?') gets only a minimal token <u>U::n.</u> ('Mmm,' line 9). Thereafter, another gap emerges (line 10) where Mari passes up yet another opportunity to add a commentary or assessment of her own. Chie perhaps picks up on the lack of topical uptake and proceeds to provide a story summary: >*Soo iu <u>uchi</u> mo aru no yo*<. ('>There are house<u>holds</u> like that too.<', line 11), a turn-shape which does not contain a further tag specifically soliciting a response. To this, Mari issues only a response particle *Hoo::::::* (line 12), which is regularly used for affective displays (Tanaka in prep.). Then, in overlap with further talk from Chie, Mari finally provides a more substantial response in line 14 in the form of additional components: >*Sorede oishii no.* ('>And is ((it)) tasty?'). Note, however, that this response represents a step-wise refocusing of topic, from the purportedly atypical division of household chores to whether the food that the husband cooks is tasty (see D. Maynard 1980 on *refocusings*). Moreover, by rushing in with the connective >*Sorede* ('>And') and speaking emphatically over Chie's voice, Mari's talk competes with Chie's slightly earlier resumption of talk (line 13).

We will see below how Chie then moves to salvage her original topical focus and resumes the gossiping activity:

(2)   **Gossip, lines 13–38** (cf. video clip [TAN-7-(2) Gossip, lines 13–38.mov])

```
13    Chie:   Sun- s[(          )] ((turns head to Mari at end of line13))
              DF    DF

14    Mari:        [>Sorede oi]shii  no.
                    and     tasty    FP
                   >And is ((it)) tasty?

15            (0.5)

16    Chie:   'N.=
              Mm.=

17    Chie:   =>Sorede<  Katsuyo   wa
                And      ((name))  TOP
              =>And< Katsuyo is

              ((intonation unit continues))
              sore  o    uzattai  tte    yutten   dakedo  [ne?
              it    OBJ  annoying QUOT   saying   CONJ     FP
              saying it's annoying, though

18    Mari:                                            [Ha?
                                                        What?

19    Chie:   Ano::
              Er::m

20    Mari:   huhh [hih
21    Chie:        [ee[to:::
                    uh:::m
22    DAU:             [huh huh
23            (0.4)
```

```
   24   Chie:   odaidokoro ga   ikko  ni:,
                kitchen    SUB  one   P
                ((there))'s ((just)) one kitchen

   25            [o-  otoko  ga   futa-=
                 DF   man    SUB  two-
                 for two- m- men=
   26   Mari:   [Aa::
                Oh::

   27   Chie:   =>aYoosuruni:<
                  in.other.words
                =>In other words,<

   28           Katsuyo  chan datte ((intonation unit continues))
                ((name)) SFX  even
                even Katsuyo

                tachi tai toki [ga aru no ↑ni::, .hhh
                cook  want times  SUB exist N  CONJ
                has times when ((she)) wants to cook but .hhh
   29   Mari:                  [Aa: Aa↓ Aa↓ Aa↓ Aa↓
                                Oh: Oh  Oh  Oh  Oh

   30           (0.4)

   31   Chie:   o↓tto [no daidokoro ni nacchatteru kara:,=
                husband GEN kitchen  P  has.become    CONJ
                'cuz the kitchen has ended up as the husband's,=
   32   Mari:         [Ao:::n
                      Oh:::::

   33   Mari:   =Hoo::::::.

   34           (0.3)

   35   Chie:   Maa, uzattai  (.) tte   ie   ↑ba,
                well annoying     QUOT  say  CONJ
                So well, talking about ((it)) being annoying,

   36           u↓zattai  no   to↑ki  mo↓= ((intonation unit continues))
                annoying  GEN  times   ADVP
                =a[ru   mitai     (ne).
                  exist seemingly   FP
                =((there)) appear to be times when ((it)) does get annoying.
2nd→ 37 Mari:     [↑Huu::: ((creaky)) ↓↑::::::nn
instance

   38   Chie:   °Soo°.         ((nod))
                °((That))'s right°.
```

The gap in line 15 may be an early sign of the trouble Mari's refocusing seemingly creates for Chie in topical development. More unequivocally, Chie shows a reluctance to accommodate the new topical line put forward by Mari, by initially proffering a miniscule acknowledger 'N. ('Mm', line 16) and quickly rushing in likewise with the connective >Sorede< ('>And<') to reinvoke an earlier contrast between the demanding and unappreciative wife versus the dedicated husband. She accomplishes this by reporting that Katsuyo is describing his conduct using a faddish term *uzattai* ('annoying', line 17). Indeed, while not directly criticising Katsuyo, the mention of the disproportionate amount of housework that the husband takes upon himself (as in lines 1–4) followed by a reporting of Katsuyo's description of the husband's cooking as annoying, in effect, constitutes her conduct as unreasonable and improper (see Drew 1998).[5] Furthermore, by presenting the contrast, Chie can be heard to be inviting a topicalization of, and an appreciation of, Katsuyo's egregiousness.

To this, Mari persists in withholding direct topical comment, though exhibiting close interactional engagement through the token *Ha?* (line 18), used as a repair initiator similarly to the employment of the particle ↑*Ee*, glossable as 'What?', and the subsequent laughter (line 20), which display that she is in accord with Chie, at least with respect to the out-of-the-ordinary or otherwise noticeable nature of Katsuyo's reported attitude. This is replicated on a nonverbal level with Mari taking on a "bemused" look and lunging forward as she utters the token. In response to Mari's show of bemusement, Chie goes on to provide an account of Katsuyo's reasoning (see lines 19–36), thereby further implicating the purported ungraciousness of Katsuyo.

Meanwhile, Mari continues to display heightened involvement and responsiveness through a serial deployment of the token *Aa* 'Oh' as newsmark to receipt Chie's account by producing them at precisely timed moments as progressive bits of new information become recognisable (lines 26, 29, 32). For instance, Mari positions the onset of her pulsed *Aa* 'Oh' in line 29 with the instant enough talk emerges to grasp the gist of the explanation that there is only one kitchen in spite of the fact that Katsuyo too occasionally wants to cook. Likewise, the potentially emotionally valenced newsmark *Hoo::::::.* (line 33) is launched at the point where the full account projectably approaches completion (line 31).

It is when Chie re-invokes the term *uzattai* 'annoying' within a formulaic expression (lines 35–36), that Mari responds for the second time with her massively lengthened and affectively loaded *Huun* (line 37):

(3)   **Gossip, lines 35–42** (cf. video clip [TAN-8-(3) Gossip, lines 35–42.mov])

```
35   Chie:   Maa, uzattai (.)  tte     ie   ↑ba,
             well  annoying     QUOT    say  CONJ
             So well, talking about ((it)) being annoying,

36           u↓zattai  no   to↑ki mo↓=  ((intonation unit continues))
             annoying  GEN  times  ADVP
```

---

5.   Detailing similar cases of complaints of misconduct, Drew (1998: 314) writes, "we can see that a report of the other's conduct – the transgression – is accompanied by an account of the circumstances of that conduct: it is through that circumstantial account that the egregious character of the other's behavior is portrayed."

```
                    =a[ru  mitai      (ne).
                    exist  seemingly   FP
                    =((there)) appear to be times when ((it)) does get annoying.
2nd  →   37  Mari:      [↑Huu:::((creaky))↓↑::::::nn
instance
         38  Chie:  °Soo°.        ((nod))
                    °((That))'s right°.

         39         Demo,  asoko::  no:=
                    but    there    GEN

         40         =o- oto[ko   wa    yoku  hataraku-
                    DF men        TOP   well  work
                    Anyway, m- men in that ((house)) are hardworking-.

         41  Mari:  ((looks down, nods))
                             [Min'na sorezore da   ne hhh
                              everyone respective  COP FP
                              Everyone unto themselves, it seems hhh

         42  Chie:  >Yoku hataraku asoko no   uchi ↑ne.<
                     well  work      there  GEN house FP
                    ((They)) are hardworking in that house, aren't they?
                    ((Toward the end of turn Chie gazes at SON and nods.))
```

This occurrence of *Huun* sounds impressionistically analogous to the first *Huun* in line 6, namely, with undulating pitch correlating with loudness characteristics and the articulation containing a non-modal, creaky period, except that this instance is not as prosodically prominent (in terms of pitch and loudness), as indicated in Figure 5 (cf. also video clip [TAN-9-Huun 2nd instance.mov] and sound clip [TAN-10-Huun 2nd instance.wav]).

Postponing for now a detailed description of the delivery, suffice it to note that it is equally if not even more expressive than the first instance in artfully communicating an appreciation of Chie's informing. That this token is taken to be aligning can be observed in Chie's turn in line 38, which explicitly ratifies Mari's response: °*Soo*°. (°((That))'s right°.) It is noteworthy here that through the use of the affirming response °*Soo*°. and by nodding, Chie not only treats Mari's *Huun* as though it had been, for all intents and purposes, a valenced, topical assessment, but fleetingly reverses her role from that of speaker to recipient.

In spite of the engaging prosody of this *Huun*, there are indications that it is nonetheless being treated as implicative of topic closure by Chie and produced as such by Mari. Whereas the various response tokens preceding this *Huun* had been produced and positioned with reference to the appearance of new bits of information (as discussed previously), this *Huun* occurs toward the end of Chie's summing up of the account of why Katsuyo finds her husband's cooking annoying (lines 35–36). It is therefore hearable as having been produced in lieu of a possibly more elaborate commentary made relevant by the extended account just provided. Such an understanding is

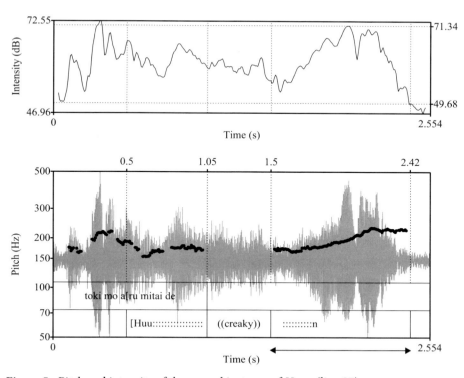

Figure 5. Pitch and intensity of the second instance of *Huun* (line 37)

reflected in Chie's further effort to secure a more substantial response with an alternative summary to the effect that men in the household are hardworking (lines 39–40). Notably, this is declined by Mari entering in overlap with a ruminative aphoristic conclusion, *Min'na sorezore da ne hhh* ('Everyone unto themselves, it seems', line 41). As is well known, aphorisms are routinely featured in the final stages of talk on a topic prior to a topic change (see Drew and Holt 1998, D. Maynard 1980). Yet, Chie recycles her just overlapped summary (in line 42), arguably in a repeated attempt to secure topical comment.

We take a moment here to inspect more closely how Mari manages to deal with the competing exigencies of showing alignment and not collaborating in the gossiping activity, by reexamining excerpt (3) (cf. video clip [TAN-8-(3) Gossip, lines 35–42. mov]). Importantly, while resisting Chie's repeated pursuits of topical engagement, the articulation of the second *Huun* provides an opportunity for Mari to enter into a manifest state of profound rumination over Chie's informing, offsetting the inherently disaffiliative character of topical non-engagement. This can be seen as realized through an assemblage of multimodal resources.

With respect to the visual conduct, although Mari's gaze is directed at Chie during this *Huun*, immediately thereafter, Mari looks down, nods once and cocks her head to one side, exhibiting a process of going into thought: a state which is sustained until sometime after she finishes articulating the aphorism 'Everyone unto themselves, it seems *hhh*' (line 41), as will be touched upon below. From this point onward, Mari appears engrossed in something by looking down and no longer gazing at any of the participants, let alone Chie. Mari also exhibits a state of auditory/aural uncoupling from the immediate physical environment through the temporal features of the production of the aphorism in line 41, which overlaps Chie's talk in line 40 rather randomly: not only are the prototypical features of interruptive talk such as increased loudness and speed (see French and Local 1983) absent, but the aphorism is produced hearably autonomously if not "out of sync" with Chie's utterance. The lack of competition or fit with Chie's ongoing talk (lines 39–40), when considered in conjunction with the abovementioned attendant visual and bodily displays, renders the aphorism recognizable as a running commentary on an independent activity of turning over in her head Chie's earlier informing. It is as though Mari temporarily retreats into her internal world, processes the prior telling, culminating in the production of the aphorism. Insofar as the aphorism engages abstractly with Chie's account while not contributing to Chie's critical evaluation of Katsuyo, it achieves sensitivity to the two interactional exigencies cited above regarding the need to show involvement as a recipient of Chie's news and preparing the ground for a topic shift.

Finally, toward the end of Chie's partial repetition of her earlier overlapped utterance characterizing the men in Katsuyo's house as hardworking (line 42), Mari reestablishes eye-contact with Chie and Chie's son through a "startled" look (eyes opening wide and focusing abruptly as though she had been roused), thereby nonverbally marking an exit from the ruminative state. All told, the gaze and other nonverbal cues attending the uttering of *Huun* and immediately afterwards appear not only to implicate topic closure but also to make publicly available Mari's entry into a ruminative state and her subsequent return to the immediate physical environment.

Returning to the point where Chie recycles her summary about the hardworking men (starting in line 42) in an nth attempt to secure topical uptake, the excerpt shows Mari simply responding with the lone-standing *Huun* for the third and even fourth times:

(4)   **Gossip, lines 39–54** (cf. video clip [TAN-11-(4) Gossip, lines 39–54.mov])

```
39          Demo,  asoko::  no:=
            but    there    GEN

40          =o-  oto[ko  wa    yoku  hataraku-
            DF   men     TOP   well  work
```
Anyway, m- men in that ((house)) are hardworking.

```
          41   Mari:   ((looks down, nods))
                              [Min'na sorezore da  ne hhh.
                               everyone respective  COP FP
                               Everyone unto themselves, it seems hhh

          42   Chie:   >Yoku hataraku   asoko no    uchi ↑ne.<
                        well  work       there  GEN  house FP
                        ((They)) are hardworking in that house, aren't they?
                        ((Toward the end of turn Chie gazes at SON and nods.))

          43           (0.8)  ((SON nodding quickly twice))
3rd →     44   Mari:   °Huu::[:::::::::::]:::::::nn°
instance                      ((begins with creaky voice, ends in modal))
          45   Chie:          [°ano otto°.]  ((nods to Mari))
                                that  husband
                               °that husband°.

          46   Chie:   ((shifts gaze from Mari to DAU at *))
                        Gaikoku:        *nami   da   yo  ↑ne.
                        foreign.countries  on.a.par COP  FP  FP
                        On a par with foreign countries, eh?

          47           (.)  ((Chie brings back gaze to Mari))
4th →     48   Mari:   [°°Huu::::n°°  ((nodding once lightly))
instance
          49   DAU:    [°°'N°°  ((nodding 4 times))
                        °°Mm°°
          50   Chie:   °'N°.  ((nodding to Mari))
                        °Mm°.
          51   Mari:   .hh  e   oniichan   nanka  sa:,
                             DF  big.brother  like   FP
                       .hh In the case of big brother ((referring to SON))

          52           ata- ma- ta-  atashi  toka:,
                        DF   DF  DF   me      like
                       ata- ma- ta- when ((people like)) me,

          53           sono,  mama no    tomodachi  n    toki ↑mo
                        that   mom  GEN   friend     GEN  time ADVP
                       in other words, even when mom's friends come over,

                       ((intonation unit continues))
                       set↓tai  shiteiru-  jya   nai?=
                       entertain  doing      COP   NEG
                       ((he))'s doing the entertaining, isn't ((he))?=

          54   Chie:   =Un.
                       =Yeah.
```

The fact that Chie's successive overtures are repeatedly met merely with the particle *Huun* from Mari (third instance in line 44 and fourth instance in line 48) reinforces the sense that the topic is exhausted, at least for Mari (cf. video clip [TAN-12-Huun 3rd-4th instances.mov]).

In comparison with the first two instances, this third issuing of the token is considerably more recessed both prosodically (as dealt with below) and nonverbally. Apart from blinking once mid-stream while articulating the token, Mari remains expressionless throughout. Chie nonetheless persists by making one final attempt at reviving the topical line with another summary statement: *Gaikoku:* *nami da yo ↑ne.* ('On a par with *foreign countries*, eh?', line 46), though she shifts her gaze from Mari to Mari's daughter (DAU in the excerpt) mid-turn at *, returning her gaze to Mari post-turn. In line 48, Marie responds for the fourth and last time with the particle *Huun*, produced nearly inaudibly, employing it as a filler. The situation is resolved by two of the participants likewise producing mini-tokens (lines 49 and 50), through which they mutually confirm an unspoken consensus that the current topic is exhausted. Thereafter, the informing sequence comes to a close with a step-wise collateral topic shift by Mari in line 51.

To deepen our understanding of the role of this particle within the process leading to the extinguishing of the current topic, further aspects of its delivery will be reviewed more

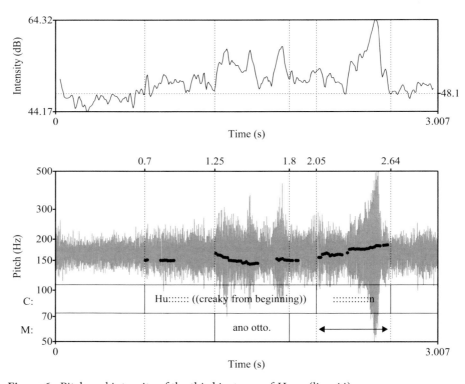

Figure 6. Pitch and intensity of the third instance of *Huun* (line 44)

closely. Here the importance of regarding speech, sound and bodily behavior as integral dimensions of the overall embodiment of action in interaction should be stressed:

> "...actions are both assembled and understood through a process in which different kinds of sign phenomena instantiated in diverse media, what I call semiotic fields, are juxtaposed in a way that enables them to mutually elaborate each other."
> (Goodwin 2000: 1490)

However, given the difficulty of describing in a single "pass" the myriad of multimodal dimensions constituting the fabric of a spate of talk-in-interaction, attention will be restricted primarily to the relative prosodic contours of the instances of *Huun* – which supplement the layers of semiotic displays already considered.

5.   Additional prosodic properties of the first three instances of *Huun*

With respect to the first three instances of *Huun*, limiting comparison to the latter part of the sound after the portion produced with creak (i.e. the parts not overlapped by Chie's talk, denoted by the double arrows ←→ in Figure 7), the pitch and loudness characteristics follow similar patterns, as is also indicated in Figure 7.[6] Specifically, in each instance, the F0 trace can be seen to rise in tandem with the surge in intensity, flattening to a plateau toward the end; the intensity terminates in a "grand crescendo".

Although it is difficult to attribute iconic meaning to a particular prosodic pattern due to its multifunctionality (see for instance Gardner 2001: 196 and Couper-Kuhlen 2009), it is worthy of mention that the three instances of *Huun* contain an identifiable terminal section, creating a perception of finality and conclusiveness (cf. see video and sound clips [TAN-5-Huun 1st instance.mov], [TAN-6-Huun 1st instance.wav], [TAN-9-Huun 2nd instance.mov], [TAN-10-Huun 2nd instance.wav], [TAN-12-Huun 3rd-4th instances.mov], [TAN-13-Huun 3rd instance.wav] and [TAN-14-Huun 4th instance.wav]). Such a perception is reinforced in part by the following features:

1. a 'swell' (see Wells and Peppé 1997) at the ending of the particle: increasing loudness reaching a "grand crescendo" followed by a sudden decrease
2. a transition from a voiceless nasal in the former part to a voiced nasal in the latter part of the particle
3. the pronounced upward pitch movement coming to a plateau at the end of the particle
4. after the loudness reaches a peak and the pitch flattens in the last stretch of the particle, the particle comes to an end quite abruptly

---

6.   Comparison will be limited to the latter part of the sound, since apart from the first instance, the opening parts of the remaining two are overlapped by Chie's talk, making it impossible to measure the pitch and intensity accurately.

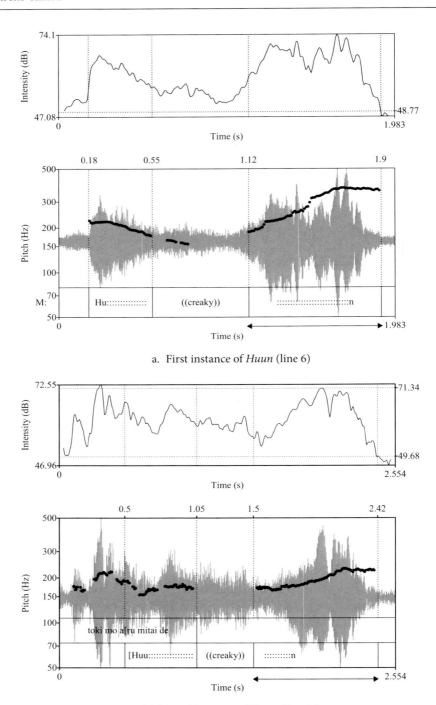

a. First instance of *Huun* (line 6)

b. Second instance of *Huun* (line 37)

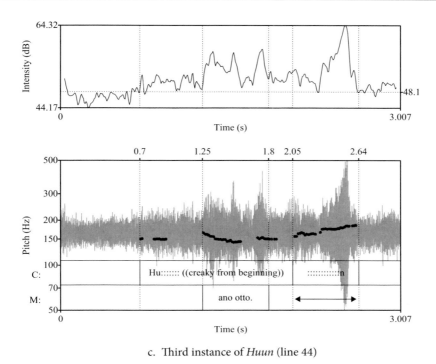

c. Third instance of *Huun* (line 44)

Figure 7. Comparison of pitch and intensity of the first three instances of *Huun*

Importantly, the prosodic ending is synchronized with Mari's head or postural movement backwards, as touched upon previously (though absent from the third instance). In the first instance of *Huun*, after the downward movement of the head nod follows the pitch declination to the baseline, the subsequent head movement to the upright 'home position' (Sacks and Schegloff 2002, Schegloff 1998) is synchronized with the pitch movement upward as the particle comes to the end. In the second instance, the "springing" bodily/head motion backward is precisely timed so that the final postural position is reached coterminously with the ending of *Huun*, followed thereafter by an attenuating "bobbing" motion of the head. Taken as a whole, it appears that these instances of *Huun* are designed to come to an ending. Through the collateral multimodal displays, it is as though Mari is putting the "final embellishments" as it were on the topic as well. Although an exploration of the possible significance of these features for participants must be left for future research, I briefly note that a discrete terminal phase such as that described above tends to be absent in many other response particles when deployed as continuers, including *Aaa*, *Hoo*, *Haa* and *Hee*, which are all prosodically designed to be indefinitely extendible with their near linear pitch contours (see Tanaka in prep.).

Finally, an exquisite pattern can be observed with respect to the relative phonetic parameters of the three instances of *Huun* in the final non-overlapped portion where the token is produced in the clear, as shown in Table 1.

Table 1. Successive reduction of phonetic parameters in the final non-overlapped portions of the instances of *Huun* (rounded to the nearest decimal place)

Huun	Line #	Duration	Min F0	Max F0	F0Δ (Max – Min)	Peak intensity
1st	6	1.7 secs.	194.8 Hz	370.5 Hz	175.7 Hz = 11.1 semitones	74.1 dB
2nd	37	1.9 secs.	166.4 Hz	230.5 Hz	64.2 Hz = 5.7 semitones	71.3 dB
3rd	44	1.9 secs.	156.3 Hz	185.2 Hz	28.9 Hz = 2.9 semitones	64.3 dB

The impressionistic observation that the three parameters – the minimal pitch, the maximum pitch and the pitch range – undergo a successive reduction from the first instance to the third is corroborated by the corresponding measurements of minimum F0 (from 194.8 Hz in the first instance through 166.4 Hz for the second, and down to 156.3 Hz in the third), maximum F0 (from 370.5 Hz through 230.5 Hz, falling to 185.2 Hz) and the pitch range (from 11.1 ST to 5.7 ST and reducing to 2.9 ST). The auditory perception of a softening of the final crescendo section across the three instances (becoming nearly inaudible in the fourth instance (cf. [TAN-14-Huun 4th instance.wav]) is likewise reflected in the successive fall in the measurements of the peak intensity from the first to the third instances (74.1 dB in the first instance, 71.3 dB in the second, dropping to 64.3 dB in the third). It can therefore be seen that the phonetic parameters of the particle are being "wound down" temporally across the sequence as another resource to implement a step-by-step extinction of the topic.

6   Concluding comments

It goes without saying that participants in social interaction orient to a fundamental normative constraint to exhibit attentiveness, alignment and affiliation with one another if social solidarity is to be maintained. In the course of an informing, such as in the telling of gossip, a recipient may on occasion refrain from participating directly in topical development, as with the example just examined. This may be motivated by any number of factors such as lack of interest, lack of access to the information, or even reluctance to collude in the activity of gossiping. Of relevance to the case dealt with in this chapter, the very act of coparticipating in criticizing a non-present third party who is portrayed as a close friend of the producer of the criticism can potentially involve a conflict of loyalties and therefore may be conceived of as interactionally delicate if not problematic. However, as Bergmann states,

"...because they (the gossip-producer and gossip-recipient – HT) have to deal with morally contaminated material, both have to get about their work with great care in order to prevent a situation in which each alone appears interested in gossip" (1993: 85).

Thus, even when withholding topical engagement, recipients face the need to attend to the competing normative obligation to concurrently exhibit alignment with the affective and evaluative stance of the main speaker.

An excerpt including four instances of *Huun* for the reception of an informing was used to demonstrate how this response particle may be employed for displaying involvement in, and appreciation of, the current speaker's talk while circumventing topical engagement or explicit evaluation of the content of talk, as well as a resource for gradually extinguishing the topic. Although far from being exhaustive, this chapter dealt with the procedures through which the *Huun*-producer attempted to juggle the multiple constraints, including:

1. showing alignment with the speaker by maximizing the expressivity of the particle through an extensive manipulation of the prosody of the token, incorporating pronounced pitch movements and loudness characteristics, in lieu of, or as compensation for lack of, topical uptake,
2. a successive reduction across the sequence of the prosodic parameters of the first three occurrences of *Huun* – in terms of the minimum pitch, the maximum pitch, the pitch range and the peak loudness (of parts produced in the clear) – employed as a resource for engendering an extinction of the topical line,
3. exploiting the particle's association with a ruminative state to mark an entry into a process of going into thought over an informing, thereby exhibiting profound involvement while temporarily severing engagement with the main speaker's efforts to secure topical commitment,
4. mobilization of a wide range of collateral multimodal resources which collectively enabled the *Huun*-producer to implement such procedures and processes, as well as making them publicly available for coparticipants (and also available for analysis).

Although it has only been possible to scratch the surface, it should hopefully be clear that a close examination of the prosodic and nonverbal displays surrounding the production of *Huun* is central to a deeper appreciation of the complex interactional processes in which the particle may play a part (e.g. in managing topical engagement and disengagement in informings), much of which are collectively implemented through a constellation of multimodal displays.

This chapter has investigated one use of *Huun*, which constitutes just one out of six response particles that share similar properties with the English *Oh*. Due to its association with a ruminative state, the particle *Huun* may be particularly suited for negotiating delicate interactional tasks in the context of informings. For instance, the subtle manner in which *Huun* may be used to introduce a topic shift as demonstrated here can be contrasted with the direct shift of topic that regularly follows some other tokens among the six response particles, such as *Hee* (Mori 2006, Tanaka in prep.) or ↑*Ee* (Hayashi 2009). More generally, it may be directed toward a display of heightened concern and focus on a topical discussion without necessarily implicating an evaluative stand on the matter at hand. The potential expressivity and versatility of *Huun* (explored further in Tanaka in prep.) make it an invaluable resource for responding in nuanced ways to informings involving socially and interactionally sensitive matters, rendering it perhaps one of the most thoughtful, empathetic and eloquent response particles among the six.

Appendix

Transcription conventions:

The excerpts have been transcribed in accordance with Gail Jefferson's transcription conventions adapted for presentation of non-English talk. In the three-line transcripts, the first line consists of the original Japanese talk; a word-by-word interlinear gloss is given in the second line; an English gloss of the line or turn as a whole is provided in the third line. In order to reflect the "rhythm" of talk, each numbered line has been transcribed to correspond to a single intonational unit.

Special symbols used in the transcripts:

In the interlinear gloss, where an English phrase is used to translate a Japanese word, a full stop is used to separate the words in the phrase. (e.g. in line 46, *Gaikoku:* is translated as *foreign.countries.*)

Double parentheses are employed for two purposes: for transcriptionist commentary (as is normally the case) as well as for supplying candidate unexpressed elements (e.g. in line 42, the subject *they*, which is unexpressed in the Japanese talk, is provided in the English gloss in the third line).

Abbreviations in the interlinear gloss:

ADVP	Adverbial particle
CONJ	Conjunctive particle
COP	Copula
DF	Dysfluency
FP	Final particle
GEN	Genitive particle
N	Nominaliser

NEG	Negative
OBJ	Direct object (accusative particle)
P	Particle
QUOT	Quotative particle
SFX	Suffix
SUB	Subject (nominative particle)
TOP	Topic particle

The entire excerpt:

(5) **Gossip, ALL** (cf. video clip [TAN-15-(5) Gossip, ALL.mov])

```
1   Chie:  De    atashi  nanka  no:,
           and   me      like   GEN
           And for ((people)) like me

2          shokuji-  (1.2)
           meal

3          gochisoo ni naru    toki   wa,=
           invite.for.meal     time   TOP
           when invited over for a meal,=

4          ((shifts gaze from Mari to SON at * and nods))
           =.hh hotondo      *ga  otto    da    yo   ↑ne?
                almost.always  SUB husband  COP   FP   FP
           =.hh ((it))'s almost always the husband ((who cooks)), right?

5   SON:   ((nodding)) °Un°.
                       °Mm°.
```

1st → 6   Mari: ↑**Huu**::::::::: ((creaky)) ↓↑::::::::::::::**nn**
instance

```
7          (0.6)

8   Chie:  >Zuibun   ii     deshoo<.
           quite     good   COP
           Pretty good, isn't ((it))?

9   Mari:  U::n.
           Mmm.

10         (1.0)

11  Chie:  >Soo  iu  uchi      mo     aru   no   yo<.
           that  say household  ADVP   exist FP   FP
           >There are households like that too. <

12  Mari:  ((creaky)) Hoo::::::::

13  Chie:  Sun- s[(         )] ((turns head to Mari at end of line13))
           DF    DF⁷
```

---

7. The turn-initial dysfluency was indiscernible.

```
14   Mari:        [>Sorede oi]shii no.
                  and      tasty   FP
                  >And is ((it)) tasty?

15        (0.5)

16   Chie:  'N.=
             Mm.=

17   Chie:  =>Sorede<  Katsuyo   wa
             And       ((name))  TOP
             =>And< Katsuyo is

             ((intonation unit continues))
             sore   o    uzattai  tte    yutten  dakedo  [ne?
             it     OBJ  annoying QUOT   saying  CONJ     FP
             saying it's annoying, though

18   Mari:                                             [Ha?
                                                        What?

19   Chie:  Ano::
             Er::m

20   Mari:  huhh    [hih

21   Chie:          [ee[to:::
                       uh:::m

22   DAU:             [huh huh

23        (0.4)

24   Chie:  odaidokoro   ga   ikko   ni:,
             kitchen      SUB  one    P
             ((there))'s ((just)) one kitchen

25        [o- otoko  ga    futa-=
             DF man   SUB   two-
             for two- m- men=

26   Mari:  [Aa::
             Oh::

27   Chie:  =>aYoosuruni:<
             in.other.words
             =>In other words,<

28        Katsuyo    chan   datte  ((intonation unit continues))
             ((name))  SFX    even
             even Katsuyo

             tachi  tai  toki  [ga  aru  no  ↑ni::,    .hhh
             cook   want times  SUB exist N   CONJ
             has times when ((she)) wants to cook but .hhh

29   Mari:                     [Aa:  Aa↓  Aa↓  Aa↓ Aa↓
                                Oh:  Oh   Oh   Oh   Oh
```

```
        30              (0.4)

        31  Chie:   o↓tto   [no   daidokoro   ni   nacchatteru   kara:,=
                    husband  GEN  kitchen      P    has.become    CONJ
                    'cuz the kitchen has ended up as the husband's,=

        32  Mari:           [Ao:::n
                             Oh:::::

        33  Mari:   =Hoo:::::::.

        34              (0.3)

        35  Chie:   Maa, uzattai  (.)  tte   ie  ↑ba,
                    well annoying      QUOT  say CONJ
                    So well, talking about ((it)) being annoying,

        36          u↓zattai  no    to↑ki   mo↓=  ((intonation unit continues))
                    annoying  GEN   times   ADVP
                    =a[ru    mitai    (ne).
                    exist    seemingly FP
                    =((there)) appear to be times when ((it)) does get annoying.
```
2nd →
instance
```
        37  Mari:     [↑Huu:::  ((creaky))  ↓↑:::::::nn

        38  Chie:   °Soo°.        ((nod))
                    °((That))'s right°.

        39          Demo,  asoko::   no:=
                    but    there     GEN

        40          =o- oto[ko  wa    yoku  hataraku-
                    DF  men    TOP   well  work
                    Anyway, m- men in that ((house)) are hardworking-.

        41  Mari:   ((looks down, nods))
                             [Min'na  sorezore   da   ne    hhh
                              everyone respective COP  FP
                              Everyone unto themselves, it seems hhh

        42  Chie:   >Yoku  hataraku  asoko  no   uchi  ↑ne.<
                    well   work      there  GEN  house FP
                    ((They)) are hardworking in that house, aren't they?
                    ((Toward the end of turn Chie gazes at SON and nods.))

        43              (0.8)  ((SON nodding quickly twice))
```
3rd →
instance
```
        44  Mari:   °Huu::[::::::::::::]:::::::nn°
                    ((begins with creaky voice, ends in modal))

        45  Chie:         [°ano   otto°.]  ((nods to Mari))
                           that   husband
                           °that husband°.
```

```
        46   Chie:   ((shifts gaze from Mari to DAU at *))
                     Gaikoku:        *nami    da    yo   ↑ne.
                     foreign.countries   on.a.par  COP   FP    FP
                     On a par with foreign countries, eh?

        47                   (.) ((Chie brings back gaze to Mari))
4th →   48   Mari:   [°°Huu::::n°°  ((nodding once lightly))
instance

        49   DAU:    [°°′N°°  ((nodding 4 times))
                       °°Mm°°

        50   Chie:   °′N°.  ((nodding to Mari))
                     °Mm°.

        51   Mari:   .hh    e   oniichan   nanka   sa:,
                            DF  big.brother  like       FP
                     .hh In the case of big brother ((referring to SON))

        52           ata-  ma-  ta-  atashi  toka:,
                     DF    DF   DF   me      like
                     ata- ma- ta- when people like me,

        53           sono,  mama  no   tomodachi   n     toki  ↑mo
                     that   mom   GEN  friend      GEN   time  ADVP
                     in other words, even when mom's friends come over,

                     ((intonation unit continues))
                     set↓tai   shiteiru-  jya   nai?=
                     entertain  doing      COP   NEG
                     ((he))'s doing the entertaining, isn't ((he))?=

        54   Chie:   =Un.
                     =Yeah.
```

References

Bergmann, Jörg R. 1993. *Discreet indiscretions: The social organization of gossip* (John Bednarz, Jr. Transl.). New York: Aldine de Gruyter.

Clancy, Patricia M.; Thompson, Sandra A.; Suzuki, Ryoko and Tao, Hongyin 1996. "The conversational use of reactive tokens in English, Japanese, and Mandarin." *Journal of Pragmatics* 26: 355–387.

Couper-Kuhlen, Elizabeth 1996. "The prosody of repetition: On quoting and mimicry." In: *Prosody in conversation: Interactional studies*, Elizabeth Couper-Kuhlen and Margret Selting (eds.), 366–405. Cambridge: Cambridge University Press.

Couper-Kuhlen, Elizabeth 2009. "A sequential approach to affect: The case of 'disappointment'." In: *Talk in interaction – Comparative dimensions*, Markku Haakana, Minna Laakso and Jan Lindström (eds.), 94–123. Helsinki: Finnish Literature Society (SKS).

Drew, Paul 1997. "'Open' class repair initiators in response to sequential sources of troubles in conversation." *Journal of Pragmatics* 28: 69–101.

Drew, Paul 1998. "Complaints about transgressions and misconduct." *Research on Language and Social Interaction* 31 (3–4): 295–325.

Drew, Paul and Holt, Elizabeth 1998. "Figures of speech: Figurative expressions and the management of topic transitions in conversation." *Language in Society* 27: 495–522.

Flowe, William C. 2002. *The form and function of prosodic stylization in spoken discourse.* Unpublished PhD Dissertation, University of Konstanz, (www.ub.uni-konstanz.de/kops/volltexte/2002/748/).

Freese, Jeremy and Maynard, Douglas W. 1998. "Prosodic features of bad news and good news in conversation." *Language in Society* 27: 195–219.

French, Peter and Local, John 1983. "Turn-competitive incomings." *Journal of Pragmatics* 7: 701–715.

Gardner, Rod 1997. "The conversation object *mm*: A weak and variable acknowledging token." *Research on Language and Social Interaction* 30 (2): 131–156.

Gardner, Rod 2001. *When listeners talk: Response tokens and listener stance.* Amsterdam: Benjamins.

Goffman, Erving 1981. "Response cries." In: *Forms of talk*, Erving Goffman, 78–122. Philadelphia: University of Pennsylvania Press.

Goodwin, Charles 2000. "Action and embodiment within situated human interaction." *Journal of Pragmatics* 32: 1489–1522.

Goodwin, Charles and Goodwin, Marjorie H. 1987. "Concurrent operations on talk: Notes on the interactive organization of assessments." *IPrA Papers in Pragmatics* 1 (1): 1–54.

Hayashi, Makoto 2009. "Marking a 'noticing of departure' in talk: *Eh*-prefaced turns in Japanese conversation." *Journal of Pragmatics* 41: 2100–2129.

Heritage, John 1984. "A change-of-state token and aspects of its sequential placement." In: *Structures of social action*, John Maxwell Atkinson and John Heritage (eds.), 299–345. Cambridge: Cambridge University Press.

Iwasaki, Shoichi 1997. "The Northridge earthquake conversations: The floor structure and the 'loop' sequence in Japanese conversation." *Journal of Pragmatics* 28: 661–693.

Jefferson, Gail 1983. *Caveat speaker: Preliminary notes on recipient topic shift implicature.* Tilburg: Tilburg University.

Local, John 1996. "Conversational phonetics: Some aspects of news receipts in everyday talk." In: *Prosody in conversation: Interactional studies*, Elizabeth Couper-Kuhlen and Margret Selting (eds.), 177–230. Cambridge: Cambridge University Press.

Maynard, Douglas W. 1980. "Placement of topic changes in conversation." *Semiotica* 30 (3–4): 263–290.

Maynard, Douglas W. 1997. "The news delivery sequence: Bad news and good news in conversational interaction." *Research on Language and Social Interaction* 30 (2): 93–130.

Maynard, Senko K. 1986. "On back-channel behavior in Japanese and English casual conversation." *Linguistics* 24: 1079–1108.

Maynard, Senko K. 1990. "Conversation management in contrast: Listener response in Japanese and American English." *Journal of Pragmatics* 14: 397–412.

Mori, Junko 2006. "The workings of the Japanese token *hee* in informing sequences: An analysis of sequential context, turn shape, and prosody." *Journal of Pragmatics* 38: 1175–1205.

Müller, Frank E. 1996. "Affiliating and disaffiliating with continuers: Prosodic aspects of recipiency." In: *Prosody in conversation: Interactional studies*, Elizabeth Couper-Kuhlen and Margret Selting (eds.), 131–176. Cambridge: Cambridge University Press.

Okada, Misao 1996. "How the length and pitch of aizuti 'backchannel utterances' and the nature of the speech activity determine preference structure in Japanese." *Berkeley Linguistics Society* 22: 279–289.

Sacks, Harvey and Schegloff, Emanuel A. 2002. "Home position." *Gesture* 2 (2): 133–146.

Schegloff, Emanuel A. 1998. "Body torque." *Social Research* 65 (3): 535–596.

Shimotani, Maki 2007. "A claim-of-reanalysis token *e?/e* – within the sequence structure of other repair in Japanese conversation." In: *Japanese/Korean Linguistics* 15, Naomi McGloin and Junko Mori (eds.), 121–134. Stanford: CSLI.

Sorjonen, Marja-Leena 2001. *Responding in conversation: A study of response particles in Finnish.* Amsterdam: Benjamins.

Takubo, Yukinori and Kinsui, Satoshi 1997. "Ootooshi, kandooshi no danwateki kinoo [The discourse management function of fillers in Japanese]." In: *Bunpoo to Onsei* [Speech and Grammar], Spoken Language Working Group (ed.), 257–279. Tokyo: Kuroshio.

Tanaka, Hiroko in prep. *Response particles in Japanese: Listener stance, multimodality and Gestalt.*

Ward, Nigel 1998. "The relationship between sound and meaning in Japanese back-channel grunts." *Proceedings of the 4th Annual Meeting of the (Japanese) Association for Natural Language Processing*, March 1998, Fukuoka, Japan, 464–467.

Ward, Nigel and Okamoto, Masafumi 2003. "Nasalization in Japanese back-channels bears meaning." *Proceedings of the International Congress of Phonetic Sciences*, August 2003, Barcelona, 635–638.

Wells, Bill and Peppé, Sue 1997. "Ending up in Ulster: Prosody and turn-taking in English dialects." In: *Prosody in conversation: Interactional studies*, Elizabeth Couper-Kuhlen and Margret Selting (eds.), 101–130. Cambridge: Cambridge University Press.

White, Shieda 1989. "Backchannels across cultures: A study of Americans and Japanese." *Language in Society* 18: 59–76.

Wilkinson, Sue and Kitzinger, Celia 2006. "Surprise as an interactional achievement: Reaction tokens in conversation." *Social Psychology Quarterly* 69 (2): 150–182.

Response tokens – A multimodal approach

Comments on Hiroko Tanaka "Multimodal expressivity of the Japanese response particle *Huun*"

Dagmar Barth-Weingarten
Hermann Paul School of Language Sciences, Freiburg, Germany

While at first sight, verbal response tokens may appear to be positioned spuriously and interchangeably, upon closer study they turn out to be placed at specific moments in the interaction (cf. Barth-Weingarten 2009) and the studies carried out so far (see e.g. Ward 1996, Gardner 2001, Sorjonen 2001, Reber 2008, the work by Golato and her colleagues; for visual responses, such as nodding, cf., e.g., Maynard 1989, Aoki 2008, Stivers 2008) have shown that the tokens themselves are highly specialized in both form and function: on the one hand, while influenced by local contingencies, their instances cluster around certain prosodic-phonetic core forms. On the other hand, certain core forms seem to accomplish specific interactional tasks. Moreover, they can accomplish various tasks at once: in their function as newsmark, continuer or assessment, they can also convey a specific stance, such as enthusiasm, subduedness or disaffiliation (e.g. Jefferson 1993, Stivers 2008, Couper-Kuhlen 2009).

Tanaka's paper contributes to this research. She focuses on one response particle in Japanese, namely *Huun*. More precisely, her paper draws attention to one form of *Huun*, namely its use as a specific alignment token. Prosodically this variant is produced with undulating pitch resulting in a sing-song-like intonational form. Interactionally, Tanaka claims it to exhibit "attentiveness and involvement with a main speaker's informing-in-progress while not engaging topically and paving the way toward an eventual topic shift" (this volume: 307). She argues that, through a range of "collateral multimodal displays, a recipient can maximize the expressivity of the token (...). On the other hand, through a successive recalibration of its phonetic parameters, coupled with nonverbal displays to create a stepped down effect, the particle may be instrumental for bringing a topic to closure while dealing with delicate interactional exigencies" (ibid.).

Tanaka supports her argument by means of a detailed multimodal analysis of four instances of *Huun* in one longer excerpt of Japanese face-to-face conversation in terms of their sequential organization, prosodic patterning as well as visual features.

In the following, I will (1) focus on the kinds of multimodal evidence used in identifying a token's interactional function, and (2) complement the analysis of visual contextualization cues in Tanaka's examples. This will lead to considerations concerning the nature of the evidence needed for different levels of granularity in studying lexical items and concerning the choice of material.

1.   Distinguishing response tokens – multimodal evidence

So far in investigating the function and use of response tokens, interactional linguists have mainly concentrated on evidence from lexical content, sequential placement and sequential consequences as well as prosodic-phonetic realization (see the references mentioned above). Yet, Tanaka's paper raises our awareness that we can, and indeed should, go beyond these sources of evidence, at least with multimodal data and when investigating the interactional function of an item with a greater granularity. To prove this, lexicalized and non-lexicalized verbal items (sound objects, Reber 2008) may be especially suitable since with these, it is most obvious that "meaning" is indeed a result of the manifold contextualization cues accompanying an item's use.

Current listeners of most languages appear to have more than just one vocal response token at their disposal. Their different segmental make-ups already suggest different uses, and this is apparently also corroborated by Tanaka's work for a range of response tokens in Japanese: *Aa* is most similar to English *Oh*, *Ee* is used as a repair initiator, *Haa* and *Hoo* as affective responses, *Hee* for an unproblematic acceptance of an informing, and, finally, *Huun* as a generally more subdued token, also able to index a contemplative state. For determining this broader interactional function, evidence based on the sequential placement of the respective token is most helpful as it shows whether an item is used in a repair or informing sequence, for instance.

A similar kind of evidence can also be used at a next level of granularity, namely for differentiating between various subtypes of the uses of a single, segmentally distinguished token: Tanaka briefly mentions *Huun* as a response to bad news (this volume: 305) and then focuses on its use as a token of alignment (for further uses see Tanaka in prep.). However, with regard to these functionally different *sub*types of individual response tokens it is the prosodic realization which gains in importance because it seems to contextualize their distinction, too (see, for instance, Gardner 2001 for subtypes of *mm*, Reber and Couper-Kuhlen 2010 on *oh* as well as Golato and Fagyal 2008 and Barth-Weingarten in press on subtypes of German *jaja*). Accordingly, Tanaka, too, describes different prosodic contours in connection with the two abovementioned uses.

Moreover, as Tanaka also shows, these subtypes of *Huun* can be further differentiated, in turn, according to the degree of involvement of the current listener with a previous informing, i.e. the stance they are taking (cf. Stivers 2008, Drew and Walker 2008). The paper shows these to range from the expression of "surprise, amazement or wonderment" (this volume: 309) and "strong endorsement" (this volume: 311) of a previous speaker's evaluation of a state-of-affairs, via alignment avoiding topical involvement and taking a stance, to signaling exhaustion of the topic.

Here then, it seems, prosody plays a key role: these different stances can all be taken in one and the same sequential position. Yet, the interlocutors need to appropriately react to them immediately. Hence, even for the participants, the on-line analysis of sequential placement alone does not suffice to identify a token's specific use. And indeed, in Tanaka's examples interactional function seems to be closely connected with prosodic form: starting off with an extremely marked prosodic pattern, which signals a positive stance, Mari later produces *Huun*s whose length, loudness and pitch movements are gradually reduced and flattened from instance to instance (compare Tanaka this volume, Table 1) indicating less and less inclination to engage topically and even prepare moving out of the current topic, as Tanaka argues.[1]

Yet, making claims as detailed as these calls for more evidence. And this is where the paper goes beyond many previous studies of acknowledgement tokens: it draws upon an additional type of evidence, namely visual cues. In her paper, Tanaka convincingly shows that investigating the visual channel opens new possibilities for microanalysis, such as when current speakers coordinate their visual behaviour with each other or with the prosodic patterns they produce (1st *Huun*), but also simply when they use it to display a certain stance (for the interactional relevance of nodding in Japanese cf. Maynard 1989, Aoki 2008). Thus, it may be no coincidence that it is only the 1st, stance-taking, *Huun* that is accompanied by an explicit, coordinated nod, rather than the other, topic disengaging ones.

In sum, we can note that determining the interactional function of a response token with different degrees of granularity may require studying different language-organizational modes. While segmental and sequential analysis prepare the ground and prosody contextualizes finer distinctions, from what we have seen in Tanaka's paper, visual cues may also provide us with the kind of evidence needed at the finest levels of granularity.

On a slightly different, but connected, point and pursuing this line of argument a bit further, this observation also has very real consequences for the kind of material to be used in studying the interactional functions of response tokens in detail: it requires modally complete data, otherwise the necessary multimodal, not to say visual, evidence will not be available.

2. Additional visual cues

While Tanaka in her detailed analysis of the *Huun* instances repeatedly uses visual cues as arguments for the interactional function of the token instantiations under

---

1. This gradual reduction can also be seen with the 2nd *Huun* instance as I will argue in Section 2 of this paper, even though Tanaka claims that its delivery is "equally if not even more expressive than the first instance" (this volume: 316).

discussion, in Section 5 of her paper, she restricts herself to complementing and systematizing the prosodic-phonetic features. In the current section, I would like to extend the visual analysis in a similar way.

Including all kinds of visual cues potentially observable for the participants sitting around a table with the material at hand, we would not only have to describe head movements and gaze behaviour but also torso and hand movements. When doing so, we can obtain the following results:

We can note that overall Mari's body movements, when she is the current listener, are very restrained – in contrast to when she herself becomes the current speaker (compare video file of Tanaka's excerpt [TAN-15-(5) Gossip_All.mov]). Also, during the *Huun*s, eye contact with the news deliverer (Chie) is maintained and Mari's torso is hardly ever moving. What differs strikingly, though, between the *Huun*s, are the nodding behaviour and the hand movements: (1) It is exactly the 1st *Huun*, i.e. the stance-taking, involved one, which is accompanied by a rather extensive and thus notable nod. (2) It is the 3rd and 4th *Huun*s, i.e. the ones shortly before topic shift, during which Mari's hands are busy "doing something else". Thus, it seems that the topic disengagement is also bodily enacted.

Table 1. Visual cues produced by the *Huun* speaker accompanying the instances of *Huun* in Tanaka (this volume)

Huun	Line number	Movements of body parts during *huun*			
		Head	Gaze	Torso	Hands
1st	6	single nod accompanying *Huun*	eye contact with Chie and her son; towards end of *Huun* blinking	– (upright back)	– (right h. remains on table, left h. remains on lap)
2nd	37	–	looks at Chie during *Huun*	– (during 1st half of *Huun*); then moves sideways back till end of *Huun*	– (left h. remains at chin; right h. supports left arm)
3rd	44	–	looks at Chie; blinking once mid-stream	– (upright back)	right h. on table (palm up), left h. keeps stroking right h.
4th	48	single very slight nod accompanying *Huun*	looks at Chie	– (upright back)	right h. on table (palm up), left h. keeps stroking right h.

Moreover, this bodily disengagement can also be observed to happen gradually: while the 1st *Huun* is bodily engaged, with the 2nd *Huun* we can note that for one, the head nod is already missing; second, Mari leans backwards, not forward as when she takes the turn later on. This backward movement could thus be taken to already indicate topical disengagement, rather than engagement, in contrast to what was claimed by Tanaka (this volume: 315). The 3rd and 4th instances then are bodily disengaged.[2]

Hence, the overall trend observable with the visual cues accompanying each instance of *Huun* in essence parallels that of Tanaka's prosodic analysis: *Huun* not only prosodically but also visually becomes disengaged and topic-shifting. Thus, while further research must, of course, reveal whether this collaboration of modes is indeed more than coincidence, there is at least a possibility that the visual analysis can support the prosodic analysis. Yet, at the same time we must not conclude that prosodic analysis is sufficient then. Especially the stance taken by a response token may be conveyed by visual cues alone (cf. Barth-Weingarten in press).

3.   Conclusion

The approach chosen by Tanaka's and the current paper suggests that the analysis of visual cues is indispensable for face-to-face interaction as they can be used to extend and complement the interpretation based on an inspection of the segmental, sequential and even prosodic features of an item.

While this approach may be especially useful with items that are little lexicalized, it may also be well worth checking its usefulness beyond response tokens. A basic prerequisite for all of this is, of course, that the multimodal aspects of the data the participants had access to are recorded.

Further questions for research are

–   what happens in 3rd position, i.e. how are particular response tokens responded to by the current speaker? Note that Chie is nodding after each *Huun* instance, but with different timings and to different extents (cf. Reber 2008).
–   what about the use and realization of response tokens in telephone vs. face-to-face conversation?
–   are there cultural differences in the multimodal use of response tokens in languages other than Japanese (cf. Maynard 1989, Aoki 2008)?

Further analysis will also lead to more general questions such as

–   what about the range of prosodic contours of response tokens – what is mere variation; what is a different contour?

---

2.   Aoki (2008) points out that head nods in Japanese also accompany topic shifts. Hence, the slight nod in the 4th instance could also be explained by the following topic shift rather than by topical involvement with the preceding topic.

– what about similar prosodic contours with other response particles? Do they contextualize something similar?

Research on any of these points will continue to reveal the fascinating complexity of human conduct in talk-in-interaction.

( )   indecipherable speech; parentheses may contain approximation of sounds
*   onset/offset of visual action
@   creak/creaky voice

References

Aoki, Hiromi 2008. *Hearership as interactive practice: A multi-modal analysis of the response token* nn *and head nods in Japanese casual conversation*. Doctoral dissertation, UCLA.

Barth-Weingarten, Dagmar 2009. "When to say something – some observations on prosodic-phonetic cues to the placement and types of responses in multi-unit turns." In: *Where prosody meets pragmatics*, Dagmar Barth-Weingarten, Nicole Dehé and Anne Wichmann (eds.), 143–181. Bingley: Emerald.

Barth-Weingarten, Dagmar in press. "Response tokens in interaction – prosody, phonetics and a visual aspect of German JAJA." *Gesprächsforschung – Online-Zeitschrift zur verbalen Interaktion* (www.gespraechsforschung-ozs.de).

Couper-Kuhlen, Elizabeth 2009. "A sequential approach to affect: The case of 'disappointment'." In: *Talk in interaction – Comparative dimensions*, Markku Haakana, Minna Laakso and Jan Lindström (eds.), 94–123. Helsinki: Finnish Literature Society (SKS).

Drew, Paul and Walker, Traci 2008. "Going too far: Complaining, escalating and disaffiliation." *Journal of Pragmatics 41*: 2400–2414.

Gardner, Rod 2001. *When listeners talk. Response tokens and listener stance*. Amsterdam: Benjamins.

Golato, Andrea and Fagyal, Zuzanna 2008. "Comparing single and double sayings of the German response token *ja* and the role of prosody – A conversation-analytic perspective." *Research on Language and Social Interaction 41* (3): 1–30.

Jefferson, Gail 1993. "Caveat speaker: preliminary notes on recipient topic-shift implicature." *Research on Language and Social Interaction* 26 (1): 1–30.

Maynard, Senko K. 1989. *Japanese conversation: Self-contextualization through structure and interactional management*. Norwood, NJ: Ablex Publishing.

Reber, Elisabeth 2008. *Affectivity in talk-in-interaction: Sound objects in English*. Doctoral dissertation, University of Potsdam.

Reber, Elisabeth and Couper-Kuhlen, Elizabeth 2010. "Interjektionen zwischen Lexikon und Vokalität: Lexem oder Lautobjekt?" In: *Sprache intermedial. IDS-Jahrbuch 2009*, Arnulf Deppermann and Angelika Linke (eds.), 69–96. Berlin: de Gruyter.

Sorjonen, Marja-Leena 2001. *Responding in conversation. A Study of response particles in Finnish*. Amsterdam: Benjamins.

Stivers, Tanya 2008. Stance, alignment, and affiliation during storytelling: When nodding is a token of affiliation. *Research on Language and Social Interaction* 41 (1): 31–57.

Tanaka, Hiroko in prep. *Response particles in Japanese: Listener stance, multimodality and Gestalt*.

Ward, Nigel 1996. "Non-lexical conversational sounds in American English." *Pragmatics and Cognition* 14 (1): 129–182.

Multiple practices
for constructing laughables*

Cecilia E. Ford and Barbara A. Fox
University of Wisconsin-Madison, United States
and University of Colorado-Boulder, United States

This study explores a range of interrelated semiotic resources for constructing a "laughable," which we define as one or more utterances proffered by a speaker and inviting recipient laughter or other laugh related displays. These semiotic resources, in and around the talk, include a range of phonetic practices we initially characterize as smiley voice, breath particles, small modulations of pitch and loudness, high pitch, audible breathing, and laryngealization, as well as visible bodily practices such as leaning, smiling, shoulder shaking and gaze aversion. We also find that particular activities are constructed as part of the laughable, including exaggerations and contrasts. The current report is thus an initial foray into an extraordinarily complex realm of social interaction.

1. Introduction

Conversation analysts have used the term "laughter" to refer to the free standing tokens *heh, hah, huh,* and the like. In addition to free-standing tokens, a variety of other speech sounds are described as practices of speech infused with laughter or "speech-laugh"; common descriptors for such phenomena include "aspiration," "breathiness" and "smile voice". While studies of the sounds of speech-laugh exist, an account of the multiple and interdependent semiotic resources, including sound, body displays, and situated activity, of speech-laugh has not been attempted before. This chapter is meant to be a first step in the direction of filling this gap. We approach the data from a multi-modal perspective as we attempt an integrated approach to speech-laugh and the larger sequential activity of constructing "laughables".

* We are grateful for comments and encouragement from Chuck and Candy Goodwin, John Local, Richard Ogden, and Gareth and Traci Walker. We want to especially thank Rebecca Scarborough for help on an earlier version of the paper. Our warmest thanks go to Veronika Drake for her tireless efforts on the formatting of this paper. The work she has done could easily qualify her for co-authorship.

Our focus is upon interactionally ratified laughables, instances when both a speaker and a recipient treat an action as laughable in their formulations of actions and responses. To count as a laughable, a turn (or part of a turn) must be produced with possibly laugh-relevant sounds and/or bodily displays, and it must be responded to with laugh-relevant sounds or bodily displays. In this chapter we report on the interactive and reciprocated construction of laughables drawn from a corpus of videotaped interactions in Standard American English.

It is essential to note from the outset that our study owes much to the extensive body of literature on laughter by Gail Jefferson. Jefferson's groundbreaking work on laughter (1979, 1984, 1985, 2004) has provided both the transcriptional foundation and the analytic tools for the research we present here.

At the very beginning of our research on constructing laughables, we focused on phonetic practices. In collecting cases of speech-laugh, it quickly became evident that, in face-to-face interaction involving doing laughables, visual practices always work concurrently with phonetic practices. In addition, it became clear that sequential context and the content of the specific turns in question were also fundamental to the construction of laughables. Evidence from our corpus convinced us that the production of "laughability", if you will, is highly monitored and is co-produced through simultaneous practices of sound and bodily displays, and such productions are consequentially situated within emerging sequences of action. The collaborative and multimodal nature of sequences in which reciprocal speech-laugh and laughter are produced demands an analytic approach of the sort modeled by Charles Goodwin (e.g. 2000, 2002). In line with Goodwin's holistic view of the semiotic systems through which interactants co-construct courses of action, we worked to analyze sounds in a larger perspective: in the context of other practices as parts of the emergent structuring of interaction. Bringing our observations together with the prosodic focus of this volume, the current chapter addresses what has been known as "speech-laugh" in interplay with other sounds, bodily displays and the unfolding activity.

In taking stock of what the descriptor "laughter" might reference, one must acknowledge the status of laughter and speech-laugh as taken-for-granted cultural categories, categories that require more concrete grounding with reference to the orientations of participants at particular moments in the flow of interaction. Interactants regularly deploy laugh-like tokens and speech-laugh in service of actions quite distinct from initiating shared displays of amusement. Thus, in addition to being identified with sequences in which mirth is apparently both displayed in one person's turn and responsively reciprocated by a recipient, speech-laugh has been associated with troubles telling and delicate formulations (e.g., Jefferson 1984, Haakana 2010).

The complexity of the construction of laughables can be seen in the following fragment from our collection. We present the fragment here with sound symbols added where speech-laugh is hearable.[1] The details of the sounds will be the subject of a later section of the chapter.

Prior to this fragment, Lucy and John have been sharing stories about shopping with mutual friends and the unusual things their friends like to buy. Lucy is describing the purchase of a ceramic "Pekinese puppy", which was odd and inconsistently painted with great detail on the back and only a "smiley face" on the front:

(1) **JL Pekinese Puppy** (cf. sound file [FF-1-Pekinese Puppy.wav])

```
24  L:    £it was like-(.) p(h)erfectly air brushed,£ on the
25        ba:ck.
26        (.)
27  L:    £θO[ka:y~ay? £
28  J:       [°mheh°
29  L:    >↑but ↑'n< ↑the~e  ↑£f::r~o~:[n:t(h),£
30  J:                                [meh hah hah hah hah
31  L:    °m:°↑.HHH[H- >it'<s ↑£like ↑th[ey ↑ra:n (.hh)=
32  J:            [°.h°            [They £sort of gave
33  L:    =[↑out-£] ↑they ↑j~ust=↑the~y ↑j~ust ↑we↓nt ↓like a
34  J:    =[up?£ ]
35  L:    =little=£smiley fa:ce:.£ ↑suh~uh li~ke hah
36        ↑hah↑↑hah↑↑hah↑↑>hah<
```

If we start our analysis by examining only the sound production of the laughable sequence, we notice that Lucy produces most of line 24 with smile voice (that is, we can hear that her lips are spread, which creates a raised first formant; see Section 4.1 for further discussion). Her production of the word *perfectly* includes lengthened and noticeably loud aspiration on the initial voiceless stop. In addition, there is laryngeal to pharyngeal constriction during *back* (line 25). At line 27 with her *okay*, Lucy again uses smile voice, but we also hear loud and long aspiration on the velar stop release, modulations of loudness on the first syllable, and the second syllable sounds resyllabified into two syllables: *ka:y~ay*, with possible modulations of loudness and pitch on the added syllable.[2] At line 29, *but* and *the* are produced with modulations of pitch and loudness, *the~e* is quite high in pitch, and *f::r~o~:n:t(h)* begins with an extremely long fricative. There is very high pitch on the vowel (close to 600 Hz), continuing with increased loudness, laryngeal constriction, and modulations of intensity and pitch. It ends with a notable release on the final voiceless stop. Overlapping with the end of line 29, John (line 30) produces laughing uptake.

In these few lines of talk, then, we find a number of salient phonetic practices associated with what we call speech-laugh: lengthened and loud aspiration on voiceless stops, lengthened fricatives, localized modulations of pitch and loudness on vowels, high pitch, and laryngeal constriction on vowels.

---

1.   See Appendix for transcription symbols.

2.   This practice we refer to as "wobble" and represent with "~". See Section 4.

However, all of these phonetic practices may be deployed in different interactional contexts to distinct ends. High pitch can indicate emphasis and stance apart from laugh-relevant stance. Lengthened and loud aspiration on stops, and lengthened fricatives, can be used for other emphatic ends. In the instance we are examining, the lengthened and loud aspiration on *perfectly*, for example, is not exclusively interpretable as laugh-relevant. Even when many of the practices are produced together on a single word (e.g., as in *front*, in Example 1), they cannot be said to be unequivocally constitutive of speech-laugh. Indeed, Hepburn (2004) has noted that crying shares many of the same phonetic practices as speech-laugh.

So although there are clearly phonetic practices we can associate with speech-laugh, for participants, any of these phonetic practices alone would not be sufficient either for the construction of a laughable or for the identification by the recipient of a stretch of activity as a laughable. What makes the moment captured in (1) identifiable as laughable, then? We argue here that it is the fully embodied, socially situated, and collaboratively managed unfolding activity that allows participants to interpret and respond to the laughability in this or in any stretch of action. In this chapter in addition to examining sound practices, we explore the visual, embodied displays done in and around speech-laugh practices, as well as the larger sequential activities within and through which the laughable is constructed. We claim that it is through the coordination of these semiotic systems – sound, body, and sequence – that laughables are co-constructed.

Identifying laughables preferred to be reciprocated is oriented to as socially consequential and at times its consequences are problematic. The impressive variety of uses to which laughter and speech-laugh are put relates to the potential for equivocality and misunderstanding of speech-laugh. This leads Gail Jefferson (2010: 8) to refer to some (perhaps all) cases of speech-laugh as "possibly laughter-relevant" (PLR). Beyond the variations in the work PLR sounds can do, and beyond the variation in recipient uptake of possible laughables[3], PLR sounds and even free-standing laugh tokens can be sources of misinterpretation. Jefferson explores the indeterminacy of PLR sounds, focusing specifically on sounds she describes as "gutturals" in the midst of speech (transcribed with "gh" in her transcripts). In the following example, from Jefferson's article, a participant produces a laugh token in response to PLR sounds in the talk of the previous speaker:

(2)   **Segment of Example 8 in Jefferson (2010)**
      (original transcription symbols maintained ($_{gh}$ = "guttural"); lines reformatted and labels with arrows added by current authors.)[4]

---

3.   See, especially, Drew (1987) on "po-faced" responses to teases.

4.   It is not clear to us how the italicized parts of Jefferson's transcript are to be interpreted. The dots between consonants ("·pth·t·k ") represent clicking sounds.

```
 1  Tom:   tch·hh He saːys th_ghhat u_ghhːm ·t        <=Gutterals in speech
 2         hhuhhh hè-ukhh huːm. ·pth·t·k He always eatsːː
 3         befoːhhre. training. hhhhhh[hhh
 4  Jill:                             [°hheeh[Yhheh.°  <=Responsive
                                                        laugh
 5  Tom:                                   [uk-ekhhe_ghh HUHːː=
 6  Jill:  =[°uh!°
 7  Tom:   [There's a frog in my
 8         throat? ·hhhhh                    <=Account for guttural
 9  Jill:  °Oh(h)[ːː.°
10 Tom:         [He always eats before train↓ing.
```

Of particular relevance to our study, this case offers evidence that the question of what counts as laughter or speech-laugh is not just a challenge for analysts; it is a problem for participants as well. In line 4, overlapping Tom's extended in-breath (line 3), Jill produces what is hearable as two beats of laughter. In so doing, Jill treats Tom's previous and overlapping actions as inviting a reciprocal display of laughable appreciation. However, at lines 7–8, Tom rejects the laughable interpretation by producing an account for his guttural sounds as resulting from "a frog" in his throat.[5] Notably, Tom delays the progress of his action to address trouble with Jill's interpretation of his stance. He provides an account for the sounds that Jill has treated as having been *built as hearably laughable*. He not only provides an account for the sounds that Jill has responded to with laughter, but he goes on to do a partial repeat of the trouble source, this time repairing it such that it is produced with no laugh-like sounds: *He always eats before train↓ing* (line 10).

With the aim of contributing further leverage to and methodological perspective on the workings of laughter, speech-laugh, and laughables, we focus on one domain of social action with which speech-laugh has regularly been associated: sequences in which amusement is displayed by one speaker and taken up by another. To this end, we collected sequences in which a speaker produces PLR sounds and/or bodily displays, and we narrowed the collection further by concentrating on sequences in which a "laughter" orientation toward the display of amusement is evidenced in a recipient response to the PLR sounds or bodily display by the first speaker. Thus, our core cases are identifiable as possibly laugh relevant (PLR in what follows) or, as we term it, "laughable"[6], based both on practices in the production of a laughable and on recipient's treatment of such actions. In other words, our core cases are ones in which recipients respond to co-participants' actions with displays of amusement.[7]

---

5.   Jefferson presents a nuanced analysis of how participants may enter into sequences in which they address the misapprehension of their talk as having been "produced to be heard as laugh-relevant" (in press).

6.   In our chapter, we use "laughable" as either a noun or an adjective.

7.   We acknowledge the circularity of trying to deconstruct 'laughter' by using laughter responses themselves as evidence of participant orientations.

2.   An initial look at multiple practices

We begin by briefly noting multiple practices in the laughable sequence touched upon earlier as Example (1). Before we introduce this example, we should acknowledge a meta-linguistic problem: An unintended consequence of our using "laughable" both as a noun and an adjective is that this usage may imply that there is a discrete and clearly bounded laughable unit in the interaction. However, laughables in our data are not uniformly or even typically identifiable with single, clearly bounded linguistic units or otherwise clearly bounded segments of action. On the contrary, what constitutes and may be reciprocally oriented to as a laughable involves diffuse and cumulative practices rather than discrete and contrastive structural slots, segments, or units. Laughable practices are regularly distributed across strips of activity rather than discretely bounded in single units.

Example (1a) – an expansion of (1) – is a typical case of the co-construction of a laughable in our collection. In our initial discussion of (1), we intentionally focused on the sound production; here we expand our discussion to include the visual and action context within and through which laughables are constructed. The much richer understanding revealed here evidences the need to attend to the full range of semiotic resources available to, and coordinated by, participants.

In (1a), John and Lucy are in the midst of a chain of stories about shopping excursions with mutual friends whom they know to be eccentric. Their stories have in common that they feature friends with odd shopping styles or unique tastes. Lucy and John have shared laughter during the previous two stories, setting a context in which a next PLR story may be relevant. Thus, the broader sequence involves chaining related tellings of laughable events. In that sense, the sequential context leading up to this segment exemplifies one of the multiple and diffuse semiotic systems that contribute to the construction and recognizability of laughables.

As the excerpt begins, Lucy introduces a next in this chain of funny shopping excursions, *I must've told you that I went to the dollar store with Sebastian Lark one time.* (line 1). In a display of recognition of the laughability of even this first unit of Lucy's telling, John throws his head back and then leans backward as he laughs (lines 4–5).

(1)   a.   **Pekinese Puppy** (cf. video file [FF-1a-Pekinese Puppy.mov])
          (Sebastian Lark = pseudonym)

```
1   L:   *I must've told you that I went to the-dollar=
2        *((L: Head lowered with hand above eyes, gaze toward J))
3        =store with Sebastian Lark one time.
4   J:   *.hh eh huh *huh huh [huh
5        *((J: head back * smile, torso lean back))
```

```
 6  L:                   [Didn't I?
```

Still 1: ex. 1a, lines 4–5

```
 7      (.)
 8  J:  [*(ehmuh)
 9      *((J: return to upright))
10  L:  [£↑Didn't I ↑tell you ↑this?£
11  J:  That would've been ama:zing.
12      (.)
13  L:  We: went-*=Oh my God you <should> have=
14         *((L: hand moves over eyes))
```

Still 2: ex. 1a, lines 13–14

```
15  L:  =£seen what he bought,£ °it w[as awful,°
16  J:                               [I can just imagine.=
17  L:  =↑It ↑wa~az: [↑£this- (.)↑ri~ih-£
18  J:              [I sa:w his room. [I kno:w what he likes.
19  L:                                [↑ri- eh hah hah
20      hah
21      (.)
22  L:  ↑.hhhh What a freak sh[ow.
23  J:                        [ehinh nyinh*nheh nheh
24                                 *((J: lateral head movements))
```

```
25 L:  ↑He ↑bought,(.)↓He bought this little, (.) this
26     little like s:l:ip-cast, porcelain, f:igurine of
27     P:ekinese, (.)P:U~p[py,       £d:↑~og.£]
28 J:                   [ah hah hah hah hah] huh
29 L:  £↑heh hihit was like ↑this bi↓g.
30 L:  [.h an' it was-
31 J:  [I believe (I saw like just bet).=
32 L:  ↑just ↑well £it was like-(.) £pʰerfectly air
33     brushed, on the ba:ck.£
34     (.)
35 L:  £θ0[ka:y~ay? £
36 J:     [°mheh°
37 L:  >↑but↑'n< ↑the~e ↑£f::r~o~:[n:t(h)*,£
38                              [*((L: forward lean toward knees))
39 J:                           [meh hah hbah *hah hah-
40                                    *((J: head to hands))
```

Still 3: ex. 1a, lines 38–40

While John is leaning and laughing, Lucy delays further telling. She does two successive checks on whether John has heard the story before (lines 6, 10). In concert with and expanding upon John's treatment of the very idea of shopping with Sebastian as laughable, Lucy uses her turn at line 10 to incorporate a more extreme affect display: her second version of the question is upgraded from a tag question (line 6) to a full yes/ no interrogative clause, and it is also upgraded affectively as she produces it with high pitch (for lines 6–11 see sound file [FF-1b-Didn't I.wav]).

John then displays verbal understanding of the extreme sort of experience shopping with Sebastian would be, in *That would've been amazing.* (line 11). The use of *would have been* also claims knowledge based only on inference and shared knowledge of Sebastian, rather than on having heard the story before. In displaying this epistemic position, John gives Lucy a go-ahead to continue the telling.

Lucy then launches a description of one of Sebastian's purchases, though even this is multiply delayed. She first repairs away from telling where they shopped (line 13: *We went-*) to produce the exclamation, followed by an elaborate pre-assessment of the purchase (lines 13–15) (see sound file [FF-1c-you should have seen.wav]).

This leads into further appreciative responses by John, and a truncated attempt at description by Lucy (line 17) which breaks into laughter as John continues to join in to assert his knowledge of the extreme taste of their friend (lines 16, 18–19), *I can just imagine [...] I saw his room. I know what he likes.* At line 25, Lucy restarts her description of what Sebastian Lark bought: the ceramic puppy, an item, which was notable because it was incongruously painted. Its back was finely painted, but its front had only a cartoonish *smiley face* (line 35 in (1)).

As Lucy sets up the first part of a contrast, she produces PLR sounds (as already noted) and also PLR bodily movements. And even before Lucy has completed the second part of the projectable contrast, John and Lucy both produce PLR sounds and bodily movements (for lines 32–40 see video file [FF-1d-perfectly airbrushed.mov] and sound file [FF-1d-perfectly airbrushed.wav]).

To provide a richer sense of the multiple semiotic systems deployed to co-construct a laughable, we will concentrate here on practices deployed by Lucy in describing the ceramic puppy and on John's interwoven responses to Lucy's actions. Among the visible and hearable practices for constructing laughability in that part of the sequence are the following:

I. Sequential context and action relations:

a. sequential context: well before Lucy details the incongruous paint on the puppy, she and John have both been doing sharing laughables. As we have noted, the entire telling comes just after two prior laughable tellings about odd shopping excursions with shared friends, which both participants treat as laughable in themselves. This makes it conditionally relevant for yet another excursion with a unique friend to be shared, among other relevant next actions. And a next shopping telling, with a unique shared friend, is precisely what Lucy launches at line 1. In other words, the position of Lucy's telling contributes to its interpretability as a laughable, even without any PLR sounds or bodily displays.

b. action relations: Lucy produces a contrast within her developing description of the ceramic puppy: the incongruity between the painting on the front and the back. In lines 32–33, Lucy offers a partial description of only the back of the puppy, projecting further and possibly distinct features for the front. In line 37, Lucy begins the now-projectable contrasting part. John displays recognition and appreciation of the developing laughable by overlapping with laugh tokens *meh hah hah hah hah huh* (line 39) and by putting his head in his hands before Lucy has completed the second part of the contrast (line 30–34 in (1); end of video file [FF-1d-perfectly airbrushed.mov]).

II. Sound patterns:[8]

a. notably long and loud aspiration on the initial aspirated stop [pʰ] in *pʰerfectly* (line 32) (cf. sound file [FF-1e-perfectly.wav]),

b. breathiness at the onset of the word *θOka:~y* (line 35) (cf. sound file [FF-1f-okay. wav]),

c. modulation of loudness on the second syllable of *θOka:~y* (line 35),

d. syllabification of the second syllable of *θOka:~y* (line 35) into two syllables,

e. extended frication on the fricative [f] in *f::r~o~:[nt* (line 37) (cf. sound file [FF-1g-front.wav]),

f. modulations in loudness of vowels (e.g., *f::r~o~:[nt* (line 37),

g. free-standing tokens interpretable as laughter or PLR sounds (lines 4, 19, 23, 28, 29, 39)

h. high pitch (lines 10, 17, 19, 22, 25, 27, 28, 32, 37)

i. loud and high-pitched inhalation (lines 22)

j. lip spreading in vocalizations (between "£" symbols at e.g., lines 10, 15, 17, 27–29, 32–33, and in many lines that follow).

III. Visual-bodily practices:

a. visible lip spreading during speech of both participants (from line 6 to end of fragment).

b. forward as well as backward leans of the torso by both participants (lines 5, 38, 40).

c. covering face with hands: (Lucy lines 13–14, John at lines 39–40).

Many of these practices have received previous, though separated rather than integrated, treatment in CA and discourse research (Trouvain 2001, Chafe 2007: 1–50, Jefferson 1979, 1985, 2010, Haakana 2001, 2010, Glenn 2003, Griffitt 2008). However, an integrated account based on the multiple and interwoven semiotic resources associated with speech-laugh remains to be attempted. In this chapter, we begin to address this gap by focusing upon multiple practices through which laughables are jointly constructed by speakers and recipients.

The next section reports on our data and method; the remainder of the chapter concentrates on the practices. We divide the discussion of semiotic systems for doing laughables into three sub-sections: audible practices, bodily-visual displays and action-sequential patterns; however, separating the descriptions in this way is not intended as a claim that they are produced or interpreted separately in social action. On the contrary, participants coordinate the practices simultaneously rather than

---

8. One of the reviewers asked: "Which of these sound features are produced simultaneously and come as bundles? Is there a hierarchical order of features, that is, obligatory and optional features for laughability?" It would be very beneficial to have an answer to these insightful questions; this is an area in which phoneticians could provide important expertise.

separately, with each system elaborating and contextualizing the other. We conclude the chapter with a summary of our findings.

3.   Data and method

Our collection is drawn from a corpus of ordinary and institutional interactions, all in Standard American English. The data come primarily from videotaped, face-to-face interactions, but we also have cases from telephone conversations. We provisionally define laughables as actions and sequences of actions which participants formulate with and respond to with possibly laughter relevant displays.

As already noted, we began by collecting moments when participants produced speech-laugh, that is, cases in which a speaker seemed to be formulating an action as laughable by deploying speech-laugh features within words, or, following Jefferson (2010), possibly laughter-relevant sounds (PLR sounds). We then narrowed the collection by focusing our attention on those cases in which the potential laughable was actually treated as a laughable by the recipient. We thus used the recipient's analysis as the grounds for our own. We did not further analyze the recipient's phonetic displays of amusement, and they thus remain technically unelaborated.

Through analyzing these cases in their sequential contexts, we identified a range of interrelated practices for constructing PLR actions or laughables, practices involving multiple systems of verbal action formulation, bodily/visual displays and sound patterns. We followed an iterative process of examining and reexamining cases in the collection, questioning our assumptions about what counts as speech-laugh and other laugh-relevant displays, and working to uncover further nuances participants had access to and contributed to in the immediate context of the developing courses of action.

We used Sony Vegas 6.0 to allow us to find time alignments between the sound and visual images. For the most part we relied on our own hearings for our analysis; in a few instances we used PRAAT to give us a sense of the acoustic properties of laughter.

Our central cases, then, are responded to with PLR displays, that is, laughter, smiling, leaning and the addition of further candidate laughables. One of our main findings is that describing the range of phonetic and visual practices that participants use for constructing laughables calls for a much finer-grained set of analytical tools than currently exists in CA research. We offer the beginnings of such an analysis below.

4.   Sounds, bodily/visual practices, and sequential patterns for co-constructing laughables

4.1   Sound features

In this section we explore the range of phonetic practices related to the percept of speech-laugh. We share our findings with caution as we see this as a rich area that requires extended, in-depth focus and documentation. What we offer here is a pointer in the direction of that documentation.

In prior CA literature, terms like "aspirated", "guttural" and "smile voice" have been useful as initial guides. That is, they have helped the analyst identify moments in the stream of talk where specific sorts of sounds are produced in ways that are perceptibly different from the norms for the same words and utterances, and different in ways that we hear as laughter-like. We find, however, that for our collection, these terms (and associated transcription symbols) are ultimately limited.

As we looked through our data and compared our initial transcriptions, transcriptions by others, and what our ears and some of our acoustic measurements were telling us, we realized that there were mismatches between the transcription of speech-laugh in CA and the phonetic properties we were documenting. In particular we noticed that the standard symbol for speech-laugh, (h) – glossed as "aspiration" – is used in cases where there is actually no appreciable increase in exhalation noise or glottal frication. Indeed, other practices, like breathy voice, voiceless vowels, high pitch, and modulations of loudness and pitch, seem to play an important role in speech-laugh.

As we saw in Example (1a) above, several phonetic practices appear to recur in our data. We list them here.

Notably long and loud aspiration after a word-initial voiceless stop is relatively common in our data. This practice comes closest to what others have called "aspiration" in the CA literature (represented with (h)). Example (1a, line 32) illustrates this practice. In this utterance, as noted above (and visible in the arrowed part of Figure 1), the aspiration after the release of the [p] closure is noticeably long and loud. It is important to note here that word-initial /p/ in English is always accompanied by some aspiration; in our laugh-relevant instances, that aspiration is longer and louder.[9]

Lengthening of fricatives is another common practice. Example (1a, line 37) also illustrates this practice, with lengthening of the initial fricative in *front* (line 37) (visible at the arrowed portion in Figure 2 below):

---

9.   For a similar observation see Chafe (2007: 42–43).

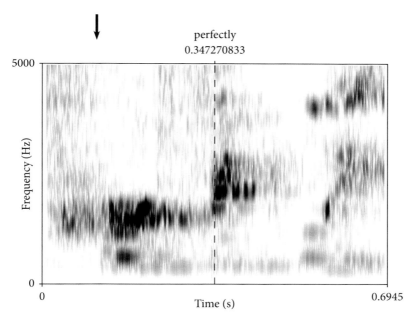

Figure 1. Spectrograph of "perfectly", ex. 1a, line 32 (see also sound file [FF-1e-perfectly.wav])

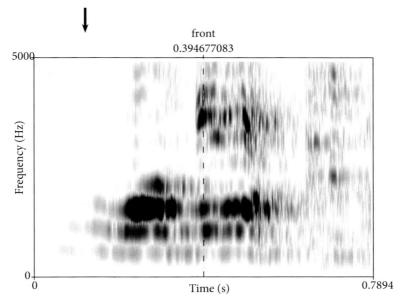

Figure 2. Spectrograph of "front", ex. 1a, line 37 (see also sound file [FF-1g-front.wav])

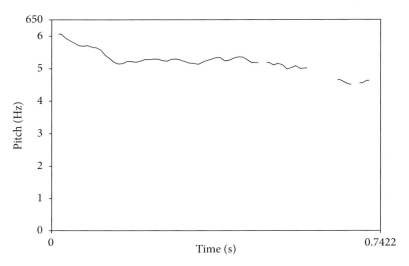

Figure 3. Pitch trace of "front", ex. 1a, line 37 (see also sound file [FF-1g-front.wav])

High pitch can be found in many instances of speech-laugh. Once again, Example (1a) exhibits an instance of this practice, especially on the word *front*. As can be seen in this pitch track of *front* (line 37), the pitch on this word is extremely high – beginning close to 600 Hz.

Laryngeal constriction can be found in some words, as in Example (1a), with constriction on *back* (line 33) (see sound file [FF-1h-back.wav]).

We have also found voicelessness at the beginnings of vowels, spreading over from a prior voiceless consonant with unusually long and loud frication. In the following example from another conversation, Laura's production of *salad* (line 3) has a notably long and loud fricative at the beginning, and the following vowel begins voicelessly.

   (3)   **Pizza vs. salad** (see also sound file [FF-3-salad.wav])
```
1   L:   [You- Yo[u take that slice of pizza ou:t.=
2   Mo:         [hehehehe
3   L:   =*[£Ea~tcyou~r s:a~[l~ad.£
4        *((L shoulders up, head down, left hand over eyes))
```

Breathiness occurs in several of our examples. Breathiness is a setting of the glottis and is distinct from aspiration, which involves the release of air after a stop consonant. Lucy's *okay* (ex. 1a, line 35) is produced with breathy voice (see sound file [FF-1f-okay.wav]).

Another practice that is common in our data is laterally spread lips (associated with smiling, but also with grimacing and with normal production of vowels such as that in "eat"), leading to raised F1 values (and possibly also a perception of higher pitch). Consider Laura's production of *chunky* (line 5) in the example below:

(4) **Chocolate chunky chocolate ice cream** (see sound file [FF-4-chocolate chunky.wav])

```
1   Mi:  ↑No::↓: >that's like the whole point.< Sh- she goes
2        and she buys like >↓what was that↓< double
3        Choc[olate,
4   L:        [£Chocolate£
5->      £chunky chocolate ice cream [with chocolate s:yrup
6        on top.£
```

Perhaps the most intriguing practice we have found in our data is what to our ears sound like local modulations of loudness, sometimes accompanied with local modulations in pitch. Chafe (2007) refers to something like this as *tremolo* (a term in music to refer to small changes in loudness); Hepburn (2004), in describing crying, refers to a potentially similar practice as 'wobbly voice'.[10] We use the term 'wobble' here. Wobble is a non-technical term, and we use it here because there has been no technical work on this phenomenon in spontaneous conversation. In this chapter we can only point to it as something interesting and deserving of further attention; clearly more careful phonetic research is needed to determine exactly what is happening in these instances.

An instance of what we are describing as wobble is given in (5), with wobbles represented by "~". Prior to this fragment, Jennifer had started a telling about a man who had come to the café where she works before the café had actually opened. Jennifer was preparing the café for opening when the man appeared.

(5) **Housemates**

(J = Jenn, T = Tere, B = Bett; lines 10–11 seem to be playful nonsense sounds)

```
1   J:   And he's like, (0.8) he tries to go in and I'm like
2        we're not open yet, and he goes .hh Uh I just
3        really need to use your bathroom. HA. (h)I'm like
4        (0.2) Fine. 'cause I had like seven minutes and so
5        much stuff to do and there
6        were al[ready like three people
7   ():         [Mmmmm
8   J:   .hhh waiting outside> Sorry. ((addressed to Beth))
9   T:   Is your (alarm clock) still not working?
10  J:   No it works.
11  T:   Mar mar.
12  J:   Mar mar mar?
13  J:   .hhh And um, (0.2) then he's like Well- I know
14       you're not open θyet, but I θwould θreally jθust
```

---

10. In more recent work, Hepburn characterizes this as "tremulous delivery" (2010).

```
15         θwant a cup of coffee. I'm like,
16         h .hh Alright, but you still have
17 ->      to wait *↑θtill £↑s:e~ven ↑o'clo~ck.£
```

When she gets to the climax of the telling at lines 15–17, Jennifer uses several laugh-related phonetic practices, specifically on *till seven o'clock*. The word *seven* is produced with small modulations of loudness or wobbles see sound file [FF-5a-till seven o clock.wav]).

We turn now to an examination of the bodily/visual practices used to accomplish the construction of laughables.

4.2   Bodily/visual displays

As we saw in Example (1a), PLR sounds are typically deployed along with PLR visual/bodily conduct. Clearly, participants collaboratively construct laughable moments through simultaneous production of sounds and bodily/visual displays. Indeed, bodily/visual movements and sound qualities are co-produced, with torso shaking related to the percept pulses of laughter, for example, and the sound and visual display of lip spreading occurring together. In this section, we report the PLR bodily/visual displays participants used in our data.

4.2.1   *Lip spreading*

Lip spreading, a recurrent PLR visual practice, can be interpreted as smiling. Thus, in our cases we can both hear and see smiling (see Haakana 2010).

In (6), both Mom and Laura's produce their talk in lines 1–4 with visible and hearable lip spreading:

Still 4: Lip spreading, Mom (mostly blocked by Donna) and Laura (far right)

(6) **Mom and Laura lip spreading** (see video file [FF-6-mom laura lip spread.mov])
   (name "Laura" deleted)

```
1   Mo: *£↑Laura goes in ~once i(h)~n *a~while with me ~and
2       *((Mo leans back)) *((Mo leans forward & then back again))
3       she-£
4   L:  *£.hhh ↑↑This ↑last ↑time *I went with her,£
5       *((L leans back))  *((L audibly slaps table top with both
                                 palms))
6       *.hh ↑£this woman was talking about having£
7       *((L leans forward))
```

4.2.2 *Leaning and/or throwing back head*

Another bodily/visual practice, recently treated in detail by Griffitt (2008), is leaning forward and back during and around laughables. Excerpt (6) also contains leans by both Mom (lines 1–2) and Laura (lines 4–7):

Still 5: Mom leaning back

Still 6: Mom leaning forward

Still 7: Laura leaning back

Still 8: Laura leaning forward

And in excerpt (1a), both Lucy and John lean forward at lines 37 through 40:

(1) a. **Lucy and John leaning** (partially reproduced)

```
37 L: >↑but↑'n< ↑the~e ↑£f::r~o~:[n:t(h)*,£
38                             [*((L: forward lean toward
                                  knees))
39 J:                          [meh hah hbah *hah hah-
40                              *((J: head to hands))
```

Still 9: ex. 1a, lines 37–40

Later in the same interaction and the continuing chain of humorous stories (not in-cluded in (1a)), John begins a story and then pauses, producing a backward lean and a backward head throw before continuing:

(7) **Backward lean**

```
1  J: A:~nd, (. ) Did I ever tell you this?
2       ((J hits table with hand, leans back & throws head back))
```

Still 10: ex. 7, lines 1–2 (John leans back and throws head back)

Laura also does a lean and head throw as she describes her experience at a Weight Watchers meeting (Example 6, line 4–5):

Still 11: Laura leans back and throws head back

4.2.3   Covering face with hand(s)

Examples (1a) and (3) are also illustrative of the bodily practice of covering ones face with one or both hands in response to a laughable.

Still 12: ex. 3, line 4: Laura responding to Mom

Still 9 (repeated): ex.1a, line 40: John responding to Lucy's telling

Face covering also accompanies the production of laughables, as in (1a), where Lucy covers her face at lines 13–15.

4.2.4   Lowering head and raising shoulders

Lowering one's head and raising or shaking shoulders is common in our data. In stills 13 a-b below, Jennifer produces *seven o'clock* not only with high-pitch and spread lips, but also with her head lowered and shoulders raised, while maintaining eye contact with Teresa:

(5)   **Housemates** (partially repeated) (see video file [FF-5-partial shrug.mov])

```
13 J:   .hhh And um, (0.2) then he's like Well- I know
14      you're not open θyet, but I θwould θreally jθust
15      θwant a cup of coffee. I'm like,
16      h .hh Alright, but you still have
17 ->   to wait *↑θtill £↑s:e~ven ↑o'clo~ck.£
18             *((J shoulders up, head dips))
```

Still 13a-b: shoulder shrug: "seven o'clock"

4.2.5   *Shaking torso and shoulders*
In (3) Laura produces the word *salad* with slight up-down movement of her shoulders:

(3)   **Shoulder shake: "eat your salad"** (partially repeated) (see video file [FF-3-shoulder up down.mov])

```
3  L~:  =*[£Ea~tcyou~r s:a~[l~ad.£
4          *((L shoulders up, head down, left hand over eyes))
```

4.2.6   *Clapping hands or slapping a surface*
In (6), Mom begins to contextualize Laura's dramatic recreation of their Weight Watchers leader's suggestion *Laura goes...*(line 1). As Mom produces *sh:* (line 3), Laura raises her arms and then begins her version of the story; on *time* she brings her hands loudly down on the table:

(6)   a.   **Table slap** (see video file [FF-6a-table slap.mov])

```
1 Mo: *£↑Laura goes in ~once i(h)~n *a~while with me ~and
2       *((Mo leans back))*((Mo leans forward & then back again))
3 Mo: she-£
4 L:  *£.hhh ↑↑This ↑last ↑time *I went with her,£
5       *((L leans back)) *((L audibly slaps table top with both
                                palms))
```

Still 14: ex. 6a, line 5 (Hands up)   Still 15: ex. 6a, line 5 (Hands slap on table)

4.2.7   *Tensing neck and facial muscles*

In another detail from Example (6), Mom leans forward and spreads her lips in (6b). As can be seen in Still 16, she also visibly tenses her neck muscles, as she produces what is treated as laughable by herself and her recipients.

Still 16: ex. 6b Tensing of neck muscles

(6)   b.   **Visible muscle tensing**

```
1 Mo: £↑Laura goes in ~once i(h)~n *a~while with me ~and
2              *((M leans forward with neck tense, lips spread))
3     she-£
```

In this section, we have reported on a range of bodily/visual practices participants deploy in constructing laughables in our data. As is evident from our ability to recycle illustrative excerpts in this section and also from the section on sound practices, sound and bodily displays are typically employed simultaneously.[11]

Importantly, like all actions in interaction, both sounds and bodily/visual displays are produced within the emerging courses of turns and sequences, and the place in which these practices are deployed is an essential component of how these practices create meaning. In the next section we move to a consideration of action combination and sequential contexts which characterize the construction of laughables in our data.

---

11.   A careful reviewer asked: "Are there any consistent patterns of co-occurring sound and bodily features?" An answer to this question would be extremely helpful in our understanding of the construction of laughable; at the moment it is beyond our study.

4.3   Action sequential patterns

Whether a laughable is prompted by a single turn or is developed over the course of a sequence of turns, what is taken up by recipients as laughable in our collection fits nicely with the categories offered by previous research on humor and laughter in talk. In our collection of laughable segments, exaggeration and incongruity are key features. Jefferson (1979) notes that contrasts are common components of laugh-relevant turns. Drew (1987) reports that actions that receive teasing responses are ones performed in an exaggerated manner. Drew also notes that contrasts are characteristic of actions leading to teases. In recent broad reviews of empirical work on humor, Carnes (2001) and Glenn (2003) report that actions or events characterized by incongruity are associated with humor, with Carnes noting that a "transient incongruity" is "a basic element of humor" (2001: 602). Interestingly, in discussing "nonhumorous situations" that nevertheless elicit laughter, Chafe (2007) also proposes a category of events that are "in some way abnormal or unexpected" (2007: 82).

Actions treated as laughable in our data involve what we can term exaggeration, extreme or remarkable tellings and incongruities. Actions treated as laughable, by current speakers and/or by recipients, regularly involve modifications of normative, expectable and/or preferred progressions of sequences-in-progress or turns-in-progress, with the producer of a possible laughable adding and even savoring an upgraded and extreme description or an unexpected juxtaposition within an otherwise projectable trajectory of action.

In this section, we provide illustrative cases of such exaggerations and incongruities.

4.3.1   *Savored exaggeration*

Recall that in (1a), John and Lucy have been exchanging tellings about shopping excursions, and Lucy starts to describe one of the odd purchases made by their mutual friend, Sebastian. As we have noted, Lucy interweaves multiple PLR sounds and bodily practices as she builds her description of the ceramic puppy. Example (8) is a partial reproduction of (1a). In this segment, in conjunction with the possibly laughable sound and bodily practices, we also find upgrading and exaggeration in the development of Lucy's extended laughable telling.

(8)   **Savored exaggeration** (see video file [FF-8-savored puppy.mov])

```
13  L:   We: went-*=Oh my God you <should> have=
14           *((L: hand moves over eyes))
15  L:   =£seen what he bought,£ °it w[as awful,°
16  J:                              [I can just imagine.=
17  L:   =↑It ↑wa~az: [↑£this- (.)↑ri~ih-£
18  J:                [I sa:w his room. [I kno:w what he likes.
19  L:                          [↑ri- eh hah hah
20       hah
21       (.)
```

```
22  L:   ↑.hhhh What a freak sh[ow.
23  J:                     [ehinh nyinh*nheh nheh
24                               *((J: lateral head
                                     movements))
25  L:   ↑He ↑bought,(.)↓He bought this little, (.) this
26       little like s:l:ip-cast, porcelain, f:igurine of
27       P:ekinese, (.)P:U~p[py, £d:↑~og.£]
```

In formulating her description of the ceramic puppy, Lucy builds on the shared understanding she and John have of Sebastian's unique taste. In a process of repair, in line 13
she cuts off the progress of the story at *We: went-* and inserts the exclamation *Oh my
God* . She employs a formulation akin to a prospective indexical (Goodwin 1996),
what he bought (line 15), thus pointing ahead to further description. In doing so, Lucy
models the stance that she projects John will share, one of amazement, *you should have
seen what he bought* (lines 13–15). After the repair and stance projection, she assesses
the extreme nature of the purchased item, *it was awful* (line 15), thereby further delaying specific reference to the object.

Having received John's displays of affiliation and his claim of prior access to
knowledge of the sorts of objects Sebastian collects (*I can just imagine* and *I saw his
room. I know what he likes,* lines 16, 18), Lucy adds the exclamation and assessment
what a freak show (line 22). This could be an assessment of Sebastian's room (just
mentioned by John) or to the shopping excursion Lucy is currently recounting. Either
way, it provides further enhancement of an extreme telling, and it continues to delay
the description of the object itself. The combination of repetition, exaggeration and
delay suggests work to extend the laughable activity, a way of savoring it or "making
it last" (Ochs 1983). Further instances of savored repetition and concomitant projection without completion (i.e., delay) emerge in line 25–26, as Lucy produces both *he
bought* and *this little* twice.

Finally, Lucy produces a possibly complete noun phrase, *slip-cast porcelain figurine of a Pekinese (.) pu~ppy* (lines 26–27). Alliteration aside[12], Lucy completes this
exaggeratedly detailed attributive adjectival phrase (*little ... slip-cast porcelain figurine*
(lines 26–27)), with *figurine* creating further projection. As she completes the noun
puppy (line 27), Lucy's noun phrase and clause could be complete; certainly nothing
further is grammatically projected. However, in continuation of what we are calling a
savored exaggeration, Lucy extends the noun phrase with *d~og. heh heh heh* (line 27).

In a case from a different conversation, Laura produces an extreme and extended
elaboration of the flavor of ice cream that she has problematically left at Michelle's
house. Just leading up to this description, Michelle has been insisting that Laura take
the ice cream home, in the interest of Michelle's diet:

---

12. But see Jefferson (1996) on poetics in conversation.

(9) **Savored ice cream** (extended version of (4)) (see video file [FF-9-ice cream.
      mov])

```
 1   Mi:  .HHH Oh that reminds me.
 2   L:   .HH[HH
 3   Mi:     [your ice cream:,=is still over at my place.
 4        (0.2)/ ((M holds gaze on L))
 5   L:   So ↑eat it.
 6        (0.2)
 7   Mi:  ↑No::↓: >that's like the whole point.< Sh- she goes
 8        and she buys like >↓what was that↓< double
 9        Choc[olate,
10   L:       [£Chocolate£
11        £chunky chocolate ice cream [with chocolate s:yrup
12        on top.£
```

While Michelle's report that Laura's ice cream is still at Michelle's is interpretable as a possible complaint (with the implied directive that Laura take it home); Laura responds strongly with a counter, the directive *So ↑eat it.*: (line 5). Michelle (line 7) follows with a strong rejection of Laura's directive, and she goes on to offer an account for why the possibility of her eating the ice cream is unacceptable, *that's like the whole point.* (line 7). Michelle then addresses Donna and Mom, beginning to recount Laura's misdeed of buying this particularly rich and tempting ice cream and leaving it at Michelle's. As she formulates her report, she displays trouble with describing the exact kind of ice cream *she goes and she buy like >↓what was that↓< double chocolate* (lines 8–9). Thus, she invites Laura to help with her word search. Laura produces the name of the ice cream with a savoring stance. She completes the in-progress noun phrase with PLR sounds and visual displays (lines 10–12), and in terms of action-sequential practices, like Lucy in Example (8), in Example (9) Laura employs repetition and exaggeration. We propose that the contrastive back and forth of directives, and the extended and exaggerated description action, form the impression of savored extreme description, with the notion of savoring carrying more than one sensory denotation in this instance.

4.3.2   *Contrast and incongruity*

We see a laughable constructed with a contrast at its core in the following formulation by Laura. Following on talk about the tempting chocolate ice-cream (Example (9)) and Michelle's will-power in not eating it (not shown), Mom suggests that Michelle would be congratulated in Mom's Weight Watchers[13] group. Mom and Laura build this connection into a laughable about the behavior of one of the leaders in Mom's Weight Watchers group. In (10), Laura enacts the talk of one leader as she adamantly commands a member of the group to put aside their slice of pizza and eat their salad instead:

---

13.   Weight Watchers is a commercial support group for weight loss.

(10)   **Pizza vs. salad** (partial repeat of (3)) (see video file [FF-10-pizza salad.mov])

```
1-> L:  [*You- Yo[u take that slice of pizza ou:t.=
2   Mo:        [hehehehe
3   L:  =[£Ea~tcyou~r s:a~[l~ad.£
4       *((L: throwing aside motion with both arms, like throwing
5       an object away))
```

Laura's formulation of this contrast functions as an exaggeration, which, for our purposes underscores the multiple forms of talk and action through which a laughable is constructed. Clearly, as we have noted earlier, sound and bodily displays are central to making Laura's talk a possible laughable, to be appreciated through reciprocal laugh relevant practices on the parts of recipients.

Another case of contrast and incongruity can be found in (11) (partial repeat of (4)), wherein Jennifer begins her story of opening the coffee shop. Recall that in this extract, Jennifer is recreating the dialog between herself and a man who wanted service at the café before it was opened:

(11)   **Wait till seven o'clock** (see video file FF-11-wait till seven.mov)

```
13    J:  .hhh And um, (0.2) then he's like Well- I know
14        you're not open θyet, but I θwould θreally jθust
15        θwant a cup of coffee. I'm like,
16->      h .hh Alright, but you still have
17->      to wait *↑θtill £↑s:e~ven ↑o'clo~ck.£
```

Jennifer's PLR sound and body practices have been described in previous sections; here we draw attention to the incongruity and contrast in her telling. Beyond the PLR practices in sound, body, and even in an exaggerated description of the man, we find two incongruous and contrasting components in the talk. First, there is the incongruity and contrast in the man's reported talk: On exiting the bathroom, he acknowledges that the shop is not open but pleads that he be granted a cup of coffee. A second contrast is used when Jennifer begins by agreeing to give him coffee but then insists that he wait till the shop opens, *but you still have to wait ↑till se~ven o'clo~ck* (lines 16–17).

Our final illustration comes from a longer sequence, in which Donna is reporting a phone call the previous evening with her college-aged son, Chuck. During that call, Chuck and another player collided and Chuck's helmet flew off. Donna animates Chuck's description of the events and his resulting injury. As Donna comes to the climax of the story, she enacts Chuck's telling, emphasizing an incongruous contrast between the blood dripping down his face and his assessment of the event as *awesome* (line 26), a strongly positive descriptor in this case.

(12)   **Blood drippin' awesome** (see video file [FF-12-awesome.mov])

```
18  D:  he said one play my helmet flew off, an'
19      a[nother guy went right into me:,              ],=
20  L:   [°Oθh Brent was telling me @about that .@°]
```

```
21  D:    =and I've got a-h .h a *scar:,=he said,>I probably
22        should of< had a stitch or two
23        [but, h .h θthere was
24        [*whh↑hh↓↓ / ((=whistle))
25        blood drippin' θdo~wn m~yθ fa~ace,[*he said,=
26  Mo:                                    [*eh heh
27  D:    =it's j~ust awesome.=
28  L:    =>eh heh< [hAH HAH hah hah hah hah .hhh
29  Mi:             [HAHHAH Huh
```

On the one hand, in lines 21–25, we have the description of a scar on Chuck's face, the potential need for stitches, and the description of the blood dripping down his face after the accident (line 25). On the other hand, we have the contrasting and incongruous (at least from a mother's point of view) assessment of the event and its consequences as *awesome* (line 27). Michelle displays a concerned facial expression as she produces the whistling response at line 24, and this offers a sense of one relevant response to the football accident and injury. It is not until Donna completes the contrasting positive assessment that Michelle and the other recipients join in doing appreciative laughter.[14]

4.4   Looking to an integrated analysis

In Section 4, we have presented an array of interrelated practices associated with co-constructing laughables in our data. While we have offered provisional and suggestive details on audible, bodily-visual, and action-sequential practices for formulating laughables as built to be reciprocated, we recognize that presenting these practices in separate subsections should ideally culminate in an integrated analysis of instances in which the semiotic systems are interwoven and mutually contextualized and contextualizing. Space limitations for the current chapter preclude reporting such integration here. However, simultaneous practices are the focus of our larger project, and we particularly invite collaboration with phoneticians to support an account for laughables in interaction. With the array of semiotic practices we have covered here, we are convinced both of the necessity for phonetic grounding in the study of laughables in naturally-occurring language use and the importance of integrating the analysis of

---

14.   As we have seen in this section, exaggerations, contrasts and incongruities are regularly constructed with simultaneous PLR sounds and bodily visual actions. However, in our collection, we find that these action formats are also used by themselves to construct successful laughables without any notable phonetic or visual 'marking' at all. It may be that such "deadpan" deliveries constitute forms of incongruity and contrast in themselves, doing something unexpected or inapposite as if doing it seriously. In addition, in some action-sequence types, unmarked laughables may be a strategy for pursuing or displaying intimacy (cf. Jefferson et al. 1977), and as such they may not always succeed in prompting laughter form recipients. We take up these potentially deviant cases in another report (Ford and Fox, in prep).

sound, visual, and action-sequential practices, in a manner that is true to the nature of activities of participants in talk.

5. Conclusions

In this study it has been our intention to contribute to inquiry into visible and audible practices of phonetics, bodily display, and sequential action, with the ultimate goal of understanding these practices as deployed within and constitutive of courses of action in which amusement is reciprocally enacted.

On the one hand, in terms of specific practices, we have found that the current state of transcription of speech-laugh needs refinement to separate out at least breathy voice, lengthened and loud aspiration on voiceless stops, lengthened and loud frication on fricatives, local modulations of loudness and possibly pitch, smile voice, and voicelessness on vowels. This inventory is far from complete, but we have added to an understanding of the range of phonetic practices at work in laughables. More detailed work by phoneticians, especially on the phenomena we have pointed to with the term 'wobble', is clearly needed.

On the other hand, we have suggested that these phonetic practices alone do not construct an action as laughable. While we began with cases of speech articulated with sounds interpretable as laughter, that is, speech-laugh, as our focus, we have situated that investigation within a richer range of semiotic systems (Goodwin 2002: 29), the systems that participants deploy and orient to in constructing laughables. The laughability of an activity is created through the deployment of a range of mutually elaborating semiotic resources (Goodwin 2000). In other words, although laughables may be thought of as having noticeable and unusual phonetic practices associated with them, we have found that they are like all other activities in being constructed through a complex web of socially situated bodies and actions. Simultaneous and associated body-visual practices and sequential organization are crucial to a complete understanding of laughables as they are produced and oriented to by participants. Ultimately, we find that constructing laughables involves constellations of action sequencing, visual displays, and sound production practices.

As a contribution to this volume on prosody in interaction, the current report is an initial foray into an extraordinarily complex realm of social interaction previously referred to as laughter-within-speech or speech-laugh. It is part of a larger project which seeks to describe many of these complexities, crucially within a multimodal approach which takes seriously the multiple semiotic resources that can variously construct laughables in different sequential environments. We offer the present study as a first exploration of, and opening into, this rich domain.

References

Carnes, Molly 2001. "Humor." In: *Encyclopedia of women and gender, sex similarities, and differences and the impact of society on gender,* Vol. 1, Judith Worell (ed.), 601–609. San Diego: Academic Press.

Chafe, Wallace 2007. *The importance of not being earnest: The feeling behind laughter and humor.* Amsterdam: Benjamins.

Drew, Paul 1987. "Po-faced receipts of teases." *Linguistics* 25: 219–253.

Ford, Cecilia E. and Fox, Barbara A. (in prep.). "Managing humor: linguistics and social action." Unpublished manuscript, available at UW Madison.

Glenn, Phillip 2003. *Laughter in interaction.* Cambridge: Cambridge University Press.

Goodwin, Charles 1996. "Transparent vision." In: *Interaction and grammar,* Elinor Ochs, Emanuel A. Schegloff and Sandra A. Thompson (eds.), 370–404. Cambridge: Cambridge University Press.

Goodwin, Charles 2000. "Action and embodiment within situated human interaction." *Journal of Pragmatics* 32: 1489–1522.

Goodwin, Charles 2002. "Time in action." *Current Anthropology* 43: 19–35.

Goodwin, Charles and Goodwin, Marjorie H. 1987. "Concurrent operations on talk: Notes on the interactive organization of assessments." *IPRA Papers in Pragmatics* 1 (1): 1–54.

Griffitt, Kira Larissa 2008. *Functions of leaning in episodes of laughter: Laughter as a visual phenomenon.* MA thesis, Linguistics, University of California, Santa Barbara.

Haakana, Markku 2001. "Laughter as a patient's resource: dealing with delicate aspects of medical interaction." *Text* 21: 187–219.

Haakana, Markku 2010. "Laughter and smiling: notes on co-occurrences." *Journal of Pragmatics* 42 (6): 1499–1512.

Hepburn, Alexa 2004. "Crying: Notes on description, transcription, and interaction." *Research on Language and Social Interaction* 37: 251–291.

Hepburn, Alexa 2010. "Interrogating tears: Some uses of 'tag questions' in a child protection helpline." In: *Why Do You Ask?: The function of questions in institutional discourse,* Alice Freed and Susan Ehrlich (eds.), 69–86. Oxford: Oxford University Press.

Jefferson, Gail 1979. "A technique for inviting laughter and its subsequent acceptance/declination." In: *Everyday language: studies in ethnomethodology,* George Psathas (ed.), 79–96. New York: Irvington.

Jefferson, Gail 1984. "On the organization of laughter in talk about troubles." In *Structures of social action: Studies in conversation analysis,* J. Maxwell Atkinson and John C. Heritage (eds.), 346–369. Cambridge, UK: Cambridge University Press.

Jefferson, Gail 1985. "An exercise in the transcription and analysis of laughter." In: *Handbook of discourse analysis,* Vol. 3. Teun A. van Dijk (ed.), 25–34. London: Academic Press.

Jefferson, Gail 1996. "On the poetics of ordinary talk." *Text and Performance Quarterly* 16: 1–61.

Jefferson, Gail 2004. "A note on laughter in 'male-female' interaction." *Discourse Studies* 6 (1): 117–133.

Jefferson, Gail 2010. "Sometimes a frog in your throat is just a frog in your throat." *Journal of Pragmatics* 42 (6): 1476–1484.

Jefferson, Gail; Schegloff, Emanuel and Sacks, Harvey 1977. "Preliminary notes on the sequential organization of laughter." *Pragmatics Microfiche.* Cambridge: Cambridge University Department of Linguistics.

Ochs, Elinor 1983. "Making it last: Repetition in children's discourse." In: *Acquiring communicational competence,* Elinor Ochs and Bambi Schieffelin (eds.), 26–49. London: Routledge.

Trouvain, Jürgen 2001. *Phonetic aspects of "speech-laughs".* Institute of Phonetics, University of the Saarland, 66041 Saarbrücken, Germany.

Appendix: Transcription conventions

a. For representing bodily actions, we use asterisks to mark the beginning of a visible action relevant to our analysis. Asterisks also mark descriptions of the bodily actions, which appear in Arial italicized font just next to the talk in question.

b. To represent verbal and vocal actions, we use CA symbols, originally invented by Gail Jefferson. Note that for qualities related to laugh (e.g., breathiness, smile voice), beginnings and endings are not discrete and clearly bounded in the talk itself. In the transcripts, we mark approximate beginnings and endings, that is, where these laugh relevant sounds begin to be evident and a point after which they are no longer evident.

£yes£	smile voice; see Section 4.1 for discussion
θ yes	breathiness; see Section 4.1 for discussion
~	"wobble"; see Section 4.1 for discussion
(h)	"laugh-like" sound within the course of a word[15]
[	point of overlap onset
]	point of overlap termination
=	no break or gap between adjacent utterances
	OR same speaker turn continuation, with overlapping talk leading to line addition
(0.4)	pause measured in tenths of seconds
(.)	micropause: a hearable pause but one that is 2/10ths of a second or less
.	low fall in intonation
?	high rise in intonation
,	intermediate contours: level, slight rise or slight fall
::	lengthening of previous sound (more colons indicates longer sound stretch)
>yes<	talk produced at a more rapid pace than previous surrounding talk
YES	increased volume relative to surrounding talk by same speaker
yes	emphasis (for English this can include modulations of volume, pitch and duration)

15. We use the "(h)" more generally than the "~". That is, we use "~" for what we feel we have begun to have a handle on, as discussed in Section 3. We revert to "(h)" for instances where the impression of speech-laugh is hearable to us, but where we do not have more acoustic or phonetic detail to add. These represent part of the analytic territory that we hope will receive more attention from specialists in phonetics and CA.

ye-	sound cut off
↑	local rise in pitch on following sound(s); marked only before sound, normally lasting a single syllable;
↓	drop in pitch on following sound(s); marked before sound, normally lasting a single syllable repeated if pitch rise continues or is reintroduced in subsequent words
( )	indecipherable speech; parentheses may contain approximation of sounds

Multimodal laughing

Comments on Cecilia Ford and Barbara Fox "Multiple practices for constructing laughables"

Karin Birkner
University of Bayreuth, Germany

The analysis of *laughables* presented by Cecilia Ford and Barbara Fox claims to be only "an initial foray into an extraordinarily complex realm of social interaction." (Ford and Fox this volume: 339) But research on laughing and humour is in fact legion. So, what is gained by examining laughing practices when so much has already been said about this topic (see e.g. Glenn 2003, Kotthoff 2006 for further references)? As we will see, it is the multimodal perspective on laughing which hitherto has not been taken into account. In the following, I will first look at the defining features of laughables and compile a number of arguments to highlight the benefits that come along with the authors' analysis. In the second part of this paper I will sketch out some desiderata for further research.

1. What is "a laughable"?

As a starting point I will first look at a general definition of what the authors consider a *laughable*: "a turn (or part of a turn) must be produced with possibly laugh-relevant sounds and/or bodily displays, and it must be responded to with laugh-relevant sounds or bodily displays." (Ford and Fox this volume: 340)

In terms of approaching the analysis either from form or function (Couper-Kuhlen and Selting 2000), the paper starts from form, considering the prosodic-phonetic practices of "speech-laugh." These include features such as smiley voice, breath particles, small modulations of pitch and loudness, high pitch, audible breathing, lengthened and loud aspiration on voiceless stops, lengthened fricatives, localized modulations of pitch and loudness on vowels, and laryngeal constriction on vowels. It is the paper's primary concern to describe the phonetic features of these "possibly laugh-relevant sounds" (Jefferson 2010, cited in Ford and Fox this volume: 342). This, in fact, is overdue, considering the impressionistic way a phenomenon as ubiquitous as speech-laugh has been treated hitherto in conversation analysis (and even more so in other approaches to language in interaction).

The same holds for the use of visual resources: The analysis also studies visual practices such as postural positions, head movements, gestures, facial expressions and gaze. Bodily displays in conversational practices have long been neglected and present one of the major challenges for future research in conversation analysis.

Last but not least, body practices are analyzed together with verbal actions and sequential patterns, thus venturing into a multimodal approach to interaction. On the one hand, laughables seem to be part and parcel of narrative sequences, as the data presented in the article suggest. The authors refer to semantic-pragmatic features such as "exaggeration, extreme or remarkable tellings and incongruities. Actions [...] involve modifications of normative, expectable and/or preferred progressions of sequences-in-progress or turns-in-progress" (Ford and Fox this volume: 360). On the other hand, a constitutive element of a laughable in the authors' sense is the reciprocation by the recipient. The authors' perspective is strictly interactional in that the analysis only includes cases that are ratified by a next speaker's uptake.

The formal features of speech-laugh are integrated into a functional approach, since the analysis tries to capture the social function behind the multimodal practices. Instead of looking at genres, e.g. jokes, or how the climax of a funny story is presented, the analysis, in line with the classic CA approach to interaction, looks at how shared amusement is manufactured as a co-constructed activity in its sequential unfolding. Laughables form part of practices that play a role in the negotiation of stance (be it positive or negative), affiliation and alignment, a field of research which still needs further exploration (cf. also Selting this volume).

A laughable is a holistic phenomenon which is difficult to reconstruct by reading the transcripts without listening to the excerpt, similar to prosodic and phonetic phenomena. It also has a cultural aspect: For readers who have not lived – and laughed – for a reasonably long time in the community the data stem from, it is difficult to grasp what is happening. Nevertheless, it seems that the semiotic resources laughables draw upon are shared at least in Western cultures.

2.   Desiderata for further research

With regard to a multimodal perspective on laughing there is still much that remains to be looked at in detail. I will briefly mention four interesting aspects without trying to be exhaustive. Taking up the last point, a first worthwhile topic is whether laughables exist in other cultures (most probably so!), and if so: What are the formal features of laughables in other communities? Are there similar types of laughables in different communities, with respect to function, form, sequential placement, etc.?

In addition to culture-specific practices, a second interesting aspect for future research is how the sequential placement of prosodic-phonetic marking contributes to the differentiation between types of laughables. The point of a joke, for example, is normally not marked by speech-laugh. A possible explanation is that since there are so many other cues, e.g. lexico-semantics, genre features, etc., the prosodic-phonetic marking by speech-laugh is not necessary. Like laughables, jokes exploit contrast and incongruity by violating expectations; they invoke a laughing ratification from the recipients (Sacks 1974), but it seems counterproductive to present a joke with laughing practices like the ones found in laughables. At what points in the unfolding interaction does speech-laugh occur? What difference does it make if it occurs before or after a "possibly laughter-relevant" verbal action?

Thirdly, the analysis shows the interactive construction of amusement. The most difficult cases of amusement, however, for participants as well as for analysts, are the cases where the prosodic-phonetic marking of a laughable is missing, but in retrospect the trajectory of the interaction shows that a laughable is ratified by the participants. This is the case in so-called "deadpan deliveries", where participants draw on shared knowledge that remains implicit in the interaction. "Possibly laughter-relevant" actions are not necessarily marked by specific prosodic-phonetic practices; in turn, the employment of the formal features typical of laughables does not always contextualize amusement. An amused uptake may be present, but lack of an uptake is often neither unusual nor troublesome. This is a typical overlap of form and function. Laughables can be presented in different forms (e.g. different sets of employed features or a total lack of marking), and yet we find the same function which the authors call "amusement." On the other hand, the same formal features (speech-laugh, so-called "wobbling", cf. Ford and Fox this volume: 353, etc.) can be found in very different functions, which do not have much in common with amusement, e.g. irony, cynicism, distance, embarrassment, etc. (see e.g. Hepburn 2004, Jefferson 1984, Potter and Hepburn 2010, Wilkinson 2007). The ethnocategory "laughter" is strongly associated with amusement; this being so close makes it difficult to grasp occurrences where the features typical of speech-laugh do not convey amusement, but distance. It remains for future research to see which multimodal sets of features are used to mark one of the above glosses and distinguish them from laughables like the ones presented in the paper.

Last but not least, the paper mainly describes prosodic-phonetic features of female speakers. It would be interesting to see whether there are gender differences, e.g. variation within certain features, such as pitch, bodily behaviour, or within the set of features.

These are only some future research topics which are prompted by Ford and Fox's paper, and the list is not to be considered a blemish, but rather an incitement. Hopefully it stimulates more enjoyable research on the multimodal organisation of visual and audible display of amusement.

References

Couper-Kuhlen, Elizabeth and Selting, Margret 2000. "Argumente für die Entwicklung einer 'interaktionalen Linguistik'". *Gesprächsforschung online* 1: 76–95. (http://www.gespraechs-forschung-ozs.de/heft2000/heft2000.htm)

Glenn, Phillip 2003. *Laughter in interaction*. Cambridge University Press.

Hepburn, Alexa 2004. "Crying: Notes on description, transcription, and interaction." *Research on Language & Social Interaction* 37: 251–291.

Jefferson, Gail 1984. "On the organization of laughter in talk about troubles". In: *Structures of social action: Studies in conversation analysis*, J. Maxwell Atkinson and John Heritage (eds.), 346–369. Cambridge, UK: Cambridge University Press.

Jefferson, Gail 2010. "Sometimes a frog in your throat is just a frog in your throat". *Journal of Pragmatics* 42: 1476–1484.

Kotthoff, Helga 2006. "Gender and humor: The state of the art". *Journal of Pragmatics* 38: 4–25.

Potter, Jonathan and Hepburn, Alexa 2010. "Putting aspiration into words: 'Laugh particles', managing descriptive trouble and modulating action." *Journal of Pragmatics* 42: 1543–1555.

Sacks, Harvey 1974. "An analysis of the course of a joke's telling in conversation". In: *Explorations in the ethnography of speaking*, Richard Bauman and Joel F. Sherzer (eds.), 337–353. Cambridge, UK: Cambridge University Press.

Wilkinson, Ray 2007. "Managing linguistic incompetence as a delicate issue in aphasic talk-in-interaction: On the use of laughter in prolonged repair sequences". *Journal of Pragmatics* 39: 542–569.

Constructing meaning through prosody in aphasia*

Charles Goodwin

Applied Linguistics, University of California-Los Angeles, United States

Despite a vocabulary that consists of only three words *Yes, No* and *And*, Chil acts as a powerful speaker in conversation. He does this, embedding his limited lexicon within larger contextual configurations in which different kinds of meaning making processes including prosody, gesture, sequential organization, and operations on his talk by his interlocutors create a whole that goes beyond any of its constitutive parts. This paper explores the role played by prosody in this process. It focuses on how Chil is able to build varied action that is precisely fitted to its local environment by using different prosody over similar, and at times identical, lexical items, here pairs of *No*'s. More generally it argues that analysis of human action should focus on the interdependent organization of diverse meaning making resources.

1. Introduction

This paper focuses on how human action is built by bringing together different kinds of resources which mutually elaborate each other. Such a perspective is relevant because within contemporary academic research different aspects of the plurality of phenomena implicated in the organization of action in human interaction – lexis, syntax, prosody, sequential organization, gesture, tools, co-present bodies, structure in the environment, indexical organization, etc. – are investigated separately by a range of different disciplines (various schools of linguistics, conversation analysis, cognitive science, gesture studies, etc.). Each gains theoretical leverage by extracting a partial from the larger whole found in actual instances of interactive action, for investigation as a nicely-bounded, self-contained system in its own terms.

---

* I am deeply indebted to Dagmar Barth-Weingarten, Elisabeth Reber, Margret Selting, Candy Goodwin and two anonymous reviewers for most helpful and insightful comments on an earlier version of this paper.

While not contesting the analytic control gained by such a strategy, the present paper will investigate two intimately related issues. First, do participants themselves in fact treat their actions as being constructed through the simultaneous use of multiple resources that provide very different kinds of structure? Despite the way in which it is common to gloss pragmatic actions with simple lexical terms, such as "request" or "greeting", and thus treat the action being investigated as a homogenous, self-contained whole, are actions in fact semiotically heterogenous in their organization? In other words, are participants systematically building action by assembling them from diverse resources with very different kinds of properties? Second, can the power and organization of even very simple human action in interaction be adequately described within frameworks that focus on single systems in isolation? Alternatively, do the diverse resources implicated in the organization of an action interact with each other to create a whole not found in any of the individual parts, and is this central to how the action is understood, what it is doing, and how it is adapted to the changing contingencies of unfolding context?

These issues will be investigated in this paper by focusing on the actions of a man with severe aphasia, Chil. Because of the severe limitations of his productive vocabulary (basically 3 words) his ability to construct action by combining his restricted lexicon with other meaning making resources, including prosody and gesture, emerges with particular clarity. It will be argued that even when his lexicon remains relatively constant (for example the repeated use of *No no*), he is able to assemble quite varied action packages by bringing together resources with diverse semiotic properties.

2.   Prosody within contextual configurations

One point of departure for the perspective taken in the current paper is earlier work (Goodwin 2000) where I argued that human action is constructed and responded to within constantly changing contextual configurations built through the simultaneous use of structurally different kinds of semiotic phenomena in alternative media (semiotic fields, including the stream of speech, the visible body and structure in the material environment) that mutually elaborate each other to create wholes that go beyond any of their constituent parts (Goodwin 2000: 1490).

The current paper will examine the powerful place that prosody occupies within such contextual configurations. I will be investigating only a few aspects of prosody, such as variations in pitch over limited lexical structures. However, consistent with the argument about contextual configurations above, I very clearly recognize that what I am glossing as prosody, is itself composed of many different kinds of mutually elaborating phenomena, which make different contributions to the intelligibility of utterances and actions. This is powerfully demonstrated by other papers in this volume. Moreover, while I will focus on Chil's creative use of specific resources, I am not suggesting that the practices being described are specific to either him as a person, or to particular kinds of aphasia. Instead, as is clearly revealed by the way in which his interlocutors are able to make sense out of what he does, his situation provides a tragic opportunity to focus on general practices used by human beings to build meaning and action in concert with each other in the midst of unfolding interaction.

This paper is a contribution to a growing body of research in a number of different fields, including interactional linguistics, the study of prosody in interaction, video analysis of interaction, anthropological linguistics, functional linguistics, gesture studies, and conversation and discourse analysis that is focusing on how diverse phenomena are used by participants within interaction to construct the details of the actions they are engaged in together (Anward 2005, Auer 2007, Couper-Kuhlen and Ford 2004, Ford et al. 2002, Haviland 1998, Heath and Luff 2007, Hindmarsh and Heath 2000, Leon 1998, Ochs et al. 1996, Selting 2008, Streeck 2009, Thompson and Couper-Kuhlen 2005, and many more). Chil's ability to make meaning in concert with others provides a powerful example of what Linell (2009) analyzes as the dialogic organization of both the mind and language.

3. Chil & his capacities and resources

In 1979, when Chil was 65 years old, a blood vessel in the left hemisphere of his brain ruptured. He was left completely paralyzed on the right side of his body and with a vocabulary that consisted of only three words: *Yes, No,* and *And.* Despite this he continued to function as a powerful actor in conversation, and indeed had an active social life in his community, going by himself to a coffee shop in the morning, doing some of the family shopping, and so forth.

How is it possible for someone with a three-word vocabulary to act as a consequential, indeed powerful speaker in conversation? Note that all three of Chil's words establish particular kinds of links with other, nearby talk. Thus, a major use of *yes* and *no* is to construct what conversation analysts call Second Pair Parts (Sacks 1992, Sacks et al. 1974). First Pair Parts, such as questions and requests, make it relevant for their addressee to produce a particular kind of action next. What the subsequent speaker says in that position will be heard and understood with reference to the contextual frame created by the First Pair Part (for example as agreeing or disagreeing with what was just said). Despite its lexical poverty, if viewed in isolation, a *yes* or *no* by Chil can be heard as participating in the construction of a complex statement by virtue of the way in which it can build upon, and invoke as part of its own semantics, the far richer structure provided by another speaker's prior talk (Goodwin 2007b). Chil becomes a competent actor by building talk and action in concert with others, a process that requires the systematic organization of language within a public environment.

Despite the limitations of his vocabulary Chil retains an extensive repertoire of other semiotic resources. First, his understanding of what others are saying is excellent. Second, he has very expressive prosody, which he produces over both his *yes*'s and *no*'s and over "nonsense" syllables such as *duh*, which seem to be spoken precisely to carry relevant prosody (Goodwin et al. 2002). Third, though completely paralyzed on his right side, Chil uses his left hand to produce a varied and important range of gestures, including pointing (Goodwin 2003b, Goodwin 2006) and hand shapes displaying numbers (Goodwin 2003a). Fourth, by living at home with his family and caretakers in the town that has been his community for almost forty years, he inhabits a world that is not only meaningful, but which can be recognized in relevant ways by those around him. He can thus use actions such as pointing to invoke meaningful phenomena in powerful ways. However, as will be seen below, his inability to accompany that pointing with relevant language can produce puzzles. Finally, unlike many people suffering from aphasia, Chil's timing as a participant in interaction is rapid and fluid. This may in fact be a by-product of the severity of his impairment, since he does not spend extensive time trying to find and produce words.

4.   Building action by combining multiple semiotic resources

Chil's catastrophically impoverished vocabulary is tied to a similar impoverishment in syntax, specifically his inability to speak utterances in which individual lexical items are organized into larger, syntactically complex wholes. He can produce units in which different numbers of *Yes*'s and *No*'s are combined (*No No*, *no no no*, *yes no* etc.), but that marks the limits of his ability to combine morphemes into larger wholes.

It will be argued that despite his limited vocabulary Chil has powerful combinatorial resources that he uses to flexibly construct relevant action.

I will begin by investigating in some detail the resources Chil uses to build action in Figure 1. In my analysis I will focus on how different kinds of semiotic phenomena, including linguistic structure in the stream of speech, prosody, gesture, embodied participation frameworks, and relevant structure in the environment are used in conjunction with each other to build relevant action. Figure 1 thus includes, in addition to a transcription of the talk,[1] images showing gesture and body position. Images give the reader a clear sense of what Chil's gestures look like, which is what is most central to

---

1.   Talk is transcribed using a slightly modified version of the system developed by Gail Jefferson (see Sacks at al. 1974: 731–733). The following symbols are used:

talk   – emphasized
.   – falling pitch
?   – rising pitch
,   – continuing pitch
:   – lengthening
–   – cut-off
((*comments*))
(1.0)   – pause of 1 sec duration
°   – low volume
[– beginning of overlap
[

the present analysis. I have tried to indicate the boundaries of each gesture with vertical lines marking approximately where each gesture begins and ends, joined by a horizontal line that marks the gesture's duration with respect to the talk in progress. This method of transcription does not encompass some phenomena that are central to some important work in contemporary gesture analysis, but is sufficient for present purposes. At the beginning of line 5, Chil places his hand over his bowl, and then during the 0.6 second silence that follows thrusts the hand forward, away from him. As Chuck starts to talk in line 7, Chil begins a second gesture, moving his hand from the bowl to point in front of him (cf. video file [GOO-Grapefruit.mov])

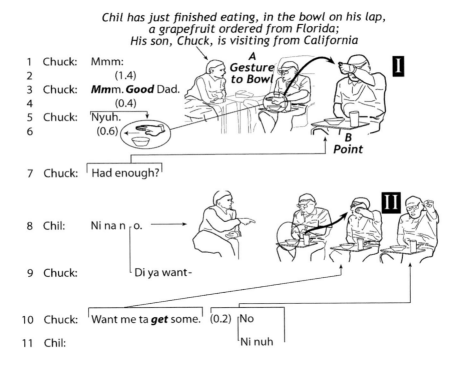

Chil has just finished eating, in the bowl on his lap,
a grapefruit ordered from Florida;
His son, Chuck, is visiting from California

1	Chuck:	Mmm:
2		(1.4)
3	Chuck:	**Mm**m. **Good** Dad.
4		(0.4)
5	Chuck:	ˈNyuh.
6		(0.6)
7	Chuck:	ˈHad enough?ˈ
8	Chil:	Ni na nˌo.
9	Chuck:	ˈDi ya want–
10	Chuck:	ˈWant me ta **get** some.ˈ (0.2) ˌNo
11	Chil:	ˌNi nuh ˈ

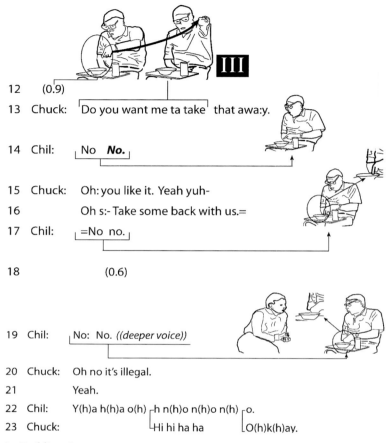

12   (0.9)
13   Chuck: ⌐Do you want me ta take⌐ that awa:y.
14   Chil: ⌐No **No.**⌐
15   Chuck: Oh: you like it. Yeah yuh-
16   Oh s:- Take some back with us.=
17   Chil: ⌐=No no.⌐
18   (0.6)
19   Chil: ⌐No: No. *((deeper voice))*
20   Chuck: Oh no it's illegal.
21   Yeah.
22   Chil: Y(h)a h(h)a o(h) ⌐h n(h)o n(h)o n(h) ⌐o.
23   Chuck: └Hi hi ha ha   └O(h)k(h)ay.

Figure 1. Building Action

4.1   Chil's pointing

My focus in the present paper is on Chil's use of prosody. However, even a cursory look
at the images in Figure 1 reveals that Chil is making extensive use of pointing gestures
here. To give the reader a clear picture of what is happening in this sequence, and prepare the ground for looking at his prosody, it is useful to briefly describe these gestures
and how they are interpreted by Chuck (Goodwin in press).

       Three times in Figure 1, at lines 5–6, 8–9 (with the second point held through line
11), and at line 12, Chil produces pairs of linked gestures. In each case the first gesture
points at the bowl on his lap. Chil then immediately moves his hand from the bowl to
shoulder height to produce a second gesture where he is visibly pointing toward

something in front of him.[2], [3] Through the way in which the second gesture is visibly linked to the initial one, it shows Chuck that what was indicated in the first gesture should be used as a point of departure for making sense out of the second. This provides some demonstration that Chil is able to combine signs in ways that display something like a topic (the first gesture) comment (the second gesture) structure. Despite his absence of language, Chil does in fact possess the ability to combine signs, here gestures, in ways that suggest that they are being organized into sign chains, i.e. an ordered combination of signs that goes beyond any of its parts in isolation.

4.2   Combined signs that are recognized as action without being understood

In the absence of conventionalized language Chuck is not able to figure out what is being predicated about the bowl. However, he does recognize, and respond to, the ordered pair of gestures as an action requesting that he do something with the bowl. Chuck's inability to decipher these signs, and figure out what exactly Chil wants him to do does not undercut the fact that Chuck attributes not only communicative intentions, but also semiotic agency to Chil.

These gestures arise within an embodied participation framework constituted through the mutual orientation of Chuck and Chil's bodies. Such arrangements create a multi-party interactive field within which other kinds of sign exchange processes, such as talk and gesture, can be organized as communicative action (Goodwin 1981, Goodwin 1984, Goodwin 2007a, Kendon 1990). The gestures are thus publicly constructed, through spatial and sequential placement, as sequences of action directed to Chuck.

4.3   Working sequentially to accomplish understanding

Chuck does indeed treat Chil's linked gestures as requests for Chuck to do something. After each set of gestures Chuck immediately proposes to Chil a candidate version of what activity the gestures might be requesting (in line 7 the first set of gestures are treated as a display that Chil is finished, something that can make relevant cleaning up, in lines 9–10, the redone gestures are treated as a request for more grapefruit, in line 13, the third set of gestures is formulated as a request to remove the bowl, etc.). In each case Chuck's guess is rejected, typically with some version of *No* spoken twice (lines 8, 11, 14, 17, 19). The prosody over these rejections will be examined in more detail below. The repetition of Chil's two-part pointing gestures in Images II and III of Figure 1

---

2.   I am using the term *gesture* to describe Chil's pointing, although in a number of important respects, what occurs here is unlike most human gesture. Space considerations forbid further discussion of this here. Space also makes impossible detailed presentation of the grounds for treating these gestures as linked, but see Goodwin (2003a).

3.   What is also interesting here, but cannot be discussed in the space given, is the way in which Chil directs Chuck's attention to the bowl.

emerges systematically through this process. Chil's *No*'s rejecting Chuck's candidate understandings are accompanied by renewed points which help sustain the relevance of the action by showing Chuck that he should continue trying to grasp what Chil is attempting to say through the gesture. They also indicate resources – what precisely is being pointed at – that Chuck should use to understand Chil.

Each time Chil says *No* he is understood as objecting to specifically what was said in the immediately prior utterance that his current reply is tied to. Through their sequential organization as replies, Chil's *No*'s indexically incorporate into their own structure the talk produced by the prior speaker (see also Du Bois 2007: 149), a sequential process that greatly expands Chil's semantic power.

4.4   What Chil was trying to say and how his signs display this

Two minutes later Chuck asks someone where his wife Candy is, and finds that she is out walking the family's dog on a street behind the house, right where Chil was pointing. Chuck now recognizes that with his linked pointing gestures Chil was asking Chuck to offer Candy some of the delicious grapefruit from Florida he had just sampled. With hindsight, the topic-comment structure of Chil's linked pointing gestures makes perfect sense. With the first point Chil topicalizes the grapefruit, and with the subsequent gesture he indicates that it should be offered to someone positioned within the trajectory of the point. He has constructed an image of the desired offer through a simple but elegant combination of two signs into a coherent image of the proposed action. However, in isolation his indexical signs remain ambiguous to Chuck, who is unable to figure out what they refer to. In Peircean terms, Chil is using his pointing gestures as a sign for a specific object, the offer to Candy. However, though Chuck recognizes that Chil is using signs, he is unable to recover that object. If Chil could produce a conventionalized sign, such as the name Candy, none of the work found here would be necessary.

Even though Chuck does not understand what Chil is trying to say, Chuck treats him, as demonstrated through the actions he produces in response to Chil's gestures, as someone who is using signs to try to say something. In Goodwin (in press) both this recognition that someone is using signs to build action, even when what these signs refer to cannot be understood, as well as the ability to construct such sign complexes in the first place, is investigated as a primordial instance of semiotic agency (see also Duranti 2004).

5.   Chil's prosody over his own talk

5.1   Chil's prosodic proficiency

Despite Chil's almost complete loss of the ability to speak lexico-syntactic signs, he nonetheless retained rich, expressive prosody. Indeed, his family and many of his interlocutors considered his prosody completely comparable to that of a fully fluent speaker.

This fact would seem to indicate that prosody and the ability to produce and combine conventionalized signs through language are in fact structurally different kinds of semiotic processes, which are intimately linked to each other within the act of speaking. This has in fact been strongly demonstrated in research on prosody within Interactional Linguistics by scholars such as Couper-Kuhlen and Selting (Couper-Kuhlen 1996, Couper-Kuhlen and Ford 2004, Selting 1996, 2000, 2008). The present paper uses such a perspective as its point of departure, and contributes to the insightful line of research for the study of prosody within emerging talk-in-interaction begun by Couper-Kuhlen, Selting and their colleagues (Couper-Kuhlen 1992, 1994, Couper-Kuhlen and Selting 1996a, 1996b, Selting 1992, 1994, Selting and Couper-Kuhlen 2001).

Consistent with the organization of prosody as having distinctive organizational features within the larger ecology of practices and resources implicated in the organization of language, there is a well-known differentiation in the effects of brain damage to different brain hemispheres. People who suffer damage to the right hemisphere sometimes retain the ability to produce syntactically correct sentences, but lose much of their prosodic ability, something that also has consequences for their ability to express emotions, and for how they engage in social interaction. Chil's profile is exactly the opposite.

5.2   The mutual elaboration of different kinds of meaning-making practices

All of Chil's utterances are built through the simultaneous, dynamic interplay of at least two structurally different kinds of semiotic processes. Borrowing a distinction made by Bateson (1972), Chil's catastrophically impoverished digital resources, the sharp contrast between *Yes* and *No* made possible by his restricted lexicon, are continuously intertwined with very rich, varied, and expressive analogic signs, his prosody. All of Chil's utterances, and utterances in general, are composite structures, built through the interplay of structurally different kinds of semiotic processes that mutually elaborate each other. Chil's rich prosody is a most important component of his combinatorial resources, and contributes to his ability to build action by combining different kinds of signs into meaningful wholes. Through prosody, Chil's limited vocabulary becomes capable of participating in the construction of richly varied utterances and actions. Chil's *No*'s in Figure 2 below provide one example.

Chil's utterances, and their prosody, are organized with respect to a developing sequence. In Figure 1 there is an extended effort, over multiple turns, for Chil to say something to Chuck, and for Chuck to try to grasp what that is. This larger activity, and the sequence through which it is developed, constitutes a major context for the prosody of individual utterances.

6. The epistemic ecology of a restricted semiotic environment and its consequences for the progression of action

Crucial to the organization of this activity is the differential positioning of the participants. Drawing upon distinctions developed elsewhere (Goodwin 1981: 149–166, Goodwin 1987), Chil is a Knowing speaker (K+) telling something to someone, an Unknowing recipient (K-), who doesn't yet know what Chil wants to tell him.

However, while Chil and Chuck are positioned within such a complementary Knowing ↔ Unknowing relationship, the structure of their situation differs in important ways from that of fluent speakers telling stories. In such a storytelling situation, the Unknowing recipient is able to immediately recognize and make use of the conventional signs being used by the teller, and the story can move forward. In contrast to this, Chuck is not able to properly understand Chil's iconic and indexical signs.

As can be seen in Figure 2, Chil's responses in lines 8, 11, 14, 17, and 19 are spoken with a variety of different pitch contours. The scale used to display pitch height from 0 to 500 Hz is the same in all of the phonetic analyses above the utterance lines in the transcript[4], with 0 placed at the level of the transcription of the talk. To make visual comparison easier, an arrow highlighting each pitch display is always placed at the 300 Hz mark. A vertical dotted line intersecting the pitch track marks the division between syllables.

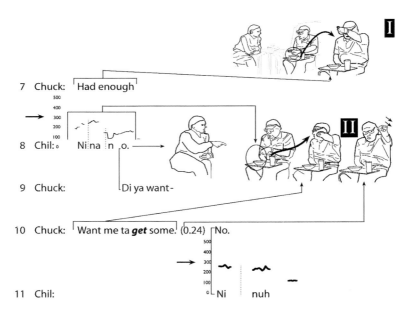

---

4.   The software Praat (http://www.fon.hum.uva.nl/praat/) was used for pitch analysis.

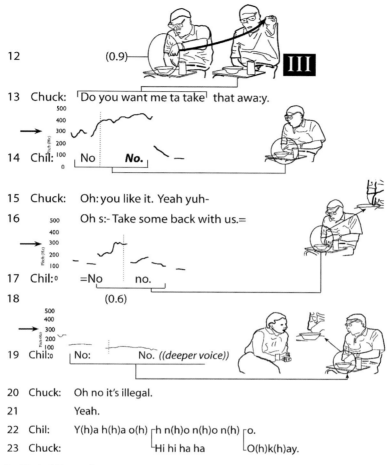

12   (0.9)

13   Chuck: ⌈Do you want me ta take⌉ that awa:y.

14   Chil: No ⌊   No.⌋

15   Chuck: Oh: you like it. Yeah yuh-

16   Oh s:- Take some back with us.=

17   Chil:⁰   =No   no.

18   (0.6)

19   Chil:⁰   ⌊No: No. ((deeper voice))⌋

20   Chuck: Oh no it's illegal.

21   Yeah.

22   Chil: Y(h)a h(h)a o(h) ⌈h n(h)o n(h)o n(h) ⌈o.

23   Chuck: ⌊Hi hi ha ha   ⌊O(h)k(h)ay.

Figure 2. Varied Prosody

7. Building varied action by combining rich prosody with limited gesture and vocabulary

7.1   A first contextual configuration

Chil constructs quite different kinds of action by combing rich and varied prosody with limited, indeed almost identical lexical structure, essentially variants of double *No*'s.[5] Line 8, after Chuck's first attempt to decipher Chil's first gesture complex, displays, in part through its high initial raise, which may be an indication of affect (cf, e.g., Selting

---

5.   Line 8, which begins with a rapid *Ni na*, has three syllables.

1994), that Chuck doesn't understand what Chil is trying to tell him. Simultaneously Chil points toward the bowl, and thus directs Chuck's gaze and attention toward the gestural complex that Chuck should use to remedy his lack of understanding.

Chuck in line 10 does respond to this, but immediately produces another incorrect gloss. As can be seen in the second image of Chil tied to the beginning of line 10, while Chuck is talking Chil keeps his arm extended in the gestures that continue to point toward the area in front of them, but moves his head to gaze at Chuck. At the end of Chuck's gloss, the place where Chil could accept what Chuck has just said, Chil does not do so. Instead, he not only continues to hold his arm in the pointing gesture that makes a subsequent response relevant rather than returning to home position, but he intensifies that gesture with a series of short stabs that continue over and past the *Ni nuh* in line 11. At the same time he moves his gaze from Chuck to gaze in the direction of his point, further marking that action complex, and what is being pointed toward, as what Chuck should attend to if he is to produce the response that Chil is seeking. Chuck takes this ensemble of non-vocal action into account. He displays recognition that his gloss has been rejected with a *No* that occurs before, and overlaps, Chil's lexical rejection with *Ni nuh*.

The continuing relevance of Chil's earlier action is visible in the organization of what happens in a number of different ways. First, essential elements of the action produced over line 8 recur in the activities that organize line 11. Thus the pitch of the two syllables that make up line 11 is at approximately the same height as the pitch over the first two syllables that began line 8 (approximately 250 Hz). Second, gesturally, the raised extended point is a redoing of the pointing gesture that occurred over line 7. There is moreover selectivity in the re-use of gesture in the second move in line 10. When Chil rejects Chuck's gloss here, he does not redo the initial point to the bowl, perhaps treating that as not problematic, but instead emphasizes that Chuck should focus on what is being indicated by the second point. Third, both insistence and visible frustration at Chuck's inability to understand what Chil wants to tell him, are displayed by the clipped syllables without a terminal contour in line 11, and by the insistent short stabbing movements of his outstretched finger. Indeed his strong, rhythmic movements here might constitute a version of prosody in a non-vocal medium. Finally, despite the fact that Chuck has produced a coherent reply in line 10 to Chil's earlier action, Chil has not relaxed the body position that he assumed as a speaker there, and thus is treating his initial action as not having come to completion by being closed with an appropriate response.

Line 14 is another two-unit *No*. Its prosody is very different from anything that has gone before, and this seems to be especially important here. Each of the two *No*'s that make up his utterance is produced in a different way. The first *No* is quite short, approximately 0.26 seconds. The pronunciation of the second takes almost three times as long, 0.68 seconds. The maximum pitch over the first *No* is higher than any of his prior *No*'s (323 Hz, versus 268 Hz for line 8 and 273 Hz for line 11), and this seems to help Chil mark as particularly salient his disagreement with what Chuck has just said. Chil's pitch then takes a very noticeable escalation during the second *No*, reaching a height of 463 Hz.

The construction of line 14 as a whole, with its variation in how each of its two *No*'s is spoken, great variation in the duration of each syllable, and its marked pitch changes which reach considerable height before finally descending, and which are quite different from any of his earlier turns, all give this utterance a very strong affective valence and display a strong oppositional position to what has just been said. Impressionistically, it seems to display strong objection, in fact outrage, at what Chuck has just proposed (taking the fruit away). Indeed, this two-syllable action with its rise-fall contour may provide an interesting parallel to what Golato and Fagyal have described for *ja^ja* in German, which they argue allows its speaker to indicate to the addressee "hold on, you didn't get it." (Golato and Fagyal 2008: 241), a reading of this pattern that is entirely consistent with what is occurring in the present sequence.[6] From a slightly different perspective, the length of the second *No* allows Chil to extend the time during which his opposition is visible, almost to dwell on it.

It seems clear that Chil is displaying objection to not only this action ("don't take my bowl away"), but more crucially to Chuck's inability to provide an appropriate frame for interpreting what Chil is trying to say. Chuck hears it this way. He begins his response with a classic change of state token (Heritage 1984), *Oh*, and thus displays that what Chil has just said has led him to abandon the assumptions that led to the gloss he produced a moment earlier in line 13.

Line 17, which objects to Chuck's *Ohs:- Take some back with us*, does not display the outrage of line 14, and is far more neutral as an objection. Each of the two *No*'s is spoken for approximately the same length of time. The first ends with moderate to high pitch (306 Hz) while the second drops noticeably (a maximum of 184 Hz before ending at 77 Hz). Taken as a whole the utterance reiterates Chil's continuing objections to what Chuck is saying (this is most salient in the higher pitch at the end of the first *No*), without, however, marking this objection with as strong an affect as found in line 14.

Chil ends line 17 by looking down at his left index finger pointing into the bowl on his lap. His posture can be seen in the image attached to line 17 in Figure 2. One import of this postural configuration, which will stand in contrast to what occurs next, is that Chil's body displays that the bowl remains relevant to the organization of the current action, and is something that Chuck should take into account in his work to build the next action that Chil is seeking.

7.2   Saying something different by building a new contextual configuration

Like so many of Chil's utterances in this sequence, line 19 is built with two *No*'s. However, though again displaying disagreement with what Chuck has said, it constructs an action that is completely unlike anything that has gone before. Instead of coming

---

6.   I am indebted to Dagmar Barth-Weingarten for drawing this to my attention.

immediately after an incorrect gloss by Chuck, it follows, after a noticeable silence (0.6 seconds), something that Chil himself just said in line 17. Lines 17 and 19 are almost identical in their lexical structure: Each is constructed in its entirety with two *No*'s. However, as shown by Chuck's gloss in line 20, which gets Chil's immediate agreement, Chuck interprets line 19 as saying something completely different from line 17, and indeed all of Chil's other utterances and associated gestural complexes. Rather than trying to get Chuck to recognize that he wants Candy to be offered some fruit, Chil's talk here is treated as drawing attention to a serious problem with Chuck's candidate gloss in line 16. Chuck lives in California, a state that prohibits the importation of citrus fruit from outside the state. Bringing some of this fruit back to California would thus be, as Chuck says in line 20, illegal.

What resources does Chil use that enable Chuck to recognize what is being said here in spite of the fact that Chil can't speak the necessary words?

Lexically, line 19 (a two-unit *No*) is hardly different from most of Chil's earlier turns. One might be tempted to argue that the *No*'s in line 19 are understood simply by treating them as operating on the last thing that Chuck said, which was a proposal to bring fruit back to where he lived. However, while this is certainly important in eventually enabling Chuck to recover what Chil is objecting to, it is by no means sufficient. Indeed, Chil himself didn't recognize the problem with California in line 17, his first response to what Chuck said. There, through both his unproblematic prosody and by again pointing at the bowl, Chil was clearly and visibly doing another version of his earlier actions objecting to Chuck's gloss of the linked gestures.

Just before speaking in line 19, Chil withdraws his finger from the bowl and lifts his head up to look directly at Chuck (see the image to the right of line 19 in Figure 2). He is no longer gesturally producing a sign indexing the bowl, as he did in all of his earlier utterances, but is instead focusing exclusively on Chuck, the source of the problematic utterance. The bowl and the point toward the region in front of them have disappeared from the sign complex and contextual configuration he is now constructing for Chuck.

Prosodically, Chil speaks the *No*'s in line 19 with a completely new, very expressive prosody. The pitch track in Figure 2 indicates this in only the most imperfect way. However, it can be seen that his pitch drops dramatically. After the initial nasal sound that begins the first *No* in line 19, the highest pitch that his first *No* reaches is 142 Hz. The second *No* descends further, with a maximum pitch of 118 Hz and a minimum of 78 Hz. Chil's pitch in this utterance is far lower than in any of his earlier turns. The utterance is also spoken with a very deep, sonorous voice. As Chil speaks his second, lower *No*, a noticeable quiver can be heard in his voice (see Ford and Fox this volume).

Impressionistically, what Chil seems to do here is display a shift in deontic, affective and epistemic stance toward the talk he is producing for Chuck. This is indexed by a very clear change in prosodic parameters. Epistemically, Chil treats what is now being said as something that he expects his addressee to unproblematically recognize. Simultaneously, he assumes with strong affect the deontic position of someone like a judge laying down the law to a person who has proposed committing a violation. By attaching this new prosody to his double *No's*, he produces what Bakhtin (1981) and Goffman (1981) have described as a layering of voices (cf. also Deppermann 2007, Georgakopoulou 2007, Günthner 2007). Within the framework of Goffman's (1981) concept of footing, Chil is using the shift in prosody to inject a new *Figure*, a typified authoritarian character, into the talk by acting as the animator or sounding box of an utterance (the authoritarian *No*) that belongs to someone else. Since the imagined author/principal of the utterance is not a concrete individual known to the participants, but a category, it could be said to constitute a category-animation (Deppermann 2007: 336). Faced with this new constellation of mutually elaborating displays which strongly contrast with the way in which Chil built his previous actions, Chuck in line 20 is able to suddenly recognize a problem with what he just said (proposing that fruit should be brought back to California, line 16), indeed the problem that Chil also discovered and expressed in line 19.

8. Chil's timing

Timing in interaction is central to its organization. Talk is constructed not only through what is said, but equally through how participants construct their own character, competence, moral worth, skill, aliveness to each other and the events they are engaged in, etc. A crucial component of this process is the ability to respond with appropriate timing to the actions of others. Various aspects of timing, including the sequencing of turns to each other, for example gaps and other delays, overlap, smooth no-gap no-overlap transitions (Sacks et al. 1974), and delays of various types within turns, such as word searches (Goodwin and Goodwin 1986), have received considerable attention within conversation analysis, linguistic anthropology and related fields.

For the moment it is relevant to note three aspects of Chil's timing within interaction. First, he is extraordinarily rapid and fluid in the ways in which he produces his own actions and juxtaposes them to the actions of others. Note the rapidity with which he produces both turns at talk (lines 8, 11, and 14) and gesture in Figure 2. On other occasions he interrupts someone in mid-utterance with a *No* to disagree with what they are saying (Goodwin 2007a). In this rapid, fluent timing, Chil differs from many right hemisphere aphasics who considerably delay their emerging utterances through extended efforts to find and pronounce words. Such delays have strong effects on the character of the interaction and the engagement of participants within it. While Chil's interlocutors may be puzzled, they are rarely bored or feel that the unfolding flow of interaction has been put on hold. Paradoxically, the severity of Chil's linguistic deficits, the almost complete lack of vocabulary, may have helped him to position himself as a very alert, alive interlocutor.

Second, Chil displays an ability to coordinate the timing of his gestures to structure in his talk that is comparable to that of fully fluent speakers. Moreover, as noted earlier, Chil's gestures frequently work to provide an account for the *No* he is speaking. The timing of the gesture with respect to specific elements of the talk is one of the practices Chil uses to establish this sequential relationship, that is, to show his addressee that the gesture should be used to grasp why a particular *No* is being spoken. In other words Chil uses temporal juxtaposition to bind different kinds of signs to each other, and position them in a relationship of mutual elaboration, in which each is used to help understand the locally relevant meaning and action import of the others.

Third, while Chil's individual contributions are produced with superb timing, the unfolding flow of the interaction as a whole, something similar to what conversation analysts describe as progressivity within turns (Schegloff 2007), is disrupted and delayed as participants put considerable work into figuring out what Chil meant with a particular sign complex. Until this is resolved in some way, or abandoned, the sequence of action that Chil is attempting to initiate through use of these signs cannot move forward. In brief, Chil produces action with rapid, fluid timing, but the organization of larger sequences of action is delayed because of Chil's inability to rapidly convey to others precisely what he means.

9.   Building action within a rich semiotic ecology

Figure 3 provides a brief summary of the resources Chil uses to build action in this sequence. Some of these resources, such as the organization of cooperative semiosis, are described in more detail in Goodwin (in press).

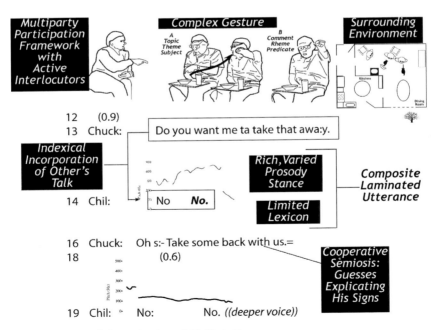

Figure 3. Contextual Organization of Chil's Action

First, while Chil has an extremely limited lexicon, the words he does use, (*Yes* and *No*) allow him to indexically incorporate the talk of others into his own actions. Second, rather than standing alone, Chil's words are linked to prosody. His utterances (and utterances in general) thus have a laminated[7] structure. While Chil's lexicon is poor, his prosody is rich. The way in which prosody and lexico-syntactic structure mutually elaborate each other to create a whole that is greater than any of its parts provides Chil with the resources that enable him to build varied, locally relevant action. Third, Chil has the ability to build complex, multi-part gestures, and these are indeed incorporated into the structure of his utterances, for example as accounts that attempt to provide reasons for why what the prior speaker is saying is being rejected, while suggesting alternatives. His success with these actions is limited by the fact that he can only use iconic and indexical signs in their construction. Fourth, with these gestures, and in other ways as well, Chil can invoke the resources provided by a meaningful environment. Fifth, Chil's actions are embedded within multi-party participation frameworks, constructed through the visible mutual orientation of multiple actors. Such frameworks create environments where other kinds of sign exchange processes can flourish. They also indexically ground the signs produced within these frameworks, something that is especially important for an actor such as Chil, since iconic and indexical signs constitute a large and important part of his semiotic repertoire. Sixth, Chil and his interlocutor(s) are using signs organized through processes of cooperative semiosis, with each sign becoming a locus for operations on it by others. Rather than simply addressing a hearer defined by the ability to decode linguistic signs, Chil is working reflexively with cognitively rich interlocutors, who use whatever signs he produces as a point of departure for further work and inference of their own. In the talk responding to what Chil has done, the interlocutor typically produces a candidate understanding of what Chil is trying to say, which Chil can then reject, accept or modify. Seventh, despite his lack of lexis and syntax, Chil participates in this process with fluent, indeed exquisite, timing. In brief, Chil is building meaning and action within a complex semiotic ecology.

10. Actions as populations of complementary, mutually elaborating signs that make possible the variety required to build relevant moves within continuously unfolding environments

An issue raised at the beginning of this paper was whether Chil's catastrophically impoverished linguistic syntax meant that he lacked the ability to build utterances by

---

7. The concept of lamination is taken from the way in which Erving Goffman used this term in his classes at the University of Pennsylvania while developing the analytic framework for the deconstruction of the speaker that eventually appeared in Footing (Goffman 1981). As a laminated entity, the person speaking in the current interaction could be animating another, quite different person, as a speaker in a strip of reported talk, while simultaneously taking up a stance toward that party and what she was being quoted as saying.

combining separate signs into novel, complex wholes. The materials examined here provide one answer to that question. First, they offer a clear demonstration that both Chil's vocabulary and his ability to combine lexical units into larger syntactically structured wholes are indeed severely restricted. Chil's non-lexical syllables also appear to be quite limited. What appears massively on transcripts of his talk are a range of *Di's*, *Dih's*, *Duh's*, and *Da's*. Moreover, though Chil can and does produce utterance units that contain variable numbers of syllables, in the sequences examined here two-syllable units were both very common and quite important.

However, despite his severe restrictions in lexical and syllable structure, Chil is able to use this basic two syllable template to build powerful, highly varied action. Chil constructs action by combining unlike phenomena – lexical structure, prosody, gesture, other forms of embodied action, and on occasion structure in the environment, – into complex wholes where each limited sign elaborates, and is elaborated by, the others to which it is tied within local action packages. There is great merit in focusing analysis on well-bounded, internally coherent self-contained domains, such as syntax, prosody, gesture, the genetic code, language as a formal, self-contained system, etc. However, in natural systems crucial processes are frequently organized through patterns of action that move across the boundaries of analytically separate modules to accomplish consequential courses of action. Further difficulties arise if one tries to locate all phenomena of interest not only within a single domain, such as language, but also entirely within the mental life of isolated, self-contained individuals. Within such analytic frameworks (which are in fact frequently used to diagnose the abilities of aphasics, as well as the linguistic competence of fluent speakers), Chil's competence to build action by combining different kinds of signs and incorporating structures produced by others, such as syntactically rich sentences, into his own action, disappears.

As an actor Chil is embedded within this continuously changing web of unfolding contextual configurations (Goodwin 2000, Kendon 2009: 363). Though he lacks the ability to produce most symbols, he is acting within a world of action structured through their presence. Chil is able to tie to, and incorporate into his own action, symbols constructed by others. He is thus able to intervene into the unfolding flow of action and reshape it in ways that allow him to accomplish what he wants to say and do.

Chil's *No's* in Figure 2 provide a simple example of this process. Lexically they are all very similar, and at times identical (lines 14, 17, 19), and as a species of action, they can all be described as disagreeing with what his interlocutor has just said. However, such a gloss, or attempt to focus analytically on just those features that define a common class of action, not only misses, but renders invisible, the great range of variation in these *No's* with respect to both their composition, and the diverse forms of consequential action they in fact produce. Through the way in which each *No* ties to different strips of talk produced by his interlocutor, each in fact says and does something different. Because Chil's prosody is rich and expressive, comparable to that of a fully fluent speaker, compositionally Chil's *No's* do not stand alone as bare lexical items but instead, through prosody, they construct a range of diverse forms of action.

Hence, what one finds here is a population of diverse, though related actions which are being organized not by the lexical and syntactic structure of the talk alone, but instead through the juxtaposition of diverse semiotic resources within an ecology of meaning-making practices being sustained through the coordinated actions of multiple participants. The utterances and other forms of action emerging within this ecology are continuously changing, through systematic transformation of the contextual configurations they emerge from. From a Peircean perspective, action is being constructed as a continuously unfolding chain of interpretants, each building from the prior and providing the point of departure for the next. The structures involved in this process are populations of related forms (for example signs marking disagreement) coupled with considerable and relevant variation because of the diverse materials and structures incorporated into each actual instance of the form. This variation makes possible precise adaptation to the local environments where each instance of superficially similar and at times identical linguistic tokens (Chil's double *No*'s for example) are being used to accomplish different, relevant tasks. The practices Chil uses are not unique to him, but instead drawn from the repertoire available to speakers in general for shaping utterances to precisely fit the constraints and contingencies of specific emerging environments. By building action in this way Chil is transformed from the almost mute participant implied by his catastrophically impoverished expressive vocabulary into a powerful, and at times, eloquent speaker.

References

Anward, Jan 2005. "Lexeme recycled: How categories emerge from interaction." *Logos and Language* 2: 31–46.

Auer, Peter (ed.) 2007. *Style and social identities – Alternative approaches to linguistic heterogeneity*. Berlin: Mouton de Gruyter.

Bakhtin, Mikhail M. 1981. *The dialogic imagination.* translated by Caryl Emerson and Michael Holquist. Austin: University of Texas Press.

Bateson, Gregory 1972. *Steps to an ecology of mind*. New York: Ballantine Books.

Couper-Kuhlen, Elizabeth 1992. "Contextualizing discourse: The prosody of interactive repair." In: *The contextualization of language*, Peter Auer and Aldo di Luzio (eds.), 337–364. Amsterdam: Benjamins.

Couper-Kuhlen, Elizabeth 1994. "The prosody of repetition: On quoting and mimicry." *Working paper of the project "Kontextualisierung durch Rhythmus und Intonation"* 28, University of Constance.

Couper-Kuhlen, Elizabeth 1996. "The prosody of repetition: on quoting and mimicry." In: *Prosody in conversation. Interactional studies*, Elizabeth Couper-Kuhlen and Margret Selting (eds.), 366–405. Cambridge: Cambridge University Press.

Couper-Kuhlen, Elizabeth and Ford, Cecilia, E. (eds.) 2004. *Sound patterns in interaction*. Amsterdam: Benjamins.

Couper-Kuhlen, Elizabeth and Selting, Margret 1996a. *Prosody in conversation: Interactional studies*. Cambridge: Cambridge University Press.

Couper-Kuhlen, Elizabeth and Selting, Margret 1996b. "Towards an interactional perspective on prosody and a prosodic perspective on interaction." In: *Prosody in conversation: Interactional studies*, Elizabeth Couper-Kuhlen and Margret Selting (eds.), 11–56. Cambridge: Cambridge University Press.

Deppermann, Arnulf 2007. "Playing with the voice of the other: Stylized "Kanaksprak" in conversations among German adolescents." In: *Style and social identities – Alternative approaches to linguistic heterogeneity*, Peter Auer (ed.), 325–360. Berlin: Mouton de Gruyter.

Du Bois, John W. 2007. "The stance triangle." In: *Stance in discourse: Subjectivity in interaction*, Robert Englebretson (ed.), 139–182. Amsterdam: Benjamins.

Duranti, Alessandro 2004. "Agency in language." In: *A companion to linguistic anthropology*, Alessandro Duranti (ed.), 451–473. New York: Blackwell.

Ford, Cecilia E.; Fox, Barbara A. and Thompson, Sandra A. (eds.) 2002. *Constituency and the grammar of turn increments*. Oxford: Oxford University Press.

Georgakopoulou, Alexandra 2007. "Positioning in style: Men in women's jointly produced stories." In: *Style and social identities – Alternative approaches to linguistic heterogeneity*, Peter Auer (ed.), 393–418. Berlin: Mouton de Gruyter.

Goffman, Erving 1981. "Footing." In: *Forms of talk*, Erving Goffman (ed.), 124–159. Philadelphia: University of Pennsylvania Press.

Golato, Andrea and Fagyal, Zsuzsanna 2008. "Comparing single and double sayings of the German response token *Ja* and the role of prosody: A Conversation Analytic perspective." *Research on Language and Social Interaction* 41: 241–270.

Goodwin, Charles 1981. *Conversational organization: Interaction between speakers and hearers*. New York: Academic Press.

Goodwin, Charles 1984. "Notes on story structure and the organization of participation." In: *Structures of social action*, Max Atkinson and John Heritage (eds.), 225–246. Cambridge: Cambridge University Press.

Goodwin, Charles 1987. "Forgetfulness as an interactive resource." *Social Psychology Quarterly* 50 (2): 115–130.

Goodwin, Charles 2000. "Action and embodiment within situated human interaction." *Journal of Pragmatics* 32: 1489–1522.

Goodwin, Charles 2003a. "Conversational frameworks for the accomplishment of meaning in aphasia." In: *Conversation and brain damage*, Charles Goodwin (ed.), 90–116. Oxford: Oxford University Press.

Goodwin, Charles 2003b. "Pointing as situated practice." In: *Pointing: Where language, culture, and cognition meet*, Sotaro Kita (ed.), 217–241. Hillsdale, NJ: Lawrence Erlbaum Associates.

Goodwin, Charles 2006. "Human sociality as mutual orientation in a rich interactive environment: Multimodal utterances and pointing in aphasia." In: *Roots of Human Sociality*, Nick Enfield and Stephen C. Levinson (eds.), 96–125. London: Berg Press.

Goodwin, Charles 2007a. "Environmentally coupled gestures." In: *Gesture and the dynamic dimension of language*, Susan Duncan, Justine Cassell and Elena Levy (eds.), 195–212. Amsterdam: Benjamins.

Goodwin, Charles 2007b. "Interactive footing." In: *Reporting talk: Reported speech in interaction*, Elizabeth Holt and Rebecca Clift (eds.), 16–46. Cambridge: Cambridge University Press.

Goodwin, Charles in press. "Semiotic agency within a framework of cooperative semiosis." In: *Multimodality in human interaction*, Jurgen Streeck, Curtis LeBaron and Charles Goodwin (eds.), Cambridge: Cambridge University Press.

Goodwin, Charles; Goodwin Marjorie Harness and Olsher, David 2002. "Producing sense with nonsense syllables: Turn and sequence in the conversations of a man with severe aphasia." In: *The language of turn and sequence*, Barbara Fox, Cecilia Ford and Sandra Thompson (eds.), 56–80. Oxford: Oxford University Press.

Goodwin, Marjorie Harness and Goodwin, Charles 1986. "Gesture and coparticipation in the activity of searching for a word." *Semiotica* 62 (1–2): 51–75.

Günthner, Susanne 2007. "The construction of otherness n reported dialogues as a resource for identity work." In: *Style and social identities – Alternative approaches to linguistic heterogeneity*, Peter Auer (ed.), 419–444. Berlin: Mouton de Gruyter.

Haviland, John B. 1998. "Early pointing gestures in Zincantán." *Journal of Linguistic Anthropology* 8: 162–196.

Heath, Christian and Luff, Paul 2007. "Ordering competition: the interactional accomplishment of the sale of find art and antiques at auction." *British Journal of Sociology* 58: 63–85.

Heritage, John 1984. "A change-of-state token and aspects of its sequential placement." In: *Structures of social action*, J. Maxwell Atkinson and John Heritage (eds.), 299–345. Cambridge: Cambridge University Press.

Hindmarsh, Jon and Heath, Christian 2000. "Embodied reference: A study of deixis in workplace interaction." *Journal of Pragmatics* 32: 1855–1878.

Kendon, Adam 1990. "Spatial organization in social encounters: The F-formation system." In: *Conducting interaction: Patterns of behavior in focused encounters*, Adam Kendon (ed.), 209–238. Cambridge: Cambridge University Press.

Kendon, Adam 2009. "Language's matrix." *Gesture* 9: 355–372.

Leon, Lourdes de 1998. "The emergent participant: Interactive patterns in the socialization of Tzotzil (Mayan) infants." *Journal of Linguistic Anthropology* 8: 131–161.

Linell, Per 2009. *Rethinking language, mind, and world dialogically: Interactional and contextual theories of human sense-making*. Charlotte, NC: Information Age Publishing.

Ochs, Elinor; Schegloff, Emanuel A. and Thompson, Sandra A. (eds.) 1996. *Interaction and grammar*. Cambridge: Cambridge University Press.

Sacks, Harvey 1992. *Lectures on conversation, Vol. 2*. Edited by Gail Jefferson, with an Introduction by Emanuel A. Schegloff. Oxford: Basil Blackwell.

Sacks, Harvey; Schegloff, Emanuel A. and Jefferson, Gail 1974. "A simplest systematics for the organization of turn-taking for conversation." *Language* 50: 696–735.

Schegloff, Emanuel A. 2007. *Sequence organization in interaction: Volume 1: A primer in Conversation Analysis*. Cambridge: Cambridge University Press.

Selting, Margret 1992. "Intonation as a contextualization device: Case studies on the role of prosody, especially intonation, in contextualizing story telling in conversation." In: *The contextualization of language*, Peter Auer and Aldo di Luzio (eds.), 233–258. Amsterdam: Benjamins.

Selting, Margret 1994. "Emphatic speech style – with special focus on the prosodic signaling of heightened emotive involvement in conversation." *Journal of Pragmatics* 22: 375–408.

Selting, Margret 1996. "Prosody as an activity-type distinctive cue in conversation: The case of so-called 'astonished' questions in repair initiation." In: *Prosody in conversation: Interactional studies*, Elizabeth Couper-Kuhlen and Margret Selting (eds.), 231–270. New York: Cambridge University Press.

Selting, Margret 2000. "The construction of units in conversational talk." *Language in Society* 29: 477–517.

Selting, Margret 2008. "Linguistic resources for the management of interaction." In: *Handbook of interpersonal communication, HAL Vol. 2*, Gerd Antos, Eija Ventola, and Tilo Weber (eds.), 217–253. Berlin: de Gruyter.

Selting, Margret and Couper-Kuhlen, Elizabeth (eds.) 2001. *Studies in interactional linguistics.* Amsterdam: Benjamins.

Streeck, Jürgen 2009. *Gesturecraft. The manu-facture of meaning.* Amsterdam: Benjamins.

Thompson, Sandra A. and Couper-Kuhlen, Elizabeth 2005. "The clause as a locus of grammar and interaction." *Discourse Studies* 7: 481–504.

Further perspectives on cooperative semiosis

Comments on Charles Goodwin "Constructing meaning through prosody in aphasia"

Helga Kotthoff
University of Freiburg, Germany

Chil's active vocabulary is severely limited. Basically his vocabulary consists of the three words *yes, no* and *and,* apart from certain non-lexical syllables. In his paper, Goodwin examines the dominant position that prosody occupies "within constantly changing configurations built through the simultaneous use of structurally different kinds of semiotic phenomena in alternative media (semiotic fields, including the stream of speech, the visible body and structure in the material environment)"(: 374). In reconstructing Chil's powerful combinatorial resources, which he uses flexibly to construct relevant action, Goodwin broadens the scope of the topics of this volume. With my comment I am going to broaden the scope even more because the author's way of taking into account the "larger ecology of interaction" has much to offer to other fields of analyzing interaction with less-than-fully-competent speakers.

1. The larger ecology of interaction

In the reception of Goodwin's work on conversations with Chil (many previous articles are referred to in his current paper), it became evident to me that as analysts of various sorts of interaction we can gain immensely from taking into account this "larger ecology of interaction" more than most of us have managed so far. All interlocutors who interact with a speaker with a limited vocabulary have to draw more extensively on other semiotic resources available in the specific context at hand than is normally the case – and that highlights these capacities of the environment.

In his paper, Goodwin draws upon the concepts of *cooperative semiosis* (: 381), *semiotic agency* (: 379) and *embodied participation framework* (: 376). Apart from speech, they include prosody, directing gaze, producing gestures and pointing to things in the environment. Chil is, for example, able to combine these signs in ways that display something like a topic (a first gesture) and a comment (a second gesture). Chuck and Chil thus create a multi-party interactive field within a larger ecology of practice.

Prosodic and gestural means always play a role in face-to-face-interaction, but Chil and his recipients make much greater use of them than most speakers ordinarily do. The special case of interacting with a person like Chil shows the power of cooperative semiosis within an ecology of practice. The compensation for his deficiencies becomes for all interlocutors, including Chil himself, a new competence.

2.   Prospects for other types of interaction with less-than-fully-competent speakers

Goodwin's work, in general and this paper, have already suggested possibilities for studies of interactions with small children and with learners of second languages at early stages of proficiency.

2.1   Cooperative semiosis with children

With regard to interaction development, some of Bruner's findings come to mind. Jerome Bruner (see his overview of his work in 1995) was, I believe, the first who made it clear that manipulating joint attention and dramatizing prosody are important strategies used by caretakers in interactions with small children and they are also among the first communicative strategies used by children themselves. Language acquisition means not just the acquisition of grammar and vocabulary, but also *a constant rearrangement within a cooperative semiosis* involving the whole family and other interaction systems. Glimpses of what these rearrangement processes are like were given by Hausendorf and Quasthoff (1987) in their studies of children's narratives. They showed how adults use the minimal verbal material they are offered by the child to build the story as very active recipients. The two authors worked with the image of a swing. With a two-year-old child the adult puts a heavy weight on the swing (i.e., offers a lot of talk). He or she basically tells the story the child initiates. Step by step the weights are removed when the child realizes more and more parts of the story him- or herself in the course of language acquisition.

Recently, studies such as that carried out by Cekaite (2010) have gone even more deeply into the details of situated verbal, bodily, and spatial practices (e.g. into how directives are performed), thereby showing how fruitful Goodwin's cooperative semiosis approach already is for language acquisition research. Cekaite focuses on parental directives requesting that routine family tasks are carried out in an immediate situational context and necessitating the child's locomotion from one place to another (e.g., requests to take a bath, brush one's teeth). As documented by the data, such directive sequences were structured using what Cekaite calls parental *shepherding* moves, that is, "techniques of the body" (2010: 2) that monitor the child's body for compliance. Focusing on *body twist*, a form of tactile intervention, Cekaite shows how parents interrupt the child's prior activity and initiate a relevant activity by perceptually reorienting the child in the architecture of the home. *Tactile* and *non-tactile steering* constituted the means for monitoring and controlling the direction, pace, and path of the child's locomotion. Overall, these embodied directives serve as multifunctional cultural tools that guide the child into reflexive awareness of the dialogic and embodied characteristics of interaction.

Currently a new type of interaction analysis is arising which sees children and adults acting more in a kind of cooperative semiosis, which is restructured over a period of years. Even literacy events are nowadays viewed as instantiations of socially and culturally situated practices in Goodwin's sense. A multimodal approach to literacy events and practices broadens the scope of enquiry to include considering how meanings are created through multiple modalities of communication, such as the embodiment of gesture, gaze, movement, words, vocalizations and augmentative communication systems, including manual signs. Yet, the difference between Chil and small children remains, firstly, in that Chil fully understands what is going on around him, including speech. This can be said of small children, if at all, to a much lesser extent. However, even small children understand more than they are able to produce. Secondly, sadly enough, with Chil we cannot expect acquisitional progress.

2.2   Interacting with second language learners

Similar processes can be observed with second language learners, although even in pragmatics most studies of second language acquisition focus on the monological development of speech acts (see the overview given by Achiba 2003) instead of analyzing cooperative semiosis.

In their early stages of second language acquisition, learners are forced to convey a lot of meaning by an as yet limited repertoire of linguistic resources in interaction with native speakers. Studies by Wagner (1996), Kasper (2006), and also the first studies of interactions with 'migrant laborers' (*Gastarbeiter*, Hinnenkamp 1982) show that also for foreign language learners the main goal in interaction is to understand and to make themselves understood. Most of the time, they manage to do so by using at least some of Chil's strategies, namely enriching utterances with analogical signs, and making maximal use of words already expressed by the native interlocutor.

Much in Goodwin's broad sense, Wagner (1996) called for a reconceptualization of second language acquisition research. He focused on describing a variety of aspects of learning-in-action captured in transcripts of recordings of naturally occurring foreign, second, or other language interactions. By means of transcript analyses, he explores the possibilities of describing learning-in-action devoid of cognitive notions of language and learning. In so doing, he suggests a reconceptualizion of second language acquisition research in a semiotic field (much in the same vein as Goodwin).

Moreover, teaching-related questions have occurred to me in reading Goodwin's paper: (a) What do embodied views of cognition reveal about interaction and learning? (b) How do learners' embodied perceptions of themselves and others support holistic understandings of teaching? The teacher is the prototype of an appreciative, competent and sympathetic recipient, very similar to Chuck when talking to Chil. Goodwin highlights many peculiarities of Chuck's recipiency, namely readiness to draw inferences from all noticeable forms of behavior, and readiness to communicate his guesses.

Language teachers need to know what it means to maximize a minimal input. This means that they should thereby move language learners into the zone of proximal development in the Vygotskian sense (as the level of potential development through problem solving under guidance and in collaboration with more capable interlocutors (Vygotsky 1978)[1].

3.   Concluding remarks

Goodwin has observed how family members – step by step – became competent interlocutors for Chil. It would be interesting to study such a socialization process in other discourse histories of teacher-student interactions. An ethnography of the development of such special interactive abilities with regard to impaired or otherwise less-than-fully-competent speakers would be important for many sorts of professional education (for nurses, teachers ...).

I have tried to point out that Goodwin's dialogic and semiotic approach gives an uplift also to socioculturally and interactionally oriented studies of first and second language acquisition.

References

Achiba, Machiko 2003. *Learning to request in a second language*. Clevedon: Multilingual Matters.
Bruner, Jerome 1995. "From joint attention to the meeting of minds." In: *Joint attention. Its origin and role in development*, Chris Moore and Philip Dunham (eds.), 1–15. Hillsdale: Lawrence Erlbaum.
Cekaite, Asta 2010. "Shepherding the child: embodied directive sequences in parent – child interactions." *Text & Talk* 30 (1): 1–25.
Hausendorf, Heiko and Quasthoff, Uta M. 1996. *Sprachentwicklung und Interaktion*. Opladen: Westdeutscher Verlag.

1.   Nowadays mostly called "scaffolding" – a process through which a teacher or more competent person gives aid to the student and tapers off this aid as it becomes unnecessary, much as a scaffold is removed from a building during construction (Wells 1999).

Hinnenkamp, Volker 1982. *Foreigner-Register und Tarzanisch: Eine vergleichende Studie über die Sprechweise gegenüber Ausländern am Beispiel des Deutschen und des Türkischen.* Hamburg: Buske.

Kasper, Gabriele 2006. "Beyond repair. Conversation analysis as an approach to SLA." *AILA review* 19: 83–99.

Vygotsky, Lev S. 1978. *Mind and society: The development of higher psychological processes.* Cambridge, MA: Harvard University Press.

Wagner, Johannes 1996. "Foreign language acquisition through interaction. A critical review of conversational adjustments." *Journal of Pragmatics* 26: 215–235.

Wells, Gordon 1999. *Dialogic inquiries in education: Building on the legacy of Vygotsky.* Cambridge: Cambridge University Press.

Author index

Subject index

In the series *Studies in Discourse and Grammar* the following titles have been published thus far or are scheduled for publication: